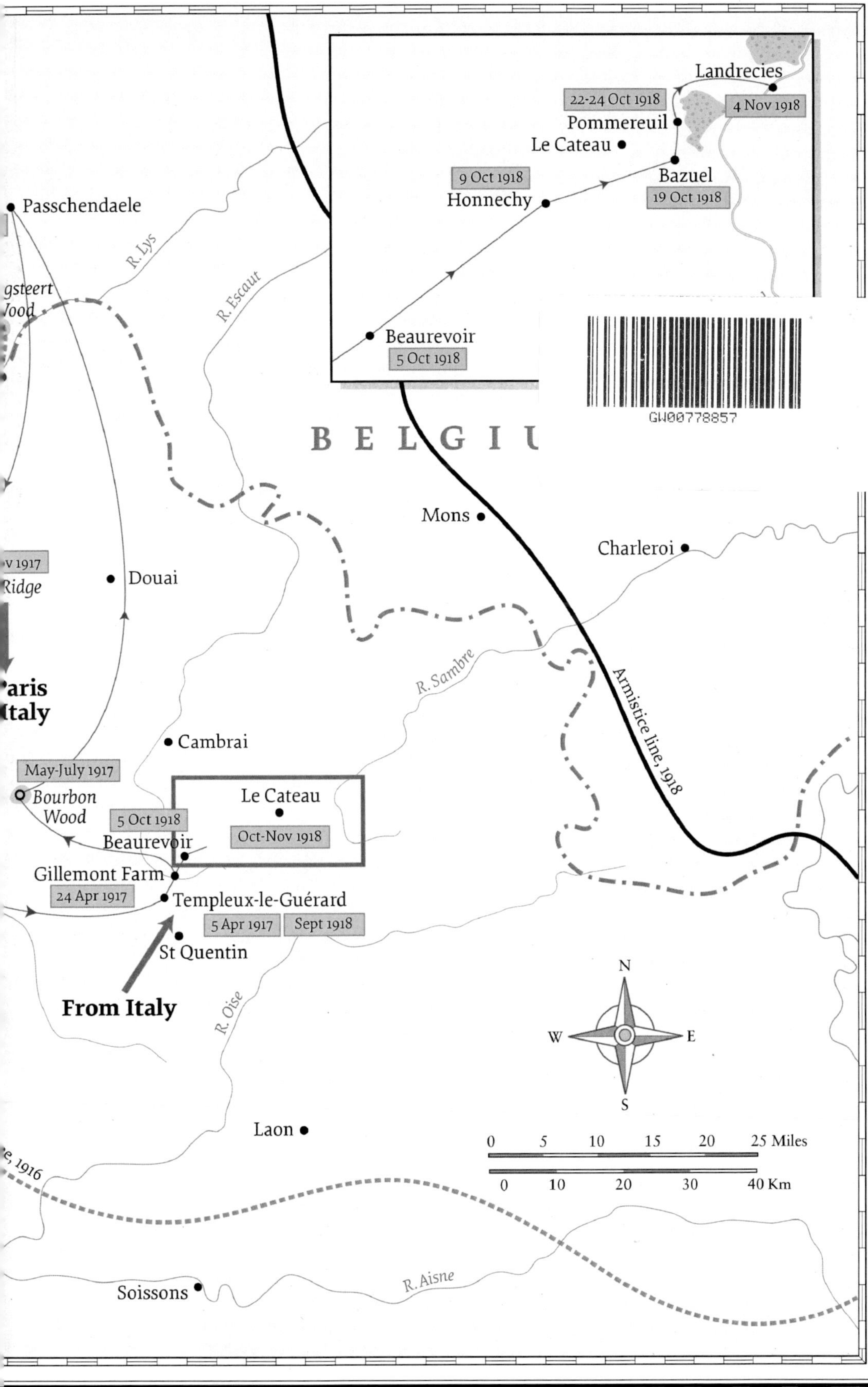

Landrecies
22-24 Oct 1918
4 Nov 1918
Pommereuil
Le Cateau
9 Oct 1918
Bazuel
Honnechy
19 Oct 1918
Beaurevoir
5 Oct 1918
Passchendaele
R. Lys
R. Escaut
gsteert
Vood
B E L G I U
Mons
Charleroi
v 1917
Ridge
Douai
R. Sambre
Armistice line, 1918
Paris
Italy
Cambrai
May-July 1917
Bourbon
Wood
Le Cateau
5 Oct 1918
Oct-Nov 1918
Beaurevoir
Gillemont Farm
24 Apr 1917
Templeux-le-Guérard
5 Apr 1917
Sept 1918
St Quentin
From Italy
R. Oise
N
W
E
S
Laon
e, 1916
0 5 10 15 20 25 Miles
0 10 20 30 40 Km
Soissons
R. Aisne

To War with the Old Gent

To War with the Old Gent

The Story of the 1/8th Battalion, the Worcestershire Regiment in the First World War

Jeremy

Nicholas Lambert

Nicholas Lambert

For Willow and Finn, trusting that your generation is never called upon to partake in such actions as these gallant men endured on our behalf, in defence of sovereignty and democracy.

CONTENTS

Endpaper maps:

The 1/8th Battalion, Worcestershire Regiment on the Western Front.

Detail of photographs on covers:

Front: Captain Alfred Rowe and Captain Osborn Walford (*Mercian Regiment Museum (Worcestershire), WOSWR: Photo Album 96*).

Back: Two graves of unknown Worcestershire Regiment soldiers in the CWGC cemetery at Pozières on the Somme battlefield (*Author*).

PROLOGUE

… I had had only 4 hours sleep since Saturday morning [this was Tuesday evening]. At 9pm I had to see the CO; left him at 9.40pm, had some cold meat and lay down at 10 pm. At 1.30 am [Wednesday] we had a cup of tea and a very small bit of tinned salmon. Started at 2.30 am and marched 6 kilometres, having to be continually putting on our gas masks as the enemy kept sending gas over all the time. We had been badly bombed too during the night by aeroplanes. We got to the jumping off point and started behind our own barrage at 5.10 a.m. The first part was quite easy for us all. We advanced about 2 1/2 miles with two battalions in front of us and had quite a pleasant country walk until it was our turn to go ahead. We passed through them, and then ran straight into it. However we pushed on and by means of our own Lewis guns and rifle fire and flanking movements gradually drove them back for about one more mile, when things got very sticky. Again the line was held up and shelling was very hot but we pushed on until we had no one on either flank as the divisions on our right and left hadn't got on as well as we did. I was getting rather anxious as the Colonel was at his Headquarters more than a mile back and I was Senior Officer. All of a sudden I saw the most magnificent sight I have ever seen, squadrons of cavalry galloping up from behind. A whole brigade of cavalry came up galloping over the skyline in squadrons right through the shelling and machinegun fire. They lost very few men considering, and we all went forward together. However we got hung up again by a railway cutting full of machineguns and had a big scrap.

The CO came up and we arranged for an artillery barrage at 2pm (we'd been on the go since 2am). I got a bit of bread and cheese, and the CO went back leaving everything to me – if we won the cutting I must decide whether to go on or not. Well, we kept fighting and before the time came for the barrage the Hun decided that he'd had enough and evacuated the cutting. We found several dead and judging from the equipment left, their casualties had been considerable. I decided to keep on. They were still shelling heavily which meant many wounded – crossing the next field my servant and I were knocked down by a shell bursting about 3 yds in front of us but we weren't touched and soon got up again though my legs were a bit shaky for the next 20 yds! But we went on and could see the Huns running but by then we hadn't a run in us especially over such rough country. They were only 400 yds in front, if only we'd had the cavalry! But they'd gone in another direction. We marched about 3/4 mile more, still under heavy fire, but we got our objective. I don't think I was ever so done in my life! I carried my pack, my loaded revolver, another one which I won in a Hun dugout, my box respirator, field glasses, spare revolver ammunition, and two Mills bombs, from 2.30am until 4pm on a cup of tea, a bit of tinned salmon and a small bit of bread and cheese! I then had to get into communication with those on our right and left. The left hadn't come up and I filled in on that flank with odd people I found:

1. Queens Bays (cavalry) Hotchkiss gun
2. Armoured cars.

I had no right to these people but they kindly said they would stay for a bit to help. Ultimately the battn on my right came up and Archie Watson who is now one of my subalterns, and at that time the only one, as two were wounded at Beaurevoir and the other the same day later on. Watson was splendid. I then sent word back to the CO, he was awfully bucked and so were the Brigadier and Divisional Gen. [Maj-Gen JRE Charles DSO]. They had the Corps Commander down; it appears they never thought we could get the 2nd objective, so were proportionately delighted!

I finally stopped at 8.30 p.m. had some cold bully and went to sleep about 10pm after visiting my sentries. A pretty good day for an old man!

The next morning we were up at 5.30am: this time in Brigade support. We continued the attack but couldn't get far as the whole line was held up and again badly shelled. We had no breakfast as they couldn't get the rations up to us as we were so near the machine guns etc. So about 9am I told the men to eat their rations, which we all did, and the CO brought Watson and me some whiskey, the first we had for two days. Sleeping out in the open and then only for short times, for you can't sleep long in that cold, one wants whiskey or something badly and we'd had no rum ration for some time.

Now you can't say I don't tell you all I can! I wonder if Harry and Matt Dixon would like to see this letter…

We went in 107 strong and after the first effort they sent me 18 reinforcements fresh from England – all young lads – that made 125 but we came out with 54 so you may gather we had a hot time. Battn orders came out with a list of mentions for good work, mine heads the list as you'll see but only because of seniority and I don't suppose I will get anything as there were no senior officers present and after all I only did my job. Still it's better than nothing to be mentioned in battalion orders.

I must stop.

This is the second half of a letter from the 'Old Gent' – Captain Osborn Walford – to his cousin on 9th October 1918. He was 49 years old. He did not 'get anything' for his work over those previous five days but he had four more battles to fight in which he led C Company over the next twenty-five days. He was to get his just rewards.

Within a month, Walford and his fellow company commanders were receiving their orders for their part in the last great battle of the War. There was a small cadre of key officers and senior NCOs who had been fortunate to survive up to three and a half years at the Front in France, Belgium and Italy, each with medal ribbons to reflect some of their achievements before that cold Monday morning of 4th November 1918. Derek Clayton in his notable work, *Decisive Victory*, explains in his Introduction the scale of the little-known Battle of the Sambre:

The Sambre was the last large-scale, set-piece battle fought by the British Expeditionary Force (BEF) on the Western Front. If the battle is known at all in the public domain, it is for the death of the poet Wilfred Owen. The battle was huge in scale: 13 divisions of the BEF led the assault on a frontage of approximately 20 miles, supported by over 1,000 guns [artillery], with initial plans presuming the involvement of up to 70 tanks and armoured cars. The engagement was therefore not dissimilar in scale to the attack of 1st July 1916 on the Somme.

The adjutant of the 1/8th Battalion of the Worcestershire Regiment, Lt GL Watkinson MC*, sent out the orders of his commanding officer, Lt Col HT Clarke DSO, with the support of his second-in-command, Major JP Bate DSO*, MC* to the three company commanders – A Coy (Captain LR Bomford MC*), C Coy (Captain JO Walford MC), D Coy (2Lt E Wedgbury DSO, MC, DCM, MM). The Sambre-Oise was the main canal from Paris to Brussels and was up to 60 foot wide and six foot deep. It had few towns on the German-held east bank. One was Landrecies and the 1/8th Battalion was given the task of leading the assault across the canal in that area and taking the town – thus they were the point battalion of the 25th Division, a singular honour. I show the gallantry awards already gained or recommended to each man at the time of those orders on the evening of Saturday, 2nd November – an * indicates a second award of that medal, usually known as a 'bar'. The six of them already had been acknowledged on fourteen separate occasions and three of them would be further rewarded for their performance at Landrecies.

Such was the intensity of the fighting that cold Monday morning that seven Victoria Crosses (VCs) were awarded across the Front, two posthumously, and a further one on the Wednesday in the capture of a town to the east of Landrecies where the Germans were still resisting. The battle cost the lives of some 1,200 infantry with estimates of about a further 5,000 wounded. These numbers were a little over a tenth of those on 1st July 1916 but, by then, the BEF (British Expeditionary Force) was a far more effective fighting force. As indeed was the 1/8th Battalion, even if only about a third of the 580 men had been in action before that day, such had been their losses from the intensity of their fighting over the previous thirty days. Raw recruits were still coming to the Front in large numbers, mainly from farms and mines.

The Battalion's *War Diary* for the 8th November recorded:

The Battalion marched to billets at PREUX – en route passing

> through LANDRECIES where they were given a magnificent reception by the inhabitants who had discovered that the 1/8 WORCESTERS had captured the town. Flags & flowers were given to the men and bouquets to the Divisional Commander (who led the Battalion) and to the C.O.

The Battalion was part of the 75th Brigade in the 25th Division. The *War Diary* of the Division recorded simply:

> 4th 75/Bde attacked, crossed the SAMBRE Canal at LANDRECIES and captured the town. 74/Bde passed though the 75/Bde and pushed out patrols.

There was so much more to these two short sentences. It was the last action of the 1/8th Battalion and a glorious way for their remarkable campaign to end.

This is the story of the Old Gent and his fellow officers and men of the 1/8th (Territorial Force) Battalion of the Worcestershire Regiment through the Great War, taken from their diaries, letters, and memoirs as well as from local newspaper stories. It tells of their extraordinary and gallant service and of their lives thereafter – involving knighthoods, suicides and even Kohima in 1944, on the India-Burmese border.

Far more eminent historians than I have written great tomes to argue the causes of the First World War, or the Great War, as it was called until the Second World War was inflicted on peoples and armies across the world. Many have eloquently and at length analysed the peace which followed and why the Great War was not to be 'the war to end all wars'. Several have provided studies of the performance and vigour of the generals; others have related tales of extraordinary heroism. Some wrote poetry at the time and afterwards; many have written detailed works on specific battles, mostly commonly the Somme or Passchendaele. Fascinating works have told us of the great cemeteries; of those who tended the wounded; of those who were shot at dawn; of the short life expectancy of young infantry officers and those who took to the skies. This work is an attempt to provide a story of what it was like to serve at the Front and in the trenches over a prolonged period, for those who never expected, when they joined their county's Territorial regiment, to serve their King and Country in a foreign field. They did so whilst demonstrating not only great endurance and considerable bravery but the British virtues of leadership, camaraderie and humour, becoming one of the most effective infantry battalions in the British Army. To compound the tragedy of their enormous losses over three and a half years, two of those in command as they successfully fought their way across the Sambre Canal on 4th November 1918, near where Captain Wilfred Owen MC lost his life, were to take their own lives in subsequent years.

This story of the 1/8th Battalion of the Worcestershire Regiment is titled: *To War with the Old Gent*. Perhaps you can try and imagine being faced with the prospect, on a cold Sunday evening in November, of rising from your sleeping bag at two-thirty the following morning to lead your men through hedges and over fields in an attack down to a canal bank two miles away, leaping into the icy water and paddling across the length of a cricket pitch on a flattened jerrycan, and then sitting on the far bank in your soaking uniform to help your soldiers across with ropes. To do this when subject to continuous machine-gun fire but with the possibility that if you are successful and survive, you may never need to fight another battle. And to do all of this, some three months into your fiftieth year. That part of the Sambre Canal was to be referred to thereafter by the inhabitants of that small French town on the far bank as the 'Red Sea' – from the blood they shed. The Old Gent and most of his men did survive and, unless they chose to serve on in the Army, they never did fight another battle. They were to spend the remaining months of their military service clearing up the battlefields of France and Flanders and burying and re-burying their fallen comrades. This is their story and a portrayal of what it was like to leave the towns, villages and farms of Worcestershire to serve your Country in a Foreign Field.

There were two seminal moments which led to the writing of this book. The first was some fifteen years ago when my mother produced a small red leather case with the royal cipher adorning the top. When asked what it contained, my mother answered 'a Military Cross' – an award for the gallant actions of junior officers and warrant officers instituted by King George V in 1915. I had undertaken some limited 'ancestry' research and knew that her father had been born in August 1899 and that he had served in the Army as a regular until the end of the Second World War, but there had been no mention of gallantry awards; instead, a story of him being offered the hand of a tribal chief's daughter on the Northwest Frontier when serving as a young subaltern in the Indian Signals Corps in the Waziristan Campaign (1921–1924). According to my surveying of the nineteenth-century censuses, his father was born in the late 1860s. I opened the case and exclaimed with a degree of amazement that it contained 'two Military Crosses!' – there was a silver bar across the white and purple ribbon. In the light of this outline knowledge of my mother's family, I asked to whom this medal belonged. My mother thought it must indeed be her grandfather. Lifting the medal from the case, I found no inscription on the reverse. However, a quick search of the *London Gazette* website confirmed my mother's belief. An additional box contained his miniatures – the MC and Bar, the British War Medal and the Victory Medal. There was no sign of the other two actual medals. There was, additionally, a set of gold chain-linked cufflinks of the Royal Warwickshire Regiment.

The second moment was in December 2021 when reading James Holland's *Brothers in Arms* which told the extraordinary story of the Sherwood Rangers Yeomanry from first light on D-Day to the time of the German surrender in May 1945. I had read Holland's edited diaries of their remarkable commanding officer, Lieutenant Colonel Stanley Christopherson DSO, MC*, the best such diaries of World War Two – *An Englishman at War*. Christopherson had left diaries of some three hundred thousand words, though not mentioning their existence to his family in his lifetime. Indeed, it appears that he spoke little of his war experiences despite participating in some thirty different actions which were of sufficient significance and intensity to be acknowledged as 'Battle Honours', let alone of being the recipient of four gallantry awards. This was all in marked contrast to my great-grandfather who left only his medals and the cufflinks; at least, that was all his family had preserved. At the age of fifty-two, on 21st February 1921, he walked out into his brother-in-law's garden in the Worcestershire village of Feckenham, spoke calmly to the gardener and went into the orchard. It was there that Captain Osborn Walford took out his wartime pistol and killed himself.

Between these two moments, I had followed almost every possible lead to uncover more about Walford's War service, where his body might lie and what had led him to take his own life. Here again, there were two seminal moments or meetings. The first followed a visit to the Worcester Records Office in 2012 to read a small book written by the Regimental Quartermaster Sergeant (RQMS) of the 1/8th Battalion of the Worcestershire Regiment – Edward Corbett's wonderful and erudite *The War Story of the 1/8th Battalion*. It was also to enquire if there was any documentation to indicate where Walford might be buried. I had been that morning to the garden and orchard of his brother-in-law, Colonel EV Sydenham DSO, at Dunstall Court in Feckenham and had inspected the inscription of every grave in the churchyard. Walford was not there. A kindly and experienced lady in the Records Office said the starting point would be to see if a Will had been recorded. It did not take her long to find the handwritten transcription of one written by Walford in July 1918, stating simply that he made his wife, Margaret (née Scott), his executrix and sole beneficiary. Importantly, it gave his address as Hanbury Mount. The lady explained that until 1961 those who had committed suicide could not be buried in sacred ground (a churchyard) nor have a Christian service. Suicide was still a crime in 1922, as is shown by an article in the *Berrow's Worcester Journal* in March 1919 under the heading 'Eldersfield Gardener's Grief – Bereavement leads to Attempted Suicide'. It stated: 'At Upton Police Court on Wednesday before Canon the Rev HW Coventry and Mr RS Bagnall, William Jackaman (54), a gardener of Eldersfield, was charged with attempting to commit suicide'. The lady explained that if the vicar consented, it was common that interment was allowed just over the northern boundary of the churchyard. I set off on the ten-mile journey to St Mary the Virgin's Church at Hanbury. It was a glorious English July afternoon and as I neared the village, I could see the church standing proudly on top of the highest hill in the area. The views from the churchyard are probably without parallel in Worcestershire, looking south with Feckenham away to the east and the full panoply of the hunting country which Walford would have known so well.

My heart sank as I parked by the churchyard. I could see that at the northern surrounds was a woodland of long standing with no room for the graves of those who had died by their own hand. A walk round the churchyard showed that the gravestones of old were of the local sandstone and few inscriptions had survived the English weather. Below the path to the main viewpoint were the graves of more recent times. To the east of the viewpoint stood proudly a white house which I understood later to be Hanbury Mount. The church itself was unlocked and welcoming. On the south wall was the War Memorial remembering all those from the village who had fallen in the two World Wars. Walford's name was not among them but then, as the inquest into his death had found, he had died because of the War, not in the War. There was no immediate indication in the church that any Walford had lived or died in the parish. There was, however, a notice on the main door stating that if anybody had any enquiries, they could ring the churchwarden, Judith Berman. There was a telephone number. I rang and explained my mission to find my great-grandfather. I said that I was on the steps of the church. Judith said she would be with me in five minutes with her 'box of tricks'. There was no doubt that she had patiently answered many similar calls. She explained that the vestry safe had been stolen some years ago and it was likely to be in the local canal together with all its records and registers. However, she did have a large notebook into which, in 1973, a thoughtful local gentleman had recorded the remaining readable inscriptions as our acid rain was fast eroding the sandstone graves. She headed quickly to the back where the 'Ws' were listed. Our eyes raced down the page. There were three Walfords and we both alighted on the name John Osborn Walford at the same time. Judith said it was the first time that a similar enquiry had showed such promise. It said only that the grave was in the area below the path, not on the detailed numbered map of the old churchyard. The wood had meant that the northern boundary had been substituted with the western one. Judith explained that this area had been blessed as 'sacred ground' in the 1930s.

Importantly, the notebook recorded the full text of Walford's inscription:

John Osborn Walford
Captain, Worcestershire Regiment
1914–1919
Died
February 21st 1922, aged 52 years

Judith and I left the church and headed quickly down below the path. It was not an area of the churchyard that I had looked at initially, having assumed that all the graves would be too recent. We scanned the faces of the oldest gravestones with no immediate sign of Walford; a number had moss, lichen and ivy covering all or part of the inscriptions. A rough-hewn sandstone grave, when cleared, showed a 'Martha Louisa Walford, wife of Robert Walford'. I said that according to the 1891 and 1901 censuses, Walford had a younger brother called Robert. A little nearer to the church was a similar rough-hewn sandstone grave. We hastened to the front to be greeted by a façade of moss and ivy. We gently pulled away this vegetation. There was a small flat area in the middle of the stone but the wording seemed to have completely disappeared. With some care we scratched away the shallow covering of moss. Just visible in the top right-hand corner were two faint letters 'RD'. In the opposite corner were an equally faint 'FE'. We had found him. We each gazed through tearful eyes at this sandstone memorial in complete silence. Eventually we hugged and as I departed Judith said that Walford's name deserved to be on the village's War Memorial.

This discovery re-energised my search for Walford's story. Neither my mother nor my aunt could recall their father ever mentioning his father, Osborn Walford. My mother could remember visiting his widow in a cottage below the walls of Warwick Castle and had a postcard picture of it. The 1881 census showed that Walford and his family were living in a smart street in Edgbaston and my own father explained that he had dealings about my grandmother's estate in the 1970s with a firm of solicitors in central Birmingham called Messrs Cox & Walford. My own knowledge of Edgbaston was limited to the famous cricket ground but looking at the map of their Victorian street showed that King Edward's School was nearby. Its website gave the contact details of an archivist whom I rang and enquired if there had been any Walfords at the school in the 1880s. It had its very own 'Judith Burman' in the guise of Alison Wheatley. She was equally helpful and, yes, Walford, his brothers and his father had attended the school although it was then in the same New Street, Birmingham as were the offices of Messrs Cox & Walford. Osborn Walford's name was not on any prize board nor prefect list. Alison asked if I could provide some details of his subsequent life to flesh out her archives. Despite extensive records of those who had served and died in the Great War, his service was unknown.

Once I had finished relating the details of his service, gallantry awards and suicide, her reaction was the same as Judith's – that he should be on the local War Memorial. In the case of King Edward's School, this was a complete building. When the school was moved from the city centre to the leafy suburbs of Edgbaston in the 1930s, the whole chapel had been transported stone by carved stone as the Memorial was an integral part of its interior. My own and Walford's good fortune persisted. Judith was on Birmingham's First World War Centenary Committee and the head of History, Paul Golightly, had initiated a short series of films to tell the story to their present generation of students of the 1914–1918 War. They had used the experiences of some notable alumni, with the films wonderfully produced by two brothers, Elliott and Zander Weaver – Old Edwardians still in their twenties. For *1916*, they had used the life of the headmaster's son, Robert Gilson, who went up to Trinity College, Cambridge in 1912, joined the OTC and left in 1914 to join up and was to die on the first day of the Battle of the Somme as a subaltern in the Suffolk Regiment. *1914* was centred on the experiences of an Oxford undergraduate and friend of Gilson's who did not immediately join up. After graduating with First Class Honours in 1915, he enlisted and, after training, was sent to France on 7th June 1916 and appointed as signals officer to the 11th Battalion of the Lancashire Fusiliers, part of the 25th Division – later to be the command under which Walford's $1/8^{th}$ Battalion of the Worcestershire Regiment was to serve from late September 1918. This fusilier officer was to lose almost all his close friends in the Great War. He was to survive and become perhaps the best known of all the Old Edwardians, Lieutenant JRR Tolkien.

Alison and Paul's enthusiasm and sympathy for Walford's story was to result in him being the unlikely central character of the school's 1918 film, *Walford's War*. It begins with a wonderful aerial view of the churchyard at Hanbury and the surrounding countryside, the home to many who were to join Walford in the 7th and 8th Battalions of the county regiment. Paul asked if I would be prepared to help with the film and to walk and talk through Walford's battlefields of October and November 1918. This had the immediate effect of me undertaking a preliminary visit to these lands between the Canal de Saint-Quentin and the Sambre Canal, armed with Major Stacke's wonderful *The Worcestershire Regiment in The Great War* – the War service across their fourteen battalions, with excellent hand-drawn maps of almost every action. It had the subsequent effect of my retirement from the world of investments in 2017 being followed within a week by joining the degree course in History at the New College of the Humanities and in 2020 of being accepted onto the Master's course in the History of War at King's College, London.

The first two tasks at King's College were to review a book on war history and, secondly, to review a document associated with war. In my enquiries at the National Archives for my book review, I entered '1/8th Battalion, the Worcestershire Regiment' into their search engine. To my surprise there was an official document and, astonishingly, it was the orders and Battle Reports of the period from the Battle of Beaurevoir on 5th October 1918 to the Armistice – all 78 handwritten pages, each signed by the commanding officer of the day. I knew already that over that thirty-day period the six senior officers of the Battalion had earned between them five Distinguished Service Orders (DSOs) and six Military Crosses (MCs). One recently promoted sergeant was to win an MC at Beaurevoir as a platoon commander. His company commander was killed that day and 2nd Lieutenant Edmund Wedgbury led that company for the following four weeks, during which time he earned an extraordinary DSO. Wedgbury had already earned a Distinguished Conduct Medal (DCM) and a Military Medal (MM) when in the ranks as a sergeant. He remains the only British infantry soldier of the Great War or any other war to win these four different gallantry medals.

Most of the men would have readily acknowledged that many such awards for officers holding commands were not often for their own specific moment of extreme gallantry but rather a recognition of a team effort – this was especially so for the DSO. Over that thirty-day period the Battalion's officers were to gain 5 DSOs and 12 MCs while the Other Ranks won 5 DCMs and 69 MMs as well as 2 Meritorious Service Medals, a total of 93 awards. James Holland lists the awards earned by the Sherwood Rangers Yeomanry fighting their way from Gold Beach on D-Day to the outskirts of Bremerhaven: eighteen Battle Honours as well as 2 DSOs, 18 MCs, 4 DCMs, 24 MMs, 6 Silver Stars (awarded by the United States) and 1 MBE. Although the 1/8th Battalion earned only fourteen Battle Honours in their whole war service and some of their awards were undoubtedly for gallant and distinguished service over a period of which these thirty days were just a part, the achievements and awards of these two extraordinary Territorial units deserve to be told. Holland, in his *Brothers in Arms,* created a most compelling tale of the service of front-line tank soldiers and commanders, of particular interest to those who have served the Crown in such armoured vehicles over subsequent decades. What follows is my attempt to tell a similar story of the service, heroism and suffering of the officers and men of the 1/8th Battalion, the Worcestershire Regiment. As with Holland's tales of the Second World War, there were innumerable regiments, batteries and battalions across the British Army who gave extraordinary service for their comrades and country in both Wars and whose stories will never be told. This book is to recognise them all and to acknowledge the suffering of so many of those who served in the years and decades after the War.

During the period of my enquiries and studies above, I undertook three of the Help for Heroes bicycle rides through the battlefields of Flanders. Their main purpose was to raise monies to help those who had been disfigured physically and mentally by their service in, or training for, Northern Ireland, the Falklands, Afghanistan, Iraq, Sierra Leone and many places not yet publicly acknowledged. They were journeys which will remain with me for the rest of my days, most notably watching a wounded young Parachute Regiment soldier get up from his wheelchair and walk across the road and pavement under the Menin Gate to lay a wreath on behalf of us all. He was walking on legs of Meccano, seemingly from his hips downwards. The Dutch schoolteachers around me were moved to tears. The following day I sat with him in the sunshine on a groyne on Dunkirk Beach after a hectic thirty-eight-mile bicycle chase from Passchendaele to the coast to make a rendezvous with a Spitfire to celebrate the end of our ride. He told me that these five days of cycling – on a hand-pedal system in his case – was the second finest achievement of his life after his passing of the P Company Course. There was no mention of his service or the action in which he had been maimed. Holland describes Stanley Christopherson's post-war life in his *Postscript.* He quotes from a 2015 interview with one of his squadron leaders: 'Stanley … was a lovely man. A very great man. A very great gentleman'. Holland continued: 'Yet there were dark moments, when Stanley would retreat. David and his sister, Sara Jane, did not understand why, but they knew to leave him alone at such times; few emerged from the war without any scars.' Of the six Worcester officers who gained their five DSOs and six MCs, in those closing weeks of the Great War, two – Lt Colonel Hubert Clarke DSO* and Captain Osborn Walford MC* – were to take their own lives over the ensuing two decades. Walford's son was serving in Waziristan at the time. He felt that his father had taken a cowardly way out and left an impoverished widow who was to survive him by twenty-four years. He never mentioned Walford in front of his own two daughters.

This tells a story of the life and trials of the infantry officers and soldiers who spent days, months or years in the trenches for King and Country, though mainly for their brother officers or fellow soldiers. A story of so many of the men who populate our family trees in the early part of the twentieth century. The vast majority did come home, many scarred by what they had seen or done, but hundreds of thousands of our relations remain in Flanders to this day – all remembered but so many as a name on the wall of one of the great memorials rather than in a grave with a headstone giving their name, rank, regiment or corps, the date of their death and, for some, a family inscription. It is a story which emphasises the importance of the local county friendships amongst the officers and their families, especially at times of injury and other difficulties. It explores what lay behind the subsequent suffering of those who lost so many of their young brother officers and men. It concludes by heralding the fascinating and important contributions in World War Two made by a number of these gallant and bemedalled survivors, such that four who served with the Battalion were to be knighted and two brothers played crucial, though differing, roles in helping to feed the nation at its second time of extraordinary peril.

PRINCIPAL CHARACTERS

Name, rank and awards at outbreak of War; awards during the War, then rank and role at the Armistice or last appointment if killed. Below is their age in August 1914, then their role in army or civilian life at outbreak of War.

Colonel Matthew Dixon DL, VD, JP retired
54, commanded 8th Battalion 1908–1911. Re-enlisted in 1914 to raise 2/8th Battalion. Retired in 1916.

Lt Col Walter K Peake OBE Lt Col, CO, 4Bn, Glouc. Regt
45, CO 8th Battalion and land agent on Hindlip estate.

Major Harry Carr DSO Lt Col, CO, 3rd Battalion
41, Regular soldier with Boer War experience, company commander, 4th Battalion serving in India and Burma.

Major Francis How TD CO, 11th Bn, Somerset Light Infantry
44, 'retired' solicitor – company commander in 8th Battalion – promoted to lieutenant 20th February 1901 and to major 15th August 1913.

Captain Hubert T Clarke DSO* Lt Col, CO, 1/8th Bn
28, Clerk to Worcestershire Old Age Pension Committee – Captain, 8th Battalion.

2Lt Jack (JC) Bate DSO*, MC* Major, 2-i-C, 1/8th Bn
20, working in an engineering company in Birmingham, commissioned 25th October 1911, promoted to lieutenant on 11th September 1913.

Leslie R Bomford DSO, MC* OC, A Company, 1/8th Bn
18, schoolboy at Wycliffe College, then medical student, Edinburgh University – commissioned July 1915 – younger brother of Douglas.

Captain J Osborn Walford MC* OC, C Company, 1/8th Bn
45, chicken farmer who had held commission in Royal Warwickshire Volunteers 1899–1903. First cousin of Col. Matthew Dixon. Captain, 8th Battalion from 5th September 1914.

Pte Edmund Wedgbury DSO, MC, DCM, MM OC, D Company, 1/8th Bn
22, worked in accounts department for Heenan & Froude – joined 8th Battalion as private on 9th May 1911, promoted to sergeant by March 1915 and commissioned 27th June 1917.

Edward Corbett MM RQMS, 1/8th Bn
43, solicitor – enlisted as private in 8th Battalion at outbreak of war. Resisted a commission.

Captain Daniel Sallis OBE, TD retired Feb 1918, Quartermaster, 1/8th Bn
49, Captain & Quartermaster, 8th Battalion from 13th May 1903 – having volunteered in 1881. Described in 1911 Census as 'Army Pensioner'.

Captain Lionel Kerwood killed, CO, 13th Bn, Cheshire Regt
28, solicitor with Alfred Kerwood & Sons, Redditch – commissioned into 8th Bn on 22nd October 1904.

Lt P Malcolm Kerwood killed, platoon commander, 1/8th Bn
24, solicitor with Alfred Kerwood & Sons, Redditch – commissioned into 8th Bn on 10th November 1909, brother of Lionel.

Captain Richard Burlingham Coy Cmdr, Officer Training Bn
30, agricultural merchant, Evesham – promoted to lieutenant on 20th May 1911 and to captain, 8th Battalion on 26th September 1914.

Douglas R Bomford wounded March 1917, captain, 2/8th Bn
20, medical student, Edinburgh University – commissioned 5th September 1914 with his cousin James – older brother of Leslie.

H Lance Evers MC* killed, OC, A Coy, 2/8th Bn
33, partner in Industrial Foundry and Engineering Co Ltd – enlisted as private in 8th Battalion at outbreak of war, rising to sergeant before being commissioned, 10th December 1914.

James F Bomford MC Captain and Transport Officer, 2/8th Bn
18, school at Bradfield College and OTC, had a place at Cambridge for that autumn having successfully completed his 'Little Go' exam – commissioned 5th September 1914 – cousin of Douglas & Leslie.

A Stanley Clutterbuck killed, platoon commander, 1/8th Bn
17, school at Aston Grammar School – commissioned 22nd October 1915, 1/8th Bn – brother of Norman.

Norman E Clutterbuck killed, company commander, 1/8th Bn
20, diamond merchant – enlisted as private soldier at outbreak of war, commissioned March 1915 into 8th Bn – elder brother of Stanley.

Sydney H Wilkes MC** Captain, 1/8th Bn – Coy Cmdr course in England.
19, undergraduate reading Classics at St John's College, Oxford – commissioned from Oxford University OTC into the 8th Battalion on 8th October 1915.

Charles R Pawsey MC* Captain, PoW – Austria, August 1918
20, undergraduate reading Classics at Wadham College, Oxford – commissioned 2nd September 1914 into 8th Battalion.

W Hugh S Chance Lieutenant, PoW 1916, Royal Flying Corps
18, school at Eton College and OTC – commissioned into 8th Battalion 11th March 1915.

Noel VH Symons MC wounded, Captain, 2/8th Bn – staff posting
19, enlisted as a sapper in the 1st Wessex Bn, The Royal Engineers in Bath and was at the Front by January 1915 before being commissioned 10th May 1915, into the 2/8th Bn.

G Laurence Watkinson MC* Captain & Adjutant, 1/8th Bn
18, civil servant – commissioned 12th (Reserve) Battalion, 31st May 1915.

Hugh W Davies DSO, MC Major, PoW – Germany, 2/8th Bn
43, fruit-grower, Pershore – Captain, 8th Battalion (from Assam Valley Light Horse) from 5th September 1914.

2Lt H Gwynne Newman Captain Instructor, School of Infantry
24, having been commissioned to 8th Battalion on 22nd November 1913 from Oxford University OTC.

LETTERS, DIARIES AND HISTORIES

The new telling of the story of the remarkable exploits of these gallant gentlemen of Worcestershire is possible because of a number of publications, mostly dating from 1919 and the 1920s; but also because of the more recent publication of letters, diaries and papers of some of the officers and soldiers involved by their families. Rather than list these key materials in the Bibliography just before the index, I believe that their details should appear here at the outset with an explanation of where they can be found and why they are important to this story. With apologies to those who have so ably taught me over the last four years through my degree and Master's courses at the New College of the Humanities and at King's College, London, this detail will not follow any prescribed referencing system. This is designed to help those less familiar with the formalities of modern histories but who may be encouraged to probe deeper into their own family history or that of the regiments or battalions in which some of their predecessors and relations served. I have not recorded the page number from which some script or a story has been borrowed from each publication – I can assure you that they are accurate. I would much rather that you read the complete text of each publication if you find this story as fascinating and compelling as I did and do.

I list them in the order in which they were first published:

The first is the digital copy of the *War Diary of the Battalion* from 1st September 1918 until 28th February 1919 from the National Archives (WO/95/2251/2) in the original handwritten form – described as the *War Diary* in the ensuing text.

The Berrow's Worcester Journal was a weekly newspaper, published on Saturdays, just eight pages each week. It provided details of all men of Worcestershire who were killed, wounded or honoured whatever their service, corps or regiment – as opposed to men who served in the Worcestershire Regiment but hailed from other counties. Many of those who died merited a paragraph which often quoted from the letters written to the family by officers in command of the deceased. As with the *History*, the exploits or demise of officers was always recalled but in the *Journal* there is much greater detail of the Other

Ranks, their pre-War employment and their families. It can be read at The Hive in the centre of Worcester or purchased electronically in six-monthly sections.

1/8th Battalion, The Worcestershire Regiment 1914–1918 was published by War Narratives Publishing Company in 1919 and sold at the price of one shilling and sixpence (7.5p). The main contributors were two of the officers who commanded the Battalion, Colonel WK Peake OBE and Lt Colonel HT Clarke DSO*. This includes a full list of the actions of the Battalion together with details of all officers and Other Ranks who were awarded medals for their gallant actions. It ends with a Roll of all who died as a result of their War service. A copy of this is held in the Worcestershire Regiment Archives. This will be referred to as the *Booklet* in the ensuing text.

An appendix to the above publication, headed *1/8th Battalion, The Worcestershire Regiment* was also published and sold in 1919 at the price of sixpence (2.5p). This includes notes of the two other officers who commanded the Battalion in action, Lt Colonel HA Carr DSO and Major JP Bate DSO*, MC*. This is referred to as the *Appendix* in the text.

(For those less familiar with the formalities of military ranks and gallantry awards, if you were awarded a particular medal on more than one occasion, the initials after your name for that award, e.g. MC, is not repeated but a star/asterisk is added. Thus, Major JP Bate above won both the DSO and the MC on two occasions, hence DSO*, MC*.)

The War Story of the 1/8th (Territorial) Battalion by RQMS Edward C Corbett MM. This was published by the *Worcester Herald* in 1919 following its publication in the *Berrow's Worcester Journal* as a series between March and June of that year. Copies are held in the Regimental Archive, the Worcester Records Office and the Imperial War Museum. It will be referred to as *War Story* in the text. Captain Laurence Watkinson MC* later claimed in a tribute to Corbett that he wrote it entirely from memory 'in a week's continuous effort'.

The Worcestershire Regiment in The Great War by Captain H FitzM. Stacke MC is now available through the Naval & Military Press in two volumes. It was first published by GT Cheshire & Sons Ltd of

Kidderminster in 1928, a time when Captain Stacke was attending Staff College. This is an extraordinary work with 515 pages of text and maps together with details of all awards made to those who served across the 14 battalions as well as a full Roll of those who died. The hand-drawn maps of all the important actions of the various battalions show the disposition of their companies with the roads, railways and housing as they were at the time of the War. They are works of art and essential to understanding the telling of this and the other battalion stories. From the 1/8th Battalion's perspective, one of their commanding officers, Lt Col Harry Carr, was on the Regimental History Sub-Committee – he commanded also the 3rd Battalion later in the War. In 1919, a War Memorial Fund was raised by public subscription with a threefold aim: to tell the story of those from the county who served and fell; to provide a Memorial Cross outside the Cathedral; and, lastly, to provide a Relief Fund for the 'benefit of the Worcestershire men born and bred, or men who served in any unit belonging to the County, the County Regiment, the Yeomanry, Territorial Artillery etc., their widows, orphans and dependents'. The *Journal* of 28th December 1918 reported on a meeting to discuss this fund-raising with suggestions that some £100,000 would be needed just for the Relief Fund as Major JM Reddie estimated 70,000 from the County served, 5,000 died and the same number were discharged wounded with about 40,000 dependents. In the end, a total of £10,157 16s 0d was raised, which would have a present purchasing power of £558,808. The *History* recorded that these monies were divided as follows:

Erection of a Memorial Window and Memorial Books in Worcester Cathedral	£1,136 18s 6d
A Memorial Cross outside the Cathedral Grounds	£1,994 11s 10d
Relief Fund for the benefit of Worcestershire men born and bred	£5,626 5s 8d
The History of the Worcestershire Regiment in the War	£1,400 0s 0d

The original copies of the History were sent with a covering letter dated 2nd May 1929 from the Secretary, CH Bird, to explain that the price of 30 Shillings (£1.50) caused a 'loss on the printing and binding alone [which] will exceed £600' and 'expressing the hope that when you have an opportunity of seeing what a magnificent work the History is, you will feel disposed to make a further contribution'. The quality and detail of the maps on a thickish tracing paper merit such a contribution on their own – and are used extensively to illustrate this story. This is referred to as the *History* in the text. I am grateful to Robert Wedgbury, 2Lt E Wedgbury's youngest son, for the loan of his father's original copy.

The *First World War: War Diary: 48 Division, 144 Infantry Brigade, Worcestershire Regiment, 1/8th Battalion – 1st April 1915 to 31 October 1917 (National Archives: WO95/2759/2).* This is the published War Diary of the Battalion for its service in France and Belgium from its landing in the early hours of 1st April 1915 until the Division headed to Italy in November 1917. The War Diary was handwritten each day, normally by the adjutant, on Army Form C. 2118 and signed at the bottom of each page by the commanding officer. Many entries are normally little more than a sentence or two with a full page or more used on days of a major action. This will be referred to as the *War Diary.* In the later weeks of the War, it included all the Operational Orders and the post-battle Narratives.

The 25th Division in France and Flanders written by Lt Colonel M Kincaid-Smith in 1918 and 1919. The 1/8th Battalion joined this Division in September 1918. It is now published by the Naval & Military Press. It is referred to as the *Divisional History.*

Brothers in War: Letters from the Western Front 1915–1918. This was introduced and edited by Nicholas Bomford and is available through Lulu (lulu.com). It was first published in 2013. It tells the War story of Nicholas' three uncles in the main through their correspondence with their parents, Raymond and Eveline Bomford who lived near Evesham. The brothers were Ben, Douglas, and Leslie Bomford who all served in the local county regiments during the War: Ben as a private soldier in the Royal Warwickshire Regiment; Douglas as an officer in the 2/8th Battalion of the Worcestershire Regiment; and

Leslie as an officer in the 1/8th Battalion, commanding A Company in the last weeks of the War aged just 21. He ended the War as Captain LR Bomford DSO, MC*. He lived until 1981 and his son, Robert, recalls that he was one of the few who spoke of his wartime exploits in his later life. I was most fortunate to be lent all the original letters by Robert Bomford, Leslie's son who still survives. This book is referred to as the *Bomford Letters* in the text below.

Captain LR Bomford wrote down his memories in his last years. They number 66 pages of type, perhaps his own, certainly with his own penned corrections. Nicholas Bomford used them in his *Brothers in War*. They and the text of a talk which Leslie gave to the Grasshoppers at the Grosvenor Hotel in Stockbridge on 6th January 1971 were lent to me by his son Robert. They give a wonderful insight into the man himself as well as into his contribution to the development of arable farming on chalk downlands and his work to help the nation's farmers improve their yields during the Second World War. These will be referred to as the *Memoirs*.

Lance's War was compiled by Jane Stanley, Lance's great-niece, and published privately in 2015. They are the diaries of Captain HL Evers MC* who served with the 2/8th Battalion and was the only officer who crossed to France with that battalion in May 1916 who was to be 'killed in action', on Friday 1st November 1918 while reconnoitring the ground for an attack the following day. His diaries portray an extremely professional Territorial officer who was a friend of both Douglas Bomford and Osborn Walford, who were also aboard the SS *Duchess of Argyle* on the night of 24/25th May 1916 when the 2/8th Battalion crossed to France. This is referred to as *Lance's War* in the text.

Letters from Flanders and Picardy 1915–1916 are those of Captain RH Burlingham and published privately by his family under the initials DHB. Henry Burlingham was second-in-command of D Company of the 8th Battalion at the outbreak of War and company commander of B Company when they crossed to France. He was to remain in that role until he was committed to No 8 Hospital at Rouen on 1st June 1916. He was a Worcestershire County hockey player before the War and had just been selected for his first England Cap in

September 1914 for a match against Germany – a match which never took place. The telegram to his wife, Mary, said simply: 'Wounded and Shell-Shock, Slight'. He was not to return to the Front but he was to regain his command just once, at a D Company Veterans Dinner at the Evesham Hotel in August 1964, aged 81. There were 28 other veterans at the dinner that night, with Burlingham as the eldest and Leonard Jones the youngest at 68. It was to my deep regret that as I completed this book, I saw in *The Times* the announcement that DHB 'had ceased to breathe' on 27th May 2022 – it would have been wonderful to have spoken to him about his father. These will be referred to as *Burlingham's Letters.*

The *London Gazette* is where all gallantry and leadership awards were formally announced, including the citations for specific awards. Additionally, all changes of substantive rank for officers are also announced in the *London Gazette.* Its website requires some perseverance as the electronic reader seems to struggle with the rank and regimental abbreviations, let alone the multitude of individuals involved. At the time of the Great War, there was also an *Edinburgh Gazette* which made similar announcements. I will refer to all such information as from the *Gazette.*

The last key resource is the Commonwealth War Graves Commission website: https://www.cwgc.org/find-records/find-war-dead/. It is a most efficient source of information about the individuals who lost their lives during the War, including those who died of their wounds in the thirty months to August 1921. This group of men were also entitled to a gravestone so familiar to those who have been to the wonderful cemeteries of France and Flanders. For those who took their lives thereafter, even as a result of their War experiences, no such honour was bestowed – as with the two senior officers of the Battalion. Information derived from this website is shown as the *CWGC* website hereafter.

The last aspect of the ensuing text is the ranks of the various officers and soldiers. Unless stated otherwise, I use the rank of the individual at the time of the action and any awards thus far attained. This is the system used in the *History* and by the *CWGC.* It does not differentiate between the rank being 'substantive' or 'acting'. Each received the pay of their 'acting' rank but at the end of the War all officers reverted to their substantive rank. The term 'Temporary' prefixed the rank of those 'acting' in the rank, normally one or two above their substantive rank. This is perhaps best typified by the announcement in the *Gazette* on 24th November 1916:

> His Majesty the King has been graciously pleased to confer the Victoria Cross on the undermentioned Officers, Non-commissioned Officers and Men:
> Lieutenant (Temporary Lieutenant Colonel) Roland Boys Bradford, MC., Durham Light Infantry. For most conspicuous bravery and good leadership in attack…

Bradford was killed the following year, on 30th November 1917 aged 25, the youngest brigadier-general in the Army. As a lieutenant colonel, Bradford was three ranks above his substantive rank and five above when he became a brigadier general. His CWGC headstone refers to him as Brigadier General with no reference to 'Temporary' or 'Acting', which is the standard for all such military graves. The *CWGC* website reflects the fact that now it looks after three of the four Bradford brothers, Captain George Bradford VC, RN; 2nd Lieutenant James Bradford MC; and Brigadier General Roland Bradford VC, MC. The fourth brother survived his service, Colonel Sir Thomas Bradford DSO.

It is for this reason that Captain (Temporary Major) JO Walford in 1918 was reduced to his substantive rank as the War ended, and he retired from the Army in 1920 in the rank of Captain, which is reflected on his gravestone in 1922. Had the bullet which struck him on 4th November 1918 proved fatal, he would have died with 'Major JO Walford' and 'MC & Bar' on his CWGC headstone. He was John Osborn Walford – John after his father, Osborn after his mother, Ellen Osborn, sister of the respected Birmingham architect, Frank Barlow Osborn. He was known as Osborn, as his son was known as Scott after his own mother and Osborn's wife, Margaret Scott – though with the full name of John Erskine Scott Walford, my grandfather.

The last aspect of this book is that the text from these sources is repeated verbatim – thus some spelling and grammar may appear incorrect. Not all authors were educated to university level and the letters and *War Diary* entries were written at the Front – at times, when shells may have been in the air. This includes ranks and their abbreviations, as well as many different ways of describing the 1/8th Battalion and other units. Letters, orders and other similar texts are laid out as similarly as possible to that in the document itself.

The photographs throughout this book are from a series of sources. The majority were taken either during training or at the Front in 1914 and 1915, perhaps into 1916. The albums presented to the Regiment Archive by Captain Pawsey and Captain Burlingham may well be photographs taken by the same camera. A further set, from Captain Paskin, can be found in the IWM. The third album is largely of those in the 8th Battalion during training whilst in England. The quality of the pictures is a reflection of the technology of the time and of time on the small contact prints which resulted. I make no apologies, I think you should see these men and their work. I am indebted to Helen Hunter at the Mercian Regiment's archive in Worcester for her patient reproduction of these albums. Additional photographs were printed in the *Berrow's Worcester Journal*, both of parades in Worcester, thumb-print formal photographs of those who died and some family groups when many sons of a single family served. Again the quality is poor by modern standards but each tells a story and helps to bring my text to life.

The remainder are of graves, memorials and battle sites which I took as I followed the Battalion's progress through France and Belgium.

THE 1/8TH BATTALION, WORCESTERSHIRE REGIMENT

The 29th (Worcestershire) Regiment of Foot was created in 1694 and was to form the 1st Battalion, the Worcestershire Regiment in the Army reorganisation of 1881. The 2nd Battalion originated as the 36th (Herefordshire) Regiment of Foot which was first established in 1701. It was the latter which brought with it the newly formed Worcestershire Regiment's motto 'FIRM'. Its origins are thought to be in recognition of its performance at the Battle of Lauffeld in Belgium in 1747, but it was only confirmed by the Inspector of Regimental Colours on 6th January 1817. An alternative origin is that it stands for 'First Infantry Royal Marines' in recognition of the service of the 29th Regiment of Foot, who, in the absence of the Royal Marines themselves, were used in that role along with the 2nd Regiment of Foot, The Queens (Royal West Surrey Regiment) at the naval Battle of the Glorious First of June, 1794 (known also as the Battle of Ushant as a battle honour). Captain Myles' *History* referred to this action, saying that 'in honour of which they are to this day permitted to carry on their Colours the device of the Naval Crown, superscribed "1st June, 1794"'.

The 7th and 8th Battalions can trace their history back to the formation of the Worcestershire Rifle Volunteer Force which was established in 1860. The Crimean War and the increasing demands of the maintenance of order in Britain's constantly expanding Empire led to an acknowledgement in the 1850s that there were too few trained troops in Britain itself, either to defend against invasion or to assist the civil powers in the maintenance of law and order.

The regulations for volunteer and Territorial battalions changed on a number of occasions before the outbreak of the First World War, initially in 1881 when the 1st and 2nd Volunteer Battalions were formed but in the main because of the demands of the Boer War and the deficiencies which it uncovered. Lord Haldane's subsequent Army Corps reforms in 1907 divided the Army into three groupings: the Regular

Army Forces Overseas; the Regular Army Expeditionary Force; and the Volunteer Territorial Forces for Home Defence. The whole of the latter into which the 7th and 8th Battalions of the Worcestershire Regiment fitted was organised in the same way as the Regular Army with its own brigades and divisions. These Territorial battalions were administered by the new County Associations under the presidency of the Lord Lieutenants – the 9th Earl of Coventry (1838–1930) in the case of Worcestershire. This system helped to ensure a strong link between the counties and these Territorial battalions of the county regiments. The County Association was responsible for the clothing, payment and maintenance of these battalions. The membership of Worcestershire's County Association as recorded in the *History* included a number of luminaries: Colonel Sir Richard Temple Bt, Lt Colonel H Howard, Colonel Viscount Cobham, Colonel The Earl of Plymouth, Colonel Sir Harry Vernon, Mr ES Albright JP, Mr TR Bayliss JP, Major F Checketts and Major SJ Tombs. The Lords Coventry and Cobham were the Lord Lieutenants of Worcestershire between them for a combined period of 58 years (1891–1949). This initiative of Lord Haldane had the effect of ensuring a much closer link between county and regiment than had previously been the case, even for the four regular battalions serving mainly overseas.

Colonel Matt Dixon

The two Territorial battalions, the 7th and the 8th, were grouped with their equivalent battalions from Warwickshire and Gloucestershire into the (48th) South Midland Division. The Division trained as a cohesive force each year but the responsibility for the training and development of each individual battalion fell very much on the shoulders of the commanding officer (Colonel EEV Wheeler for the 7th and Lt Colonel Matthew Dixon for the 8th). Each battalion was strengthened by an adjutant found from the regular battalions (Captains C Richardson, GMC Davidge and PU Vigors in succession from 1910 for the 7th and Captain Percy Whalley from April 1914 for the 8th). As a measure of their ability, Davidge was to command the 1st Battalion for the last two years of the War, earning a DSO and Bar, while Captain PR Whalley was to command the 3rd Battalion in 1918, earning a DSO. The combination of those at the head of the County Association and these commanding officers ensured that each battalion not only became officered by the children of their friends, relations and acquaintances from across the county but also that there were enough to provide officers for the four Territorial battalions once each was divided into two, the 1/7th and 2/7th, and the 1/8th and 2/8th in the early months of the War. Such links were typified by Captain Lance Evers' mother recording in her diary that when Lance was on leave in April 1917:

> Our Lallot [Lance] went to Worcester by the 8.27 train as he had many things to do. He rather wanted to go to Captain Vigors's funeral, so he and Captain Walford met at the club and went together. Lallot said it was very impressive. Two generals were present and many officers and soldiers stationed at Worcester and all done in an impressive manner. After lunch he and Captain Walford and Captain Davies went to Tardebigg to see Colonel Dixon…

Captain Phillip Vigors MVO was attached from the 18th Regiment of Foot, The Royal Irish Regiment but lived at Cedars, Fernhill Heath. The *Journal* recorded that before and during the War, he and his wife hunted extensively with the Worcestershire Hunt. He left over £13,000 in 1917 so he was a wealthy man in his own right. His grave can be found at St Michael and All Angels Church at Martin Hussingtree.

We find some of our officers and Other Ranks in the pages of the *Journal* in June and July of 1914. The 27th June edition was full of shooting results with the Quartermaster, Major Sallis, featuring in the prizes together with Captain Clarke of Worcester, so presumably HT Clarke, as well as Lts Hemming and Bendyshe – sadly, neither were to survive the War. There was JE Rayer in the bows of the Worcester Coxed Pair at the Stratford-upon-Avon Regatta – and happily rowing again in the regattas of 1919 as Captain JE Rayer. Major FAW How, the son of the Bishop of Wakefield and an alumni of Uppingham and Keble College, Oxford was playing lots of cricket, seemingly always being on the winning team despite being run-out a number of times, calling into question his fitness and judgement, not exactly ideal for a senior officer. Happily, he was playing again in the summer of 1919 and an interesting line appeared in the scorebook of the Rev M. Powers XI v. The Hon. Peggy Coventry's Viginti XI:

FAW How c. Martin b. Walford 55 – but it was not the Old Gent, rather his son, the recently commissioned 2Lt JES Walford, who was also to score 50 when opening the batting for the Viginti XI.

It was customary for battalions to leave their colours in the safekeeping of the local cathedral when departing on overseas operations. The 8th Battalion, being a recent creation, had no such precedent. Instead, they placed them at the Shirehall. The *Journal* reported: 'To the strain of the Marseillaise played by the band (under the conductorship of Mr Ernest Davies), about 80 members of A Company of the Battalion marched to the Shirehall. They were under command of Lt Col Peake, and were accompanied also by Capt. and Adjutant Whalley, Capt. HT Clarke (commanding the company) and the colour-bearers were Lt Burlingham and 2Lt Bate...'

DEPOSITING THE COLOURS OF 8th BATTALION WORCESTERSHIRE REGIMENT, AT THE SHIREHALL.

I am sure that Clarke would not be expecting to be the commanding officer of the 1/8th Battalion over four years later when the colours were recovered, nor having 2Lt Bate as his second-in-command. All five mentioned were to survive their service.

On the 24th September 1914, the *Worcester Daily Times* reported under the title 'Recruitment meeting in Ombersley':

> A meeting was held in the Ombersley Schools (pictured today) on Saturday night to appeal for recruits for the 8th Battalion (Reserves) Worcestershire Regiment. Those present included Lord and Lady Sandys, the Revd J., Mrs and Miss Webster, Captain Walford, and many others. The platform was decorated with plants and flags lent by Lord Sandys, and in a conspicuous position was Ombersley's Roll of Honour consisting of the names of 40 young men of Ombersley who have already offered their services to their country.
>
> Lord Sandys, in introducing Capt. Walford, mentioned the many dissentions which were rife in the country two months ago – the Ulster question, etc. – all of which, no doubt, the Kaiser had looked upon as favourable to himself. These had now vanished, and the whole Empire was one in heart and soul, and in determination to come to grips with Germany and remove her baneful influence from Europe. Even the Suffragettes [Walford's sister Ellen being one] had renounced their crusade against society, and had taken up the womanly work of caring for the sick and wounded. He expressed the determination of the Empire to see the war through to the bitter end, and reminded them that, in order to bring the campaign to a successful issue, great sacrifices must be made, and men must offer themselves whole-heartedly for their country's service. He asked the young men to enlist, first for liberty, secondly to support our Army, fighting against tremendous odds, and thirdly to revenge those who had fallen so nobly and heroically.
>
> Captain Walford said that as far as the supposed origin of the war was concerned, peace might easily have been kept; but the German Emperor had long ago made up his mind to fight England, and, thinking that now was his opportunity, he had fanned the flame, and declared war on France. The Germans were a clever and scientific nation, but utterly untrustworthy. He hoped no one would imagine this was going to be either an easy or a short affair. We should have to strain every nerve and endeavour. Only by continuous enlisting

Captain Osborn Walford – The Old Gent

could we hope to make up the wastage of war. There were millions arrayed against us and what seemed to us a huge loss by the enemy was as nothing in comparison with our much smaller losses. If we had but taken Lord Roberts' advice, and had been able to put a million men in the field the war might have been shorter, but now, having determined to crush the enemy, we must be prepared for a long struggle, which must not be ended as long as we had a sovereign to spend and a man to send out.

He was glad to see that Ombersley had done so well, and hoped she would send still more of her sons to help our heroic brethren, who, simply because they were comparatively small in number had to take such awful risks as were entailed in a frontal attack. He was glad to tell them he was going to the Front himself, and he hoped he should meet some of them there.

A nation like England, who could command the esteem and respect of the enemies of a few years ago, and the love of all parts of her Dominions – India, South Africa, Canada, Australia – and of the whole world, was not the nation to go under to Germany, and we were determined that the terms of peace should be dictated by us in Berlin. War was no doubt hard on the women, but the women of England knew how to stand up against difficulties, and were willing to send their loved ones away in defence of their loved native land. He was sure the young men would respond to their country's call, for how could they bear to think, in the coming years, that they stayed quietly at home while others fought for them.

Lord Sandys proposed a vote of thanks to Captain Walford.

The Vicar, in seconding it, said he hoped that everyone there would ponder on the eloquent and inspiring speech they had heard. They might not be able to join on the spur of the moment, but he had no doubt that many would join after pondering it over. They might be quite sure that the women left behind would be well cared for, for all who were physically unfit to go and debarred by age, would do all they could to look after the wives, mothers, and children left at home.

Captain Osborn Walford, then aged 45, was active across the county over these early months of the War. He attended a lecture in Hanbury given by Mr B Vernon in early September entitled 'The War, its causes and possible consequences'. The same week, he was on the platform at the Salters Hall in Droitwich at the Mayor's appeal for men and funds. He supported other speakers and pointed out that 'Worcester, Droitwich, Bromsgrove and Birmingham had still a number of young men who could enlist'. He was reported by the same newspaper as attending the Sixth Cathedral Parade on 1st November 1914, together with Col Dixon, Captains Griffiths, Mitchell and Cliff with some 1,550 on parade. Then in December the *Bromsgrove Messenger* reported that 'Back in the county, through the kind offices of Mrs Coleman, of Hanbury Rectory, HM the Queen sent 100 flannel shirts and 500 pairs of socks to Captain Walford … for the men of E Company

8th (Reserve) Battalion, the Worcestershire Regiment. These were distributed, and three cheers for Her Majesty were heartily given by the Company'. As Major Creak's sister reported that the Battalion were in good spirits during her visit to Malden in Essex at that time, it appears that Walford had been designated by his cousin, Colonel Matthew Dixon VD, as being more useful back in Worcestershire than in awaiting invasion or zeppelins down on the Essex coast.

Hugh Chance remembered his application to be an officer in the autumn of 1914. He reported to the Regiment's Territorial headquarters in Worcester to be interviewed by Colonel Matthew Dixon who stood 6'8" tall and by Major John Reddie who we will come across again as the Secretary to the County Association throughout the War. Chance recalled that 'after an interview I was accepted and assigned to one of the eight companies parading on the small barrack square adjoining the Territorial HQ in Silver St., Worcester. We had no uniforms, few small arms and very little equipment but the Bn [Battalion] was keen as mustard and had recruited a fine bunch of volunteers'. He could not join the Battalion until his commission was confirmed – in March 1915 – by which time the 8th was stationed at

Northampton. He was posted to D Company with whom he served for a year, the last months of which were based at Tidworth, with training on Salisbury Plain. He observed that in 1915 when the 8th Battalion was divided into two – the 1/8th available for overseas service and the 2/8th for Home Service – the latter lost many of their best NCOs and soldiers to the 1/8th when they were sent to France at short notice on 31st March 1915. As such, and with dissatisfaction at his company commander, Chance applied to the commanding officer and to the Adjutant to join the Royal Flying Corps. He said that despite his size, he was accepted. Thus ended a brief service in the 8th Battalion. He recalled the second-in-command as being Major Francis Checketts and the adjutant as the 39-year-old Captain PW Vigors. Checketts was to be the first commanding officer of the 2/8th Battalion and took them to France in May 1916 but was invalided home shortly thereafter. Captain Vigors was posted to the 1/7th Battalion. He died on 2nd April 1917 back at home. His death and grave are recorded on the *CWGC* website but the *History* does not include him on its Roll of Honour.

Colonel Matt Dixon and Lt Col Francis Checketts

It is early to discuss deaths, but it is the memory of those who made the ultimate sacrifice that causes us to parade on or near the 11th November every year and to wear our poppies and, in an increasing number of cases, their medals. We remember them for many reasons and not just because King George V implored us to do so in his message sent to the next-of-kin of all who died in the service of their country, on a scroll headed by the Royal Cipher:

> He whom this scroll commemorates
> was numbered among those who,
> at the Call of King and Country, left all
> that was dear to them, endured hardness,
> faced danger, and finally passed out of
> the sight of men by the path of duty
> and self-sacrifice, giving up their own
> lives that others might live in freedom.
> Let those who come after see to it
> that his name be not forgotten.

The *History* records the 9,463 names of the those who served in the Worcestershire Regiment who were killed in action; died of wounds; died of illness; died in training accidents; died as Prisoners of War. 505 of them were officers and 8,958 were soldiers – we will come to that ratio towards the end of this tome but a battalion, at full strength, had some 30 officers and 1,000 men. So three per cent of those serving were officers, whilst over five per cent of those who died were officers in the regiment. The names in the *History* were compiled from two publications by HM Stationery Office: *Officers died in the Great War* (1919) and *Soldiers died in the Great War; Part 34; The Worcestershire Regiment* (1921). The names of those who died subsequently due to the War are not officially recorded, nor are their names found on the great memorials in towns and villages across the country. If their death was after 31st August 1921, they were not entitled to such an honour, nor to a War Grave.

Corporal Leonard Lipscombe, in one of the wonderful Imperial War Museum interviews in their *Sound Archive*, related how he was coming to the end of his four-year Territorial service at the outbreak of the War. He said that all those in his circumstances were immediately extended in service by an extra twelve months. He crossed to France with B Company the following March. These interviews are thoroughly recommended both for what they tell of a soldier's wartime service but also of working life at the time. An example is Private Charles Mitchell of the 1/7th Battalion who was farming in Devon until he reached the aged of 18 in December 1916. Although in a protected industry, he was quick to enlist and he gave a good resume of his training at Sandhills Camp on the edge of Salisbury Plain and then his service with that Battalion from January 1918 until the Armistice. He was not interviewed until 1986 but his memory was still good. He was one of seven brothers to serve across the armed forces and they all came home. As we shall see, many families were not so lucky.

Soon after the outbreak of War it was realised that whole reinforcement battalions, not just the British Expeditionary Force (BEF), were required to reinforce the battalions already in France and Belgium. At that stage it was believed by many – in contrast to Walford – that the War would be over by Christmas (1914) although the authorities still needed to know which Territorial officers and soldiers were in 'critical' employment and, thus, were more important back in Britain. All members of the 8th Battalion were asked if they could and were prepared to serve overseas. Most of those who could were badged to the 1/8th Battalion while the remainder formed the cadre on which the 2/8th Battalion would be established.

As the War started in August 1914, all Territorial battalions were at their Summer (Training) Camp so such a reorganisation was much more easily achieved. The 8th Worcesters were in Minehead on the Somerset coast for their Summer Camp when War was declared. They returned by train to Worcester on the following day – 5th August – and after four days of busy preparations, they entrained for their War stations – primarily to guard against invasion on the North Sea coast. With its sister battalion, the 7th, the 8th routed via Swindon to Danbury in Essex. After a month they were billeted in Maldon for the winter months. One factor that could not easily be addressed was that the senior officers, the warrant officers (WOs) and many of the Senior Non-Commissioned Officers (SNCOs) were mature in age. Promotion in peacetime was very much 'dead men's shoes' and retirement was the usual mechanism which triggered opportunity for the next generation. This meant that many of the commanding officers and their potential replacements were well into their forties, a number approaching fifty – on average some ten years older than their present-day contemporaries and twenty years older than those in such roles by the end of the War.

The first *Journal* after War was declared was that of 8th August. The first letter was from Sir Richard Temple:

> WORCESTERSHIRE TERRITORIALS:
> CHAIRMAN'S APPEAL
> Sir – There is a deficiency in the Territorial Forces of this County of 259 men, of which Worcester contributes: Yeomanry 51, R.F.A. [Royal Field Artillery] 29, and Infantry 57. Redditch: R.F.A. 47, Infantry 31. Kidderminster: R.F.A. 10, Infantry 30; and there are smaller deficiencies in other places. I am therefore writing to you to make these facts public in the hope of inducing Recruiting Committees in all places, especially those above mentioned, to become particularly active in the matter of obtaining recruits for the Territorial Force of this County in view of the very grave situation throughout the Continent of Europe. May I hope, also, that those in a position to actively join in the defence of their country may not let so important an occasion pass of proving patriotism of the Loyal County of Worcester is no idle boast.
> RC Temple
> Chairman, Worcestershire Territorial Association,
> 16, Silver Street, Worcester
> 3rd August, 1914

On the same page, 5, of that *Journal* edition is an article under the heading of *TERRITORIAL RECRUITING*:

> Worcester Companies Filling Up

> On Wednesday [5th] a special appeal was made for recruits for the Worcester (Headquarters) Companies of the 8th Battalion Worcestershire Regiment. There was a ready response. B Company is full, but 15 more men can be accepted in A Company.
>
> A special effort is still needed to bring the Droitwich and Stoke Works ('E') Company [Captain Walford's] up to strength, and recruits are still being accepted for the Redditch, Evesham, Malvern and Pershore Companies.
>
> Among the recruits in the Worcestershire Companies is Mr EC Corbett, solicitor, who returned from Spain a few days ago. He enlisted as a private.

We will hear much more of Mr Corbett and he was not to remain a private for long.

The following week's *Journal* reported on the *TERRITORIALS AT CATHEDRAL – Impressive service on Sunday:*

> Over a thousand Worcestershire Territorials (about 800 members of the 8th Battalion and over 200 Yeomanry) responded to the invitation of the Dean and Chapter to attend a special service at the Cathedral on Sunday. They marched from Rainbow Hill, headed by the Droitwich Bugle Band, under Bugle-Major Bourne, and the 8th Battalion band, under Bandmaster WE Davies. Col. Peake was in command of the 8th Battalion, being supported by his full complement of officers, and Capt. Cheape (Adjutant) was in command of the Yeomanry in the absence of Lord Dudley…

The following day, the Battalion was on the move, with the *Journal* reporting:

> The road to Shrub Hill Station on Monday evening was lined with an excited crowd as the 8th Battalion of the Worcestershire Regiment marched through on their way to the station. Four companies, made up from men from Worcester, Malvern, Upton, Pershore, and Evesham, left shortly after six, and the remaining four companies, representing Kidderminster, Bromsgrove, Droitwich, and King's

> Norton, started just before seven. As they marched to the station they all joined in popular songs, and some blew penny trumpets. At the station the police had the greatest difficulty in keeping platforms from being overcrowded. Relations were allowed on the station to say 'Good-bye', but there were many other ordinary spectators who eluded the vigilance of the force. There were a few tearful faces among those left behind, but the general note was one of hilarity. One of the departing soldiers tenderly fondled a carnation given him by his sweetheart. There was a great waving of handkerchiefs and cheering as both trains left the station. Over 500 men left by each train.

The *Journal*'s edition of 12th September had a headline '8th Battalion full' with a draft of 53 men from Redditch arriving that morning. The *Journal* was to become a source of continual news of the progress of officers' careers in the *Local News* section, as on 7th November 1914 with an update on recent promotions which, for the 8th Battalion, included:

> The undermentioned to be captains:
> HW Davies (late Second-Lieutenant Assam Valley Light Horse);
> JO Walford (late Captain 1st VB [Volunteer Battalion 1899–1903], the Royal Warwickshire Regt.);
> AW Odgers (late Lieutenant of this Battalion).

The undermentioned to be second lieutenants:
DR Bomford
RH Stallard (late Cadet Shrewsbury School Contingent, Junior Division, OTC)
JF Bomford

Douglas Bomford, Dick Stallard, James Bomford

All these officers are to feature in this story, were to survive the War and to accumulate eight gallantry medals between them. There are some interesting previous regiments in which they served although there is no evidence that Walford reached the rank of captain before resigning his commission in 1903. The same 12th September edition listed the officers from the county who had already laid down their lives for their country – seven from the 2nd Battalion, six from the 3rd Battalion and eight others, together with three Naval officers. The prospects for those reaching the Front were clear, with fifteen of those who died being subalterns, five captains and one major.

Conscription did not start until 2nd March 1916 under the Military Service Act and was for all men between 18 and 41 years of age with the only exemptions being widowers with children; ministers of religion; those working in reserved occupations such as agriculture, mining and politics; and conscientious objectors. Military Service Tribunals were established to consider special exemptions and these were all published in the weekly *Berrow's Worcester Journal* under the title 'Before the Tribunals' which helped to ensure no special treatment. Such applications were for a wide range of reasons including, in June 1916, for the eighth son of Mr & Mrs Radcliffe, Thomas aged 38. The family firm made munition gloves and five sons were already at the Front, with two 'joining in a fortnight'. The exemption was approved. Two Radcliffes died serving in the Worcestershire Regiment, Sgt Edgar of the 1/7th Battalion and Henry Percival of the 1/8th. Both names can be found on the Thiepval Memorial without family details so no link can be easily established.

The possibility of being conscripted came with its own issues. Captain Walford was not the first man in Feckenham to take his life when 'of unsound mind' because of the War. The *Journal* reported that James Edward Dicks, a single man of 36 years, a sandblaster from The Square in Feckenham was, in his father's words, 'rather funny in the head over Conscription, but he was very well in bodily health'. The inquest recorded that 'the buckle part of the strap was tight around Dicks' neck'. Was he afraid of being wounded or being killed or of not doing himself justice before his fellow men? Fear started for some well before reaching the Front.

2Lt Bate and the Machine Gun Section

There was little hiding place from conscription. The *Journal* regularly published lists of names and addresses under the heading 'Army Reserve', announcing that:

> THE RECRUITING OFFICER, 9, BROAD STREET, WORCESTER asks for information regarding the following men as to whether they:
> Have joined the Army

> Are excepted from the provisions of the Military Service Acts, 1916
> Are in possession of a definite Certificate or Badge exempting them from liability for Military Service
> Are in a Certified Occupation
> Have moved to another District, etc. etc.

Once training was complete and the Battalion had been posted to Essex and the marshes to the north of the Thames, the main concern for the younger officers seemed to revolve around their personal modes of transport, in the main, their motorcycles. There was undoubtedly a degree of competition between them as to the model and power of their motorcycle as there would have been in all previous wars about officers' horses. An example is from the memoir of 2Lt Hugh Chance – a friend of 2Lt Douglas Bomford in the 2/8th Battalion:

> Douglas Bomford was the proud owner of a Bradbury motor bike which one foggy evening deposited me into a ditch without damage to the bike or its rider. My own Douglas had been left behind at Maldon; it was a horizontally-opposed two cylinder model and a great improvement on its predecessor.

2Lt Hugh Chance, of Blackmore Park in Herefordshire, wrote his wartime memoirs in two parts – *Subaltern's Saga* and *Subaltern's Saga Part Two* (about his time as a Prisoner of War). He was still at Eton in the autumn of 1914 but decided, with less enthusiasm than many of his fellow Etonians, to enlist soon after his 18th birthday on 31st December 1914. His early memories are at his first camp near Northampton where the mess was the local pub and their main tipple was 'sherry and bitters' – all quite a challenge for a young man with a 'sheltered' upbringing. When the 1/8th was preparing for service overseas, the 2/8th (within the 61st Division) was sent to Essex to replace them and defend it against the Zeppelins. He remembered a number of actions:

> One night when we were watching a film in the local cinema we heard a great roaring, and rushing out into the street we found a

huge Zeppelin airship flying very low overhead. Some bombs and incendiaries were dropped round the ironworks near the harbour and a light left burning in Battalion H.Q. brought another shower which fortunately did no damage apart from destroying a wooden carpenter's shop and killing a blackbird. This was the first of a series of Zeppelin raids and our initial experience of enemy action. A few months later the Brigade was under canvas near Epping and one of the Gloucester battalions was having a guest night. Suddenly over the forest appeared a Zeppelin flying low, and the bomb-dropper must have been surprised to find himself over a large, tented camp. Anyhow he forgot to remove the safety pins from the bombs which he let fly, and although several fell and buried themselves deeply in the ground, no one was hurt and the only casualty was the Gloucesters' mess tent which was set on fire by an incendiary. [2Lt LR Bomford wrote in his *Memoirs*: '…and it said that the Germans chucked out the man responsible'.]

As we had only a few antique Lee-Metford rifles and no ammunition – the Gunners were equipped with Crimean muzzle-loading guns – there was no means of retaliation, and the Zep flew off unharmed. At this period of the war the East Coast anti-aircraft defences consisted of two Rolls Royce cars each mounting a small pom-pom, and the Zeps which were brought down in flames were set on fire by early night-flying B.E.2c.s – Leefe-Robinson being awarded a V.C. as being the first man to cripple and destroy one of these huge but useless airships.

Chance and his fellow subaltern Harold Pilkington were keen for action but their application to transfer to the Royal Flying Corps proved to be just before they heard that the 2/8th Battalion was heading to the Front. Chance's memoirs are a fascinating insight into the training and flying of the Great War. He had 44 operational hours before his plane was damaged by enemy fire and he had to land behind enemy lines. He spent the two remaining years as a Prisoner of War, the focus of his *Part Two*. He took up a place at Cambridge upon his release from his PoW camp and then went into the family glass and lighthouse business, Chance Brothers. He was High Sheriff of Worcestershire in 1942 and was knighted for his services to education in the King's Birthday Honours of 1945. He was a member of the Royal Commission for Scottish Affairs in 1952 and was made a CBE for his services to the political and public life of the Midlands. He died in 1981.

OFF TO THE FRONT

By the Christmas of 1914, the War on the Western Front had become static. The BEF (British Expeditionary Force) held the ground in front of Ypres and the French had maintained control of Verdun fortifications in the south. Once the initial German advances of August had been in part reversed, both sides had dug trenches such that there was a continuous line from the Channel to Switzerland – some 500 miles. The Germans were content as they held the railway line from Metz to Lille as well as the coalfields of Lens and the industrial centre of Lille. As the retreating forces, the Germans had chosen the ground on which to base their defence, including Vimy Ridge, Aubers Ridge and the high ground to the north of the Somme river. The main German focus was on their Eastern Front where Generals Ludendorff and Hindenburg were having greater success against the Russian and Polish armies as well as propping up their ally, Austria. German policy was to defeat the Russians in the east before switching substantial forces back to the west. To this end, they had begun the transfer of twelve Divisions from Flanders to the east as early as the autumn of 1914. If the Germans were to be cleared from French and Belgium territory it was for the French Army with the support of the BEF to make the attacking moves.

Field Marshal, 1st Earl Kitchener of Khartoum had been amongst the first to realise that this would be a long-protracted war, certainly not 'all over by Christmas'. He understood also that a considerably larger Army would be required and a huge recruiting campaign was quickly organised, initially to ensure that the Regular Army and the Territorial Force were at full strength. Kitchener wanted a further 60 Divisions and by the end of 1914 a total of 1,186,000 men had volunteered – the only requirement to be a soldier was to be at least 5 foot 3 inches tall and be able to expand their chest to 34 inches. In France, General Joffre agreed with Kitchener and General Sir John French, the commander of the BEF, to reorganise their forces such that the British would occupy the ground from the Channel to the Somme and the French everything to the south, though initially leaving some divisions facing Vimy Ridge and to the north-east of Ypres. Major Archibald Wavell, then a brigade major, later Field Marshal Earl Wavell, wrote in his biography of Field Marshal Viscount Allenby, *Allenby, a Study of Greatness*, 'the French were confident; the enemy, who had counted on a speedy victory, must surely have been disheartened; and the great Russian masses would be irresistible when they got on the move.'

This reorganisation of Allied forces meant that the BEF was responsible for a much greater frontage than hitherto and much of the remaining divisions of the TF (Territorial Force) were required to cross to France, initially to man the trenches in the quieter sections. The early TF battalions to cross were those formed of men who had signed up to the Imperial Service Obligation, an initiative of Lord Haldane in 1910 for the very purpose of supporting any overseas Expeditionary Force. The two Worcestershire Territorial battalions had enough men to form at least four battalions and the 1/7th and 1/8th were posted to France soon after the first of the 1915 battles took place, that of Neuve-Chappelle (11–13 March). The Allied strategy was to launch attacks from inside the shoulders of Ypres and Verdun with the threat of encirclement to the German forces. Little ground was gained at Neuve-Chappelle because the initial gains were not exploited due in large part to the lengthy chain of command in the BEF. They suffered 11,652 casualties.

Within a fortnight the 1/7th and 1/8th Battalions had crossed to France. On the second day of the 1/8th Battalion's occupation of front-line trenches and just 14 miles to their north was the first use of poison gas on the Western Front – when the Germans made use of a gentle easterly breeze to release 160 tons of chlorine gas into the face of largely French colonial troops from Algeria. This began the Second Battle of Ypres which was, by the end of May, to reduce the Allied buffer in front of Ypres by three of the five miles previously held in front of the city wall – mostly key high ground such as Hill 60. The cost to the Allied forces was some 90,000 casualties, equivalent to six Divisions, emphasising the need for the Territorial Force brigades and all the Volunteer Battalions to be made ready for the Front as a matter of urgency. Ypres was never to be occupied by German forces, remaining the northern shoulder of the Allied front line.

***

When undertaking my research, I came across a recording of the wonderful work – *Suite for the Fallen Soldier* – by Phil Mountford and Kathy Gee to mark the centenary of the Great War, recorded in St John the Baptist's Church in Feckenham, the village of Walford's suicide. Two of the poems by Kathy Gee have particular resonance with this story of the 8th Battalion, the first of which is the imagined responses to his mother of a young private who has just enlisted:

Every mother's son

Ma, you ask me who will have to go,
and I say, me and Bert and Harry,
lads from farms and factories,
from schools and shops and offices.
You fold your hands and sigh 'You'll have to fight
some other mother's son' and I say … 'yes'.

You ask, 'where will you be'? and I say
'I can't tell you. We will go to places
you have never heard of,
and the 8th Battalion is going to win the war!'
I tell you that I won't be home for ploughing,
that the little ones must tend my pigeons now.

You ask me 'How will I know that you're alright?'
I tell you all about our training, how
the fields of France will feel the tramp of British feet.
I say 'The Hun will know the ring of bayonet
on steel, and once they've tasted our artillery,
we'll see their armies run'.

You ask, 'What will you miss the most?'
and I say 'cricket, buttercups in Seven Acre,
moonlight with my sweetheart, High Street
on a sunny day.' I say 'Our kitchen, Ma, and you
and Grandad, little Tom and Winnie
round the table. That's where I belong'.

At last, you frown and ask, 'But why'?
And I say 'England needs me.
How can I sit back as others fight to keep us safe?'

Kathy Gee, *Suite for the Fallen Soldier*, 2016

The 1/8th Battalion embarked on SS *Invicta* from Folkestone after dark on 31st March 1915, landing at Boulogne at 1.15 hrs the following morning. Its sister battalion, 1/7th, undertook the same journey some 75 minutes ahead of the 1/8th aboard SS *Onward*. The 1/8th Battalion had thirty officers under the command of Lt Colonel WK Peake.

Walter Peake was born on 5th February 1869, so was aged 46 when he led his battalion across the Channel; six months older than Captain Walford – the Old Gent. He was the younger son of John Peake, the vicar of Ellesmere in Shropshire, and followed his brother, Harold, to St Edward's School in Oxford. Detailed scanning of the School's *Chronicle* shows that neither played in any of the main sports teams – cricket, rugby, football or rowing. No prizes on Sports Day and not a prefect either. Walter won the junior school prize but nothing else of note. This is a theme that will play out amongst the gallant officers of the Battalion – few of those who were to distinguish themselves over the next three years had notable school careers, perhaps more team players than sports or house captains. Walter left in 1887 and went on to the Royal Military Academy, Sandhurst before being commissioned into the Royal Berkshire Regiment in November 1889. He was promoted to Captain in 1900, joining the Worcestershire Regiment and becoming adjutant of the Volunteer Battalion until May 1907. Promotion was slow in a peacetime army. The 1911 Census shows him as 'Land Agent' on the Hindlip Estate, living there with his wife, Hilda, who was ten years his junior, as well as with three staff – a cook, a lady's maid and a groom. In that year he succeeded Col Matt Dixon as commanding officer of the 8th Battalion with the rank of Lieutenant Colonel and, having made himself available for overseas service, he was given command of the 1/8th Battalion as they arrived in Boulogne. He was one of the Old Gents. Peake must have been with the Royal Berkshires on Gibraltar at the time of the 1901 Census because his wife was living with her widowed mother in Bridgnorth and with their only child, a daughter, Joan.

All but one of the twelve officers with the rank of Captain and above were to survive the War although just one – Captain HT Clarke – was to see service with the Battalion in those last weeks of the War. The exception being Captain Lionel Kerwood who was transferred to command the 13th Bn, The Cheshire Regiment on 25th September 1916. He was killed just twenty-six days later and is commemorated on the Thiepval Memorial. Of the eighteen subalterns, seven were to die before the War was over, with just two still serving in those last weeks – Lt JP Bate who commanded the Battalion in its second-to-last action, and 2Lt RJCW Hawtrey whose last action was when he was wounded in the attack on Beaurevoir on 5th October 1918 while still a platoon commander. By comparison, the 2/8th Battalion which embarked for France in May 1916, was to lose just one of its officers over the remaining thirty months of the War – Captain HL Evers MC*, perhaps the most professional of all their Territorial officers. He was a 2nd Lt when he left for France in 1916 and was killed on 1st November 1918 scouting the ground for the next day's action near Valenciennes. Perhaps the most telling factor was that the 1/8th Battalion was to lose a total of thirty-one officers between March 1915 and the Armistice, one more than their full officer strength when they embarked for service overseas. However, in contrast with the overall statistic that 60 per cent of those that were killed or died of wounds did so as a result of the daily grind of trench life – shelling, sniping and wiring parties – some 67 per cent of the 1/8th Battalion officers who died did so in set-piece battles, with just 33 per cent dying from disease, accidents and the vagaries of trench life.

Lionel Kerwood

Lance Evers

The *Divisional History* noted that unlike the other Territorial battalions in the 48th Division, a good proportion of the officers serving in Worcestershire with the Battalion in the summer of 1914 crossed to France with them in March 1915 – 'the existing CO and two majors but also with four of the seven captains and eight of the nine lieutenants', supplemented 'with ten new second lieutenants'. *The Worcestershire Regiment in The Great War* by Captain H FitzM.

Stacke MC and the booklet entitled *1/8th Battalion, The Worcestershire Regiment 1914–1918* published in 1919 provide a good overview of the Battalion's service in France and Italy. They give snippets of the constant actions and shelling to which the trenches and rear areas were equally subject, as well as the details of the major actions in which they were involved, until the last month which was one of near-constant action. Their service in France and Flanders from April 1915 to October 1917 was always alongside their sister battalion, the 1/7th, frequently exchanging positions on the trench duty roster. They provide a real flavour of life in the quieter sectors at or near the trenches which was the substantial experience of the majority of all those who served on the Western Front. Much has been written about the major actions and battles – the Retreat from Mons (1914), the Battle of Loos (1915), the First Battle of the Somme (1916), Vimy Ridge (1917) and the Third Battle of Ypres of 1917 (better known as Passchendaele). Even when these great battles took place, the rest of the Front had to be defended or used as the base for diversionary attacks. This is where the majority of the British Army saw action.

The 1/8th Battalion, though from a rural county, had few from farming stock and none of the local aristocracy, unlike the county's Yeomanry Regiment. Of the thirty men that formed the officer's cadre of the Battalion as it crossed to France, there were three regular officers: the commanding officer (Lt Col WK Peake), the adjutant (Captain PR Whalley) and the Quartermaster (Major D Sallis). Six had graduated from Oxford University – in order of the date of their matriculation: FAW How (Keble 1889), FW Hemming (Jesus 1906), GLJ Slater (Keble 1907), KM Mylne (Keble 1908), HG Newman (Keble 1909), and CR Pawsey (Wadham 1913) – and three from Cambridge: SH Clark (Trinity 1886), HS Wilson (King's 1904) and JJ Paskin (St John's 1912). Before the Battle of the Somme, they were joined by four more from Oxford – RF Amphlett (Oriel 1898), T Stinton (Magdalen 1904), SH Wilkes (St John's 1914) and JR Willis (Balliol 1914) – and two from Cambridge: HHG Bennett (Clare 1910) and HH Milward (Downing 1913). Four were to die in action (in order – Wilson, Slater, Amphlett and Hemming) by April 1917. None of them were to be involved in the six battles in the last month of the War.

Beyond the thirty officers who crossed the Channel on 31st March 1915, there were almost a thousand Other Ranks. The *War Diary* recorded 27 officers and 912 Other Ranks as disembarking at Boulogne with the battalion transport and machine-gun section with 2 officers, 84 Other Ranks and 78 horses doing so at Le Havre. The main structure of the Battalion was the four rifle companies, each of some 200 men, commanded by a Major or senior Captain, each of whom would have joined before the War. The Battalion was part of the 48th (South Midland) Division under the command of Major General Henry Heath and in the 144th (Gloucestershire and Worcestershire) Brigade. It was to remain under these commands until it departed from Italy in September 1918 to return once again to France. Upon their initial arrival in France, such Territorial Divisions were given additional training much nearer to the Front. In the case of the 48th Division, this 'instructional tour' was near Bois Grenier in the flat countryside to the south of Armentières. To get from Boulogne to the Front, the two battalions (1/7th and 1/8th) followed a well organised and travelled passage. Troop trains to Cassel and then short marches to villages beyond the famous Cassel Hill where the Grand Old Duke of York is supposed to have marched his men to the top and down again. The view from the top is magnificent in all directions but notably to the south-east where the Division was destined. A day of parades for General Sir Horace Smith-Dorrien, Commander 2nd Army, was followed by a twenty-mile march in persistent rain to Bailleul. Five days of training and route marching preceded the seven-day 'instructional tour'. This was at the Front and the Battalion was subject to a degree of sniping and shelling though suffered no casualties.

Jack Bate

On 17th April the 48th Division was ordered to relieve 4th Division on the Front between the River Warnave and the Wulverghem-Messine Road, covering the southern end of Ploegsteert (the renowned Plugstreet) Wood. The 1/8th Battalion, perhaps due to being junior to and less experienced than the 1/7th, was initially held in reserve at Nieppe on the northern edge of Armentières. The *History* explained that the two battalions swapped roles on the 21st and then back again on the 25th, thus confirming a four-day cycle of being in the front-line trenches and then in reserve, a mile or so from the Front. This interchange was to continue in this same area for more than two months, typical for such battalions when no major attacks were planned. This does not mean that there was no action nor casualties. Indeed, the 1/7th were the first to lose a man on 19th April – their third day at the Front. That same day their LCpl Beagin earned their first gallantry medal, a DCM, laying wire over exposed ground. Heavy fire caused him severe injury but he 'pluckily completed the work' – the first 'immediate' award for the 48th Division. Sadly, he was to die of those wounds on 2nd June.

An interesting letter from the commanding officer's wife to the *Journal* on 1st May shows that the families of the officers and men of the Battalion did not know where their men were stationed:

> A WILD RUMOUR CONTRADICTED
> Sir, – As wife of the Commanding Officer of the 8th Batt. The Worcestershire Regt., I should like to say that I have received no news which would lead me to suppose that there is any foundation in the rumours prevalent in the district concerning the 8th Battalion.
>
> If there are any casualties among the officers and men, the wives or parents will be notified by the War Office. The Secretary of the Territorial Force Association also receives a report of all casualties direct from the Territorial Records Office, and he will send a notice of all reports to the local Press.
>
> I do hope that no notice will be taken of any future rumours.
> HILDA M PEAKE
> The Court Farm, Hindlip, Worcester.

Ploegsteert

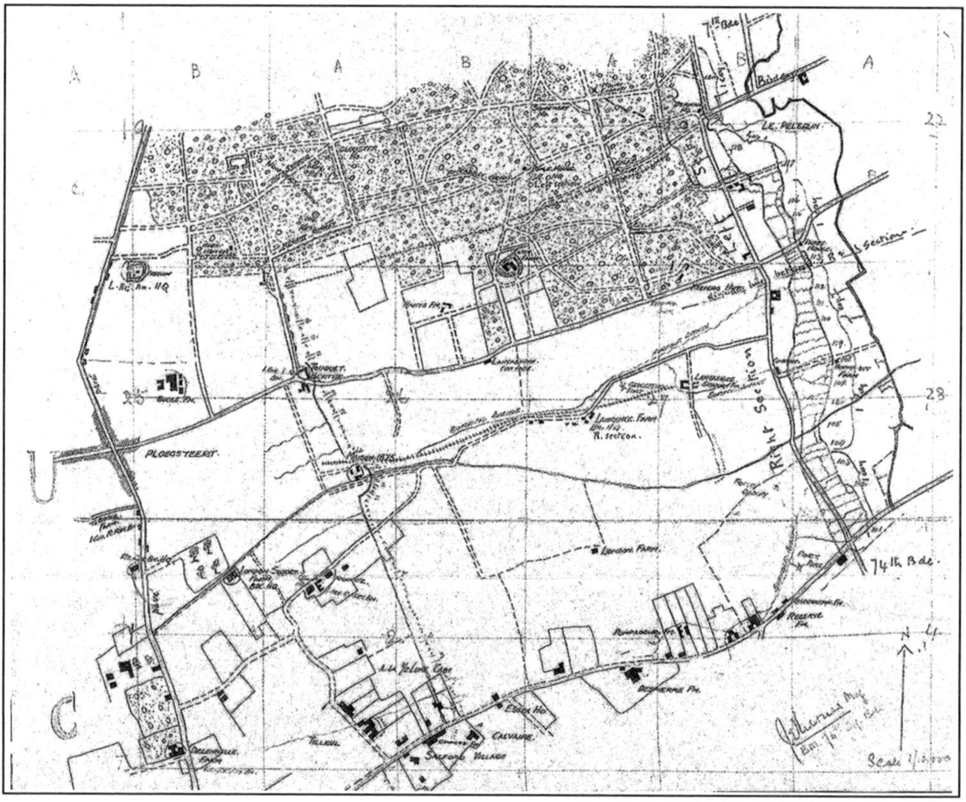

1/8th Battalion's area of responsibility, April–June 1915

Mrs Peake was, at the time, managing the Allsopp family's Hindlip estate in place of her husband until she retired in November 1915. Lord Hindlip, then 36, went to the Front in August 1914 as a King's Messenger with Lord Harry Dalmeny and the Duke of Westminster, amongst others, before becoming a staff officer in the 12th Division in December 1915. He was awarded an OBE in 1919, having been twice Mentioned in Despatches.

Across the page is part of a letter from a soldier of the Battalion to his mother, showing the importance of the censorship work of the company officers:

> 8th WORCESTER'S QUAINT NOTION OF LUCK
> A member of the [1/]8th Battalion, writing to his mother in Worcester says he has been in the trenches, but he tells her not to worry. 'It is only by luck that you get a bullet or by carelessness. It is the shells that put paid to a good many round here and about where we are. The [1/]7th Worcesters have only had only one killed and four wounded so far, so it is not very dangerous. It is when they attack that a good many of the chaps get killed.'

Private Alfred Danks

The second part of the letter he writes when in the trenches, saying 'We have only had one wounded so far'.

The first man of the 1/8th Battalion to lose his life was Private A Danks of D Company on 2nd May. The *Journal* recorded that he left a widow and was from 72 Albert Road, Redditch but the *CWGC* website gives no family details.

The publication of such letters in the *Journal* continued. The following week included one from Pte C Williams to his parents Mr & Mrs O Williams of the Forester's Arms in Malvern. The content would have given a good picture to other parents and loved ones of what life was really like in the front-line trenches. It is difficult to judge if this was the editor's intention but he seemed to include several from the soldiers of the local Territorial battalion. This text illustrates life in a trench in a quiet section:

> We have just finished our five days in the trenches, and at present we are out for about four days, which we can do with. The first day in the trenches was rather quiet – only a few rifle shots would pass over the parapet to keep you awake, and at night there were a few artillery duels on our left, and which made you think there was a War on. The second day we used our trench mortars on the Germans, which caused a few casualties to them, as they could be seen carrying the wounded out on our right. After we had used our trench mortar, they began to use theirs, but they could not get the range of our trench, so there were no casualties on our side. The following night was very quiet – only a few rifle shots from snipers would whizz over our heads occasionally. The third day our artillery shelled their trenches, which caused a few more casualties on their side, and their artillery shelled a village just behind our lines, which happened to be the village we had just left, so we were lucky. They also shelled a wood which we formerly occupied, but we are now on the right of it. The only damage they did was this – they managed to hit a watering-cart. On the third night the Germans tried to play a trick on us. They started shouting and kicking up a row, as though they were making a charge at us, but we were up to it. Our men gave them rapid fire, which quietened them down, and after that

> not a shot was fired … there was no Malvern fellows amongst the casualties I am pleased to say.

A number of aspects arise from this letter. It is well-written for a private soldier but at the early part of the War, promotion was difficult. This was to change as casualties mounted. The second is the comment on 'Malvern fellows', showing the close community of each company. Again, this was to change as the War progressed, with huge drafts from other counties like Norfolk in 1917 and again in the autumn of 1918. Private Williams was to survive the War. The letter was followed by one from an unnamed officer of the Battalion which told of other key work at the Front:

> I am having two easy days, as it is my platoon's turn to dig. In future we are to have some rest nightly in turn. We start at dusk and get up behind the line by dark. Then we dig second line trenches for a few hours and come back long before daylight, have hot tea or cocoa etc. (the men had rum in it last night), and go to bed till nine or ten in the morning. We are under fire the whole time we are digging, as the bullets come over from the front line to say nothing of the snipers, and often make us jump a bit as they hiss over, but they are almost all high and no one has been hit, though we have had men at work a week … in the day everyone who has nothing special to do rests, but yesterday we could not sleep in the afternoon as the Huns very inconsiderately dropped half a dozen shells or so, not aimed at us, about 300 or 400 yards from our house, and of course, they made a noise, though they did no harm. They make a hole in ploughed land about six feet wide and three deep. We are in a farm and our other officers are in a chateau only a few yards off. Many of the men are in a barn, but some prefer to make huts of turf, straw and ground sheets or anything they can get.
>
> Everyone is very cheerful. Our men are absolutely splendid under fire. They were sent out in front of the trench within a few minutes of reaching it, for listening posts, wire entanglements, repairing parapet and so on, but the Germans did not fire on them as they had working parties out themselves.

These letters give a very good idea of life in a quieter sector of the Front.

CANON AND MRS. WILSON AND THEIR FOUR SOLDIER SONS. (Photo Dowty, Worcester.)

Canon & Mrs Wilson and their four military sons

The only serious enemy attack was on the day before the Division was relieved, 25th June. It was recorded that one German officer reached their trench line where he was killed. This, however, does not tell the full tale because an inspection of the Battalion's Roll of Honour shows that over this nine-week period one officer and thirteen Other Ranks lost their lives. The officer, Lieutenant Malcolm Kerwood, and one of the soldiers, Pte Ingram, were killed in that German attack. The remainder are described as 'Died of Wounds' or 'Le Touquet' which would usually mean that they died at the main hospital on the coast, thus again 'of their wounds'. However, a study of the wonderful records of the *CWGC* website shows that most are described as killed and can be found in the Calvaire (Essex) Military Cemetery, south of Ploegsteert Wood. The nearest village is Touquet which no doubt led to the earlier confusion and possible misinterpretation of how they might have died. These casualties show a constant rate of attrition – there were no 'soft' areas of the front line. A new phase of trench warfare had started, initially with news from Cuinchy, the Ypres Salient and St Eloi that the digging of tunnels and mines had begun. The 'officers and men were constantly on the alert for the dull sounds of pick and shovel at work under their feet' – undermining.

The action on the 24th/25th June was a good example of the constant attempts to unsettle the enemy made by each side. It began just after midnight with two patrols under 2Lt A Plaistowe and Lt PM Kerwood. They were met in the mist and high vegetation by stronger German patrols – the Front was not yet the devastated fields of mud and leafless, even branchless, trees. Sharp actions started with short-range shooting and bombing (grenades). Kerwood was killed – hit in the head and chest – and two of his four men were injured. Plaistowe was injured but succeeded in bringing his party back to their own trench line. One of Kerwood's party, LCpl TC Fox, although severely wounded, attempted to bring Kerwood back. Unable to carry him, he worked his way back to his own lines and returned to Kerwood with 2Lt K Mylne and Private R Jeff. They brought him back but Kerwood had already died of his wounds. Fox and Jeff were awarded DCMs for their gallant work and Plaistowe was to receive the first of his two 'Mentioned in Despatches' (MiDs). Fox was to be wounded four times, the last in October 1918, but survived the War. His employers and fellow workers presented him with a 'handsome clock' for this award of a DCM.

Pte Richard Jeff

The Germans were quick to follow up with an immediate bombardment as their patrols advanced. The 1/8th Worcestershire's musketry from their parapets was enough to repel this advance although the bayonet was needed to stop and kill their leading officer. The overall toll from these actions was Lt PM Kerwood, Privates W Ingram and F Leek killed and Lt A Plaistowe and 16 men wounded. Lt Kerwood, whose eldest brother Lionel was the Battalion's second-in-command, was qualifying to be a solicitor in a London chambers when the War started, probably with a view to practising with his father and Lionel in Redditch, the firm known then as Alfred Kerwood & Sons. His school magazine, *The Old Bromsgrovian*: 'About midnight on a foggy night, suspecting trouble, he had gone out to patrol the front line of trenches, when he suddenly came upon a strong German bombing party advance to the attack. He threw a land bomb which gave the alarm, but was himself shot in two places and died instantaneously. The Adjutant writes "He was an extremely conscientious Platoon Commander. And his name had been sent in for promotion only the day before."' His body was taken to the cemetery at Bailleul and buried next to other officers who died around that time. His grave has no family inscription and the *CWGC* website has no details of age or parents. The firm's name would be changed after the War to Kerwood & Co as there were no qualified sons to continue the practice after the death of his brother, Lionel, in 1916. There appear to be five sons and the second, Clifford, joined the Royal Artillery Company (the HAC) as a private soldier in 1916 after graduating from Oxford University and working for the Local Government Board in Whitehall. He was invalided out the following January after contracting tuberculosis.

Malcolm Kerwood on front left and Lionel front right

Cpl Bertram Warner kept a diary in his Army Notebook over this time and tells of day-to-day life in the trenches during these early months in B Company under Captain Burlingham:

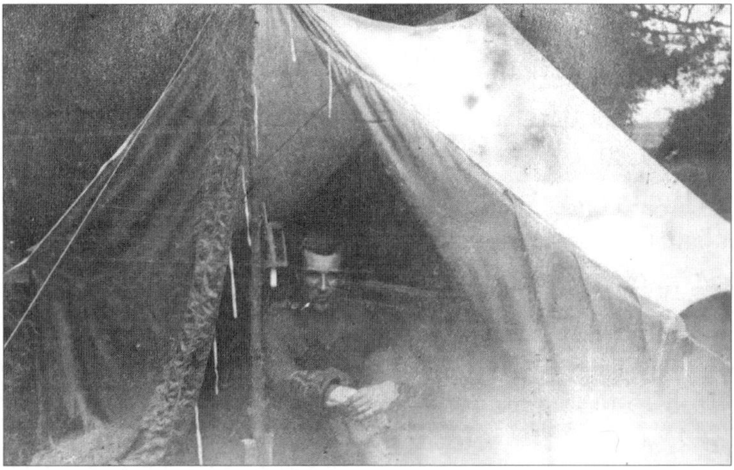

Monday 17 May 1915
Very wet morning. Wash, shave etc & slack inside. (Received parcel from home and 2 from Alice and letters from Mr G & Mary & Mrs Marsh). Inspection in afternoon, stand to in trench at 9. Beastly wet and mud awful. Rigged up good shelters with waterproof sheets, mine and Cpl Sharp by side of maxim gun stand and fairly dry. Set return to sheds about 10.20. Slept till 3.30 then rum ration and more sleep.

Officer's haircut by Percy Whalley

Tuesday 18 May 1915
More or less wet, slack day, only inspection and try new respirators. Stand to at 9 in barns, on duty for a start, but relieved and sleep all night.
Wednesday 19 May 1915
Up at 7 & parade 8.30 & go to Nieppe & get bath, return at 12. More or less wet day. Fall in (after general clear up) to relieve 7th [Bn] C Coy at 7.30 and go to Fort London carrying next day's rations. No 7 Platoon up in loft. We on straw bags etc. Stand to at 2.45-3.45 (first light).
Thursday 20 May
Fine morning, very hot. Did various jobs in trenches, mostly brick bottoming. Slack afternoon. Usual fatigues for rations, water. Stand to 7.15-8.15 (last light).
Friday 21 May
Stand to 2.45. I & 4 others & Lt P[laistowe] & Sgt H put up wire in front. Sgt Wild [Wylde] killed & another, also 5 stretcher bearers (1 killed – Pte S Harris). Work on firestep & fatigues, stand to at 7.45-8.15.
Saturday 22 and Sunday 23 May
Stand to 2.45 & finish wire in front. Lovely day. I very slack as no tools. Sleep in afternoon. Stand to at 7.45 for hr. Rattle in barn. Capt B. made a fuss & No 7 [platoon] got I days extra duty. Warned of batteries in rear at 12.30 and 3.30. None off at 12.30, rapid fire on left in front of wood & very heavy bombardment by new Batteries, left and right, range excellent, also shrapnel, weak reply in wood. Go on with firesteps, & slack in afternoon after gum boots, blanks etc are collected in order to move to Nieppe for Divisional Reserve. Brigadier round in the morning. Relieved by 7th [Bn] about 8.30 & march to Nieppe by platoons. No 7 singing all the way. Arrive nearly 10, very warm, go to same billets, no beer and get last drop of coffee.

It is interesting to consider for these same days the letters written by his company commander, Captain HR Burlingham. He wrote almost every day to his wife, Mary:

Monday 17 May
I had a glorious lot of letters this morning, and parcels too, quite a long one from Claude. I have just been cutting one of the subaltern's hair with clippers, I never laughed so much in my life, he is quite bald and white on the top. I cut patterns on him first. A great big Indian bearded soldier has just come in to enquire the way to his mountain [artillery] battery, which is somewhere round here; they are fine looking men.
Tuesday 18 May
Thank you so much for your letter and parcel, the sausages were A1. We had the fowl for lunch today, as we had asked a gunner subaltern into the meal with us. He is by himself here and in charge of a mountain battery with native Indian driver. We got talking and found he had a yacht at Heybridge, and knew the Browns at Maldon.

The mouth-organs are a great acquisition to the Company, and we now have a really good band; four or five mouth organs, a kettle drum (biscuit tin), a tin whistle and a triangle (entrenching tool).

We go back to the trenches tomorrow night, May 20.
Thursday 20 May
We are back again in London Farm for four days, we took over last night. The last two days have been very wet, and you should see the mud, its simply awful.

I have just had a telephone message from Captain SH Clark. He says the Germans opposite him are waving white flags and calling out 'Peace in two days', however, knowing them we are preparing to be attacked tonight.

They are shelling a farm to our right which is deserted, we light fires there daily, so that they can think it is occupied.
Saturday 22 May
One of my sergeants [Wylde] was killed yesterday, he was a very nice chap, and had held a commission in the Buffs. His father I believe is Bank manager at Malvern.

Some of K[itchener]'s Army at last put in an appearance, and his Artillery is behind us now, a mixed blessing. This morning at 3 a.m. when you were fast asleep, we were putting barbed wire around this fort, I tore my puttees pretty badly, and had to darn them with

thread, very large stitches I am afraid.
Sunday 23 May – Whit Sunday
I had the [Brigadier-]General round this morning and he professed himself very pleased with all that had been done, after his visit I had to go to the fire trenches to see Captain Clarke. I am taking over his section of the trench next time. I went all round with him and saw everything there was to see and brought Captain Creake back to lunch in our dug-out, which is called 'Sum House'.

We move to our bath billets tonight and shall be glad of the mental rest. Goodbye, I am going to sleep.

'Capt B' in Cpl Warner's diary must be Captain Burlingham in B Company. The wiring events are too similar to be a coincidence. These two accounts show the drudge of the life of the Other Ranks when compared with those of the officers in command of them. Burlingham's other letters include much detail of recreational rides round the countryside during their time in reserve as well as visiting local hostelries with brother officers. Perhaps it is not surprising that the following summer, the then Sergeant Warner applied for a commission. With the commanding officer's support, this was agreed and he was posted to the 1/5th Bn, The London Regiment, on a trial basis before he could be sent to Officer Cadet School. His papers at the Imperial War Museum do not continue after that time but the *CWGC* provides the answer. He was indeed commissioned as he was killed as 2Lt Bertram Warner on 12th April 1917 aged 28, the son of John and Alice Warner of Wadden House, Croydon. He is commemorated on Bay 9 of the Arras Memorial, so his body was not found or, if found, not identifiable. His two brothers, Archibald and Evan, both lost their lives in the War, Evan at Ypres on 14th December 1914, aged 34 as a sergeant, and Archibald on the first day of the Battle of the Somme, aged 32 as a second lieutenant, having been commissioned from the Artist's Rifles. Archibald was buried at Hébuterne, where his younger brother had served over the previous winter. The inscription on his grave – They Shall Shine As The Stars For Ever & Ever – was paid for by Mrs Norah Marriage (previously Warner) who had remarried a vicar in Essex. Evan's grave has no inscription.

The other feature of Captain Burlingham's letters was his noting whenever another officer went on home leave and sometimes bemoaning the fact that it was not his turn. That should not have been the case as the *Journal* reported on 26th June that 'The parents and friends of the members of the 8th Battalion will learn with pleasure the fact that, after 11 weeks of active service, the officers and men of the Battalion are to be given a short leave in order to visit home. This leave has actually started, two officers and eight men having been sent home last weekend, and other batches of ten will follow every other day'. The two officers in this first batch were Captain SH Clark, of Redditch, and Captain RH Burlingham of Evesham. Burlingham was born on 11th October 1883 so he was 30 when the War started, and 32 by the summer of 1916. He had married Ursula Mary Slater in 1910 and was described as an agricultural merchant in the 1911 Census. There are no references to children in his letters but his son was commanding a company of the 8th Battalion at the start of the Second World War so he must have been born before 1914. Perhaps married officers and men with young children were given priority when it came to home leave? The *Journal* reported Burlingham as being home on leave again in mid-November.

After two months in the trenches or in immediate reserve, the Brigade was relieved on 27th June and began a march back to Burbure for two weeks of rest and training. The Divisional Commander, Major General Heath, fell ill and returned to England where he died in late July. He was replaced by the newly promoted Major General Robert Fanshawe, of the Oxfordshire Light Infantry. He had been awarded a DSO in the Boer War. He was to remain the Divisional Commander until June 1918 when his actions during the Battle of the Piave River in Italy were not in accordance with his Corps Commander's wishes; the then Lt General Sir Frederick Lambart, 10th Earl of Cavan, dismissed Fanshawe and posted him back to England. After the War Fanshawe was restored to Divisional Command, of 69th (2nd East Anglian) Division. He was widely respected by those who served under him and he became Honorary Colonel of the 1/7th Battalion of the Worcestershire Regiment. He was to die falling from his horse in 1946, aged 83.

Both of Fanshawe's brothers were to attain the rank of Lt General and receive knighthoods – Lt General Sir Edward Fanshawe KCB and Lt General Sir Hew Fanshawe KCB, KCMG. General Sir Hew was to command V Corps from October 1915 until July 1916 when Haig relieved him of command and replaced him with his elder brother Edward – probably a unique event in the annals of the British Army. Such were the vagaries of senior command in the War and the need to apportion blame for failure. General Sir Edward was subsequently relieved of command of V Corps after failures during the German advances of Operation Michael in March 1918, although he was restored to Corps command (XXIII Corps) that August. Also relieved of his Corps command at the same time was the highly decorated Lt General Walter Congreve from XIII Corps, who was to retire as General Sir Walter Congreve VC, KCB, MVO in 1924 without a hand and having lost a son, Major William Congreve, VC, DSO, MC, in July 1916 in actions at Longueval where he won his posthumous VC. His younger brother was to win a DSO in Norway in 1940 but lose his life in an action off the French coast the following year. The Fanshawe and Congreve families were amongst a number with gallantry and leadership running deeply through their veins, although even they were not immune to the loss of some of their commands.

The 1/8th Battalion and the 48th Division were relieved the following day by the 12th Division and retired to the Lille area, a march of some ten miles. Much of their rest period was taken up with digging trenches near Vermelles in the area just to the north of Loos. The summer of 1915 was the time when the British Army in France and Flanders was being rapidly expanded. A new 3rd Army was formed under Lt General Charles Munro who had crossed the Channel in August 1914 as Commander, 2nd Division and been promoted to command I Corps that December – thus in under twelve months he had risen from Divisional to Army command. Both the 1/7th and 1/8th remained with 48th Division and joined the rest of the 3rd Army in the area to the north of what would become the Somme battlefield. On 19th July, the Battalion was designated to the defence of Hébuterne, immediately north of the Serre Road some ten miles to the south-west of Arras. It was to remain there for almost a year.

Hébuterne, July 1915–June 1916

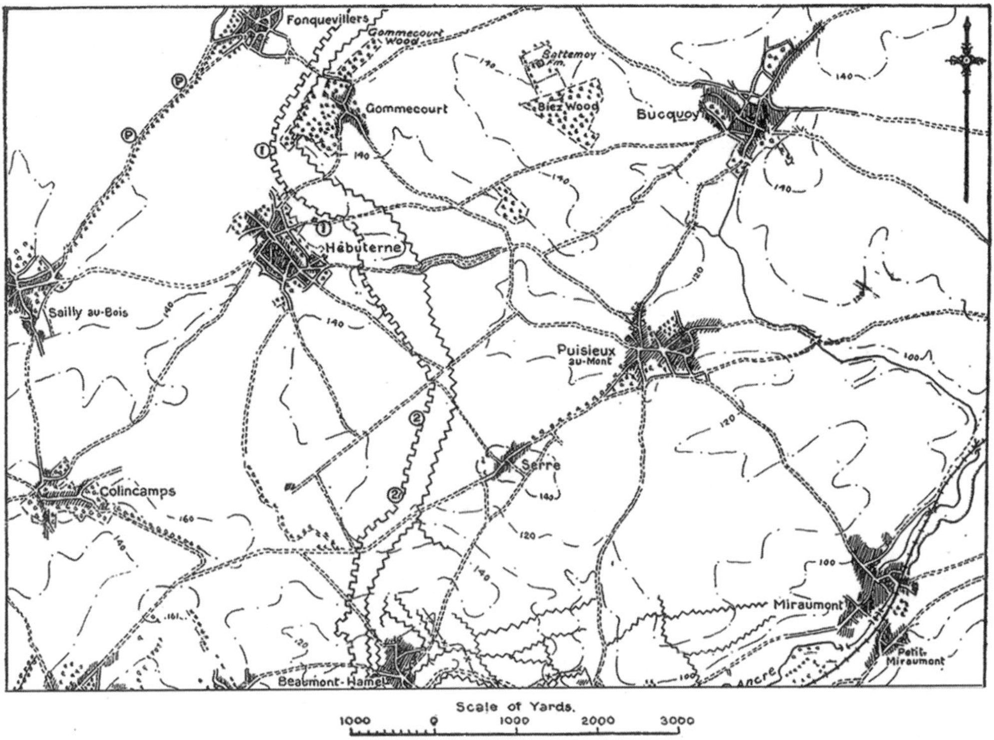

Hébuterne was a quiet part of the Front with the opposing trench lines some way apart. The British trenches were on the east side of the village and dominated the immediate area to the west, giving them excellent viewing over their German counterparts which should have ensured accurate artillery bombardments. All the ground to the immediate rear was in orchards or the village, so out of direct line of sight of the German artillery observation officers. Thus the German bombardments were largely speculative. Corbett described the trenches as 'new and unfinished, but admirably designed' (by the French troops who had been responsible for this area since the German withdrawal after the First Battle of the Marne in September 1914 to the high ground to the north of the River Somme). The contours of the opposing lines were dictated by the boggy nature of the ground … 'the first thing to do was to consolidate the trenches and prepare them for the winter, a prodigious and interminable task.' All other things gave way to this and now the memorable order was issued 'The comfort of the men must be the last consideration'. Corbett continued: 'we all became sappers, the shovel was our weapon of war; we carried brickbats instead of bombs and the sandbags became our oriflamme' – the battle standard of the medieval kings of France. This may seem rather elegant language for a soldier who was by then a CQMS (Company Quartermaster Sergeant) but Edward Corbett was not a standard Other Rank. A tribute written by Captain Sir Laurence Watkinson when Corbett died in 1952 aged 81 (making him 43 when War broke out and 47 as it ended with him still serving in the Battalion): 'He joined us well beyond the permitted age after a life spent all over the world, often in the turbulence afflicting growing states, including those of the South American Republics. He was widely admired and it was fascinating hearing him on the soldiers of France, of Spain and of Germany … he was a first class soldier, time and again he evaded commissioned rank'. He was another of the Old Gents of the Battalion. He was forthright in his views, as shown by the ensuing paragraph in his *War Story*:

> The dominant notes of war are neither glorious fisticuffs nor gruesome bombardment, but the incessant toil and bodily discomfort.

> The gentlemen at home who strike for an eight-hour day or forty-odd-hour week can scarcely realise that for months on end we worked anything from twelve to twenty-four hours a day, never had a bed to sleep on, furniture of any kind, houses to live in, seldom a decent roof over our heads, and hardly ever dry clothes, and that we throve on it. The health, vigour and joviality of all ranks throughout these terrible winters were amazing. Cases of sickness were almost unknown, pleurisy and pneumonia did not occur.

Corbett was described in another unattributed tribute in the Regimental magazine, *FIRM*: 'I never saw him in any but a cheerful mood; he was tireless and never seemed to sleep; no matter what were the conditions of the weather or the mud, he always saw to it that his company ('A') had hot food in the trenches and their regular rum rations'. These are a soldier's views of life and conditions in the trenches. Some readers may believe that the bunks and furniture of *Blackadder Goes Forth* were commonplace but certainly not for the Other Ranks.

The Battalion was not immune from shelling which took a modest toll, some six private soldiers being killed in the remaining six months of 1915, during which time the only significant British attack of 1915 was undertaken. The Battle of Loos was fought from 25th to 28th September and lost – lost in that no enemy ground was captured and retained and that the British suffered almost 60,000 casualties to German losses estimated at some 26,000. The Battalion were fortunate not to be part of the attacking infantry at Loos, some of which suffered up to eighty per cent casualties. Instead, patrolling in No Man's Land was a regular occurrence as it had been at Ploegsteert. It was to cost the life of another young subaltern in a firefight on 14th September: 2Lt HS Wilson, the son of Canon Wilson, the Vice-Dean of Worcester. Hugh Wilson himself had graduated from Cambridge University and was teaching at Rugby School when the War broke out. Both his full brothers were to survive the War and later to be knighted. His elder brother, Sir Arnold Talbot Wilson KCIE, CMG, CSI, DSO, MP was to volunteer to join the RAF in the Second World War and was killed as an air-gunner (pilot) in a Wellington over Dunkirk in May 1940, the first MP to be killed in action in that War – at the age of 56. His younger brother, Steuart, was severely wounded twice in the Great War when serving with the King's Royal Rifle Corps, losing both a kidney and a lung. He survived to be knighted for services to the Arts Council of Great Britain as its music director.

Hugh Wilson

Interestingly, Corbett noted:

> … an appalling feature of this war has been the brutal wastage of brains. Gladstone [the old Prime Minister's (1868-74, 1880-85, 1886 and 1892-94) eldest son's son and himself an MP of four years standing when he joined the colours in August 1914. He was killed by a sniper in April 1915 and was, with King George V's permission, disinterred and buried in the family's local church in Hawarden in Flint]; Raymond Asquith [the then Prime Minister's (1908-16) eldest son who was killed in the later days of the Battle of the Somme aged 37]; Neil Primrose [second son of the Liberal Prime Minister (1894-95), Lord Rosebery, who was himself an MP for seven years but was to be killed at the Third Battle of Gaza in November 1917 when aged 34 and the recipient of an MC], all killed as Platoon Commanders; compare their capacities with those of the average Staff Officer.

Perhaps this was more the view of a senior and worldly Other Rank of the intellect and performance of the staff officers with whom he worked or came into contact. Corbett's choice of 'brains' was not the only immediate family of Prime Ministers to lose their lives in the War. The 3rd Marquis of Salisbury (Prime Minister: 1885–86, 1886–92 and 1895–1902) was to lose five grandchildren in the War, including three by his son William who was, at the time, the Bishop of Exeter. The only other Prime Ministers between 1868 and 1916 had no children – Benjamin Disraeli, Arthur Balfour and Henry Campbell-Bannerman. Both of Lloyd George's sons served, as did four subsequent Prime Ministers – Lt Colonel Winston Churchill, Major Clement Attlee, Captain Anthony Eden MC and the thrice-wounded Captain Harold Macmillan. There is a book to be written here – it is an extraordinary commentary of that time that those of privilege, ability and brains were often the quickest to enlist for military service in their country's hour of need. Only Churchill had been a professional soldier before the War.

Early in their time at Hébuterne the commanding officer, Lt Col WK Peake, was invalided home. The *Journal* of 25th September reported that he was 'making good progress towards recovery. An additional operation, not of a serious character, was found necessary, and has had the desired effect, so that the present expectation is that the patient will be able to get about in a fortnight's time'. These senior Territorial figures had not expected to serve overseas nor to see sustained action. They were sending friends and sons of friends from across their county to their deaths. Their battalions were intended more for keeping peace and order on the home front. Peake had begun his command in 1911. The commanding officer of the 2/8th Battalion, Lt Col Francis Checketts, was to be similarly invalided home within six weeks of their arrival in France in May 1916, not to return. In the case of the 1/8th, Peake was to return to command, remaining in post until September 1916. The *Divisional History* recorded that by that September, Lt Col Peake was the last of the Territorial commanding officers at the outbreak of War still to be commanding their battalion. A commendable achievement for a man in his 48th year – another of the Old Gents. He ended the War as a full Colonel, having been

Mentioned in Despatches and awarded an OBE. He was to write some of the early sections of *1/8th Battalion, The Worcestershire Regt 1914–1918*. He described the action in which Wilson lost his life:

> During August numerous patrols were sent out almost nightly, and eventually the track of a German patrol was carefully noted, and it was decided to endeavour to capture it. At this time there was long grass in 'No Man's Land' and it was decided that the patrol should crawl out in daylight and place itself athwart the track of the German patrol with both wings thrown forward. The patrol consisted of two parties of one officer and 10 other ranks each. Lieutenant Wilson in command of the west wing and Lieutenant Pawsey in command of the right. About half an hour after darkness fell the Germans were heard approaching, but instead of coming along the track as expected, they came upon Lieut. Wilson's left flank. This necessitated him bringing up his right flank to enable him to bring full fire to bear on the enemy, and also caused delay and placed Lieut. Pawsey's party in echelon in his right rear. He then, according to plan, stood up with the utmost gallantry, and challenged the patrol and was at once shot dead. Owing to the darkness it was difficult for Lieut. Pawsey to gauge exactly what was happening; but he at once took action and brought his patrol up in line with the other party, and this saved the situation. Heavy fire was kept up for some time, and the Germans eventually retreated. Lieut. Hawtrey shortly after brought up a stretcher party, and Lieut. Wilson's body was brought back to our lines. His loss was keenly felt by all ranks… [Pawsey was recommended for the MC for this and other good work, duly received.]

This incident highlights a number of factors of life at the Front during the relatively quiet year of 1915. Patrolling was a constant requirement and almost all were led by young officers. As with Lieutenant PM Kerwood at Ploegsteert, it was a significant factor in the lifespan at the Front of the subaltern officer averaging just six weeks. Commanders were not short of volunteer officers despite the risk because a successful or gallant action would often lead to the award of

Grave of
Hugh Wilson

a much sought-after Military Cross. The comment about 'long grass' demonstrates that although there was much artillery shelling of trench lines, the countryside had not as yet been cratered and destroyed as was to happen in this area and across the Somme Front the following summer.

Battalions operated on a cycle of time in the trenches and a similar time in reserve – usually four days, often rotating with the same battalion over a prolonged period. Time in reserve was spent near the Front and well within artillery range. Captain RH Burlingham described on 5th August that he had 'just been taking General Nicholson and the CO round my trenches. I am responsible for 600 yards of the British Line! And I have only 160 men and 3 machine guns, it needs constant vigilance. The trenches here are an absolute maze, and it is quite easy to get lost, you can wander about for hours. You see that the French first had them, then the Germans, then the French again and now ourselves. Each time more trenches have been added according to a different situation.'

The main scourge of life in the trenches was enemy artillery. As such, men being killed or wounded in such incidents frequently did not merit a mention in the Battalion's *War Diary*. A letter published in the *Journal* of 25th September by a private soldier of C Company, GH Taylor, provided those at home with a picture of life under such shelling, even in a quiet section of the Front:

> The small town just outside here [Hébuterne] is very much damaged, and not a single house is left untouched by the German shells. They send us a few every day, and yesterday one of our chaps had a very narrow escape, as a shell burst less than ten yards from him, making a large hole in the road. Luckily, the concussion from the shell laid him flat, and by doing so, he escaped all injuries, save a bad shaking up. A fragment from the same shell found a victim who was some distance away and, by last night's news, he was in a critical condition.

That same edition reported the letters to the parents of Pte J Thomas of 14 Platoon – from Major RHH Creak (acting CO), the padre, Captain PC Thomas, his platoon commander, Lt HS Benjamin, and Pte W Brough on behalf of the platoon. Lt Benjamin reported:

> He was hit in the left thigh by an anti-aircraft shell core. I was on the spot a few minutes after it happened and I can assure you that everything that was possible was done to save his life. The doctors assure me that he did not suffer very much.

Another sad example occurred on 6th October 1915 when the only *War Diary* entry between the 1st and the 10th was on the 5th but just to record: 'Major RJ Rawson 1/4th Gloucester Regt was appointed to the temporary command of the Battn. owing to the absence of Lt Col Peake, who was in England on sick leave'. However, it was on the following day that Pte Alfred Tudge from Bromsgrove was wounded in a heavy artillery barrage. He did not remember anything of the shell which wounded him and due to suffering many 'turns' he was taken back to England, to Woodcote Convalescent Hospital in Epsom and then to 4th London General Hospital. He was eventually discharged as medically unfit in 1917 but was awarded a Silver War Badge which had the inscription in the band around the royal cipher and crown: 'For King and Empire + Services Rendered'. This could be worn to show that a man had served and was not a draft-dodger. In September 1928, life became increasingly difficult for 40-year-old Alfred Tudge and he lost his job in Cheltenham as a travelling salesman for an ironmonger, Messrs Sharpe and Fisher. His wife, Mary, reported that Alfred had not been in good health since his Army service. For a year he had suffered bad headaches and had become 'nervy'. He was dismissed on Friday 14th September and the following morning he left home at 8.30. His wife presumed that he had gone to work as he had not told her of his dismissal. He did not return that evening. A farmer found him the following morning, slumped at the base of an oak tree. He had a .22 pistol with one spent cartridge and a wound above his right ear. He had a letter with him:

> My darling Mary – We have had a bust-up at the shop. They said that they paid me every penny that was due to me, and can (which you know is a lie) pay me no more. I am in difficulties and can't face you, darling. Mother will help you, I am sure, to look after the darling child. God bless you till we meet again. Your loving husband, JIM.

Tudge was not the only member of the Battalion who would use his pistol in such a way once the War was over.

Another private soldier – W Carey, an assistant schoolmaster before the War – wrote to a friend about life at the Front when not in the trenches. The *Journal* published on 30th October the following excerpt:

> We are at present out of the trenches, but this does not mean getting a rest … the whole of this work, of course, is done under shell fire, as, although invisible to the enemy, they know we are about, and so send a number of shells over each day. During our last period of support we had to parade at 6.30 am for inspection, shaved and cleaned our rifles, etc.; breakfast, 7 am; work 8 am until noon and 1 pm until 5 pm. All the work done in the village [Hébuterne], which is two or three hundred yards behind the line, and consisting of trench-digging, road-mending, laying down water pipes, etc. Being so close to the trenches, the village has been rather badly knocked about. Where the houses have been entirely demolished we have used the bricks to pave the trenches, but where they have only had half the roof blown off, or a few holes made in the sides, we use them as billets. No civilians are allowed in this village, so we can't get anything stronger than water to drink. I strolled into the cemetery the other day (we were picking up the road just outside), to see what effects the shells had had on the [local] graves. Several of the vaults were blown open. In most cases the remains had been removed, but one contained the skull and a few old bones of what, according to the stone, was a young lady buried in 1837. The village where we are now [Bus-les-Artois], has not been damaged at all, and there are plenty of estaminets [cafés which sold alcohol], where we can get a drink between the hours of 11 am and 1 pm and 6 pm and 8 pm. The first period is not much use to us as we are working from about 8 am to 5 pm. One or two places keep beer, but it is rotten stuff. The chief drinks are vin blanc and vin rouge. The price is about one franc a bottle, and as the wine is rather sour, we sweeten it with citron or grenadine. Champagne varies in price, according to the quality, from 3 to 5 francs. There are one or two small shops where we can get tinned goods, but the prices are very high. I have sent home, by one of our Sergeants, the 'nose' of a German shell.

Other than providing a very good description of life immediately behind the Front, it also shows the breadth of social class in the ranks

– not only is this well-written but the talk of champagne would more likely feature in an officer's correspondence. The comment on the local cemeteries is of particular interest – that of Hébuterne is at the back of the village. I have visited many near the Front where an annex has the graves of our dead. Each cemetery holds many family vaults, each marked with the names of multiple individuals. Few, if any, predate the War so must have been repaired or renewed, probably at the same time as the village church and the houses. These cemeteries are not beside the church in this area of France, rather on the edge of the village.

Corbett told of the work spent on finding and preparing billets for that reserve time. They were assigned the small village of Bus-les-Artois, some two and a half miles behind the trench line. The front-line companies in each battalion relied heavily on those in the Headquarters Company as well as those like Corbett, their company quartermaster's team. Bus-les-Artois offered 'barns well supplied with hay to live and sleep in … here we wintered and very comfortable we were'. The barns in Picardy were constructed of wattle and daub over an oak framework and many were very substantial in size. Corbett bemoaned the lack of repair equipment from the sappers so they made their own tools and used the nails from the ration boxes and biscuit tins. They puddled their own daub from the local clay and 'stole wattles [hazel shoots] from the woods'. Time in the billets was for rest, cleaning and repairing equipment and rifles and for drying uniforms and boots. Training and sports competitions were organised as well, when the battalion was taken back 'out of the line', which was normally after several months.

The drying of clothing and boots was crucial to the health of the troops and Corbett is forthright in his views on 'trench foot' as being an avoidable affliction. He referred to it as being 'very like malaria, but far more painful'. He went on to explain:

> Trench-foot was a great puzzle to soldiers, and still greater to the Medical Corps but to the alluvial miner it is an old friend. It arises from checked circulation in wet feet. So long as your feet are free they can endure harmlessly any amount of damp: they are designed

> to do so: but wind tight puttees round your feet, get both shrunken with wet, and in two days or so your feet will simply die. The cure for a bad case takes several months and is very expensive, and the pain is terrible.

He referred to 'this scourge, which occasioned scores of thousands of cases of sickness', so one would expect it to be a considerable focus of the generals, the commanding officers and the medics. The result of each case would normally have meant replacing an experienced soldier with a raw recruit. Corbett explained the Battalion's solution: 'hot drinks and bare feet for half an hour or so once a day'. He claimed that over the winter of 1915/16 the Battalion had only one case of trench-fever – 'a man with very poor circulation' – and that the next-door battalion had fifty cases that same night. The *Divisional History* supports this assertion when noting that across the whole 48th Division, 'together with 6/Gloucestershire, 8/Worcestershire with 33 admissions, had the lowest number of men sent down to the field ambulances during January 1916'. Was this a case of the Battalion being more disciplined than others at following standard procedures, or was its low infection rates not noted by Brigade or Division staff officers and its practices not passed on across their commands as lessons to be learned? 2Lt LR Bomford, who joined A Company in January 1916, remembered that one Army solution was 'the issue of rubber thigh boots when going into wet trenches'. However, he continued, 'these were usually damp for a start, and sooner or later one tripped up on uneven trench floors and knelt or fell down and got water in the boots'. It appears that these boots were soon dispensed with and 'you went into the trenches, however wet, in boots and puttees'. He confirmed CQMS Corbett's account of the Battalion's discipline – 'you had to make your men remove these [boots and puttees] daily and rub their feet with boracic powder'.

A second observation by Corbett is equally of interest. Through the winter, the enemy's 'fortifications were growing – not in our haphazard undirected way, when one regiment destroyed what its predecessor had done, to have its work altered by the next: but on a definite, able plan, admirably conceived and sedulously carried out. We watched

Serre grow to a stronghold with terrible Gommecourt as a bastion to the right and the Quadrilateral to the left. It looked impregnable, and so proved to be so, for it was never taken'. Was he being wise after the event or, more likely, was there a lack of trench discipline imposed by Brigade or Division to build effective and coordinated defensive structures? The first observation is that the Germans were, in 1915, building defensive lines that were to last until they had removed Russia from the War when they could concentrate all their forces on the Western Front. The Germans had the coalfields and heavy industry of France and Belgium under their control, they had no plans for any serious attacks in the British sector. As such, they employed copious quantities of concrete and steel to build bunkers of several storeys and greater comfort than those of the British. In contrast, the British trench line was a more temporary holding structure that would be superfluous once a wide-fronted attack had been successful. Indeed, in the southern half of the Somme Front, the trenches were unused from early July 1916 until, in some cases, March or even August 1918. If that explains the logic of the superiority of the German defences, it does not give comfort to those Divisions who were to be at the forefront of the northern half of the Somme Front on the morning of 1st July 1916. Did General Sir Douglas Haig not know what CQMS Corbett had witnessed, or was Haig confident that his artillery would successfully isolate these strongholds and that they would be encircled by infantry penetration through the less-well-defended areas to their flanks? I will not seek the answers which so many more eminent military historians have studied and opined on over the last hundred years. The intelligence reports which accompanied the Battle Orders for Divisions, Brigades and Battalions do indicate that the strength of the German defences in the Serre and Gommecourt areas were understood; and patrols in the days before the attack had reported the ineffectiveness of the British artillery to make significant damage to the Germans' defensive wire obstacles. However, Serre and the Quadrilateral Redoubt were within the Green Line of the First Day's objective so Haig must have believed that the capture of these great defences identified by Corbett was well within the capacity of the 31st Division. It was to suffer 3,800 casualties on the first morning of the battle, failed to capture any of its objectives and was withdrawn from the line the following day.

The winter of 1915/16 was cold and muddy but with few serious incidents. Much of the time when in reserve was spent digging new trench lines rather than training. When the Battalion's position was adjusted to the north of Hébuterne in February 1916, they found trenches which had 'been badly revetted and without proper drainage; and the bad weather of the preceding month had dissolved the footways into troughs of mud'. This is the image which has come down the generations. The *History* told of an attack in mid-February but the Battalion's Roll recorded the deaths of seven Other Ranks on 3rd January. No incident is recorded in the *War Diary*, and the *CWGC* website shows that no bodies were found, as each death is recorded on the Thiepval Memorial. It must be assumed that this was the result of an artillery bombardment with a direct hit on a trench or working party, from which no bodies could be identified. Although there were two sergeants and a corporal amongst those killed, it merits no mention in the *History.* A Facebook post by Lisa Bayliss records that her great great-uncle was one of the sergeants, Harry Edwards, and that he was the last of three brothers to be killed in the War. This is in part a reflection of the times because if an officer had been amongst their number, the incident would have at least been described in the footnotes of the *History*. Corbett, however, comes to our rescue in a paragraph headed 'the Major's Sang Froid'. The conjecture that the loss of these men must have been due to a bombardment was correct, as 'the worst thing that befell us in this place was the direct hit of a shell in which were eight NCOs and men of "C" Company, who were all buried'. It took thirty hours to dig them out, an operation under full observation of the Germans and thus subject to heavy fire. All were dead and they left the mound as their grave. The company commander, Major FAW How, 'earned the affection of us all by his energy and amazing indifference to shot and shell'. He was Mentioned in Despatches, presumably for this incident. The Roll only records seven deaths that day, so Corbett's memory may have failed him on this occasion. Major How gets few mentions through this book because he was soon to head for staff jobs. He was to be found commanding the

11th Bn, The Somerset Light Infantry who were in France from May 1918, returning to the 8th Battalion the following May and eventually being promoted to the rank of (substantive) Major on 12th November 1920 – some 17 years after being promoted to Captain. However, he had to retire from the Army on 20th September 1921 'having attained the age limit' – another of the Old Gents. He died at The Larches, Worcester Road, Droitwich on 23rd April 1930, leaving a widow, Myra, who outlived him by 47 years.

The attack of mid-February is well described by Lt Col Peake and shows the difficulty of coordinating defence at night and with their own distant artillery:

> During the evening of February 17th the Battalion relieved the 7th Battalion in the line in front of Fonquevillers and Hannescamps, the relief being completed about 10 pm. All four companies were in the line, 'A' Company being on the right. All the trenches were water-logged, and the communication trenches between the Front and support lines being impassable, it had been impossible to reconnoitre the front line in daylight. Two sections of No. 1 Platoon were holding an isolated post just to the North of the Fonquevillers – Essart's Farm road, the only approach to the post being along the road, which was swept by enemy machine-gun fire. At one end of the trench was a small dug-out. Running forward from the parapet was an old French sap [ditch].
>
> At 12 midnight the enemy opened a very heavy bombardment on the post and all along the road with a few shells on the rest of the Battalion front. The only artillery support we had was one 16-pounder Battery belonging to another Division, which owing to all the telephones at that time being connected by a single line, it took 42 minutes to get on to. One of the earliest [German] shells burst on the parapet, knocking out the Lewis-gun, killing one sentry, and mortally wounding the other, and another shell seriously wounded the sentry at the entrance to the dug-out. The enemy barrage then lifted and formed a 'box' round the rear and flanks of the post and a raiding party rushed down the sap onto the parapet. This was the first intimation the men in the dug-out had that it was

> anything more than a bombardment, and while one fired at the enemy through a hole in the roof, the others started up the steps, only to be met by several bombs which stunned them all and wounded several, and when eleven of them recovered consciousness, they found themselves prisoners in the enemy trenches. When a few minutes later one of the support Platoons arrived to re-inforce the post, all they found was two seriously wounded men, one of whom died later.

This raid seems to have been remarkably well coordinated, more so than similar British attempts described earlier. The Roll only records one death 'of wounds' on 21st February, Private J Matthews who now lies in Doullens Communal Cemetery Extension No 1. There is no mention of his family in the paperwork, and no private inscription was added at the base of his gravestone. Doullens is some ten miles from the trench line and indicates the site of the hospital where he was tended but died. There is no other death recorded on the Roll for the 18th February, which leaves the soldier killed by the Lewis gun unknown. Reviewing the records of the nearby CWGC cemeteries provides no further help. The Sucrerie Military Cemetery at Colincamps does not hold members of either Worcestershire battalion until 5th March. It is interesting sorting the 885 graves by date as it shows the various battalions and supporting arms who operated in the immediate area between 26th July 1915 (35-year-old Private William Tarver of 1st Bn, The Royal Warwickshire Regiment) and 28th August 1918 (32-year-old Sergeant John Mullins of the 1/8th Manchester Regiment) although there also lies Private Alexander McIntyre who died on Christmas Day 1918, a 50-year-old Cameron Highlander who had transferred to 245th Prisoner of War Company, Labour Corps. Between these soldiers are listed those from New Zealander, Canadian, Australian and South African battalions, demonstrating the reach of this War. Neither is there a soldier from the Battalion buried in the Hébuterne Military Cemetery at this time. It is unlikely that the Lewis-gun sentry was not killed as reported by the commanding officer. The remains should have been present with the two wounded soldiers who were rescued that night. Either his body disintegrated as the shell found its mark or it was not known which of the remaining soldiers had been taken prisoner until sometime later. The last place to enquire is the Thiepval Memorial, listing those who were killed in that area of the Front for whom there is no known grave. Here we find a Private William Bradley of the 1/8th Bn Worcestershire Regiment who is recorded as being killed on 18th February 1916. He is not listed in the Roll of the *History* of the Regiment nor of the Battalion but this must be him and we know exactly how and when he died, almost to the minute. To give the scale of the losses of the War, it should be noted that ten William Bradleys were killed and have no known grave in the Thiepval area alone.

Private William Bradley

It is only possible to trace who might have been taken prisoner from the local newspaper, the *Journal*, in part because none were officers or SNCOs. On 4th March, two weeks after the incident, the *Journal* recorded that A Company commander, Captain HT Clarke, had written to a number of the parents of those missing:

> PTE. HARDWICK
> Mr E Hardwick, of 57, Bath Road, has received a letter from Captain HT Clarke, the Officer Commanding 'A' Company of the Battalion, regretting to report that his son, Pte R Hardwick, was taken a

> prisoner on the 18th, adding that he believed he was unwounded. He joined the 8th Battalion before the war broke out and was employed at Messrs. Dent, Allcroft and Co. before mobilisation. He is a well-known local athlete, and has taken part in many wrestling displays in the YMCA and at St Peter's Young Men's Club. He was home on leave a month ago.

There were similar reports for Pte S Portman, Pte G Bates, Pte T Beese, Pte Harold Chambers, Pte Ricketts, LCpl A Pegg, as well as Pte William Bradley and Pte [Her]Bert Griffiths, his friend. Clearly, Bradley had not been taken prisoner but had died soon after capture and had been buried by the Germans. The letters, all from Captain Clarke, show the trouble which the company commanders went to when casualties occurred. It shows also that the Battalion was still almost all men of Worcestershire. Harold Chambers' brother William must have been in the same Company, even the same platoon, as he is recorded as having written home to describe the action as well as to allay fears that his brother had been badly wounded:

> Just a line to tell you how Harold is. I hope you will not worry about him, because he is quite safe and well. I expect you will have heard from the War Office before you get this letter, but you can believe me he is all right. I was not 30 yards from him when he was made prisoner, but owing to the heavy shell fire from the enemy, we could not get out to help them. He won't be lonely, because there were about 10 of them gone with him. I expect we shall soon hear something about him.

Three weeks later in the *Journal* there were reports of families having received letters from their sons who were held prisoner in Munster – Pte Ricketts, Pte Green (not mentioned above) and, under the heading 'SERGT WEBB'S 16 WOUNDS', he must be the tenth man captured:

> Mrs Webb of 36a, Britannia Square, Worcester, has received a post-card and letter from her son, Sergt HA Webb, of the 8th Battalion,

> who is a prisoner of war at Munster, Germany. He says in his letter (29th February): 'I am badly hit in the left foot and leg, and have one finger of the left hand broken and blown about. In my right leg there are only a few holes, and my right hand is nearly all right. I have 16 wounds, but only four are bad ones. Taking things all round, I am lucky to be alive. The Germans are treating our wounds just as they would treat their own soldiers, and they feed us well. There are several other Englishmen here, and I have Green of my platoon, who is also wounded. The Englishmen have treated us to a few luxuries which they have received in parcels. That makes life worth living…

The publication of this letter would have been helpful to all families who had sons or husbands at the Front who may have been captured. From the *Journal*, we have been able to identify ten of the eleven men given in the *Booklet*'s table as being taken prisoner that night.

The spring of 1916 did not bring much relief. The two battalions continued to rotate on a four-day cycle in a section of the trench line opposite Serre – 'deeply gloomy trenches infested with rats – with alternate periods of frost and thaw interrupted by periods of heavy snow'. The Battalion was holding the trenches on 19th March when the Germans attempted a raid. The ensuing artillery wounded five Other Ranks but the trenches suffered severe damage. Over this month, the Roll records the deaths of a further eight private soldiers with Cpl GA Mackie dying of his wounds on 3rd April. A number are described as being 'killed in action' or 'died of wounds' but others have no such detail on the *CWGC* website. These may well have died of illness brought about by the weather, mud and workload. The *History* records that 2Lt JE Jordan, a 40-year-old subaltern of the sister 1/7th Battalion, as dying of disease on 9th February 1916. The real tragedy for the 1/8th Battalion was the death of the Adjutant, Lt Gilbert Slater, hit by a stray shell at night (29th/30th April) when sending a message to Brigade headquarters. On May 1st, the commanding officer had the following written in the *War Diary:*

> Lt Colonel WK Peake, Commanding the 8th Bn., the Worcestershire Regt, wishes to place on record his deep appreciation of the faithful

& untiring services rendered to this Battalion by the late Lieut GJL Slater during his time as Adjutant. The Commanding Officer is confident that his own grief is shared by all ranks of the Battalion over Lieut. SLATER's death in action on the night 29/30 April 1916.

2nd Lieutenant LR (Leslie) Bomford will feature increasingly as this story progresses. He was at medical school in Edinburgh when the War started. His elder brothers were already serving: Benjamin (born in August 1891) was working in the family agricultural machinery business, Bomford and Evershedan, as a clerk. He volunteered at the outbreak of War as a private in the 14th Service Battalion of the Royal Warwickshire Regiment (The Birmingham Pals), enlisting on 24th September. He did not cross to France until November 1915; however, within four months he was found unfit for front-line duty and posted as a clerk to the base at Etaples on the coast. The cause of his fitness issue is not recorded, but a letter from Leslie to the parents who had recently visited him in a Rouen hospital indicates that he 'had a mishap. Partial burying is quite a common thing. When you hear a shell coming you crouch down in the bottom of the trench. If it pitches just on the side of the trench it knocks earth down to partly bury you'. This sort of incident was an almost daily occurrence for soldiers on the front line. It could have both physical and mental implications for those buried, as in Benjamin's case. His deterioration was continuous and an operation of some sort was required. He was eventually discharged from the Army in August 1917 and he died, probably of tuberculosis, that December, aged 36.

James Bomford

Leslie's other older brother was Douglas, who was twenty when he and his cousin, James, enlisted, receiving their commissions on 5th September 1914. Douglas had been a medical student at Edinburgh University at the time. Both cousins were posted to 2/8th Battalion of the Worcestershire Regiment. The Battalion crossed to France on the night of 24th/25th May 1916. James remembered that on the first night their boats were turned back halfway across due to submarines. He became transport officer, in charge of all the horses and vehicles. He remained in that role for the rest of the War and was awarded an MC in the New Year's Honours List of 1918. Such medals were awarded either in the New Year's Honours or the King's Birthday Honours in recognition of outstanding and other gallant service over a prolonged period. Douglas was a platoon commander in A Company alongside a friend, 2nd Lieutenant NVH Symons, and under the command of Captain JO Walford, then approaching his 47th birthday and referred to in letters by Douglas as the 'Old Gent'. Walford was to spend the last year of the War in the 1/8th Battalion, as a company commander alongside Douglas' younger brother Leslie in the Battalion's last great action. Douglas served with great distinction until his leg was shattered by a machine-gun bullet in a night attack on the 6th/7th April 1917 trying to seize Hill 120, some three miles to the north-west of St Quentin. He was still receiving hospital treatment eighteen months later in Blyth in Northumberland when the War ended. He did not return to his medical studies, instead devoting his whole working life to agricultural engineering, remaining chairman of the aforementioned Bomford and Evershed until two years before he died in 1968. He married his cousin James' sister, but there were no children. An indication of the close connections of the officers of a county regiment or battalion, similar in ways to the soldiers of the Pals Battalions, is best illustrated by a letter written by Captain Walford to Douglas' parents after the 2/8th Battalion's early actions around Aubers Ridge and Neuve-Chappelle in June 1916 and their participation in the British diversionary attacks made shortly before the Battle of the Somme:

Osborn Walford and Noel Victor Housman Symons

Dear Mr Bomford,
Your son Douglas may have told you that he is my Company (A) and I feel I must tell you how splendidly he is doing. We have just been in the trenches for four days on our own and he has been my right hand man. By his courage, initiative and personal attention to detail he has proved himself a natural soldier of a high quality. Probably he has told you that we had a little trouble with the Huns, who attacked and bombed a party out of a crater which we had to hold. We recovered it but lost two killed and one severely wounded. Douglas

showed great coolness and courage. I don't know what I should have done without him. He ultimately led the party to bomb them out again. Fortunately our rifle and machine gun fire had driven them out, but he did not know that when he set out, and I know he would have gone on just the same if they had still been there.

I am fortunate to have such an officer and if I may I should like to congratulate you on having such a son.

I hope some day to make your acquaintance.

In the meantime I am yours very sincerely,

J. Osborn Walford (Captain)

One can imagine the pride with which such a letter was received and the comfort it will have given that their son was doing so well. The detailed description of the actions and Douglas' bravery may equally have caused concern. It is also an indication of the time available when the Battalion was not in the front-line trenches. Walford would also have written to the families of the two soldiers who were killed. He did make the acquaintance of old Raymond Bomford when on leave that November. A letter from Douglas to his parents confirmed the meeting and his feelings for the Old Gent:

Dear Father and Mother

Many thanks for your letters. I am so glad you liked Capt. Walford. He really is one of the best and I always feel, if one is doing a little job of any sort, he would come and if necessary bring his Company with him if one got into any difficulty. He has been more to me than one knows how to express since we have been in France…

This indicates a level of camaraderie and respect which will be explored further. Douglas was 22 at the time and Walford was 47, nearer in age to Douglas' father Raymond, who was then 61. Walford was not having as good a time of it; in *Lance's War,* Lieutenant HL Evers noted in his diary on 12th September 1916 that 'the Old Gent is in bed with malaria' and on 14th September that 'the Old Gent is in hospital at Merville with trench fever'. This may confirm Corbett's views on trench fever being very similar to malaria except more painful

– perhaps making it difficult to distinguish between them. Walford had spent about seven years on the Gold Coast of West Africa before the War, so a recurrence of malaria was certainly possible. On 19th October Evers noted that 'The Old Gent complains of gout and in the evening is taken away to hospital'. Between these two bouts, Walford must have been granted some leave as Evers wrote: 'Hear from home – they are delighted to have seen the Old Gent'. Evers continued his entry of 19th October: 'Personally I feel his soldiering days are over out here'.

Evers, who was 35 at the time of these actions, was the sixth of eight brothers from Stourbridge and was a partner in the Industrial Foundry and Engineering Company Ltd. He signed up as 2778 Private Evers, rising swiftly to Sergeant before being commissioned in November 1914. He was undoubtedly a very professional soldier who was to earn two MCs. His observations of Walford's struggles and possible withdrawal from the front line were made in a matter-of-fact and sympathetic manner. He was clearly a friend of Walford's, referring in a letter to his mother to 'going to dine with Captain Walford for the celebration of his 48th birthday (though 47th by my calculations)'. He makes two other diary entries related to Walford: in July that 'I seem likely to be a Captain soon and hope to be 2nd in command of A Co. and thus under Walford'; and on 1st October, 'I shall be glad to see the CO, Davies, the Old Gent and Odg back again [from leave]'. That Walford should feature so significantly as the C Company commander of the 1/8th Battalion in the last weeks of the War is, perhaps, all the more remarkable given these health problems from which he suffered. There must have been plenty of staff jobs available to him.

LIFE IN THE TRENCHES

We must return to 2Lt LR Bomford as the 1st July 1916 approaches. Born in December 1896, he was too young to enlist at the outset of War and in April 1915 headed to Edinburgh University to study medicine. He joined its OTC (Officer Training Corps) and having completed his first set of exams, was commissioned into the 3/8th Battalion that July. There is an interesting set of correspondence with his older brother Douglas once Leslie had decided to enlist, starting with a sharply-worded recommendation that he should seek a commission:

Mersea Island 7th June 1915

Dear Les,

Officers will be needed very badly; everyone who knows anything tells us this. They also say that for anyone with brains and education to go into the ranks is a mere shirking of responsibility, and with the possibility of conscription coming shortly it is most essential that you either go into something or get married, and though some of our friends and relations seem to go in for the latter course I think you had better go in for the former (it would be jolly bad luck on the unfortunate lady you know)…

I feel sure I could get you a commission under Major Garnett in our 3rd line of the 8th Worcesters. No doubt you will turn up your nose at this, but there is no need to do so, you can't expect to take a commission one week and go into the trenches the next even if you come from the swagger of Edinburgh University OTC. Of course you will be a regular nob at the theory of the business and very likely know more than a good deal of what field officers do, but you will have absolutely no experience in handling Tommy Atkins [colloquial for the average private infantry soldier] and he will lead you about by one ear accordingly, and when you are put in a ditch half full of mud and water with 40 men under you to do whatever harm you

> can to the other people in a similar mess 50 yards from you, I don't see that a lot of crammed knowledge of attack and defence tactics, outposts, etc., goes far…
>
> I hope you have not attached your heart to the kilts ['the Argyll and Sutherland']. The Worcesters have a better reputation than any Scottish regiment (though of course the Scots are splendid fellows) and, besides, petticoats are most indecent things for a soldier to wear, especially in a high wind. You will like Major Garnett very much. If you can settle with Father and let me know I will write to him at once.

Two points of interest come from this letter: that married men were thought likely to avoid the initial conscription; and that the brothers thought that parental permission would be needed for Leslie to forsake his university medical studies. Douglas was quick to follow up his letter with another:

> I have written to Major Garnett today. If he cannot get you one [a commission], I shall write to Colonel Dixon and he will get you one somewhere, I know.
>
> They will not keep you out on account of your size, as you are quite up to standard, so I don't think you should worry any more. A few months of soldiering will soon fill you out. (Leslie was 6' 2" so height was not an issue but, presumably, he was quite skinny.)

Leslie was to write to his father the following Sunday:

> Douglas told me that he would be home on Saturday so I expect he has given you the news. He got me an interview with Major Garnett at Worcester so I shall be coming down to England after the exams, that is Monday night…
>
> I suppose you would have no objection to my trying for one [a commission]…

Ray Bomford, Leslie's father, was quick to respond – by telegram:

We do not object to commission. Bomford.

After a brief spell with his brother Douglas in the 2/8th, Leslie was posted to the 1/8th Battalion, joining them in France shortly after his 19th birthday in January 1916 as a platoon commander of No 2 Platoon in A Company. He was to stay with the Company for the remainder of the War, as its company commander in the last actions. His first company commander was Captain HT Clarke, who was to command the Battalion for the last year of the War. Bomford noted in his written memories after the War that he 'had two Sergeants, Edwards and Wedgbury and about 30 men in all'. Sergeant Wedgbury was to become an increasingly important part of the Battalion's story – perhaps its most remarkable soldier – eventually commanding D Company in several actions in the last month of the War. It is extraordinary that from a single company, three such notable commanders should arise, earning nine gallantry medals between them – Clarke, Bomford and Wedgbury.

2Lt Bomford's letters provide some interesting observations of life at the Front when not in the trenches. He started by asking for his parents to settle the bill for his revolver; officers were expected to provide their own personal weapon. In Bomford's case, he bought one from the Army which his Quartermaster (J Thomas) had to pay for, so a cheque payable to him was required from his parents. This meant that an officer owned and, thus, retained his revolver once military service was complete.

An important task for company officers when in billets or in reserve was to censor the letters of their soldiers. Bomford wrote: 'some of them write jolly funny letters and most of them are in one style as if they have been made up by a formula. A few of the more superior ones write quite a good letter'. His comment about a formula is usually interpreted as an indication that several soldiers asked the brighter men of their platoon to write letters for them. This may have been in part because they knew that their platoon commander would read it or, perhaps, to impress parents, spouses or girlfriends with their written English. He confirmed another widely-held view of trench life, that they 'are infested with rats and in the dugouts are a lot of mice. My platoon has a dog, a sort of strong diminutive collie that is dead nuts on the rats'. Later, he reported to his mother, Eveline, that the dog, by then named Paddy, killed 'about a dozen [rats] a day. This sounds a lot but really isn't very many when you consider the number of rats and mice about'. It was not any unhygienic actions of the troops that caused the infestation of rats, rather the bodies left unburied. Corbett reported inheriting the Hébuterne trench line 'from our gallant Allies. We did not know what they were – one remembers a gallant Serjeant surveying with wonder the seventeen corpses laid out on the parapet – but we learnt: oh yes, we learnt'. (The 'parapet' is the raised earth bank at the front of the trench. The 'parados' is the lower earth bank to the rear of the trench – both to provide additional shelter when being shelled, the parapet also to guard against German snipers.) Bomford continued with a lesser-known fact: 'It is one of the dogs used for dragging carts so it is very beefy when it comes to digging.'

Harvey Carter

It was not always the British who initiated raids on enemy trenches as the Battalion found out in their first month in France. An example is recorded in the *History*:

> Shortly after midnight on May 21st [1916] a subaltern of the 1/8th Battalion, 2/Lieut HGC Carter, while visiting his posts along the front line, encountered an advancing German patrol. In the fighting which ensued the subaltern and his orderly were both severely wounded by bombs. Despite his wounds the subaltern managed to

> reach the nearest post and gave orders for fire to be opened; then he struggled back to the post on the right and there gave similar warning before fainting from loss of blood.

The *Journal* of 1st July recorded the citation for the MC awarded to Carter for his part in this action. The wording is almost identical to that in the *History*, though also mentioning that he was the son of Mr WF Carter of Bromsgrove and that he was an old Bromsgrove schoolboy – with him opening the batting for the 1st XI in July 1914.

The *Journal* that day also recorded the death of Private Alfred Edward Turner of the Worcestershire Regiment (Territorial Force) on Sunday 18th June – it was never specific as to the battalion for security reasons. What is different about this announcement is the cause of death: '... died in No 4 London General Hospital on Sunday from shell shock. As stated last week, deceased was admitted to hospital on the 6th inst. and subsequently brought over to this country... The funeral took place at Bromsgrove this Saturday at 2.30 p.m.. The Town Band, wounded soldiers from Blackwell Sanatorium, the Volunteer Training Corps, the Ambulance Corps and the Boy Scouts attended'. There was no hiding such a cause of death. Indeed, most weekly editions of the *Journal* recorded names under 'Wounded: Shell Shock' – in this edition, just beneath 'Wounded: Concussion Shell'. Pte Turner had not been in a major battle, rather subject to constant sporadic shelling and patrolling. Shell shock was openly being acknowledged before the Battle of the Somme. It was not just the Other Ranks as in this same month Mrs Burlingham received a letter from her husband, Captain RH Burlingham, including: 'I expect you will see my name in the papers, as "wounded. Shell-shock"'.

There were two main tasks facing those battalions not at the Front: trench-digging and road repairs. Bomford described a night when 'our line was re-dug about 200 or 300 yards in front of the old front line. The Huns weren't a bit pleased. They were caught napping a treat'. The *History* recorded this as, on 17th/18th May in front of Hébuterne, '580 of all ranks [of the 1/8th Battalion] dug an entirely new piece of the front line with support and communication trenches: about 50,000 cubic feet between 9.30pm and 2 am.' Shortly afterwards, Bomford noted that 'on Sunday I had to take a party of 100 men to a village near here to work on road mending. Some of them had to put the stones on the road, while the others dug them from quarries. Rotten luck on the men doing navvy's work wasn't it, especially on Sunday'.

In reserve, sport was a source of entertainment and diversion. Corbett recalled that A Company had some cricket equipment, 'the source of constant strife between the Quartermaster and Transport Officer' – but it always made its way to the next camp. He remembered a match against the Hampshires which was a 'great win, for Hants were put out for 50-odd, while A Company made over 270. Corporal Jew and Lance Corporal Cuffe making 150 on the first wicket' – perhaps the highest partnership of the War. Bomford wrote home to inform them that 'the importance of football is not so much in the quality of the game as in the diversion for the men'. In April: 'I had a very good football match yesterday. It was an inter-platoon game, part of a scheme for all the Battalion. My platoon turns out quite a hot stuff team, only my Sergeant bungles matters rather. He runs it; I have nothing to do except playing. We won by 1-0 after a very fast and exciting game … the unaccustomed hard exercise pulled holes in most of us after the trenches, and I think I'm by no means the only one who is stiff today'. This is an interesting reflection of their fitness just three months before the Battle of the Somme. One of the key observations on the performance of the British infantry on the first morning of the Somme was that they walked across No Man's Land. In many parts, as near Thiepval, it was all uphill to the German trenches. Walking was ordered by the generals who believed that the week-long barrage would have destroyed the Germans' will to fight; but it would seem that few of those troops would have been fit enough to have run, especially with their kit and rifles, even if they had been ordered to do so. Any exercise was only possible when away from the front line and much of it seemed to have been on the initiative of the junior officers. Bomford told his mother: 'the other day we had some sports, I suggested them and the whole job fell on me. It meant a lot of work but they went off splendidly … 120 men in teams … [with some] ordinary games and some funny ones like cockfighting (one man mounted on another's back in a melee) and boot races … we gave so-called prizes, things like writing pads, three handkerchiefs and cigarettes. A dozen events only took three hours which is very good'. Bomford would be disappointed if I did not mention that his A Company won with 37 points with the next best getting 21!

Bomford told a most poignant tale of cricket, probably in June 1916:

> Cricket out here is often very amusing. The other night (on the only bit of field we could find) two platoons of our Coy played the other two. Our team was almost all from my platoon and one man from the other. This one man was the County Professional for Worcestershire and as you may imagine he was hot stuff. Of course on our wickets [pitches] there's about as much in luck as in skill, but all the same he made a big difference. I have two brothers in my platoon, they are both over six foot and both rather retiring, but just the men for real work. One of them in this match started his score with three sixes, then 1 and another 6. Before he came out the other brother went in and for a while there was a very amusing combination.

It is not possible to ascertain if Bomford had more than one pair of brothers in his platoon at that time but on 21st July he was writing the following letter:

> Dear Mr Lowe
>
> It is with deepest sympathy that I have to inform you of the death in action of your two sons, 2853 Pte C.H. Lowe and 3190 Pte H.J. Lowe.
>
> In these two I have lost two of the best men in my platoon. They were popular with their comrades, always cheerful and fearless, and their loss is deeply felt by me and their comrades.
>
> We were digging a trench behind the old German front line and they were hit almost simultaneously by German shells. Their death was instantaneous and painless. They died for the old country on a victorious battlefield and although your loss is terrible it is something you may be justly proud of.

With the deepest sympathy of myself and all no. 2 Platoon.
I remain, yours sincerely,
L.R. Bomford. 2nd Lt., 1/8th Worcesters

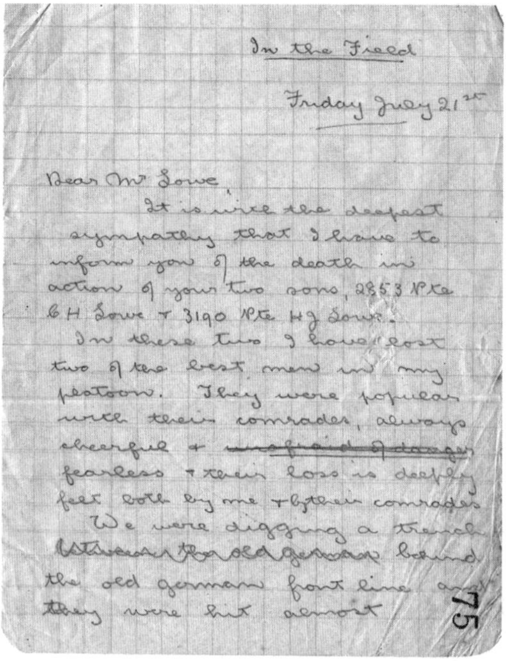

In the Field

Friday July 21st

Dear Mr Lowe,
It is with the deepest sympathy that I have to inform you of the death in action of your two sons, 2853 Pte G H Lowe & 3190 Pte H J Lowe.
In these two I have lost two of the best men in my platoon. They were popular with their comrades, always cheerful & ~~unafraid of danger~~ fearless & their loss is deeply felt both by me & by their comrades.
We were digging a trench ~~between the old german bound~~ behind the old german front line and they were hit almost

75

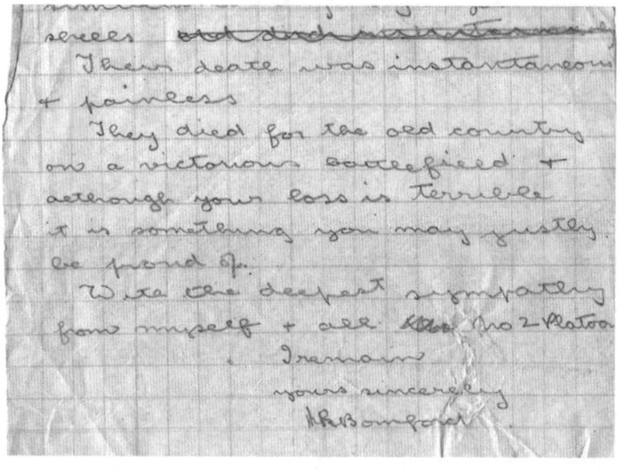

shells ~~[illegible]~~
Their death was instantaneous & painless
They died for the old country on a victorious battlefield & although your loss is terrible it is something you may justly be proud of.
With the deepest sympathy from myself & all ~~[illegible]~~ No 2 Platoon
I remain
yours sincerely
L R Bomford

The Berrow's Worcester Journal of 29th July recorded that Charles was a member of the Samome Walk Baptist Church and played cricket in the church team, taking 5 wickets for 7 runs in one of his last matches for the Baptists against Himbleton in August 1914.

Their names appear one above the other on the Thiepval Memorial. The *CWGC* website records that they were 24 and 26 years old, sons of

James and Lucy Lowe of 14 Rogers Hill, Worcester. As an indication of the closeness of the county society from which these soldiers and officers came, Bomford's mother received this letter (with the above letter enclosed, hence it being now within Bomford's own papers):

> Dear Mrs Bomford,
> One of our people has received a letter notifying the death of her sons on the same day in France. The letter is signed L.R. Bomford, 2nd Lt, 1/8 Worcesters. I wondered if this is one of your sons. If so I should like to write to him asking him to send full particulars as possible of their deaths.
> Would you be good enough to let me know if this is one of your boys. I hope they are all right.
> Give to Mr Bomford our very kindest regards, accept the same for yourself and believe me, yours sincerely,
> W.H. Condy [Reverend]

This correspondence will have brought the harshness of war to Bomford's parents who at the time had three sons in France. Writing the officer's letters as platoon, company or commanding officer will have taken their toll over the months and years at the Front. The Roll of the 1/8th Battalion totals 31 officers and 376 Other Ranks – though we know that Pte Bradley needs to be added to this list – so many such letters had to be written.

A study of the *CWGC* website records the Lowe brothers deaths as being on 20th July. It lists other members of the Battalion who died that night:

Private RF Andrews	buried Bapaume Post Military Cemetery, Albert
Private Henry Webb	Thiepval Memorial
Private Charles Henry Lowe	Thiepval Memorial
Private Harvey James Lowe	Thiepval Memorial
LCpl WG Pountney	buried Warloy-Baillon Communal Cemetery Extension
Private R Farmer	buried Warloy-Baillon Communal Cemetery Extension

Private Joseph Simmonds	buried Warloy-Baillon Communal Cemetery Extension
Private Arthur Butcher	buried Warloy-Baillon Communal Cemetery Extension
Private Charles Waite	buried Daours Communal Cemetery Extension

The *War Diary* recorded just seven men being killed in the action, including those who died of their wounds. When the Lowe brothers are added to this list, we have nine who died but the news of casualties further down the line may not have reached Battalion Headquarters by the time the *Diary* entry was made. The Warloy-Baillon Communal Cemetery Extension is some five miles from the Front so those four men would have died of their wounds at the Casualty Clearing Station. The Bapaume Post cemetery is on the western edge of Albert, two miles from the action. I visited it to see if there were also graves marked with:

A Soldier Of The Great War
Worcestershire Regiment
Known Unto God

The brothers were killed early in the bombardment and the working party continued digging the communication trench for a further three hours and that 2Lt Bomford, their platoon commander, went back to the site to ensure that no gas casualties remained, it seems unlikely that the bodies of the dead were left on the battlefield. Bomford's *Memoir* said that four of his platoon were killed by shells that night. That does assume that there were enough remains of those hit by shellfire to retrieve. It is possible that they were buried nearby; the wooden crosses were War-damaged in 1918 but when the graves were opened in the early 1920s, the decayed uniforms bore some insignia to identify at least the regiment. Given the harrowing story, I felt the need to attempt to discover if they were at least buried side by side.

Gas Attack, 19th–20th July 1916

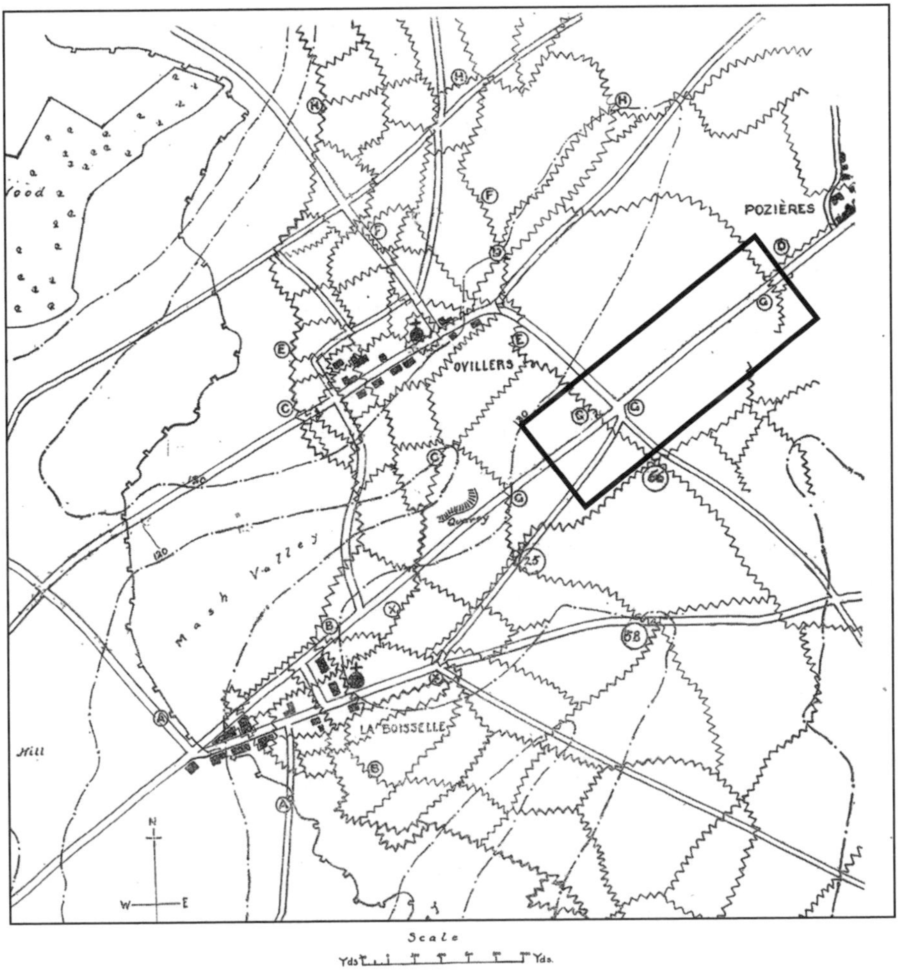

REFERENCE.

German Trenches .... 1st July 1916.

British Front Line .... " " "

(N.B. British reserve & support trenches are omitted.)

Ⓐ Ⓐ Front from which 10th Worc. attacked night 2nd/3rd July.

Ⓑ Ⓑ Line consolidated by 10th Worc .... dawn 3rd " .

Ⓒ Ⓒ Ⓒ Front line of 32nd Division .... 10th " .

Ⓓ Ⓓ Line occupied by 3rd Worc .... night 13th/14th.

Ⓔ Ⓔ Line taken over by 1/7th Worc .... night 15th/16th " .

Ⓕ Ⓕ " established " 1/7th Worc .... night 17th/18th " .

Ⓖ Ⓖ Ⓖ Communication trench in which 1/8th Worc were gassed ... night 19th/20th " .

Ⓗ Ⓗ Ⓗ German position attacked by 1/7th Worc. night 20th/21st " .

At Bapaume Post cemetery I found only Private Edwards' grave and none from the Worcestershire Regiment 'Known only unto God'. The map showed two other cemeteries near Ovillers-la-Boisselle, the Gordon Dump to the south and the Pozières British Cemetery a few hundred yards further up the main Albert to Bapaume Road. The Gordon Dump cemetery has 624 graves but none bore the above inscription. I drove on to the Pozières cemetery – a substantial structure with full-height walls allowing for the names of the missing to be listed on the internal walls from the March to August 1918 actions – from the German advance in Operation Michael until the commencement of the Battle of Amiens. The *History* has a map showing that the working party were repairing a 1,200-yard section of the main Albert-Bapaume road up to a point some 300 yards short of the edge of Pozières. The village of Pozières itself was attacked by the 48th South Midlands Division and the 1st Australian Division on 23rd July 1916 and captured the following day. The senior officers of the $1/8^{th}$ Battalion were undertaking a reconnaissance for this battle at the time of the working party. While it might be assumed that this Pozières cemetery was initially for the dead of the Pozières battle, there are 218 graves which pre-date it – including Lt Norman Gough, 2Lt John Gorrie, Private G Adams and Private FC Powell of the $1/7^{th}$ Battalion on 19th July. The cemetery holds 2,760 graves of which 1,382 are unidentified, with the names of over 14,000 of the missing from 1918 on the walls. The cemetery is on the northern side of the road at the furthest point reached by the $1/8^{th}$ Battalion's working party. Again, I walked each line of graves and was almost at the end when I found the inscription 'A soldier of the Great War Worcestershire Regiment' but it was just a single one. However, further down the very same row were two other graves, side by side, each bearing that same inscription. Could these three be those of Webb and the Lowe brothers? Were the brothers together in death? Between them were graves dated 23rd July. We know from the *Journal* that Webb was also in A Company and that the company commander wrote: 'It is sad for us to lose any of our good comrades out here, but especially so, I feel, when we have lost one of those who have not only "done their bit" (and more) out here, but were making every endeavour before the war to prepare for service to their country when need should arrive'.

The site of the cemetery and the proximity of the working party was too much of a coincidence. I saluted the three graves and left the cemetery. I set off to report back to the most helpful CWGC assistants – Conor and Keiran – at Thiepval. I know that CWGC cannot and will not exhume those in the graves of unknown soldiers, even where there are relatives to provide DNA. This work will have to suffice as the memorial to the Lowe brothers.

Ptes Charles and Harvey Lowe

THE BATTLE OF THE SOMME

After the failure of the British attack at Loos in September 1915, it was the turn of the Germans and Austrians to try and seize the initiative in 1916. They had taken Poland from the Russians and the Austrians were about to renew hostilities against the Italians at Trentino. On the Western Front, General Falkenhayn decided that a decisive advance into the French sector would dismay the British. He moved ten Divisions to the ground in front of the fortress at Verdun together with 542 heavy guns and 2.5 million shells. Operation Judgement was delayed from 10th February by heavy rains, with the bombardment eventually opening on the 21st.

At a conference in Chantilly in December 1915 the British and French had agreed that, in Joffre's words, 'Decisive results will only be obtained if the offensives of the allied armies are delivered simultaneously or at least on dates that are close enough to prevent the enemy from transporting his reserves from one front to another'. Falkenhayn's attack had to be overcome before any coordinated attacks could be launched. In the end, the Battle of Verdun lasted throughout 1916 with some 337,000 casualties on each side, of which the Germans lost 143,000 killed and the French 162,000. By mid-March the battle had reduced to one of constant attrition rather than all-out attacks and it allowed Joffre and the new British commander, General Alexander Haig, to agree on a major assault across the rolling chalk of Picardy astride the River Somme in mid-summer. The main thrust was to be undertaken by the 39 divisions and 1,700 heavy guns under General Ferdinand Foch, with the British in a supporting role. After Verdun their roles were reversed as the French had only 10 divisions to commit, with the British fielding 11 on the first day and employing some 50 divisions by the Battle of the Somme's closure in November. To give an indication of the changing scale of the British contribution, the BEF started the War with just 6 divisions.

The British had become responsible for the whole Front north of the Somme so the vast majority of Kitchener's volunteer army was required in France. Walford and the 2/8th Battalion crossed in late

May as part of the newly formed 61st Division which was given responsibility for ground near Neuve-Chappelle to allow for the release of more seasoned troops for the Somme offensive.

***

By passing over the best-known date of the Great War, 1st July 1916, in the above narrative, it would seem that the Battalion were not involved in the early days of the great Battle of the Somme. That was not the Corps Commander's intention. The *History* recorded that on 21st June the Battalion moved into close billets in Coigneux, perhaps three miles from the Front. The 48th Division were to be the reserve Division of the VIII Corps. The *War Diary* in the early years of their time in France recorded the number of officers and men on duty on the last day of each month. Remembering that they arrived in France with 29 officers and 996 Other Ranks, it is perhaps surprising to see that on 30th June 1916 the Battalion strength was recorded as 38 officers and 869 Other Ranks but that present at the Front were just 28 officers and 789 Other Ranks on the eve of the largest British assault of the entire War. Indeed, they would only have 23 officers on duty if it was not for five subalterns 'reporting for duty' between the 5th and 10th of June – notable amongst them being 2Lt Sydney Wilkes. By starting with the 29 officers when the Battalion arrived in France on 1st April 1915, adding the subsequent subalterns 'reporting for duty', it is possible to work out from the *War Diary* who the 38 officers might be but not to narrow it down to the 28 actually on duty that day. The main reason for the difference is that the *War Diary* did not always list those on leave, wounded, on courses or transferred to Brigade or Divisional staff roles. It might be thought that the former would be very limited before such a great battle.

What is extraordinary is that on 3rd July, the *War Diary* recorded that 8 new subalterns arrived on the 1st, the very day that the Battle of the Somme started. It is difficult to imagine they would have been employed had the Battalion been sent into the assault in those first few days of the battle, although two, 2Lts EL Bishop and HH Milward, had some experience as they had been wounded at Loos with the

3rd Battalion the previous autumn. The *War Diary* recorded all their Christian names as well as which company they would be joining – both rare in such entries. They were sent two to each company – Bishop and Milward to A; Burn and Raikes to B; Clutterbuck and Dupre to C; Tullidge and Wickham to D. Over the following weeks it is possible that all 16 platoons were commanded by a young officer, probably for the only time in the whole War. Despite this, three more young subalterns arrived the following week. The *War Diary* entries for the 6th and 7th July make interesting reading:

> The following three officers reported for duty from 8th Reserve Battalion (the 3/8th): 2/Lieuts. STUART WILLIAM LEWIS, WILLIAM HARRY GRIFFITHS, FRANK WALDRON.
> The following two officers evacuated to Hospital: 2/Lieut. STUART WILLIAM LEWIS suffering from Shell Shock, 2/Lieut. FRANK WALDRON suffering from rheumatism.

It is written in a very matter-of-fact way. Neither were to be found on Battalion duty again. Lewis was an only child from Malvern Links and would have been just 20 when he reached the Battalion. The *History* recorded him as being 'wounded' that day, perhaps an act of kindness for him and his family. 2Lt (Acting Major) Frank Waldron was awarded an MBE along with four other members of the Worcestershire Regiment, all gazetted on 3rd June 1919, so a worthwhile role must have been found for him.

On the morning of 1st July, their Division (the 48th) received orders to move forward to Mailly-Maillet (a mile to the west of Beaumont Hamel) in readiness to exploit the expected success. From there, their Brigade (the 144th) was ordered forward at 9.30 hrs and:

> There, little more than two miles behind the lines, the Territorial battalions [1/7th and 1/8th] waited throughout the first day of the battle, listening to the thunder of the gun-fire and expecting the orders to advance … throughout the night and the ensuing day the Territorials remained in their reserve positions while throngs of wounded came back past their lines. At last, on the evening of

> July 2nd, came orders for the Division to attack: the 144th Brigade would come up on the right of the two surviving battalions of the 88th Brigade and in conjunction with them would attack the hostile salient at Y Ravine [now in front of the famous Newfoundland Memorial at Beaumont Hamel].
>
> The 144th Brigade marched forward after dark, and the 1/7th Worcestershire were already filing up 'Withington Avenue' towards 'Constitution Hill', in preparation for an attack at dawn, when counter-orders came. The Territorial battalions were turned about, and after struggling with difficulty out of the communication trenches, the troops marched westward again and reached their bivouac of the previous night at about 4.30 a.m. Thence on the following afternoon the Brigade marched in grilling heat back to Coigneux.

That was the Battalion's experience of the initial British attacks and slaughter of the Somme. They all survived the day but one can only imagine the graphic thoughts of the officers and men as they waited for their orders over a period of 36 hours. However, one officer, 2Lt VR Fox-Smith, was attached to 144 Brigade's Trench Mortar Battery and was involved on the 1st July as a forward observation officer (FOO). After the War he wrote down his observations of that fateful day. His detachment was stationed directly in front of Serre, between Hébuterne and Beaumont-Hamel and had undertaken its part in the bombardment as dawn broke. Fox-Smith then took up his OP station, watching at 7 a.m. as the 'Bombardment reached a crescendo and a smoke barrage was now included. Then two minutes later the Stokes Mortars joined in a hurricane bombardment of thirty rounds a minute'. He watched then as disaster unfolded:

> Meanwhile at 7.30 the Officers all along the line blew their whistles and began to lead and help their men over the parapet.
>
> At the sight of our troops the Germans poured out of their dugouts with rifles and machine guns. The latter were dropped into prepared emplacements and were in action as soon as our men began to walk across No-man's-land. Then their artillery began dropping shells along No-man's-land. As our troops moved forward they were mown

> down by machine gun and rifle fire. High explosives and shrapnel tore into them…
>
> … a good proportion of our troops were young and many barely trained. They walked slowly towards the enemy in formation, in open order as if still on parade and carrying their rifles at the port. They moved slowly – no doubt due to the weight they were carrying on their backs. Our troops were ideal targets for the Germans…
>
> I could not believe what I was witnessing; it seems like a mad, long nightmare dream. Still the waves on No-man's-land with its carpet of mangled corpses and dying men which were regularly churned by the German high explosives.

Fox-Smith was to be awarded an MC for his actions at Passchendaele and he survived the War. It is not clear when he typed this or who placed it at the Imperial War Museum in 1976. He was to spend his 21st birthday on 19th July near Ovillers walking through the battlefield of a few days before as the British advance continued in that central area. He wanted those close to him to know what he witnessed but he was clearly very bitter about what the generals ordered their troops to do at the Somme. It is in contrast to Corbett's more measured writings as well as those in LR Bomford's *Memoir.* It is, however, the story which so many historians have latched onto when considering the tactics and strategy employed by the British generals. Fox-Smith was the only member of the Battalion to actually witness the slaughter. To his credit, it did not affect his performance at Passchendaele.

On 4th July, the 48th Division was ordered to support the 93rd Brigade of the ill-fated 31st (Territorial) Division in the front-line trenches near Serre. The *History* recorded:

> There the fighting had been desperate, and the defences had been wrecked by heavy shells. Dead men lay everywhere, and the task of clearing and repairing the trench-line was difficult and nauseating … the Territorial battalions held that line in succession for twelve days, and those trenches long remained in the memories of the officers and men, as their worst experience of the horrors of the field

of a great battle. During that period [4th-7th July] Lieut. CR Pawsey showed great bravery in repeatedly rescuing helpless wounded men out in 'No-Man's-Land' during daylight.

Symons wearing his Military Cross

Pawsey was the first member of the Battalion to be awarded an MC and by this time only one other officer, 2Lt Harvey Carter, had also won an MC – for actions on patrol on 21st May 1916. 2Lt NVH Symons was to gain an MC for a single daylight rescue in No Man's Land with the 2/8th Bn. Perhaps recommending Pawsey for a Bar to his MC, when the Battalion had so few such awards, counted against him. There were probably so many such incidents across the Front in these early days of the Somme that Pawsey's heroics had become more commonplace – although Symons' action was on 22nd August 1916.

Charles Pawsey, like almost all other officers including Lt Col Peake and Captain Walford already mentioned, was not a schoolboy hero. He was at Berkhamsted School from 1909 to 1913, becoming a prefect and reaching the rank of sergeant in the school CCF. He was not a man of Worcestershire, rather the son of one the Royal Navy's ten Paymaster Generals. Additionally, he had been one of two subalterns to be Mentioned in Despatches in the 1916 New Year's Honours alongside the 19-year-old 2Lt Alan Plaistowe, the commanding officer (Lt Col WK Peake) and company commander Major FAW How. Pawsey was not to be rewarded for his actions in No Man's Land.

Bomford remembered the scene:

> The front line was terrible, all mud and corpses. The only way to get along the line was to walk on the bodies. You couldn't get them out of the mud. The trenches had to be abandoned, all troops moving back to the second line.

The scale of this devastation is perhaps best illustrated by the statistics from the nearest cemeteries, Serre Road Cemetery No 2 where there are 7,127 graves but according to the *CWGC* website, 4,944 are unidentified. The nearby Serre Road Cemetery No 1 has 1,728 unidentified graves of the 2,426. The names of these missing officers and soldiers are recorded on the Thiepval Memorial at the centre of the Somme battlefields. Private Charles Westcott was the only Battalion casualty over this period.

Corbett recorded a more telling tale of the scale and impact of the terrible defeat of these initial Somme attacks under the title 'In the Lost Battle':

> In the sector we now took over the scene was incredible to disciplined troops. The defeated regiment had raided the stores of emergency rations, and the formalities of 'handing over' were neglected. In a sap [ditch] off the communication trench a dripping Satyr, surrounded by empty rum-jars, was issuing mess tins full of spirit to all who came. All order, all soldierly pride seemed lost in the bitterness of defeat and disaster: these were not soldiers, but spectres of despair, who lurked and died hourly in that battered and reeking charnelhouse. Corpses and fragments of corpses lay everywhere: their blackened faces glared at us from the parapets: tattered limbs

> and unnameable members strewed every stinking trench: untended wounded lay groaning in the open: the RAMC [medical] men were in a deep dug-out and would not come out to their work. No attempt had been made to clear the trenches of the dead or to bring in the wounded from No-Man's-Land. Every man we could spare went on that dreadful duty, and piteous cases were brought in. Living men were rescued who had been lying there for seven, ten, and even fourteen days, blistered by the sun, soaked by the rains, chilled by the frost, crazed by fever, tortured by pain and vermin, the maggots crawling in their gangrened wounds, but still indomitably alive, faintly cheerful, piteously grateful for our aid.
>
> We had to examine the water-bottles of the dead and wounded and pour away the spirit they often contained instead of water. Countless men had 'gone over' in the assault with their rifles unloaded and bayonets unfixed. Small wonder that in one brigade which attacked along that line three of the battalion commanders found death and the fourth committed suicide.
>
> These things were evil to see and shameful to tell of. One cannot tell all the shame. But it is well that those who love the glory of war should learn also what a lost battle is like.

This was written shortly after the War rather than in letters or diaries at the time – it is not a criticism of the generals, rather of those commanding the battalions which they replaced. Letters with such content would not pass censorship. Others have examined the Battle of the Somme in greater detail which is not my purpose here. Clearly Corbett still felt very strongly some three years after the battle. The images which will have become ingrained in the memories of those tasked with clearing the battlefield of the dead and wounded undoubtedly had serious long-term effects on many of those involved. On the positive side, it showed the importance of having well-disciplined battalions in reserve which were able to cope with this seemingly senseless loss and destruction and which could still operate effectively at the Front, continuing to prosecute the general's orders to attack over the ensuing months until the battle ended 141 days later with the British in relative supremacy.

To emphasise the good fortune of the Battalion both not to have been committed as a third line of attack in the first days of the Somme and then of becoming inoperative after the gas attack of 19th/20th July, the entry in the *War Diary* of 25th July provides a sober reflection:

> Capt HG Newman, Capt CC Davies, Lt JR Blake, Lt A Plaistowe, [all photographs below] temporarily attached to 6th Bn. Gloucestershire Regt as Coy Commanders to replace their heavy casualties of the week & 2Lts WOH Williams, BH Tullidge, JC Wickham & SH Wilkes as platoon commanders.

A review of the *CWGC* website finds the names of two subalterns and three company commanders (Capt GE Elliott, Major CE Coates and Capt EW Bird) from 1/6th Bn killed over that single week.

GAS

It is interesting at this juncture to follow Bomford's references to gas attacks in his letters. In January 1916 he wrote: 'we have to carry smoke helmets and tear goggles with us all the time in readiness for any gas or lacrymonious shells the Boche may bless us with. I don't think there is the faintest chance of any but still they make us do it'. By early February, he wrote: 'we are getting gas alarms but we have never had any gas. I don't know whether they are false alarms or whether there is stray gas around from some other part of the line. What wind we have has been from our lines to the Germans so they can't be trying any tricks'. There are no further references until 22nd July when he mentions that 'I'm temporarily suffering from a slight gassing' – the day after his harrowing letter to Mr Lowe. The *History* recorded:

> The 1/8th Battalion had met with disaster. After three days in Divisional Reserve at Bouzincourt the Battalion had received orders, on 19th July, that all four companies would form a working party that night. The work to be done was to dig a new communication trench up the main road from La Boisselle to the position in front of Pozières ... which was the furthest ground held in that [easterly] direction.
>
> At 9 p.m. the four companies moved off, marched through La Boisselle in the darkness, deployed along the road and commenced to labour. Little more than an hour's work had been done, when [at 11.10 p.m.] the enemy's guns commenced to shell the line of the road. The troops continued their work as best they could, throwing themselves down at intervals when the shells struck near. Some of the shells exploded, but most of them made so little noise that the troops took them for 'duds' [confirmed by Bomford in his Memoirs after the War]: the muddy ground, they thought, must account for the enemy's fuses not working. Presently, 'funny stink' said someone 'what's is it? ... Gas?'... 'no, gas doesn't smell like that.' The work went on. More shells, softly thudding, fell along the line of the road.

> Then at last the sickly smell became overpowering and men started to vomit. It must be gas the officer (Captain JP Bate) decided, gas of a kind hitherto unknown; however the effects did not seem very serious; the work must go on. The work went on till nearly 2 a.m. Then, their task practically accomplished, the four companies made their way back. Visible casualties had not been very heavy – 7 killed [actually 9] – the two Lowe brothers, plus Privates Webb, Andrews and Farmer – who died of wounds – and Waite, Butcher, Simmonds and Lance Corporal WG Pountney [who are each described as having 'Died of gas Poisoning' on the Roll and each now buried in a different cemetery, presumably depending at which stage they died – dressing station, aid post or hospital], and 7 wounded by shell-fire; but 36 others were affected by the gas and had to be supported back to a dressing station nearby, whence they went to hospital. The four companies tramped back to billets and about 5 a.m. the men threw themselves down to sleep.

It is here that it is appropriate to introduce another of those officers who will figure so prominently in the Battalion's exploits in 1918. Lt Colonel Peake recalled in the *Booklet* the 'Gassing of the Battalion'. He explained that 'Company Commanders were absent making a preliminary reconnaissance of the trenches in the neighbouring Ovillers, which the Battalion were to take over the next day, and the only Captain available was Captain Bate, who was sent out in charge of these parties'. John Percival (Jack) Bate was to suffer from his gassing that night and for many years to come.

Bomford added some flesh to this story with his own experiences:

> I had four men in my platoon killed by direct hits and then we realised they must be gas shells quite new to us, the second time they had been used and we had no warning. The 'stockinet' gas masks we had were primitive and the only way to get men out of the valley was to take off your gas mask. You couldn't see at night in them. After we had got the men out at dawn I tossed another subaltern for who should go back to look for the wounded. I went. I got back to the Battalion camp, but a lot of the men collapsed on the

way. The Doctor couldn't understand what had happened, and a few men died.

Sec.-Lt. L. R. Bomford,
Evesham. Gassed.

Corbett, who as CQMS would not have been in the trench-digging party, provided some evidence that not only were the gas masks inadequate for the task but also that warnings of impending gas attacks by the Germans were not passed down to the Battalion. The Germans would only have used gas when the wind was in the east so that it did not blow back into the faces of their men in the Front trenches and outposts. Corbett started by recording that the Battalion was moved to this part of the Front by lorries – the first time in their 15 months at the Front they had not had to march. He continued that the trench-digging operation was done in coordination with the 1/7th Warwickshires:

> The masks were put on but the damage had been done.
>
> The enemy found a new way of disseminating gas by means of shells. They had first tried it a few days before on an East Country regiment and had done fearful harm. Warning had been sent round, and the Warwicks had received it, so the Battalions working near us were prepared and suffered few casualties. But our Usual Channels had 'let the matter lie on the table' for two days. To be exact, our H.Q. received the warning that midnight, just about the time when the gas bombardment was taking place six miles away.

It might be considered an important aspect of the disaster which should have been included in the *History* so that those involved who survived the War, as well as their families, would know the full story. It begs the question as to whether a cover-up or a degree of incompetence or ineptitude was perpetrated after the War? And, if it was in this instance, were there other similar mistakes that were glossed over a decade later as Stacke's work was nearing completion? Stacke's *Preface* outlines how the *History* was written, no doubt the way in which similar regimental histories were produced in the 1920s:

> The basis of the account of each fight is to be found in the Official War Diaries … kept by each unit and formation … day by day. All the important facts or events were entered – or should have been entered … it is from these Diaries that the initial narrative of the work of the battalions has been compiled. The Narrative in the War Diaries is necessarily bald and official in tone. The writers seldom had the time or space to record in detail the many gallant deeds which redeem the record of slaughter – the official accounts of many of those brave actions were published in the contemporary 'London Gazette'. The official 'chits' of these decorations were collated with the general account and in most cases worked into the text (<u>it has to be said, mainly in the case of officers</u>).

Stacke went on to explain perhaps the most important phase of the production of the *History*:

> The third stage of the work was the checking and correcting of the account by individual survivors of the various engagements. Unlike the majority of historical works these records of the last war concern intimately many hundreds of living officers and men. Some such process of personal revision was therefore essential.

There are listed the members of the Regimental History Sub-Committee who, presumably, oversaw the final draft. Its chairman was Major-General DE Cayley CB, CMG whom Wikipedia records as having served throughout the Gallipoli campaign and then being in command of the aforementioned 88th Infantry Brigade at the Battle of the Somme. He was to suffer gas attacks twice in 1917, the second during the Battle of Passchendaele. He was further promoted in March 1918 to command the 29th Infantry Division.

From the above, it is possible that this failure to record that the warning of possible gas attacks was passed neither to the Battalion nor to the companies at the Front was due to later editing. Either it did not get into the *History* for the sake of time or space or because it reflected badly on those involved; or it was not thought important by Stacke himself; or it was subsequently removed at the behest of the commanding officer of the time, Lt Col Peake or, indeed, by General Cayley and his committee. Peake was not a well man and died in 1923 – some six years before final publication. The *War Diary* of that time is different to its records of the previous days. For 15th July there are two entries, one written at 12 noon and another at 8 p.m., the latter ending with: 'The Bde was under orders of 32nd Div. until the morning 16th, when 48th Div. moved to BOUZINCOURT'. There is then a blank line – the first for several months. Then, on 16th:

> The first day of 48th Div's share in the great offensive. Even now it could hardly be called 'field fighting' nor 'open warfare'. For it chiefly consisted in 'nibbling' trenches bit by bit. [There is then a raised note, thus added later, which appears to say '5 7 d SE. X2 and 8'.] The 7th Worcs were in the line with the 4th Glosters on their left, 49th Div to the left of them & 145 Bde to right of 7th Worcs. The 6th Glosters were in Bde Reserve, and the 8th Worcesters in Div. Reserve. All ranks looked eagerly to the day when their turn should come to meet the enemy in fair fight after the comparatively tame and wearying monotony of the trench garrison work for 16 months. But the Battalion was disappointed. For on the night 19/20 July when the old German line now occupied by the Bde had been reconnoitred, & the Battn was prepared to take over in the afternoon [of 20th July] a digging party strength 18 Officers and 580 OR working on a New Communication trench on the ALBERT-POZIERES road 57D S E X 9 was caught in a barrage with 5.9', 4.2', & 77 MM shells, but they were the least part of the barrage, the major portion being

> gas shells of a type which had not hitherto been encountered. They exploded with but slight noise – so slight as to be mistaken by many for 'blinds'. Consequently many men were late putting on their tube helmets, & none realised the danger early enough, for the smell of the gas employed was a novelty to everyone. Of the 598 of the ranks present only 18 were entirely unaffected by the poison. The barrage lasted from 11.10pm – 1.45am. Capt JP Bate in command of the party handled the situation in a cool & skilful manner; as a result of this & of able co-operation of the other officers present, the party continued as far as possible at work, till 1.55am & returned to billets in excellent order. Casualties 7 killed & died of wounds 7 wounded. 2 Off. 36 OR suffering from gas poison – most of whom were attended to at a dressing station nearby, whence they were conveyed to F. Amb in ALBERT.

War Diaries are not written up on pre-numbered pages so a page can be quietly removed as appears to have happened here. The date (July 19th/20th) seems to have been added later and is in a different hand. Also, it would be at least a week before it was known that '598 of the ranks present' had, excepting 18, been affected by the gas. The remainder of the entry provides interesting detail about the effects of the gas but clearly a page has been removed or lost. As Lt Col HA Carr, who succeed Peake as commanding officer just three months later, was a member of the Regiment's History Sub-Committee, he would have been able to ensure that the detail of the gassing could be added accurately to the *History*, without apportioning blame. The *War Diary* continued:

> The full effects of this gas poison did not manifest themselves until some 10 to 12 hours afterwards when the men turned violently sick. All question of relieving the 7th Worcs in the trenches had to be abandoned, only 18 men being fit for duty, beyond transport, headquarters & quartermaster's details who hadn't been in the digging party. The effect on the cardiac action was such as to make all exercise or exertion impossible & complete rest was ordered by the ADMS [Aid Detachment Medical Sergeant]. Men who appeared unaffected

went about helping their comrades or doing their ordinary work & would collapse suddenly & unexpectedly. Even several days later when many appeared to have recovered, light exercise caused a setback. ([Added later] Between 20th and 25th 79 ORs were also sent to Hosp suffering from gas poisoning).

Corbett provided greater detail of the impact on the Battalion of the gas attack:

The scene as the Battalion returned soon after dawn was appalling. On the long march some had fallen by the way, others lay down to rest, but hundreds returned, some staggered, many apparently unhurt. It was a new gas [later reported by Bomford as Polygene]: instead of attacking the lungs it had plainly affected the heart. We administered the only stimulants we had – tea and rum mixed – and brought the men out of the huts where the fumes of their breath poisoned the air. As time passed and the poison bit, men fell down by the scores. They fell as they stood, or walked, or worked. We were ordered to fall in to go to the Line: one Sergeant-Major, apparently quite well, as he went to rouse the men, fell senseless to the ground. The ADMS arrived, prescribed tea and rum, and sent the worst cases to Hospital. Over 80 went, and most of those returned to us in two or three months, cured, and did good service. Some died, some had to go home … only three died immediately (listed above), but 536 were affected, some of whom died later. The last recorded case passed away in his sleep five months afterwards … only 150 men were left available for duty. These went up to Ovillers to carry bombs and ammunition to the firing line, an arduous duty which brought them several casualties.

Phosgene (cobalt chloride) was the gas involved and proved to be the most lethal of the various gasses used by the Germans in the War, with estimates of those it killed ranging between 76,000 and 85,000. It was first used by the French in 1915 and was an important industrial product before the War, rather than a chemical developed especially as a weapon of war. It smelt like new-mown hay and was heavier than air, so would sink to the bottom of the trenches. The safest action, beyond fitting your gas mask at the first mention of gas, was to stand still – thus keeping your head as high off the ground as possible but also keeping your breathing short and slow. As such, those that July night will have suffered badly because they were ordered to continue to dig and move earth for several hours after the shells fell. The gas was accompanied by a misty cloud, but this would not have been obvious to the Battalion as the shells were dropped on them at night.

There is no indication from the Roll as to who it was who died 'five months afterwards' and the Roll in the *History* does not distinguish between those who died from gas poisoning and those who died from their wounds – all such cases are described as 'd. of w.'. There are some listed in the *History* but not on the Roll; the first amongst them may well have been Pte Walter Cottrill who died on 20th October 'at home' of 'pneumonia following wounds' and was buried at Astwood Cemetery in Worcester. Pte John Dowles was buried in Besford Churchyard after his death on 21st November 1916. An inquest recorded that he 'died from asphyxia following on gassing whilst on active service'. He was 30 and was buried with full military honours. His death is recorded in the Roll in the *History*. Another possibility is Lance Corporal Frederick George Coles who died on 13th December. The *History* states that he died at 'Home' which means back in Blighty. He was 30 and his parents lived in Dartmouth – so nowhere near Worcestershire. His mother, Mrs Emma Jane Coles, paid for an inscription on his headstone – HE GAVE HIS LIFE, THAT WE MAY LIVE IN PEACE. This, in turn, provides more information – that Mr William Coles, father, had probably died and that the family had some money. The latter point was one of contention because families were asked to pay 1/2d per letter, so a total of 7s 6d (37.5p) for Mrs Coles, or £16.50 in 2023. Perhaps it was this or a lack of a next of kin in the early 1920s when the great cemeteries were being laid out, but only about a quarter of graves have a family inscription. Perhaps all these three died as a result of the gassing or the associated shelling. As in other instances during the War, if any had been an officer, greater detail would be available, probably meriting at least a footnote in the *History*.

The Battalion was rendered effectively inoperative for several months. It is not surprising that there was anger that the warning message was not passed on correctly and in a timely manner. Indeed, Corbett told of disagreement amongst the authorities as to how these soldiers should be treated:

> The Military Authorities insisted that nothing was the matter with us [perhaps indicating that Corbett himself has been affected by the gas]: the Medical Authorities, including the D.M.S. and the principal specialist in heart cases, insisted that the men were in danger. This absurd dispute lasted for nearly two months, during which time the remainder of the gassed men received no treatment (except when they collapsed) and was terminated by a compromise which sent them down the Lines of Communication. This neglect robbed us of their services for nearly five months.

Lt Col Peake expanded on the travails of the gassed:

> The medical authorities, not thoroughly understanding the effects of this new gas, thought that the majority of the men would shortly recover and a week later the whole Battalion was dispatched by bus and train to a convalescent camp at Cayeux-sur-Mer on the coast, near the mouth of the River Somme. While there, repeated efforts were made to have the Battalion examined by some expert in gas poisoning, but to no effect: and after 10 days there the whole Battalion was taken by bus and train back to the Somme. It detrained at Acheau and was conveyed by bus to Bouzincourt and bivouacked in fields to the west of the village. Between the dates of the men being gassed and arriving back at the Somme area the Battalion had received a draft of 200 men, and there were at this time about 400 all ranks fit … the Battalion [later] proceeded with the rest of the Brigade north again, and took over the trenches opposite Beaumont-Hamel. Whilst there an expert was sent down from General Headquarters to examine the 'gassed' men, who were bivouacked with the rest of the transport west of Mailly-Maillet. After 10 days in

> the trenches the Battalion was drawn out to rest at Bus, and whilst there they were inspected by the G.O.C. Division (Major General Robert Fanshawe) who, for the first time, saw the terrible effects of this gas poisoning. A few days after, an order was received from General Headquarters to dispatch to convalescent camps the officers and men still suffering from the effects of the gas, and it was many months before they were fit to rejoin the Battalion.

Bomford, in his memoirs, stated simply that he went to hospital on a stretcher (on 1st August) and the remainder of the Battalion went to the coast to recover – presumably the 536 identified as suffering from the effects of the gas. Bomford's letters of the period talk of a gradual decline: 22nd July to his father:

> I'm temporarily suffering from slight gassing … the gas doesn't affect you at first except for a bit of a choking sensation, but when it comes on six or seven hours later, it affects men pretty badly. It first affects the lungs and then causes heart depression. Thanks to the fact that neither my lungs nor my heart are feeble I have shaken it off pretty easily. The great thing is to rest and eat nothing for 24 hours or so, this leaves me a bit feeble but with a huge appetite that I can now gratify.

Then 27th July, again to his father: 'I've quite recovered from the effects of gas. I did about six miles yesterday and was none the worse for it'. It was another four days before he was stretchered to hospital. He recorded later that he was invalided our and spent a month at Chatham Hospital, and was then sent home. The *History* reports that Lt CR Pawsey, Lt LR Bomford and 2nd Lt CT Lodge were the officers mainly affected – without mentioning Captain Bate. However, four officers were added to the casualty list from that night in mid-September – Captain JP Bate, Captain CC Davies, 2Lt HR Ryan-Bell, 2Lt GH Smith. Bate and Davies were put in charge of two companies totalling 424 men who were sent to No. 5 Convalescent Camp, Cayeux-sur-Mer, with orders to get the men fit again by gradual training.

Bomford's summary of the next few months provides an interesting example of how the stages of recovery were organised:

> I remember if my motor bicycle [a Connaught two-stroke] didn't start immediately, I had to lie on my back for ten minutes. I remember going partridge shooting before a Medical Board decreed light duty, and I went to east Coast defence at Cromer [on the north Norfolk coast]. The Monmouth Regiment, a peculiar lot, was there: half were convalescent like me back from France, half didn't intend to go back to France. I was given a detachment at Runton, a few cottages and a path down to the sea. I overstayed my leave and went back to our 3rd line [3/8th Battalion] at Catterick in Yorkshire, a beastly cold and draughty camp. All I did there was to take the convalescents for a march each day. We went to a convenient wood and waited until it was time to return. At some point when I was back I was billeted at Cheltenham and saw brother Douglas, who was there after shrapnel in his neck. [He then attended a 'Bombing' course on Clapham Common before returning to France on 17th February 1917.] I was sent back to France and very luckily to the 1/8th Battalion and to No 2 Platoon again … at Peronne.

This gives an impression of an enormous structure back in England to deal with the sick and wounded, of being moved regularly around the country, presumably by rail, and then of hoping that you would get your old job back or, at least, return to the same company. This was not necessarily the case, nor even to the same battalion – as Captain Walford was to find out later in 1917. The whole tale shows the implications of a simple mistake or misjudgement, taking hundreds of men from the Front for several months. It is a telling indication of the damage an effective gas attack caused. The shelling killed four men, but the gas 'dud's' took a whole battalion from the front-line for months.

Whilst the Battalion was recuperating, the commanding officer, Lt Col Peake, was invalided home to England due to ill-health and he handed on command of the Battalion. He was to recover some months later and in July 1917 he was given command of the 4th Battalion, the Gloucestershire Regiment. This he retained until the following August when he was promoted to Colonel. The *Chronicle* of his old school, St Edward's Oxford, recorded him in May 1919 as being acting Brigadier in Blyth, Northumberland. He was rewarded with an OBE for his war service and only retired in February 1922, becoming too old for further service at the age of 53. He died on 4th January the following year at a nursing home in Newbury.

Harry Carr

Lt Col Peake was succeeded by Lt Col Harry Carr, a career soldier who was transferred from the 2nd Battalion to take command. He was born in September 1872 in Rawalpindi and was staying with his grandfather, Ralph Carr-Ellison, at Dunston Hill Hall, a wonderful Georgian house on the edge of Whickham in County Durham at the time of the 1881 Census. His father was Lt Colonel Ralph Carr who commanded the 36th of Foot, later the 2nd Battalion of the Worcestershire Regiment in the 1870s. Carr married Elsie Putnam in 1913. His brother, Captain Martin Carr, was killed at Aisne on 18th September 1914 having married Elsie's sister on 6th August in Aldershot, some six weeks before he was killed. Both brothers had served in the Boer War, with Harry having served also in Malta, Bermuda, Ceylon (Sri Lanka) and India. He was in Burma as the War started and was commander

MARRIAGE OF MISS GWENDOLYN PUTNAM AND CAPT. CARR, OF THE WORCESTERSHIRE REGT.

of W Company of the 4th Battalion when it was ordered to Gallipoli in 1915. In intense fighting over the first days of May, including a full company bayonet attack, the 4th Battalion was to lose three captains and 10 Other Ranks, in addition to over 70 wounded. Major Carr, as he was then, was awarded a DSO for his part in the action. He had just passed his 44th birthday when he was appointed to command the 1/8th Battalion – yet another of the Battalion's 'Old Gents'. He was the Battalion's only member of the landed gentry serving, albeit the third of eight sons. Captain Hubert T Clarke became his second-in-command. Between Peake and Carr, Major Lionel Kerwood took command for the month 12th September to 12th October. An Old Malvernian and a solicitor before the War, he was then promoted to command the 13th (Wirral) Battalion of the Cheshire Regiment, part of the 25th Division which will feature significantly in this story over the last weeks of the War. The Battalion had lost 18 officers as casualties on 7th July in an unsuccessful attack by the 74th Brigade at the Somme. Their commanding officer, Lt Col LH Finch DSO, was wounded. His successor, Lt Col PS Hall, won a DSO during a brief two months in command. Under Major Kerwood they were part of a major assault on 21st October on Regina Trench, just north of Le Sars. The Divisional history said simply: 'On the left of the brigade the 13th Cheshires, when nearly all their officers became casualties, slightly lost direction…' Kerwood's name is recorded on the Thiepval Memorial, giving just his battalion, rank and date of death. He was 30 when War broke out, so fourteen years younger than Lt Col Carr on his promotion to battalion command. As with Captain JC Bate, he was at Malvern College. His short obituary in the *Malverian* said:

Lionel Kerwood and Clement Davies

> **Lionel Kerwood (No. 7 [House] 1900–1902)** Middle V – Remove: Minor Scholar. Lea Shakespeare [prize].
> **Solicitor 1908. Major Worcestershire Regiment.**
> Major Kerwood had always taken a keen interest in military matters. Twelve years ago he joined the Volunteers in Redditch. He became a captain and was instrumental in raising a Company of Territorials at King's Norton. He afterwards raised funds for a drill hall, which was opened about four years ago. He went to the Front a year and eight months ago, and was killed in action on 21st October whilst in temporary command of a battalion of the Cheshire Regiment.

He had married Grace Sheldon, also of Bromsgrove, in the summer of 1913. He must have impressed as a young officer to be considered for command when just thirty but it must be remembered that we were in the third month of the Battle of the Somme at the time. His young widow remarried in London on 16th November 1918 and was christening her son, Timothy O'Donovan, in the same church, St James's Piccadilly, a little over a year later.

Sydney Clark

Corbett said of Major Kerwood that 'the loss of no officer was more regretted by us than of this accomplished and beloved officer. No death was more lamented'. Praise indeed from the ranks. Kerwood's transfer to the Cheshires followed that of three other of the senior officers who crossed the Channel in March 1915. Corbett recorded that Major RHH Creak – another solicitor who was born in 1864 so the oldest of the Old Gents and a bachelor – 'most beloved and accomplished of officers', had 'been taken from us' that winter and 'the imperturbable' Major FAW How and Major SH Clark – a prep-school headmaster from Barnt Green, born in Gibraltar on 12th July 1867, attended Marlborough College and Trinity College, Cambridge – 'left us' in the summer of 1916. As such, the six senior officers – Peake, Creak, Kerwood, How, Cotton and Clark – of the Battalion when they arrived in France had been killed, transferred to staff jobs, or invalided away within 18 months and before much of their real fighting had taken place. Corbett did not mention the adjutant, Captain Percy Whalley, but he was quickly promoted to brigade major, for six months in 144th Brigade and the next six months in 143rd Brigade. He was commanding the 3rd Battalion by mid-September 1916 and earned a DSO the following August at Westhoek, Ypres. His medal collection shows five (campaign) bars on his Boer War medal. Such experience was difficult to replace, indeed nobody with pre-War service was to join the Battalion in the remaining 25 months of the War. Additionally, three notable young officers – PM Kerwood, Wilson and Slater – were also dead. Lt Col Carr in his forties and Captain Clarke at just 31 were the only officers much over twenty-five left in the Battalion. This would remain the case until the 'Old Gent' himself joined the Battalion in late 1917 at the age of 48, together with a number of commissioned NCOs.

This dearth of experience amongst the officers required compensating strength and experience amongst the warrant officers and senior sergeants, at least until the younger officers had been fully blooded. This, to a degree, required a lack of desire from the senior NCOs to take a commission which would mean a change at least of battalion, more normally of regiment. At the apex of the NCO structure was the RSM (Regimental Sergeant Major) and here the Battalion appears to have had some luck. RSM H Heath is recorded as being Mentioned in Despatches in June 1916 and then received an MC, listed as *France 1918* (*general*), thus for continuous and valuable service. He served as RSM for all or for the vast majority of the Battalion's tours of France, Belgium and Italy. They lost only two senior NCOs in action, CSM J Heydon at Louverval in June 1917 and CSM WH Wheeler at Beaurevoir on 5th October 1918. The latter was Mentioned in Despatches as a Lance Corporal in the New Year's List of 1916 and awarded a DCM in October 1917 at Ypres as a sergeant. He had made good progress through the ranks. He was amongst just seven Other Ranks killed in action to have won a gallantry medal – a DCM or an MM – and only one of these died before June 1918. Perhaps another indication that the best NCOs survived for all or the majority of the War. A further strength of the Battalion was that the Major and Quartermaster Daniel Sallis who crossed to France in that role, remained as such until early 1918. He was the oldest man serving, being 51 when War broke out. He was Mentioned in Despatches in January 1917 and raised to a 'higher rate of pay' the following January. As with RSM Heath and RQMS Corbett, Major Sallis did not merit a mention in the *History.* These men are all likely to have been in their forties when the War started and would have been a steadying influence on the Battalion throughout their wartime service.

Only Corbett's life is easy to trace before the War and shows clearly that he could have taken a commission before or during the War. He was born in 1870 in Worcester to Frederick, a solicitor as well as a farmer (of 150 acres) and a timber merchant, who lived to 97. The RQMS, Edward, was a solicitor in both the 1901 and 1911 Censuses and was known to be Secretary to the Worcester Chamber of Commerce immediately before the War. This meant also that he was in England on the relevant dates but he had business before and after the War in South America. He is recorded as returning from Argentina aboard the SS *Amazon* on 13th December 1913 and having travelled to Argentina and Mexico after the War. One brother, Sir Geoffrey Corbett KBE, CIE gained a double first in Classics at Oxford before joining the Indian civil service and becoming a founder member of the Himalayan Club. Corbett came from a large and gifted family, having four sisters and three brothers. His legal qualification explains the eloquence of his *War Story* but not why he was not an officer. He had his 48th birthday in August 1918, perhaps the third-oldest man in the Battalion after Majors Sallis and Walford. The RSM, H Heath, was to succeed Sallis and Clemo as the Quartermaster in 1918. Heath was the youngest of the Old Gents, being a mere 37 when the War ended, but the worldly and military experience of those at the apex of the Other Ranks' command structure proved crucial to the success of the Battalion in almost all that they did in the trenches and in attack.

RETURN TO THE FRONT IN THE COLDEST WINTER

The gas attack back in July 1916 did not mean that the Battalion would not participate again in the Battle of the Somme. Mitchinson's *Divisional Diary* stated the official strength of the Battalion still down at 24 officers and 470 men at the beginning of October and 22 officers and 613 men by the end of October, some three and half months after the incident. It should be remembered that full strength was 27 officers and 1,000 men, although Mitchinson understood that the War Office lowered this to some 800 men in the summer of 1915. Mitchinson went on to provide some interesting analysis of the home areas of those serving across the Gloucestershire and Worcestershire battalions, with only 20 per cent of the 148 fatalities across 144 Brigade in September and October being those from or having lived in the two counties. The new drafts since the Battalion had landed in France had not in the least been confined to those coming from the Reserve battalions back in England. At the end of July 1916, so immediately after the gas attack, the Battalion had a strength of 29 officers and 778 men, with 2 officers and 113 men in hospital suffering from the gas. They received 122 men in three drafts that month, hence the numbers being only a few below the month-end average of the previous year of a little over 800. By the end of July 1916, the Battalion had received eight drafts totalling 394, thus indicating about half the original average strength had been replaced. Of those, 31 are recorded as being Battalion men returning from hospital. All these figures seem very precise but when you take a month-end 'strength' total, remove those declared killed, wounded or missing during the next month, add back any from new drafts, you do not get to the 'strength' figures at the end of the following month. In addition, there were often 80 or 90 on leave or training to take from these numbers at any one time, even at the end of June 1916 as the Somme offensive approached. This constant change of personnel emphasises the importance of having time to train in at least company strength on at least a monthly basis.

The *War Diary* reported drafts of 75, 50, 74 and 23 men in July, and 150 from the Worcestershire Yeomanry in September joined the Battalion to bring it up to effective strength. After a period of training for the Territorial battalions of the 48th Division, the sister battalions, 1/7th and 1/8th, went back to their old trench line at Hébuterne for four days which cost the lives of Privates WH Leek, W Savory and AW Knight due to shelling. At the end of the month the Battalion moved to Contalmaison for a night and then marched via Martinpuich to Le Sars with trenches astride the Bapaume Road. Immediately to their front right was the infamous hill, the Butte of Warlencourt. This had been an area of intense and heroic fighting for over a month. Two notable VCs had been earned, one to the aforementioned Lt Col Roland Bradford MC of the 1/9th Durham Light Infantry at the site of Eaucourt L'Abbaye a mile to the south of the village of Le Sars on 1st October and another to 2nd Lt Henry Kelly of the 10th Duke of Wellington's Regiment on 4th October in the village itself, the Germans having captured it the day after Bradford's action:

> For most conspicuous bravery and good leadership in attack, whereby he saved the situation on the right flank of his Brigade and of the Division. Lieutenant-Colonel Bradford's Battalion was in support. A leading Battalion having suffered very severe casualties, and the Commander wounded, its flank became dangerously exposed at close quarters to the enemy. Raked by machine-gun fire, the situation of the Battalion was critical. At the request of the wounded Commander, Lieutenant-Colonel Bradford asked permission to command the exposed Battalion in addition to his own. Permission granted, he at once proceeded to the foremost lines. By his fearless energy under fire of all description, and his skilful leadership of the two Battalions, regardless of all danger, he succeeded in rallying the attack, captured and defended the objective, and so secured the flank.

2Lt Kelly's citation for his Company's attack on the Flers Trench – the same trench line occupied by the 1/8th Battalion just four weeks later – reads:

Operations around Le Sars

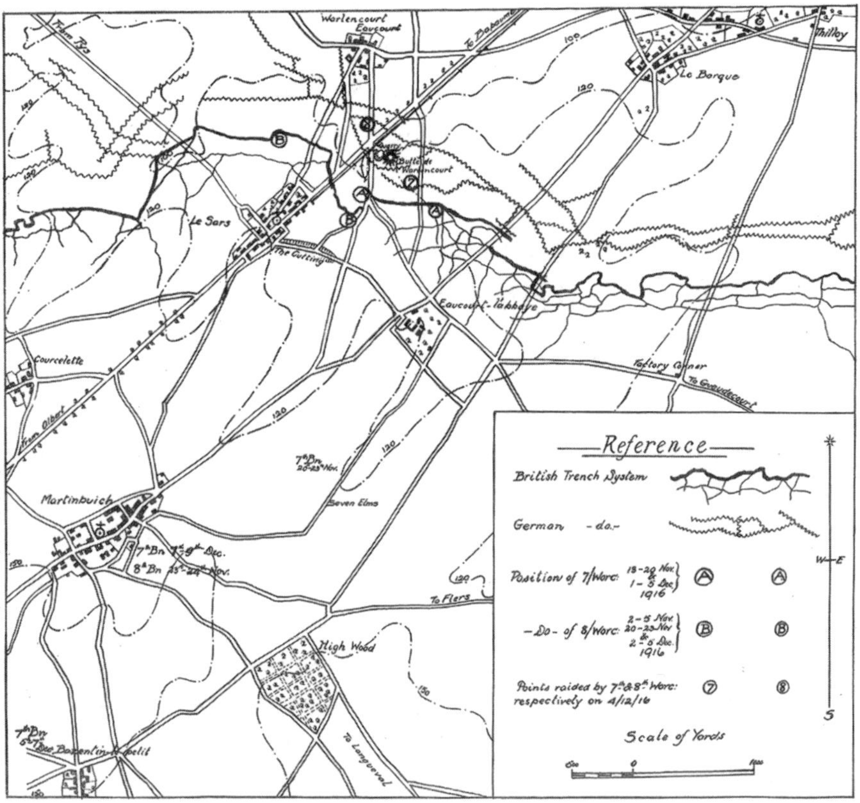

Map showing the proximity of the trench lines around Butte of Warlencourt

> For most conspicuous bravery in an attack. He twice rallied his company under the heaviest fire, and finally led the only three available men into the enemy trench, and there remained bombing until two of them had become casualties and enemy reinforcements had arrived. He then carried his Company Sergeant Major, who had been wounded, back to our trenches, a distance of 70 yards, and subsequently three other soldiers. He set a fine example of gallantry and endurance.

Le Sars was important because it was on a ridge which afforded views to the east and to the spires of Bapaume – interrupted only by the Butte of Warlencourt. It was however just three miles up the Albert–Bapaume road from where the Battalion had been gassed some three and a half months earlier – a measure of the British Army's progress. It had been initially captured in early October by the 23rd Division as part of the Battle of Transloy – one of the many phases of the ongoing Battle of the Somme. It was delayed for two days by incessant rain so one can only imagine the state of the ground and the trenches when the 1/8th Battalion took their turn in these front-line positions. A letter in *The Times* printed in John Lewis-Stempel's wonderful *Where Poppies Blow* and written in July 1917 told how quickly nature can recover even from man's remorseless artillery barrages and slaughter:

> Rarely outside the tropics have I seen more butterflies, whites and tortoiseshells and peacocks and skippers and little crambite moths. The kingly swallowtails are here too, but so far I have chanced this summer to see only one, and that was not among the flowers, but on the bare white hill of the Butte of Warlencourt when the King was there. The royal butterfly sailed round and round the little party and, as if recognising kinship, more than once made to settle on the King while he stood looking at the graves of the gallant Durhams.

Perhaps the incessant rain helped nature's recovery, but the best description of the seven weeks the Battalion was to spend near Le Sars with the 48th Division came from the commanding officer himself, Lt Col Harry Carr DSO, in his *Notes* written shortly after the War:

Our Battalion was one of the first to take over the Front Line (on 1st November) and the last to be relieved. During the whole of November and December (until the 16th), the Battalion alternated between miserable tented Camps near Mametz Wood, when in Divisional Reserve, waterlogged half-blown in trenches in the vicinity of Martinpuich, while in support and heavily shelled trenches in and around Le Sars Village while in the line. The weather was vile, consisting of heavy rain for days alternated with hard frost and snow. Although the Battalion was never called upon to attack, casualties while holding the village of Le Sars were considerable, while the work of getting up trench stores and rations over almost impassable roads and shell-hole areas under continuous shell fire imposed a great strain on the men, to which they responded nobly.

German view from Butte of Warlencourt to Le Sars

This single paragraph sums up so well the experiences of many both at the Somme and the following year at Passchendaele. Martinpuich was a mile from the front-line trenches and Mametz Wood a mile and a half further back. The whole area had been subject to continuous battle and barrage for four months so any movement was difficult. Movement laden with rations and the wood and iron posts for the trenches would have been interminable, even without the constant fear or actuality of German shelling. The attraction of the Butte's views to the east were key for the British but, having stood on top of what remains of the heavily-shelled hill over a hundred years later, one can see that the Germans could observe the whole area of the Battalion's life and work for those seven weeks. It seems rather inadequate for the Colonel to finish with 'to which they responded nobly'. It is at these times of difficult replenishments that Major Sallis, RSM Heath and CQMS Corbett will have been key to the Battalion and to maintaining its discipline.

During the Battalion's time at Le Sars, the announcement in the *Supplement to the London Gazette* dated 11 November 1916 included a number of awards for Other Ranks. Notable in the list of Military Medals (MMs) were three members of the Battalion:

2221 CQM/Sjt. E.C. Corbett, Worcs. R
1426 Sjts. E. Wedgbury, Worcs. R.
2231 Sjt. S.P. Maylett, Worcs. R. (below, holding citation)

There are no citations for MMs so the particular actions for these awards are not known. Corbett in *War Story* makes no reference to his award, nor to being wounded at this time, on 3rd December. He was taken back to England on the 7th with what the *Berrow's Journal* recorded as gun-shot wounds in the arm and leg. This was quite normal; such awards tended to be celebrated more by those around the individual than by the individual himself. MMs, as with MCs, could be awarded also for continual gallant and valuable service rather than just for a single action. As Sergeant Wedgbury was to be awarded a DCM in the New Year's Honours of 1st January 1917, it is most likely that his MM was for a single incident. Those who received awards in the New Year's and King's Birthday lists were always for gallant and valuable service over a prolonged period. Wedgbury's DCM recommendation will have been working its way through the system in November 1916. Wedgbury will take centre stage in this story in the last weeks of the War, by then commissioned. As a company commander in October and November 1918, he wrote Battle Reports each evening. Those after two notable actions make no mention of his own remarkable exploits in his report for the day. Both were to be properly acknowledged in due course. This modesty, if that is the correct word, contrasts with the desire of young officers for their fellow subalterns to be rewarded for particular exploits, notably successful raids or helping to retrieve wounded soldiers from No Man's Land. An illustration can be found in the letters of Douglas Bomford and the diaries of Lance Evers. The tales revolve around the actions of Lieutenant NVH Symons who was serving in A Company of the 2/8th Battalion in the early months after its arrival in France towards the end of May 1916. His full name, Noel Victor Housman Symons, gives a hint to a more renowned relation, AE Housman, the classical scholar and poet – his mother's elder brother. His father was the headmaster of King Edward's School in Bath. He was one of the few in the 2/8th Bn who had prior battle experience. He enlisted in his then local engineer battalion, the Wessex Engineers, and was writing to his father on 6th January 1915:

> We marched from our farm billet on Tuesday, the 5th inst., from 8.30 am to 3.30 pm and it was such severe marching that when the

destination was reached only about six of 40 were left. Today we covered 10-11 miles of cobbles and most of us are absolutely dead lame. We are now in the thick of it, and shells are literally bursting all around us.

'Sym'

Symons' fellow platoon commander, Douglas Bomford, wrote to his own parents on 27th July:

Symons, with whom I have worked pretty closely for some months did a very fine thing the other day [the 19th]. He went down to a part of the line where another battalion [the 2/7th] was in occupation, in charge of a carrying party, and while there saw a wounded man out in front of the trench about 30 yards. The regiment in occupation had been there all day and were waiting for night to fetch him in, but Symons went straight out in daylight and brought him in under fire. He found the man was badly wounded and had already been

> lying there for two days and nights. We are all hoping he may get the Military Cross for this. In South Africa [Boer War] it would have been a VC but this war is different.

It was different in part because the MC was only instituted in 1915 for young officers and warrant officers. Bomford's letter of 8th September included:

> I think I told you Symons had been wounded and we are all very annoyed that he had not had the Military Cross. Well, he has been given it now, it took a long time to come through, that was all.

This does seem to be a separate incident because later in the same letter Bomford wrote:

> That night Symons was wounded by a piece of the first shell of the bombardment. It hit him [Walford] on the behind but did not go through, and it was the last shell that hit Symons … we heard that the shrapnel in Symon's arm had broken the bone, but he seems to be doing well all the same. He had a brother [Lt Clement Aubrey Symons, 10th Bn, the Gloucestershire Regiment] killed at [the Battle of] Loos and it would have been rather awful if he had gone too. I think he is one of the finest fellows I have ever met … Captain Walford is rather bad with rheumatism and could not walk this morning. I do hope he will not go sick, he is such a figurehead in the battalion and he has done a very great deal for me and several others of us.

Bomford's assessment of Walford and Symons seem apt. Walford was to become a company commander in the 1/8th Battalion, alongside Douglas' younger brother, Leslie. Symons was to be wounded again on 24th August 1916, losing a hand from a shell at the end of a sustained three-hour bombardment, ending his service at the Front. Once recovered he became the officer in charge of drafts, those being brought from depots in England to the bases in France.

Walford wrote of this incident, published in the *Bath Chronicle*:

> He walked with me to the dressing station and stood it very well. He was, as always, plucky and cheery. He is a great loss to me, and yet I cannot help being glad and hope that he will get back to England and not come out again. He has done splendidly out here, and certainly deserves a VC for his very gallant action the other day in bringing in a wounded Gloucester man in daylight, and has done many other gallant actions, and his duty always. He has done more than his share and if anyone else had done half as much I believe the war would be over. He has been with me for eight months, and will be a great loss to me and to his men, who will follow him anywhere and think very highly of him.

It is interesting that Walford should be glad for Symons if his wound meant that he would not have to come out from England again. As with Burlingham in the 1/8th Bn back in the spring, Walford was probably wishing such a wound for himself or a home posting.

Lt Lance Evers recorded his feelings on 28th August:

> On getting back heard that Sym had got the Military Cross. This is splendid. He will be pleased. He jolly well deserves it too. He got in a wounded man from NML [No Man's Land] in broad daylight and had to go back to fetch a stretcher too.

A few days earlier he wrote 'The 7th had done a raid on their second night in and had done well but Geoff Tomkinson, who ought to get an MC, hope he will, and two other officers were wounded'. Tomkinson did get an MC but a New Year's List one for overall gallant and valuable service. Captain Evers, as he became, was to win the MC twice. He was badly wounded gaining the first at Aisne Farm in front of Ypres on 27th August 1917 so there is no diary entry for that period. He described the action in a long letter to Douglas Bomford some ten days later. There was no mention of awards although he was to receive an MC with a citation:

> Although severely wounded at the commencement of the attack, he continued to command his Company for three hours, and did not

leave to have his wound attended to until he had seen his Company established in their position after the attack.

There are no diary entries in October 1917 while he was still in hospital, during which time his MC was gazetted. That hospital was Selly Oak in Birmingham, probably the University's Great Hall which was a VAD hospital during the War. Selly Oak was to become well-known in the early twenty-first century during the Afghanistan and Iraq conflicts. Evers returned to France on 24th June 1918 and was again in the thick of the action two months later at the Passage of the Lys. He was not wounded so there are full diary entries but nothing of awards. The Regimental *History* recorded:

> Meanwhile C and D Companies under Captain Evers made their way across the Meuse Bridge in time to come in on the flank of the retreating enemy and to inflict many casualties. Then they worked eastwards along the riverbank and joined the other two companies near Le Nouveau Monde…

The citation read:

> During the crossing of a river and subsequent operations, this Officer behaved with great courage and dash, and on two occasions led out-flanking attacks on machine-gun positions. His inspiring example greatly contributed to the success of the operations.

These words are all that any young officer would want to achieve when he is called to action. Evers' only reference to his second MC, won for this action, is in his diary on 4th October: 'On my return I find I have got a bar to my MC which is very nice. Dick [Stallard] comes in after dinner'. He was to be killed some four weeks later, two months before the award was gazetted. His final diary entry is poignant and shows that these junior officers were very keen to be well thought of by their brother officers and their soldiers:

> I find that A Coy is very anxious for me to take them into the show

> which is highly complementary. In fact, my reputation is, I think, higher with the battalion now than it ever was – and Dick's too. Get to bed in the cellar and sleep well.

Seven days later his mother wrote a devastating entry in her diary:

> Still no letter but dear old Guy [brother of Lance] who came in during breakfast told me there was no room for anxiety, that posts must be difficult. I felt easier and attended to the fowls and ordered dinner early so that I might go to Birmingham to keep an appointment. I was in the sitting room preparing to get ready when the door opened and dear old Percy [another brother] came in with sorrow, love and pity in his face. I knew at once and asked no questions. He told me that our precious Lance was gone in that terrible attack, shot through the heart... This blessed son has gone from our home, his noble heart, all his tender thoughtfulness taken from us, his life given for us all. He was such an example of courage and steadfastness – so true of heart ... and we must live without him ... treasure after treasure taken, our only hope is God and the desire to carry out His will. Oh! May we be helped to bear our sorrow...

And some three weeks later, sixteen days after the Armistice, his sister Rose wrote:

> Today has been a terrible heart-breaking day. Sometimes I feel I cannot go on and today is one of them. Everything is dark and hopeless and I feel utterly incapable of facing life with any courage at all...

An extraordinary example of the thoughts of those at the Front as they faced their great tests, their humility when succeeding in their trials, the awards that came their way, and, although a different ordeal, how difficult it was for those loved ones left at home.

There was a real desire to acquit yourself well in front of and for your friends, brother officers and your soldiers but there was so much respect from those around you when your achievements were publicly acknowledged. It may be a stronger sentiment in the Territorial battalions and regiments as so many of the young officers heralded from the same county and all seemed to have mutual friends serving near them. This desire to think of others before oneself is well illustrated when Douglas Bomford wrote to his parents while still recovering in England in the autumn of 1918 about his younger brother Leslie:

> Just a line to say I have heard from Les and he has got a bar to his MC (perhaps you have already heard). This really means a good deal more than it sounds. You see, when a man has one MC and earns another, they never give you another one [medal] but give him a bar [to go across the ribbon of the first medal] instead, so it means just the same as two MCs.

In return, Leslie's letter to his father in 1917 includes: 'I suppose you know Doug was recommended for an MC but some fool knocked it out.' Then in July 1918, when Leslie received his first MC, his reaction was to include the news in a letter to his father only as a postscript but also to think first of his elder brother:

> PS. They have given me an MC. It makes me feel very fed up because poor old Doug didn't get anything. He deserves it miles more than I do.

Returning again to Le Sars and early November 1916 – the last few days of the First Battle of the Somme – we find Corbett at his most florid in describing the conditions. He portrayed the difficulties of just living and feeding in graphic detail. His general description of trench life is more widely understood, especially from films such as the early parts of *1917*. The black and white photographs of the time, notably of Passchendaele, provide glimpses of the mud and of the floundering horses and men. Over the winter of 1916/17, such glimpses were the widespread reality of almost all troops operating anywhere between the old 1914–1916 trench lines and the new hard-won forward lines as at Le Sars. They were the norm and Corbett described it well:

> Our indefatigable General [Fanshawe] had secured the best place in the whole Line – the front seat in the orchestra stalls. The vast curve of the battle-front ran out at the middle into a sharp little apex under the Butte of Warlencourt … and here, right under the Butte were the 7th and 8th Worcesters. The famous tumulus towered above us like Cruckbarrow above the Depot … and never had the mind of prophet, poet, or maniac conceived a scene so wild, desolate, and hideous as that which it surveyed.

Corbett's narrative is less that of a senior Other Rank, more of a war poet. He continued:

> For miles there stretched one vast rolling sea of pitted mud. The villages had disappeared, most of the trees were smitten down, the few scattered trunks that remained were dead. No green thing grew, no birds flew over, not even a rat was to be seen among the corpses that strewed the ground. Not even thorns or thistles could grow in the accursed tract, for the rage of man was more desolating than the wrath of God. The only signs of life were tiny companies of men struggling and staggering through the mire, lost in the desert they had made. And here, there, and everywhere arose the smoke-clouds and vast mud-spouts of the ceaseless bombardments; the air trembled and the mire quaked with the roar of the guns and the howling of the shells. It was the abomination of desolation, a picture of the last men struggling with the Powers of Hell in the death-throes of the world – the dream of Ragnarok fulfilled.

This was written over 100 years ago culminating with the reference to Norse mythology – the end of the world of gods and men.

Under the title of 'Rations in the field', Corbett continued:

> The chief difficulty at Le Sars lay in taking rations up. The unpaven roads were so deep that four horses were required to a single limber with a half-load – say 1 cwt [50kg] per horse – and were quite often blocked by floundering vehicles and dead horses. Then the sacks had to be carried by a party of men, some 70 strong, for miles, a terrible

task where it required great efforts to draw one's foot out of the mud.

More optimistically, he observed that 'presently a railway was made to Martinpuich from which we only had two miles to carry them'. This short excerpt tells of two important aspects of infantry warfare. Firstly, it helps to explain why a battalion was made up of 1,030 men but had just four fighting companies, each of 200 men. The work of the other 250 or so men was in part to undertake this strenuous task of keeping those at the Front supplied with food, water and ammunition. The second point is Corbett's observation that the Engineers and Pioneers had already built a workable railway to within two miles of the Front. This was most important for getting the heavy artillery shells to the batteries near the Front.

As to the food itself, Corbett explained:

> Once the food was up we lived well, for a cave was found in which the company cooks were installed, and hot stuff was issued four times a day. [Even he described the food as 'stuff'.] In all troubles and difficulties we continued to mother the men, and it paid, as the following returns of sick sent back from this part of the Line during one tour of four days will show:

Australians	110
Warwicks	80
Gloucestershire	50
7th Worcesters	8
8th Worcesters	2

Thus, it was possible with a strong team ethos and an efficient and disciplined Quartermaster's department to ensure an effective fighting force could be kept in front-line trenches in the worst of conditions and weather. We need to hark back to the experience and dedication of the triumvirate of the forty-somethings: Carr, Sallis and Corbett. Corbett gave an outline of his own work at this time:

> We had a different system of economy from that usually followed. There was one man in each Company whose duty it was to mother

> the men – the CQMS. In the Line it is about the only duty he has, and properly executed, will keep him busy for 25 hours a day, eight days a week. Obviously his place is with his men and was so with us. But in the Service at large he was kept at the Quartermaster's Stores and simply forwarded food to his Company. But that is only the beginning of his duty: he should see it cooked and eaten: he should know the men's wants and likings and give them what they like; he must see that they get their food warm, know their ailments and their weaknesses, comfort and coddle them, look after their socks and their poor wet feet, and treat them like the dear good children that they are. He cannot leave these things to the CSM [Company Sergeant Major] and the M.O. [Medical Officer]. The Sergeant-Major has enough work of his own to do; the Doctor only comes in when the Quarter bloke [CQMS] has failed.

This was written shortly after the War, not in the immediate aftermath of Battle of Transloy. It is perhaps understandable as to why Corbett had just been awarded an MM and that he would later be promoted from CQMS to RQMS. He would have been an invaluable resource for any company commander who, when in the trenches, had more than enough to keep him busy without worrying if the men would be fed, ammunitioned and maintained to the highest levels attainable in such conditions. For these two miles a CQMS would have been as vulnerable to artillery shells as the front-line trenches, though without the comforting trench walls of Flanders mud. It is possible to envisage the lack of encouragement to seek a commission made to a man as capable and intelligent as Corbett by the Battalion's senior officers. Men like Corbett were much too important to let slip as few men commissioned from the ranks returned to their own regiment or battalion. The distinction between officers and men was not nearly as clear cut in a Territorial battalion as it was in the Regular Army. There were many cases where one brother was an officer and another in the ranks – as with Douglas and Leslie Bomford whose elder brother, Ben, was a private in the Royal Warwickshire Regiment. Corbett illustrated this well in recalling the death of the first NCO back in Ploegsteert – Sergeant Wylde of Worcester:

> This gallant soldier (who before the war had held a commission [in the 4th Bn The Buffs – Royal East Kent Regiment from 1909–1913]) had received his commission with the rank of captain two days before we sailed [for Boulogne] but sooner than lose a chance of service on the Western Front he obtained leave to resign it. And he was one of the first to fall – betrayed by his great stature on one clear dawn.

Perhaps a giveaway in the Battalion's Roll of Honour is that Wylde was one of very few in the ranks with three Christian names – Charles Gilbert Andree. His military number of 2220 means that he enlisted immediately before Corbett (2221) – probably on the same day in August 1914, both as private soldiers. He was the son of Mr and Mrs CA Wylde of Bank House, Malvern, and manager of the local branch of Lloyds Bank. Wylde was perhaps one of the few sergeants to have an inscription in Latin on his headstone: 'Pro Rege et Patria, Requiescat in pace' – 'For King and Country, rest in peace'. He was not a man of Worcestershire. He was born in London in 1891, was at Chatham House School in Kent in 1901 and was in a boarding house in Paddington in 1911 with the profession of a bank clerk. However, he resigned his commission in 1913 when he took up a place at Lloyds Bank in Worcester – hence joining the Worcestershire Regiment.

Grave of Charles Wylde

Corbett explained early in his *War Story* what a mix of men and skills the 1/8th Battalion was:

> The Eighth was a microcosm of the whole. We had men from British Colombia, Natal, the Indies, North and South America, Spain and the Levant, a rancher from Rhodesia (who having lived for years in the saddle was rejected by the Yeomanry as unable to ride), sailors from the Seven Seas, and an adventurer known to the Patagonian police [probably Corbett himself] – but all men of Worcestershire. In the ranks were doctors, dentists, artists, surveyors, schoolmasters, craftsmen of all kinds, and so many lawyers that the General Officer said that we ought to be called the Devil's Own [a reference to the nickname of The Inns of Court Regiment].

This showed the strength and versatility of these Territorial battalions. The 1/8th gave themselves an additional advantage in 1914, as Corbett remembered:

> We had been inspected by the King and by Sir Ian Hamilton. We had been reformed into the new four-company establishment. The two City (Worcester) Companies were amalgamated into A Company; Evesham, Pershore, Upton and Malvern formed B Company; Bromsgrove and King's Norton became C Company; and, Droitwich and Redditch [formed] D.

These were 'Pals' companies based on the groups who had attended the various local drill halls in peacetime. Once established in France, the Battalion attempted to ensure that all those returning wounded as well as new recruits could preserve this structure. Corbett complained that the Reinforcement Authorities, particularly in Rouen, 'neglected men's feelings in this respect often [leading] to very distressing results and showing how little they appreciated the meaning of the Territorial system of recruiting and its enormous value of morale and discipline … they didn't know what his mate means to a man.' Field Marshal Lord Kitchener and General Sir Henry Rawlinson had recognised the importance of locality and had put it at the core of the recruitment drive from August 1914. Corbett told a story of the Battalion in 1916 to support his claim about this key aspect of the Pals and Territorial battalions:

> A soldier of Ours was given employment which would have kept him out of action. When we went back in the Line he asked to be relieved, that he might be with his mate. This was granted, and next day they were killed by the same shell. Immortality crowns the friendship of Nisus and Euryalus: they deserved it less than Privates Hodges and Bray.

The Roll shows that these two private soldiers died on Sunday 2nd April 1916, the Battalion's only casualties that day. They now lie buried in neighbouring graves I.F. 49 and I.F. 50 in Sucrerie Cemetery in Colincamps. The *CWGC* paperwork of the time gives no Christian names, no age, no parentage, no family inscriptions but at least they were buried and are not just names on the Thiepval Memorial. Ernest James Bray was from Leominster, born in October 1894 and was working as a 'hallboy' in Crown East in 1911. William George Hodges was the same age and from Powick. I wonder if anybody has ever been to visit their graves – other than me?

Alan Plaistowe

As to the main action during the Battalion's tour of Le Sars, it came on 5th November when the neighbouring 50th Division attacked and, for a while, held the Butte of Warlencourt. The Battalion, under heavy suppressive artillery fire all day, provided supporting machine-gun fire to those forging the attack on the Butte into the teeth of gale-force winds. As was their practice, the Germans launched a strong counter-attack – in this case, just after midnight – and regained their lost ground and the all-important Butte. Two subalterns earned themselves MCs that day, both severely injured, but staying at their posts for some twelve hours when the Battalion was relieved by the 1/6th Gloucesters. Lt Plaistowe who undertook gallant raiding back in Ploegsteert was again sent forward, this time with Sgt Crump. Under the barrage, they reached the quarry immediately to the north of the Butte and located wounded survivors of the Divisional attack. They were able to escort them back without incident. The *History* notes that Sgt Crump was awarded a DCM for this and other actions. However, it does not appear in the lists in either the *History* or the *Booklet*. A Private JW Crump of the Worcestershire Regiment was awarded an MM which was gazetted on 8th January 1917. It does not give his battalion but it is possible that his substantive rank at the time was that of private and that he was an acting sergeant. Unlike officers, it shows substantive rather than acting ranks in the *London Gazette*.

The casualty numbers for the battalion on 5th November gives an indication of the effects of prolonged and heavy artillery barrages: 12 killed; 3 officers (2Lts Raikes, Keen and Griffiths) and 61 Other Ranks wounded – some 10 per cent of the 800 men likely to have been in the trenches that day. In all they lost 28 Other Ranks at Le Sars over the six-week period in those exposed trenches. The First Battle of the Somme finished officially on 18th November. Despite this barrage, the gas attack and the normal attrition of front-line trench duty, the 1/8th Battalion had survived reasonably intact. They were fortunate not to have had to undertake a frontal attack. Over their 18 months at the Front they had lost four officers and 58 Other Ranks killed or died of wounds. However, well over half of the men of the fighting companies would have been wounded or gassed or both.

2nd Lieut. W. H. Griffiths, Worcester. Wounded.

Lt. R. T. Keen, Worcester. Military Cross.

RAIDING

The *War Diary* contains a series of reports under a 'Scheme for raid on enemy line' written by Captain JP Bate and sent to 144 Inf Bde with a covering letter from Major HT Clarke, who was commanding the Battalion at the time. It gives an idea of both the planning and the equipment involved in these raids on German trench lines which were the bread and butter of life for junior officers in these prolonged periods at the Front when no major battle was being fought:

144 Inf. Bde
The attached Scheme for a Raid on the enemy's line during the next tour in the trenches is submitted for approval, please.
HT Clarke Major
Comd. 1/8 Worc. Regt.

28.XI.16
Remarks:
2 officers to accompany raiding party
Escort for prisoners?
Is there any wire in front of enemy trench, provision to organise Bangalore Torpedo?
3 mins Barrage along front trench at first and then lift and form pocket – & on exit on front trench again.
Is there a machine gun here?
Signal for exit to be sent up so barrage can go to frontline again.
Telephone
Trench probably bad like ours & a series of posts better to go along parados [earth mound behind trench – parapet at the Front]

SCHEME FOR RAID ON ENEMY LINE
Ref: LE SARS trench map 3A and sketch map herewith.
OBJECTS: 1. To kill Germans
2. To take prisoners
3. To obtain information.

IDEA: To enter GALLWITZ TR[ench] at point where track leaving our line at M16A 8580 into enemy frontline at M10D1537; to proceed from that point to junction of enemy frontline and SUNKEN ROAD and then to return. During time of occupation of enemy line, barrage to be kept by fields. [The next section detailing barrage is all crossed out, presumably by the Bde; with replacement by their instruction in 'Remarks' above.]

STORES Required

2 BANGALORE TORPEDOES
16 CLUBS
6 LONG PATTERN WIRE CUTTERS
24 BOXES No. 5 GRENADES
24 ELECTRIC TORCHES
2 6FT LADDERS
2 8FT LIGHT TRENCH BOARDS (for bridging [trenches])
400 yds TRACING TAPE
30 GRENADE CARRIERS
6 'P' BOMBS

COMPOSITION OF RAIDING PARTY

LEFT STOP
Corporal & 4 men, 2 rifles and bayonets with six bombs each. 2 bombers 12 bombs each. Bombers bayonets & clubs & wirecutters.
ADVANCE PARTY
Sgt and 6 men. 2 rifles & bayonets, 2 bombers with clubs and bayonets, 2 carriers with clubs and bayonets.
MAIN PARTY
2Lt Wilkes and 6 O.R., 6 bombers with 6 bombs each, also 'P' bombs. Armed with clubs and bayonets.
EXIT GUARD
1 officer and 1 NCO and six men with rifles and bayonets. 12 bombers (to supply main party), 2 6ft ladders, 2 bridges and tracing tape

PARADOS PARTY
1 NCO and 3 men to go along keeping touch with main party.

Strength: 2 OFFICER
25 O.R.
1 platoon in support 30 yards from gap.

Bate's plan had only one officer, 2Lt Wilkes, in the initial plan. The wording for the officer in the Exit Guard has been added, presumably at the brigade's instigation – with officer strength increased by one. It is clear that bayonet and grenades (bombs) are the main weapon in such a raid.

ORDERS

Party will assemble at junction of track and LE SARS TR: NORTH at Zero-1 ½ h.

Party will leave assembly trench at Zero-1h, proceed along track and take up position 50 YARDS from enemy wire at Zero-15.

At Zero time, barrage will start. A BANGALORE TORPEDO will be exploded in wire, and an entrance made.

'A' party (Left Stop) will move to left and make a stop 20 yds from point of entry.

'B' party (Advance Party) will bomb down trench in direction of SUNKEN ROAD.

'C' party (Main Party) will keep in touch with Advance Party, and do as much damage as possible.

'D' party (Exit Guard) will place ladders in trench and prepare the way for a rapid exit.

If condition of trench is bad the raid will be carried out along the parados, using the 2 8ft bridges.

The party will not stay in the trench longer than necessary.

The support platoon will cross NO MAN'S LAND 50yds behind raiding party, during raid, it will be 30yds from entry point. The officer in command of it will be responsible for keeping touch with Exit Guard.

Zero time, if possible, 9 AM on a foggy morning. If weather not suitable, about 4 AM.
JP Bate Capt.
1/8 WORCS
28.11.16

Then a letter from the commanding officer of the 1/7th Battalion:

SECRET

Headquarters
144 Inf. Bde.

30.XI.16

Ref: RAIDS
When this Bn. was last in the line the enemy had various small posts out at night in front of BUTTE TRENCH about M17a63.

I would propose to locate one or more of these posts exactly and to capture them at night by means of a party of 1 officer & 20 O.R. who would move out from MAXWELL TRENCH and be supported by 1 officer & 10 O.R. & a LEWIS GUN.

For artillery support I would ask for a 2 minute rapid barrage on the point selected followed by a 10 minute slow box barrage.

I cannot give the exact objective until this Bn. returns to the line & I ascertain the present state of affairs.
DM Tomkinson
Lt Col Cmdg.
1/7 Worcs Regt.

Jack Bate lighting a cigarette

The raid took place on the night of 3rd/4th December. Captain Bate wrote a report which is verbatim in the *War Diary*:

> During the day usual enemy shelling round LE SARS. At night a raiding party left our lines according to Scheme previously drawn up and approved, but owing to the fact that our own shells were constantly bursting in SMALL WOOD (M10.C.93) the raiding party was unable to advance past the front edge of wood and could not enter the enemy lines as arranged. Six or seven shells also burst behind SCOTLAND TRENCH. 25% of our own shells burst in NO MAN'S LAND & half of this percentage on percussion. The party returned with no casualties – useful information was obtained. 2Lt SH WILKES was in charge of raiding party & 2Lt WH REYNOLDS in charge of supporting platoon. Patrols under 2Lts NE CLUTTERBUCK & JE RAYER also went out and brought in useful information.

This scheme and the report provide an indication of the work and planning involved in undertaking a raid on the German front line. The coordination with the artillery is crucial and, on this occasion, their shelling plan was inaccurate and caused the failure to enter the enemy trench line. It is interesting that Captain Bate chose 2Lt SH Wilkes to lead the raid. Clearly there was trust in Wilkes' abilities which he was to show again and again over the ensuing two years. Sydney Wilkes was born at Dudley on 9th April 1896; he was at Oxford University when War broke out and immediately joined the OTC. He was commissioned into the 1/8th Battalion on 9th October 1915 and crossed to France to join it on 1st June 1916.

BATTLING TOWARDS THE HINDENBURG LINE

The 1/8th Battalion entered 1917 having been at the Front for 21 months but having not been committed to battle as a complete unit – largely due to their planned assault at the Somme being cancelled, followed by the gassing of the night of 19th July, resulting in the Battalion not being up to fighting strength until late November. The Battle of the Somme ended on 18th November after the five-day Battle of Ancre. One of the coldest winters of the century was setting in and survival became the main theme. Britain, having had a winning draw at the Battle of Jutland, was able to enforce a blockade of all German ports which was to last for the remainder of the War, U-boats excepted. Back in Germany the potato crop had largely failed and troops at the Fronts were always a priority. The population was left with a crop normally fed to cattle and sheep – turnips. The ensuing famine and freezing hardship had a marked effect upon morale at home in Germany.

As in late 1915, the Allied commander gathered at the French headquarters in November 1916 to consider their 1917 offensives. Initial plans were to continue to press across the chalk downs of Picardy and then for the British and their Imperial allies to press forward in Flanders in front of Ypres and to the north in order to 'clear' the Belgium coast and recapture the German bases, Ostend and Zeebrugge. It was from these ports that their U-boats were operating with increasing effectiveness. However, the replacement of Joffre with General Robert Nivelle resulted in a change back to the 1915 strategy of attacking from the shoulders. For the British this was to be initially in front of Arras and to seize the high ground of Vimy Ridge – successfully attained by the Canadian Corps on Easter Monday and Tuesday, 9th/10th April. In the early spring the Germans continued their retreat from the Somme battlefields in order to occupy the Hindenburg Line, a newly-constructed and heavily-fortified area of high ground along the Canal de St-Quentin – with three prearranged lines of defence.

British forces were ordered to harry them throughout their withdrawal and it is in this role that the 1/8th Battalion were to undertake their first battalion-scale assaults.

***

The Battalion was clear of the trenches at Le Sars before Christmas when they retired to a 'camp' near Mametz Wood – less than a mile south of where they were gassed some five months before – for six days, protected by a mile of mud in each direction such that a cart would not pass. All supplies had to be manhandled to the battalions and brigades held there in reserve. Their duties mostly included digging away the mud – Corbett says that it was 'tantamount to removing the parish'. Relief was not far away and they were at Fricourt on Christmas Day but held their celebrations a few days later at Baizieux, a place remembered by Corbett 'as not convenient for an orgie, but we did our best: pigs were again procured, plum puddings and fruit was sent from England and Colonel Carr provided the beer'.

The Territorial battalions of the 48th Division 'soon afterwards were entrained for a blessed rest down the lines'. The 1/8th stopped at Pont Remi and marched through a snowstorm to Doudelainville for a fortnight's rest and training. Corbett observed that 'we could buy vegetables and even poultry, and lived well amongst nice people. Never have we been so kindly welcomed. It was very much in the country' and, more cynically, that 'we are never allowed to be billeted in or around a town: that privilege is reserved for Scots and Colonials, whose conduct is much more restrained and seemly than that of Territorial infantry'! On 28th January they were moved back towards the Front. Reality struck as soon as they left their billets: 'the weather was very severe [and we began by] sitting for three hours by the roadside in half a gale of wind and 15 degrees of frost … we travelled all day in carriages with no windows to Cerisy … to stables with floors compounded of frozen muck and mud.'

2Lt LR Bomford returned to France on 17th February having been in Chatham Hospital at Cromer in Norfolk and in Catterick as part of his recovery from his gassing. He was fortunate in that he got back to his own battalion, indeed to his old platoon in A Company. While it might seem beneficial to all that officers returning from being wounded or indeed from a course did so to their own regiment or battalion, this was very often not the case. Other battalions, particularly after a mauling at German hands, would need a new cadre of officers. Bomford confirmed the severity of the winter, as did his brother Douglas who returned after a shrapnel wound in January: 'it has been fairly cold, it was down to 22 degrees [-6°C] one night' in the nearby 2/8th Battalion. The brothers were near enough to attempt a meeting. Douglas wrote:

> (3rd March) I heard from Les yesterday. He is somewhere near us and I am going to set out on my gee [horse] tomorrow to try and find him. It will be the first time I have ever seen him in France if I can. (7th March) Les is not far away. Cyril Holcroft and I rode over last Sunday (4th) and found he was in the [trench] line, so missed him.

This was his last letter home before he was badly injured on the assault of Hill 120 on Good Friday, 6th April, when hit by a machine-gun bullet just before midnight – as his friend, Lt Dick Stallard, confirmed in a letter to Douglas' father, Raymond. However, Leslie's letter to his mother, Eveline, dated only 'Monday', confirmed that the brothers did meet before Douglas' War-ending injury:

> The best news I've got for you is the fact that I've seen Douglas. It was jolly hard work. I had to cycle about eight and a half miles. It doesn't sound much but on an army bicycle and French roads I very nearly walked it the second time. It wasn't eight and a half all told, but eight and a half there. He is still in charge of [C] Coy looking very fit and quite cheery.

Leslie clearly saw Douglas the following day as well as he continued:

> I went over there yesterday and the day before. Yesterday I didn't see him for long as he had to go off on a working party.

While it is natural for brothers to make the most of the few opportunities to see each other at the Front, the same applied to brother officers. As the War went on and home leave was attained, it was a regular occurrence for officers to visit the homes and families of their colleagues, as the letters of the two Bomford brothers and Lance Evers illustrate:

Douglas to his parents – early October 1916: I am glad that you liked Capt. Walford. He is really one of the best.

Evers to Douglas's mother – 1/12/16: I am very sorry we had such a short time at Salford Priors on Tuesday and that we didn't have much time to talk. I wonder if you know how well we all think Douglas has done.

Douglas to his sister Betty from Rouen Hospital – 26.4.17: I am glad you saw Evers. He would give you a lot of news that we are unable to write; even here we are under the Censor. He is a great chap, the kind you can rely on for absolutely anything.

Leslie to his father – 20-4-17: I'm glad to hear that Evers has been over. He is a nice fatherly old fellow [aged 36]. They seem to do jolly well for leave in the 2/8th, we have no officer's leave in our division just now.

Leslie to his father – 15/11/17: [Lt] Dick Stallard is now on leave in England, I wonder if you've seen him. [No letters from the Bomford parents to their sons survive, so such questions cannot be answered.]

Ernest Williams (HQ. 144 Bde. Italy) to Raymond Bomford – 13/9/18: You can imagine my surprise and pleasure to discover your little boy!! serving in this Brigade. I knew nothing about it until he was decorated the other day on parade with a Bar to his MC. I fancy that I was living with you about the time he was born. I am commanding the 144th while the general is away for three weeks.

Evers diary of 28/9/16: The Old Gent gets his leave… He promised to go down to Stourbridge and see the family.

Evers diary of 7/10/16: Hear from home – they are very delighted to have seen the Old Gent.

Evers diary of 28/10/16: Write letters to mother and Ernest. I ask the latter to go and see Douglas, now at the Russian Hospital

[St Mary's Russian Hospital for Officers, 8 South Audley Street, Mayfair].

Evers diary of 12/11/16: Had a letter from mother to say that they had seen Sym [Lt NVH Symons MC] at home and liked him very much.

There is a charming photograph published with his diaries with Evers, Captain AW Odgers, Douglas Bomford and Sym with Evers' mother Isabel in the centre – all in uniform and 'sam browns' with only Sym displaying an MC ribbon.

Symons, Evers and Douglas Bomford recovering from wounds

This is a sample of the connections across the county of Worcestershire of a group of officers in the 1/8th and 2/8th Battalions, with an age range at the end of the War of 21 to 49, who shared the support of each other's families. There will have been other meetings and letters, most especially when one of them was in hospital recovering from wounds, or battle stress:

Evers diary of 2/12/16: Catch the 10.37 to London with mother and Rose. Douglas meets us at Paddington and we get rooms and lunch at the hotel there. Then we meet Sym and the three of us go by train to see the Old Gent at The Holmwood. He is getting better but is very thin and cannot walk much. Isabel wrote in her diary that day: About 11 o'clock they all came in having had a pleasant visit to Capt. Walford who seemed an old gent when they first got there but after their pleasant talk seemed much better and declared himself five years younger.

The importance of such visits is difficult to fully appreciate. The Old Gent did not get back to France until July 1917 and then to the 1/8th Battalion and to Leslie Bomford, rather than to the 2/8th and Douglas, Symons and Evers. Given his achievements in 1918, the camaraderie shown by these younger officers for Walford cannot be overestimated. He would not have wished to let down their obvious affection – and he didn't.

Douglas was taken back to No 8 Hospital, Rouen:

Dear Sir [Ray Bomford] –,
I am writing to tell you that your son Lieut. DR Bomford, 2/8th Worcesters, is a patient in this hospital seriously wounded with a compound fracture of the femur. Although the wound is serious his general condition is fairly good and there is no immediate cause for alarm.

I have told him that I am writing to you and that I shall say that he will write himself when he feels stronger.

He does not want you to be anxious about him. Every care will be taken of him and I hope that he will soon improve.

Yours faithfully,
K. Roscoe, Matron

Douglas was to be more reassuring three days later:

I am much better and feeling myself again. I don't think there is any danger of losing the leg now, certainly not if things continue as they were doing.

> I fear I shall be in this ward for some time, weeks at any rate if not perhaps a month or two…

The War was over for Douglas, he never returned to France – and he was to be in Rouen Hospital for at least six months.

The action at Hill 120 in early April 1917 where Douglas was wounded occurred as the Germans were making an organised retreat to their pre-prepared and formidable Hindenburg Line. 'The great drama of The Somme was over: the curtain had fallen on that vast and tragic stage … but our indomitable enemy, defeated, outworn, but unshaken, fell back, not in confusion or disorder, but methodically, subtly, and scientifically to a new and even more formidable front'. Corbett went on to describe their move forward to the new Front:

> Across the Somme we entered a new pleasant country – woods, green pastures, a fine brook, all untouched by war except the railway, which was cleverly disabled, and the villages which had been systematically destroyed, even fruit trees being felled or girdled. Some of the bridges had been blown up, others mined and left as traps. If a house remained it was mined…

This may have been sound military tactics but the wanton destruction will have been in the minds of those negotiating for compensation at Versailles in 1919. Corbett continued:

> One [house] of which had been occupied by our HQ for eight days, blew up the next day [18th April 1917] under the 6th Glosters, killing all the HQ officers. Delayed action mines were under crossroads, railway tracks, everywhere, and for weeks after the enemy's retirement we could hear explosions about the countryside. This was fair in war (if not very chivalrous) … amidst this desolation lived poor peasants homeless, starving, but delivered. Their delight at seeing us was piteous. We fed and clothed them and sent them back across the 40 miles of desolation that lay behind us, that desert that we had made.

This rather sums up the futility of war and the impact on innocent bystanders.

An examination of the *CWGC* website identified the 'Glosters HQ officers' – from the 1/6th Battalion of the Gloucestershire Regiment – and showed it probably was 'all the HQ officers'. They were one of the other Territorial battalions which made up 144 Brigade throughout their tour of France and Italy. The commanding officer was 28-year-old Lt Col Thomas Walker Nott DSO and the adjutant was his younger brother, 23-year-old Captain Louis Cameron Nott MC – devastating news for their proud parents, Mr and Mrs Louis Nott of Stoke House, Stoke Bishop, Bristol. Amazingly, rank took precedence over family and those who committed them to the Villers-Faucon Communal Cemetery placed between them Major Robert Finlay Gerrard, attached from the 4th Battalion, The Royal Scots, presumably the second-in-command. Thus, the Nott brothers lie in graves D53 and D55. A communal cemetery is the town or village's local cemetery. Away from the major battlefields these were used as burial grounds, assuming there was space; usually in a separate area, now walled off. Permission of the local mayor and priest was required. The Nott brothers' parents later linked them by the inscriptions which they chose for their headstones. For Louis:

He That Believeth In Me
Though He Were Dead
Yet Shall He Live
John 11.25

and for Thomas:

Them Also
Which Sleeps In Jesus
Will God Bring Them
1. Thess. 4.14

The Nott brothers were from a large family with six sisters. The *CWGC* website shows that their only brother also served in the 6th Bn, The Gloucesters, and had been killed near Hébuterne on 27th April 1916, aged 21. For his grave, his parents choose another bible passage:

His Servants Shall Serve Him
And They Shall See His Face
Rev. 2. 3&4

Beyond the commanding officer, the second-in-command and the adjutant, also killed in the explosion were Lt Leonard King MC from Bristol; the medical officer, 37-year-old Captain Everard Harrison, husband of Sara from Leicester; and the padre, 39-year-old Reverend Matthew Burdess, the rector of St Thomas's, Port Clarence near Middlesbrough. It was at times like these that officers from other battalions needed to be brought in to steady the ship.

It was at about this time that a letter appeared in the *Journal* under the title: PROBLEMS OF NERVE SHAKEN SOLDIERS. The subject was to become an increasing problem to the Army and to some of the officers and men of the Battalion.

Dear Sir,

A stirring article in the issue of 'Truth', Feb. 9th, entitled 'Mad-Houses for Soldiers', has brought into fuller daylight the great injustice being done to the soldiers suffering from nervous breakdown after severe battle stress. The facts of their case, too little realised, were brought by me (as being in touch with medical and Parliamentary efforts made by the War Office on their behalf) before a small but intelligent audience at the Ladies' Club, Malvern, last week.

That 1,300 beds have been commandeered in asylums for sick, wounded, and mentally confused soldiers, whose affliction is likely merely to be transient, if properly managed, has aroused the greatest interest and dismay. As 'Truth' remarks: 'For officers in the same state all kinds of interesting methods are resorted to for linking up again with stable normal life the transiently shattered thread of consciousness'.

I have myself visited Napsbury Asylum near St Albans, Herts, and found 200 soldiers of the rank and file were there. The Under-Secretary for War admitted on September 30th, 1915, that all that is done for the uncertified nerve-stricken soldiers is to place them under the same medical management and advice that is dealt to those persons certified as lunatics. For men to be placed in such a position is a far greater risk than for officers, as I pointed out, since they have to depend on their own exertions for a livelihood. The Board of Control, ie. The Lunacy Commissioners, may have the best intentions, but it is not their proper function to deal with the uncertified.

Recently I saw the excellent results of a system at Heather Morland Sanatorium, Llandrindod Wells, taken over last September by the excellent and progressive administration of the Red Cross. This system I had long ago seen near Zurich. Rest gardens for sun and air bathing, aided by massage, sulpha waters and special diet, were there admirably provided in all simplicity. The good effects after 10 days stay, whose arrival from Harrogate I witnessed, with faces grey and warn, with shattered nerves and terrible foot wound, gout supervening, was incredible and delightful to realise…

Those who heard me speak at the Club have since asked me to read the paper to their own circle. Surely, therefore, it is time that public

meetings should be held to ventilate discussion on this important subject of placing our soldiers in the annexes of our asylums.
M. Beadon
February 17th 1916

The generals and politicians continued to struggle to agree a solution between the two extremes detailed above. The key was to return to the Front as many of these men as possible, but only if they could make a valuable contribution. Having a cadre of trusted officers and senior NCOs in a battalion was, perhaps, the most important aspect as it would have helped to minimise the numbers having to be withdrawn from the Front to hospitals in France and back in Britain. There are no numbers in the 1/8th Battalion's *War Diary* or *History* of those who suffered from shell shock. Corbett makes no mention of a problem, indeed he was always quick to point out the numbers of sick in the various battalions in the Division – most usually with the 1/8th having the lowest numbers. Losing your entire headquarters leadership in a single blast would not have helped.

THE BATTALION GOES ON THE ATTACK

The last phase of the advance to the Hindenburg Line approached, and with it the first battalion-scale attacks for the 1/8th. Lt LR Bomford's letters are sparse over this period but the reliable CQMS Corbett sets the scene:

> The formidable Mont St Quentin had fallen, the 143rd Brigade occupied Peronne, and we advanced up the pleasant Cologne Valley in bitter weather, and had a smart brush at the taking of Villers Faucon. On the 5th April we fought a fine open battle…

The *History* recorded for '1st April and the following two days' that the Battalion sent out forward patrols … but Ronssoy and Lempire were strongly held. All the next day (the 4th) snow fell and at midday orders arrived. The Battalion was to launch an attack to cover the flank of 145 Brigade's attack on Ronssoy and Basse Boulogne at dawn the next morning. They were to attack Templeux-le-Guérard and a conspicuous mound some 250 feet high to the north-east of the village. The commanding officer, Lt Colonel Harry Carr, 'rode out' together with his four company commanders, captains HG Newman, JP Bate MC, CR Pawsey MC and A Plaistowe – all had been subalterns two years previously when the Battalion crossed the Channel. The snow and poor maps gave no scale of the Mound, nor knowledge of the quarrying at its apex.

In the early hours of 5th April, the Battalion advanced through the village and deployed with A Company (Newman) to the right, B (Bate) in the centre and C (Pawsey) on the left 'up the steep northern side' with D Company (Plaistowe) in reserve, perhaps because their commander was only 20 years of age:

Templeux and Gillemont Farm, April 1917

> B Company… scaled the slope of the Mound [a steady gradient of 800 yards, steepening near the top], closely followed by the remaining platoons of A Company. The top was found not to be flat but split by several chasms [the quarry with sides of 50-60 feet in Corbett's estimate] – from the far side of which the enemy fired rapidly. The enemy positions were taken one after the other by turning movements skilfully executed by C Company from the left and A Company from the right [with B Company sweeping the crest with a machine gun].

Corbett, more dramatically, recorded:

> The second [crest] was similarly handled, the crest was crowned, and the enemy lost this Gibraltar to sheer superiority of tactics. We pursued him more than a mile to Toine Wood, a small copse full of men and strengthened by two machine-guns. Lt [GH] Smith of B Company attacked it with his platoon of 24 men, beat down the enemy's fire with his musketry and Lewis gun, and carried it with the bayonet without losing a man.

Major Clarke, then second-in-command, recorded that the 'line was consolidated on the objectives by 8 a.m. and the Battalion was relieved by the 2/4th Lincolns at 2 p.m.' Lt Smith got no reward for his work but Captain Bate and Captain Pawsey won Bars to their MCs. Two new officers – 2Lt RF Amphlett and 2Lt WH Reynolds – were wounded, the former mortally, with 11 men killed and 37 wounded. Sgt WE Edwards and Cpl H Gisbourne took charge of the platoons of the wounded officers and each received a DCM for their actions and initiative. The importance in this attack of a platoon's private soldier's gallantry and sergeant's drive is exemplified by the award of eight MMs in addition to those two DCMs, with another for Pte W Jelfs:

> For conspicuous gallantry and devotion to duty. He displayed great courage and initiative in assisting his Company Commander [Captain Pawsey] to carry out a reconnaissance under heavy fire. He was severely wounded.

Pte W Jelfs
DCM

This was a theme which we will see again and again in such battalion attacks in the autumn of 1918. Reynolds, who had joined the Battalion on 1st July 1916, survived and was the adjutant in many of the Battalion's last actions in October 1918.

Corbett remembered that the 'General was delighted … we had carried a stronghold for which he was prepared to sacrifice five hundred'. The *History* closed saying 'the following day was celebrated as a complete holiday'. The 'General' was still Robert Fanshawe DSO and he was awarded a KCB (Knight Commander of the Bath) for his Division's success that day, taking all their objectives for the loss of just 200 men. However, this was just the warm-up act for the main and last battle before the Germans were to spend a year in and behind their Hindenburg Line with the British entrenched before them.

Pte Frederick
Bruton

A wonderful postscript to this battle and for those who died in the action. The Imperial War Museum has a small file entitled: *Letter concerning a Soldier's Grave, First World War.* It contains a very small faded photograph in which a cross can just be made out. It has also a photocopy of a birth certificate for a 'boy', Frederick Edwin Bruton, dated 'Sixth May 1887'. His father, Edwin, was a hairdresser in Great Malvern. The last document is a letter from 'Base HQ, Dunkirk, British Troops in France' written by hand. It reads:

> Dear Mr Bruton
> Col HT Clarke & myself were visiting our old lines near Templeux le Gerard and Gillemont Farm a few weeks ago & I came across your son's grave on the crossroads where I had my Coy HQ the morning that we attacked the quarries at Templeux.
> I was not commanding B Coy at this time but I had done so for six months & knew your son well – one of the best of fellows.
> I thought perhaps you would like a photo of the grave – it was a dull and wet day unfortunately & the negative is very thin – but you can see that the grave has been tended – a French girl living in a hut close by who had been a prisoner all through the war told me she put flowers on the grave every day – I promised I would write & tell you of her kindness.
> If there is any other information you would like I will gladly do my best to furnish it.
> Yours sincerely
> HG Newman Capt.
> 1/8 Worc Regt

One presumes that this was written when the Battalion was still in France in the months after the War as Pte Bruton's grave was untouched. The tragedy is that Pte Bruton's name is now found on the Thiepval Memorial so his grave or its identity was lost from the records after the War. Perhaps he is still lying untouched where he was originally buried and the girl kept her secret when the Imperial War Graves Committee staff came round the battlefields after the War. It is difficult to think other than this sort of letter and care would have only happened in a county Territorial regiment. Lt Col Clarke and Captain Newman had been in France and Italy for about four years by then. It might be assumed that similar photographs of some of the other graves from those of the Battalion who fell in the Templeux and the next action were sent to families in England but no others have come to hand. A remarkable gesture.

The Battalion's work in front of the Hindenburg Line was not finished. Again, Corbett sets the scene under the paragraph title 'the night of Gillemont':

> This spot is of famous importance. Situated on the crest of the land which looks right down on Bony and the Hindenburg Line in the part where the great St Quentin Canal by passing through a tunnel, ceases to be its moat … we were to have the honour of attacking supported by the (6th) Gloster battalion…

The *History* reported that the three companies designated to launch the attack – A, C, D – were encamped in the same quarries at Templeux which they had captured some 18 days before. B Company (Bate) were sent to man the trench line. A Company (Lt NE Clutterbuck) with 2Lt LR Bomford leading 2 Platoon were designated to seize a small copse to the right. C Company, now with Captain FW Hemming and D Company, still commanded by Captain A Plaistowe, 'were to carry the spur'. Their attack was launched on 24th April at 3.45 a.m. under a heavy artillery barrage. A Company's way was checked by thick wire and they had no artillery support. Bomford recalled:

> My objective with 1 and 2 Platoons was a farm [Quennemont] on the right flank. On reconnaissance there was no barbed wire but during the night it was wired. Just on our side of the wire was a steep bank giving good cover. The Germans opened heavy rifle and machine-gun fire and I got a bullet through my tin hat which took a groove out of the left side of my head and knocked me out. The tin hat saved my life. Some of my men tried to cut the wire but after taking casualties had to return. The two platoons retired to the front line before it was too light.

In a letter to his mother dated later that day, Bomford wrote:

> Rejoice with me, I've just stopped a lovely little one, or rather redirected it. A bullet hit my tin hat, cut my head just a little and went on again. That was at 4.30 in the morning and now I'm back at the C.C.S. [Casualty Clearing Station] some way behind our lines … my sleep for the last two nights hasn't been exactly what it might have been, so the thought of a bed and sheets has a considerable attraction for me at the moment although it is only tea-time.

This letter is clearly an attempt to allay fears at home when the 'wounded' telegram arrived – which it did, dated 26th April to Bevington Hall: 'Regret to inform you 2nd Lt LR Bomford 8th Worcester Regt admitted to No.2 General Hospital Havre. Gunshot wound to the head, not serious'. Bomford demonstrated a degree of post-trauma hysteria in his first and last sentences. Perhaps a mixture of relief that it was not worse and great sadness at the other loss of life.

Captain Hemming (another of the subalterns to cross the Channel on 31st March 1915) commanded the main assault. Corbett described the action:

> The enemy's fire was heavy as we advanced. Captain Hemming was wounded but continued to lead the attack until close to the works he was killed outright [the first company commander to be killed in the Battalion]. His maddened men rushed the works, drove out the enemy and the Farm was ours. Meanwhile A Company were having heavy fighting by the copse. But the Glosters were unable to advance far, in spite of the gallant efforts of that renown Battalion; the Division to the right did not advance at all, and we were isolated. A battalion of the enemy passed round to the left and attacked us in the rear, while another counterattacked in front. The two companies – C and D – in the Farm sallied out and after a desperate struggle, cut their way back to the reserve company – B – on which they reformed and drove the enemy back.

The commanding officer, Lt Col HA Carr DSO, later wrote:

> At Zero, 3.45 a.m., both attacks were launched, but the preliminary attack on our right (A Coy) was soon held up by superior forces and was not pressed.
> The Main attack, in spite of the distance – 800 yards from our front line to the Farm. – and a very heavy fire from Machine Guns and rifles, was successful, and the Farm was captured by the leading platoons of C and D Companies, led by Captain Plaistowe. During the advance the supporting platoons of C and D Companies suffered severely from the Hostile Barrage and from Machine Gun fire from the left flank, where the 6th Gloucesters had failed to enter the German Trenches on the Hill, which was their objective. Captain Hemming led his left Supporting Platoons in a gallant attempt to deal with these Machine Guns but was killed while leading his men, with nearly all his NCOs, and the few survivors of the supporting platoons were compelled to fall back upon the original front line. Here they were ultimately joined by the remnants of the platoons of A Company, who had lost their officers – Lieuts. Clutterbuck, Bomford and Potter – and had been held up in their advances towards the Farm by the heavy fire from the left flank. The result of this was that Captain Plaistowe, with D Company and two platoons of C Company were left without support in the captured position, behind which a heavy hostile barrage was now being put down, making communication almost impossible, and breaking the telephone wire which had been gallantly run out from Battalion Headquarters, and it was 6.45hrs before the situation as regards the failure of the supporting Platoons to continue their advance was realised. Lieut. Gilbert was then despatched to reorganise the survivors and support Captain Plaistowe, but, owing to the heavy barrage and the loss of all leaders, it was found impossible to do more than hang on in our original front line.

A brother officer wrote to Hemming's father, Mr FJ Hemming, a Worcester solicitor:

> It is with the greatest sorrow and regret that I write to tell you that Frank was killed in action on the morning of the 24th. He gallantly led his Company in an attack on a farm which was strongly held by the enemy. During the early stages of the attack he was slightly wounded in the shoulder by a bomb [grenade], but he carried on, and finding his left flank exposed, sent back for his support platoons to come up on the left, as he had something for them to shoot at. He drew his pistol and shouted 'Come on lads!' and was leading them forward when he was hit in the head and died instantaneously. It was a dreadful shock to all of us when we got the news, as Frank was such a splendid fellow in every way. It will be a great blow to you, and to his mother and sisters, and you have our most heartfelt sympathy. You have one consolation in knowing that he died a 'hero's death'. I have had a talk with his runner who was with him at the end. Every officer, NCO and man of the Battalion sympathises with you and shares your loss.

The servant, perhaps his 'runner', also wrote:

> As being with him as his servant for over two years, it is a blow to me, and I know it must be an upset for you all. The Captain was killed in the early morning of the 24th, while leading the Company in an attack on the Germans, and he was wounded in the arm. Still going on, he had another wound, and still calling his Company on he got a fatal blow from a rifle grenade which burst near him. I can assure you that he did not suffer any pain, for death was instantaneous. It hurts me very much to write this message to you, for I feel very sorry for you all. He died a brave soldier's death, pushing back the Germans. The Captain will be much missed by the Battalion, and he will be by me, for he was always a good friend to me since I came into the Country [France] over two year ago. It is blow to me; I don't feel the same chap.

To be considered as a 'gentleman' and 'brave', though dying a heroic death, was the best that a young officer could hope to achieve. Frank Hemming had achieved much in his 29 years, becoming head boy at the Royal Grammar School in Worcester before being awarded a scholarship to Jesus College, Oxford to read mathematics. He was keen to follow his father into the law and gained a 2nd Class in his Intermediate Law Examination the following year, 1910. But he also had a calling for Army service and received his commission into the Territorial Force in 1912. The *Berrow's Journal* continued at the time:

> He went through a special course of signalling and on one occasion at the annual camp was signals officer to the Brigade of which the Worcestershire Territories were a part. In this and other ways he proved himself an exceptionally earnest soldier, to him it was a serious calling, not a recreation, as, in peace time, some regarded it. He was promoted Lieutenant in 1913 and it was natural when War broke out, that he should take up an active service with zest. He went abroad with the Battalion two years ago last Easter, and during that time he shared in a lot of hard work. Some time ago he was gassed with some men of the Battalion [presumably July 1916], and a fortnight ago he was reported slightly wounded [at Malakoff Farm on 11th April], but did not absent himself from duty. He was promoted Temporary Captain in June 1915 which was later confirmed.
>
> When War broke out he was working with his father and was already beginning to show in the profession that industry and thoroughness which had been prominent in his career at school and college and in his application to military matters. He had been home on leave twice and on the second occasion had acted as best man at the marriage of a brother officer, Lieut. RT Keen MC [to Miss Mary Abell of Ronkswood]. Sympathy will be extended to Mr & Mrs Hemming and their daughters on their heavy loss.
>
> Other letters which Mr Hemming has received indicate how keenly his son's loss is felt. One writer says 'I have been serving with him since our arrival in France, and no one knows more than I do the gallant work he has done. His Company [C] was always the happiest in the Battalion, the smartest on parade and the finest in action – all this due to the splendid example he set his men who would follow him anywhere. He died encouraging his men to drive the Germans back from a position they were attacking. I can honestly say that I

have never seen men so deeply affected by the death of an officer as all of C Company are by his death…

The *Berrow's Worcester Journal,* to give it its full title, was published intermittently from 1690 and continually since 1712. All the above excerpts of letters and biography of Captain Hemming were issued in May 1917, and it was later to publish Corbett's memoirs. It produced photographs of many who died as well as family groups where many members were in the service of the Crown. The Royal Grammar School reported at the Centenary of the War that Hemming's parents had presented a Cup in his memory for the 'most deserving cadet of the OTC' and it is still awarded to this day.

Frank Hemming

This ground in front of Gillemont Farm is little changed today, except for a Route Nationale, running north-south just behind what was the start-line for the attack. The track up to the farm remains and has some cover from a rough hedge-line in the early stages. Thereafter, it is open flat ground with a deep dry valley immediately to the left of the centre-line of the attack which would have given shelter from machine-gun fire from the farm until the last 200 yards. It is not clear that much use was made of this 'dead-ground', rather the attack was launched directly into the enemy fire, albeit in darkness. Looking today, and knowing the effectiveness of the German machine guns, it is remarkable that the attack even reached the farmhouse and buildings – due very largely to the bravery of Captains Hemming and Plaistowe. A much more numerous force would have been required than just two companies to hold such an exposed piece of ground.

View of Gillemont Farm from Startline

Last 200 yards to Gillemont Farm

At this stage it is worth considering the role of the commanding officer – and that Captain Plaistowe was just 20 years of age. Lt Col Carr wrote his report in 1919 for the families of those who fought with the Battalion over the previous four years. I am reminded of the citation of the then Captain (Acting Lt Col) Adrian Carton de Wiart DSO, Dn Gds:

> For most conspicuous bravery, coolness and determination during severe operations of a prolonged nature. It was owing in a great measure to his dauntless courage and inspiring example that a serious reverse was averted. He displayed the utmost energy and courage in forcing our attack home. After three other battalion Commanders had become casualties, he controlled their commands, and ensured that the ground won was maintained at all costs. He frequently exposed himself in the organisation of positions and of supplies, passing unflinchingly through fire barrage of the most intense nature. His gallantry was inspiring to all.
> —*London Gazette*, 9 September 1916.

It begs the question as to whether Lt Col Carr should have led a counter-attack with the remains of A, C and D Companies as well as some of Bate's B Company. Instead, he sent out a young Lt Gilbert – competent as he may have been as he ended the War as Captain and adjutant, having earned himself an MC. Lt Col Carr made no assessment of his own leadership that day, instead continuing:

> Meanwhile, at 7.15 a.m., a hostile counter-attack developed from the North and South-east of the Farm. This was successfully repulsed with heavy loss, but was followed at 8.15 a.m. by a heavier attack from the North, North-east and South-east of the Farm.

After the initial counter-attack was repulsed, Plaistowe must have been wondering when the British counter-attack was coming. Carr had missed his opportunity. Instead, in Carr's own words:

> Owing to the failure of the Battalion on our left [through the

dead-ground], and to the retirement of the remainder of the supporting platoons, Captain Plaistowe's men were practically isolated, and after gallant resistance in which every officer was killed except Lieut. Pittard, who, though badly wounded, reorganised and extracted the survivors, and fell back on our original Front Line, where they successfully maintained themselves until relieved by the 1/7th Worcestershire Regiment after dark.

Lt Col Carr was to write to Plaistowe's father: 'Had he lived, I would have recommended him for a DSO… He will ever remain a tradition in this Battalion as a "very brave gentleman"'. However, there was no mention by Carr of his own role or of any attempt by him to influence the battle. He concluded those years later that:

> In the light of our experience that day, it was obvious that the Farm could not be held unless the high ground to the North was in our hands. The attack of the leading platoons of C and D Companies was brilliantly carried out, and the position was maintained to the last.

In the light of Carr's apparent lack of personal leadership that day, it is perhaps not surprising that Bomford was to write to his mother on 2nd October: 'We have a new Colonel, he is a very cheery old soul but that's all I know about him. He couldn't very well help being better than the last'. However, in his defence, a three-battalion (1/7th Worcesters, 1/4th Gloucesters, 1/4th Berks) attack was launched that evening with the same objective with only the 1/7th Worcesters still holding their ground in the face of the German counter-attacks the following morning. The commanding officer, Lt Col FM Tomkinson, was to be awarded a Bar to his DSO for his leadership that night.

The losses that day were very heavy. Both company commanders, Hemming and Plaistowe, were killed together with four platoon commanders – Lts AR Swallow and AG Richards, 2Lts FG Potter and CG Eaton, the latter commissioned on 26th December 1915 after being a lance corporal in the Queen's Westminster Rifles. Great gallantry was displayed by 2Lts GH Jones, the signals officer, and RM Pittard who was wounded but took command of his company – both being awarded MCs – while the twice-wounded Sgt W Pitt and LCpl A Woodward took charge of their respective platoons and coordinated the defence. They received DCMs. Lt Clutterbuck was also killed, leading A Company, meaning the Battalion had seven officers killed that day as well as, according to the *War Diary*, 16 Other Ranks – a ratio of 2:1 when at the start of the attack the ratio would be almost 30:1. Seemingly a clear demonstration of the life expectancy of young officers when attacking over open ground. The *History* reported two officers (Bomford and Pittard) wounded together with 67 Other Ranks as well as 63 missing. Total casualties of 153 from some 600 who started the twin attacks in the early hours of that morning. However, when the Roll is reviewed, the total killed, died of wounds or died in captivity was actually 52 Other Ranks although a post-War schedule divides the casualties that day as:

Company	**A**	**B**	**C**	**D**	**Total**
Killed	8	-	12	17	**37**
Missing/killed	-	-	4	17	**21**
Missing/prisoner	-	-	4	11	**15**
Wounded	5	2	18	48	**73**
TOTAL	**13**	**2**	**38**	**93**	**146**

This will mean that the Battle Report for that night recorded the above figures but when the battlefield was cleared, the bodies of some 21 of the 67 missing were found, with 15 taken prisoner, so 31 must have been lying wounded or having been taken back to a casualty clearing station without Battalion HQ having been informed. This changes the ratio to 7:1 – still a heavy toll on the young officers. Perhaps it is not surprising that Bomford was so relieved to have only been wounded.

The post-War schedule records the home town or village of all the 58 who died as a result of the battle. They show a picture of the officers coming from across the country (Birmingham, Henley-on-Thames, Worcester, Warrington and all the three from D Company from London – Highgate, Wandsworth, Highbury) yet of the 51 men from the ranks, only 4 came from outside the immediate recruiting area – from Kent, Exeter, Paignton (Devon) and Plymouth. This shows that the 1/8th remained very much a county pals battalion – although this was to change significantly when the replacement draft arrived on 7th July.

Corbett noted the heroics of CSM Ward who 'performed a great feat of endurance that night. With his thigh shattered, unhelped and alone, sustained only by his unconquerable heart, he crawled back for seven hours to our lines and was saved'. The Battalion was well and truly blooded and could look all others in the eye. The Germans, true to their training, had launched a counter-attack as soon as was practical. Corbett concluded:

> Next day we were relieved by the seventh Worcesters, who captured the Farm after another bloody fight [2 officers and 12 Other Ranks killed, 5 officers and 90 Other Ranks wounded and 29 missing: total casualties 138]. The Division who relieved us soon lost it and the 48th had to retake it for them. So the fighting went on around it for a year until the Germans had their great advance [in their Spring Offensive of 1918 – Operation Michael].

One has to go and walk round the present-day Gillemont Farm to see the views it commands in all directions to fully understand the strategic importance of this place. It was the reason why such loss of life was involved on both sides in order to hold or to capture this invaluable piece of ground. The ten-month advance from the Ancre

River below Thiepval had ground to a halt at the feet of the Hindenburg Line – a distance of some 29 miles.

When following Captain Hemming to his grave, in the British cemetery at Templeux-le-Guérard, we find only eight members of the Battalion – three officers, the 29-year-old Francis William Hemming, son of Francis and Lucy Hemming of St John, Worcester and an alumnus of the Royal Grammar School, Worcester; Captain Alan Plaistowe whose parents lived in Highgate and who, despite all his previous actions, was only 20; and Lieutenant Norman Eckstein Clutterbuck, with no age or parental details given on the *CWGC* website. Corbett reminds us that his younger brother, 2Lt AS Clutterbuck, had died the previous July. However, the *Ancestry* site shows that Norman Eckstein and (Arthur) Stanley were the two sons of (Councillor) Clarence and Florence Clutterbuck who were living in Handsworth in Staffordshire in 1901 and 1911. Norman was born in July 1894 and was a private in the Royal Warwickshire Regiment before his commission. He was married in November 1915 to Ida Silverman and crossed to France on 4th June 1916. His brother, Stanley, crossed to France exactly two weeks later but was killed on 14th July 1916, aged just 19. Their parents had two more children, Edward and Olive, but the loss of the two elder sons must have been devastating. It is not clear as to why neither son has any age or parental detail on the *CWGC* records as their British Army World War I Medal Rolls Index Cards provide their father's name and address as well as that of

Norman's widow. Perhaps this is the reason why neither grave has a family inscription. This does seem an oversight by Sir Fabian Ware's IWGC teams as this additional information was available in London.

The Clutterbuck brothers, Stanley and Norman

The *War Diary* records on 28th April:

Burial of bodies of Captains Hemming and Plaistowe, Lt Clutterbuck, LCpl Morton, Ptes Rodney, Hughes and Wheeler at L1 d99. A service was conducted by Rev JB Frith CF and attended by CO and all available officers.

Rev J Brien Frith, a Cambridge man (Pembroke 1904) was the rector of Shrawley, just north of Worcester, when he volunteered in 1916. He had twin sons who both served, were awarded MCs and were killed in the Second World War: Captain Robert Brereton Frith MC when serving with the Worcestershire Regiment in Eritrea in 1941 and Major John Brereton Frith MC in Burma in April 1945.

War maps show L1 d99 as being beside the road running west-south-west out of Templeux, which is not where they are all now. Forms will have been filled in by the Battalion to record these burials and sent to what was then the Graves Registration Committee. It is assumed that LCpl Morcombe was incorrectly written as 'LCpl Morton' on the form. His and the other bodies were exhumed on 11th July 1919 and moved to their present 'concentration' cemetery. His mother, Mrs MG Morcombe of 4 Malvern Road had The Day Thou Gavest Lord Is Ended as the inscription. Confusingly, the map reference used in 1917 – L1 d99 – was recorded at the exhumation as 62C.L.1 750 850 E, which was then changed to 62C.L.1.b.5.7. It is not surprising that the Imperial War Graves Commission, as it was then, became an organisation of 721 people in France and Belgium in 1919.

But where are all the others who were killed? Lt AG Richards, 24, from Wandsworth in London and Pte John Bishop, 32, whose wife Florence lived in Wolverhampton, are at Villers-Faucon Extension – so beside those officers of the 1/6th Glosters killed in their HQ building. This still leaves many unaccounted for. Seeking 2Lt AR Swallow leads one to the Thiepval Memorial and by sorting the 71,501 names into 'date of death' you find that 128 officers and soldiers were killed on that day alone who have no known grave. Of those, 3 officers and 37 men are listed as from 1/8th Battalion, giving a total in the three places of remembrance of 51 men. The Roll lists 50, of whom Private TE Millward is known to have died as a Prisoner of War on 2nd October 1917 and is buried in Cologne. In the end, there were 56 members of the Battalion recorded as being killed that day or dying of their wounds. They are buried or commemorated in 9 different cemeteries – a demonstration of the network of casualty stations between the Front and Rouen where the most severely wounded would have been taken. There are seven names missing from the Roll – published in 1919 – but all are named in the back of the *History* – published in 1929. I mention this because it demonstrates the difficulties for families in the years after the War in finding their loved ones or even knowing whether they had a grave.

The Roll has 31 officers and 374 Other Ranks, so 405 names in all. The *History* by 1929 had discovered another 35 in the intervening years, of whom two are officers – including Captain James Robert Blake, another Old Malvernian (with Lionel Kerwood and Jack Bate), the son of JEH Blake, the senior curate at the Malvern Priory and vicar of Bretforton. He was commissioned on 7th January 1915, having been an architect, and crossed to France with the 1/8th Battalion two months later. He was attached to the 14th Battalion when he was reported 'missing & wounded' together with his commanding officer on 25th March 1918. The *Journal* announced his promotion to Captain on 15th November 1918, when he was still 'missing' but he was never found. Blake was not gazetted as killed by the *Malvernian* until the following March and his name is now found on the Arras Memorial. He had twice been Mentioned in Despatches. The other was 2Lt FM Walton who died in February 1919 and is buried in Cherbourg. There is no explanation as to whether he died of wounds or of sickness. It does record that his body was exhumed in October 1935 due to building developments and that he was 5ft 4 inches tall. It seems that all those in that cemetery were moved to the extension of a nearby communal cemetery.

Of the thirty-three Other Ranks missing from the initial Roll, it makes one wonder what the families knew at the time – what did their telegram say? Did it just record them as missing or dead? Taking two examples from early in the alphabet we find that Pte Thomas Abbey died of illness in Italy on 1st June 1918 and is recorded on the *CWGC* website, which shows no next-of-kin. The next is 16-year-old Pte William Bruton who is buried in Chelmsford Cemetery. He died on 17th February 1915 when the Battalion was based in Suffolk and Essex on anti-invasion and anti-Zeppelin patrols. His parents, William and Susan of 26 Happy Landing North, St Johns in Worcester, would undoubtedly have known. Perhaps there are good reasons of security that families did not know where their men were killed or died until after the War. It was, after all, not until August 1932 that the Thiepval Memorial was finished and unveiled by the Prince of Wales.

This chapter should not end without a further mention of Lt Alan Plaistowe, killed three months after his twentieth birthday. A pupil of Highgate School, so an Old Cholmeleian, from 1908–1912, he had not been awarded any gallantry medal yet he was mentioned six times in the Regimental *History*, the same number as the Old Gent. He would have been entitled to wear an oak leaf on his campaign medal ribbon had he survived. He had been Mentioned in Despatches on two occasions for his constant leadership of raids on enemy trenches. It was he, Bate and Pawsey who seemed to be most called-upon in those first two years before the Battalion was committed to serious frontal assaults. One can only wonder what Plaistowe might have achieved had he lived through the Gillemont battle. His father was a 'jam maker' from Highgate in north London. He had three sons and the eldest, Lt Richard Reeves Plaistowe, was killed serving in Gaza with the 1/5th Norfolks exactly one week before Alan. His younger brother was a subaltern in the Oxs & Bucks Light Infantry and survived the War.

A HOT AND QUIET SUMMER

The Battalion occupied the site of Gillemont Farm on the night of 29th April and then, with the whole of the 48th Division, was transferred from the 4th Army to the 5th Army which meant moving north up the Front of the Hindenburg Line after three weeks' rest near Velu Wood. With their sister 1/7th Battalion, they then moved forward to the area to the east of Lagnicourt, some ten miles to the north of Gillemont Farm. They would be back in this area the following year as they approached the scene of perhaps their greatest triumph, marching past the quarries of Templeux-le-Guérard on 4th October 1918. Gillemont Farm has been completely rebuilt and remains a substantial and working farm between the main A26 road north of St Quentin and the American military cemetery at Bony. Perhaps, after the infamous Mouquet Farm (known to the soldiers as 'Moo Cow Farm') in front of Thiepval, Gillemont was to be the most fought-over farm on the Western Front. There had been one even better-known farmstead in the history of warfare, that of Chateau d'Hougoumont to which the Duke of Wellington attached so much importance at the Battle of Waterloo a little over 100 years before Mouquet and Gillemont farms were to cost so many lives. Each provided the only shelter in the wide-open landscape of these great battles.

Corbett reported that the British front line was a 'chain of outposts' rather than an organised set of interlinking trenches. He told a strange tale which seems to have been somewhat embellished. It does, however, introduce another gallant young officer:

> One night two serjeants walking about unarmed found themselves in the face of six Germans who rushed at them. They picked up a rusty rifle which happened to be loaded and killed two. Lieut. SH Wilkes and his batman running up killed three more. The sixth escaped.

'A rusty rifle which happened to be loaded…' sounds a little implausible but we were not there and cannot judge. Corbett finished his notes on the Gillemont Farm area, noting:

> It was a most adventurous place and just suited [Major-General] Sir Robert Fanshawe – (commander 48th Division) – who spent his nights among us, walking from post to post and hoping (no doubt) for deeds of high impress.

We came across Lt Wilkes patrolling at Le Sars and we will do so again as he was to win the Military Cross on three occasions. The first, in the King's Birthday Honours, was gazetted on 4th June 1917 for his actions over the winter months of 1916/17, perhaps concluding with this incident.

However, the main British focus had already switched further north with the wonderful capture of Vimy Ridge by the Canadian Corps and the less successful Battle of the Scarpe which moved the front line from the edge of the town of Arras forward by some 4,000 yards.

In early May 1917, some 25 months since the Battalion crossed to France, we have Lt Col Harry Carr in command of the Battalion; Major Hubert Clarke as his second-in-command; Captain Jack Bate MC commanding B Company; Douglas Bomford (2/8th) recovering from wounds at No 8 Hospital, Rouen; Leslie Bomford (1/8th) at No 2 Hospital, Le Havre; Captain Osborn Walford (still 2/8th) recovering in England but now in Worcestershire; Sgt Edmund Wedgbury DCM MM (1/8th) on a commissioning course; Captain Lance Evers (2/8th) on leave in England; 2Lt Laurence Watkinson still with 12th (Reserve) Bn in England. Of the remaining senior officers who had crossed the Channel at the head of the Battalion on Maundy Thursday some two years before, Lt Col WK Peake had been rested and was soon to be commanding the 4th Bn, the Gloucestershire Regiment; the adjutant, Percy Whalley, was commanding the 3rd Bn, the Worcestershire Regiment; Major Lionel Kerwood had been killed commanding the 13th Bn, Cheshire Regiment; Captain AS Creak had become a Draft Conducting Officer within six weeks of crossing; and Captain WEL Cotton had been seconded to Staff Duties within three weeks of his arrival in France, and was to be Mentioned in Despatches three times in the last year of the War and to win an MC. Later he was to command the amalgamated 8th Battalion from 1923-27 and become High Sheriff of Worcestershire. The only person with the rank of captain or above at the time of the Channel crossing was the present second-in-command, Major HT Clarke. It is interesting to find that on the parade through Worcester on 23rd August 1919, Major FAW How, Major SH Clark TD and Captain RH Burlington who had all crossed back on 31st March 1915 were representing the 8th Battalion that day. It is difficult to trace them between those two dates – SH Clark commanded briefly between Peake and Carr but must have been soon on his way to a staff role, as HT Clarke had been promoted to second-in-command on Carr's assumption of command.

Isabel Evers wrote in April 1917 that her son Lance Evers, Walford and Captain HW Davies (Adjt – 2/8th) had been to visit Colonel Matt Dixon at Tardebigg 'who for a short time had been their (2/8th) CO in France. He was in much better health than when they last saw him'. Colonel Dixon (1860–1931) had commanded the 8th Battalion from 1908–1911 and was then the founding commanding officer of the 2/8th from 1915 to 1916. He had handed over command to Lt Colonel Francis Checketts before the battalion crossed to France at the end of May 1916. He would have been 55 years old by then. Colonel Dixon's mother was Anne Walford (1832–1909), sister of John Walford (1834–1899) who was Captain Osborn Walford's father. It is considered in his family that Walford's enlistment at the outset of War when aged 45 was strongly encouraged by his first cousin. Walford had served in the 1st Volunteer Battalion, Royal Warwickshire Regiment from 4th November 1899 until he resigned his commission as a Lieutenant on 28th November 1903, so he had some military experience. His father, John Walford, was a Lieutenant Colonel in the same battalion of the Royal Warwickshire Regiment and a first recipient of the newly instigated Victorian Officers Decoration – gazetted on 23rd December 1892. He was a Birmingham solicitor, founding partner of Messrs Cox & Walford with offices in New Street. In those days, King Edward's School was in the Charles Barry and Augustus Pugin buildings in New Street. It is not surprising that Osborn Walford and his brothers attended the school. Thus, the Dixon and Walford families had strong links to the Volunteer and Territorial county battalions of Warwickshire and Worcestershire over several decades. Captain Hugh Davies was another Old Gent, a bachelor fruit-grower from Pershore who seems to have served with the Assam Valley Light Horse in the Boer War. He was 42 at the start of the War and was the adjutant of the 2/8th Battalion when they crossed to France in May 1916. He was to receive a DSO and an MC before the War was over.

The Battalion had earned only three Battle Honours up until May 1917 – the Somme 1916, Pozières (when they were gassed) and Le Transloy (for their time in Le Sars). It is not clear in which battle these two – Templeux and Gillemont Farm – gallant and costly actions were later attributed. The King announced the award of Battle Honours through Army Orders in 1922 and 1923 to all the regiments involved. Neither of these battles were specifically listed, despite the heavy losses over a number of weeks at the latter. They were now a battle-hardened battalion. They would add a further eleven Battle Honours to their Colour before the War was over. The only change of key personnel would be in the autumn when Captain Hubert Clarke took over command of the Battalion with 23-year-old Captain 'Jack' JP Bate being promoted to his second-in-command. Walford would join from the 2/8th and Wedgbury would complete his officer training and, despite being badged to the Glosters, would soon be back with the Battalion and adding to his medal collection.

Lt LR Bomford returned to battalion duties after his wound when they were at Bourlon Wood – 'a quiet line in unspoilt country … further south than we had been before'. He received news that he had been Mentioned in Despatches:

> Lieut. (Acting Captain) Leslie Raymond Bomford. During the period under review this officer has done continuous good work as a Platoon and Company Commander. By his personal example in action and in his devotion and initiative at all times he has displayed high qualities of leadership.

This would entitle him to put a bronze oak leaf on the ribbon of his campaign medal (the Victory Medal in the case of World War

One) when he received one and, until then, he could wear it on his uniform next to any other medal he may have. In Bomford's case, he had no other medal but he could pin it to his uniform above his breast pocket, though no photographs show him so attired.

The focus of attacks in the British sector through the summer of 1917 moved north from the Hindenburg Line, first to the Arras and Vimy Ridge area and then to the Messine Ridge, before Ypres and Passchendaele. The Battalion would spend six weeks in glorious weather in this quieter area to the east of Bapaume. Due to the British and Canadian losses at Vimy Ridge and at the Scarpe and with the impending Messine and Ypres campaigns, commanders at all levels were discouraged from risking their troops. The Battalion needed this time to allow the new intake of young officers to get to know their men and to hone their skills. Bomford and Corbett gave some wonderful insights into life on this Front. The fact that it was in lovely summer weather rather than in the rain, snow and mud of the previous winter made it easy to organise supplies and keep up the troops' morale. Corbett recalled that the Battalion was, not surprisingly, reinforced. In addition, another company commander was posted away: 'Capt Newman has left the [A] Coy to instruct in some Corps school since I left. Capt. T Stinton, who came to France a full-blown captain a short time back, is in command. In some ways it's rather a shame that a man who has spent all his time in England should get a Coy, but he's a very nice fellow and isn't superior to getting guidance where experience is needed' – a sign of good leadership. He was also ten years older than Bomford. Thus, within two months, three company commanders had been killed and another sent away on a staff posting. A huge challenge for any commanding officer.

The *War Diary* recorded that on 4th May there was a ceremonial parade and presentation of DCMs to Sergeant WE Edwards:

> For conspicuous gallantry and devotion to duty. He assumed command of his platoon and in the face of heavy fire at close range succeeded in gaining his objective. He was largely responsible for the success of the operations.

and to Cpl Gisbourne:

> For conspicuous gallantry and devotion to duty. He assumed command of his platoon, and in spite of very heavy hostile fire succeeded in reaching his objective.

(Harry Gisbourne was present at the D Company 50th Anniversary Dinner in 1964 and 'carried his proudest war time souvenir … the DCM'.)

The CO read out on parade the reports upon which these were granted and also the reports upon which the bars to the MC were granted to Captains Bate:

> For conspicuous gallantry and devotion to duty when in command of his company. He led his men in a most gallant manner, and was largely responsible for the success of the operations. He set a fine example of courage and determination.

and Pawsey:

> For conspicuous gallantry and devotion to duty. After establishing superiority of fire in a very difficult position, he gallantly led the final assault and personally captured two unwounded prisoners.

They had been rewarded for their gallantry and leadership at Templeux-le-Guérard on 11th April. All these awards were announced in the *Journal* on Saturday 23rd June 1916 with the full citation in each case; thus all in the county would know of their gallant actions. Only in the case of Sgt Edwards were family details given: 'Son of Mr J Edwards of North Malvern'. This parade gives an indication of the time – 23 days – between an action and the announcement, even if they were not formally gazetted until 18th June. Each would have been presented with a medal ribbon to sew onto their uniforms. The medal itself would follow later. Cpl Harry Gisbourne had a good summer because, as the *War Diary* recorded, he shot down a German plane 'with a Lewis Gun in Havrincourt Wood. The aeroplane fell down in the 20th Divisional area. The observer was killed and the pilot wounded'. Gisbourne was to be invalided home on 6th November 1917 and given an honourable discharge from the Army the following November. One difficulty is that the Battalion had another Gisbourne – Sergeant Albert Gisbourne, who was killed in October 1918 having just earned himself an MM in Italy. Albert is just recorded as being 'Gisbourne' by the CWGC on the Vis-en-Artois Memorial halfway between Arras and Cambrai. Had these Gisbournes been officers, the person who shot down the plane would have been better identified – not an occurrence limited to the Worcestershire Regiment.

The *Journal,* always wanting to celebrate individual success on the battlefield as well as listing the casualties, gave space in June 1917 to what amounted to a family announcement, under the title DCM FOR TERRITORIAL SERGEANT:

> Mrs [Mary] Pitt, of 17, Spring Gardens, St Paul's, Worcester, informs us that she has received news from France that Sergt. Pitt, Worcestershire Regt. (T.F.) has won the DCM, that his comrades have written congratulating him on gaining the decoration, and saying that they are proud of him for his brave work. He was out in France for two years and two months and was home on leave four months ago. He went back in February, and was then wounded in the left arm. He was bleeding for 13 hours and says that he wonders that he is alive. He is going on as well as can be expected. He is at the Royal Infirmary, Perth, Scotland, and says the Scottish people are very good to him. He is in his 30th year. He went through the South African War [2nd Boer War] when he was a lad. He has a brother, Corpl. Frank Pitt (also in the same battalion), who has also been out for two years and four months. They both volunteered on the outbreak of war. He has another brother, Drummer Jim Pitt, in the band, and yet another brother, Thomas Pitt, who was in the Worcestershires in France, and is now home discharged. His father, Mr Thomas Pitt, jnr, and Sergt. W Pitt, work at the Worcester Gas Works, and Corpl. Frank Pitt and Drummer Jim Pitt worked at Messrs. Williamson's, Worcester.

Sgt. W. Pitt,
Worcester.
Awarded D.C.M.

Visiting Munition workers in Worcester

A wonderful story of family service. It did not mention that Willie Pitt, as a private, had been twice Mentioned in Despatches (November 1915 and May 1916). It noted that he served in the 'South African War when he was a lad' – which indeed he was as he would have only been 15 when the War ended in May 1902. It is pleasing not to find any of the family on the Battalion's Roll of Honour at the end of the War. Perhaps as a sign of the times, there was no mention of Sgt Pitt's own family, his wife Ellen, a glovemaker whom he married when he was just 18, and their three daughters, Florence May, Lilly Beatrice and Ethel Janet, who would have been ten, eight and six at the time of the *Journal* article. They too must have been very proud. Pitt was to live until April 1957.

Bomford wrote also that a new subaltern had arrived, (Lt JH) Myhill who came from Essex, was tall, thin and about 35. 'He is a nice old boy but lacks initiative; he simply runs our mess splendidly'. This has two implications: the county was not providing a sufficient number of new young officers; and, that if Bomford and Myhill are the only officer platoon commanders, there was greater pressure on the SNCOs who would be commanding the other two platoons. In addition, this is the period when Sgt Wedgbury was away at his Officer Cadet School, No 8 in his case. He left battalion duty on 10th

March 1917, so before the two big actions, and was commissioned on 27th June. To make matters worse, Wedgbury was commissioned into the Gloucestershire Regiment. This was common, usually due to the perceived difficulty of commanding SNCOs who had, until then, been friends. He was to serve as a platoon commander in the 1/2nd Battalion of the Glosters before returning to the 1/8th on 21st October as a platoon commander in D Company. This meant also that he missed the Battalion's two major actions in the 3rd Battle of Ypres, known to all as Passchendaele. There was however plenty of time for him to cover himself in further glory.

Corbett told an amusing tale of the Battalion's exposure to the Guards battalions by Buire:

> Most of the places in this valley have Welsh names, thinly disguised under fantastic French spelling. We were in distinguished company here. Not only were the 1st Division present, but even the Guards, making railways and roads, but as soldierly as ever, and the spirit of emulation entered our rude breasts. We would be 'posh' too, and never was seen such a camp as ours, with equipment laid out in parallel lines, and even the kitchen buckets 'dressed', the cowls of the cooker funnels all pointing in the same direction and the smoke blowing out at the same angle.

A story surely embellished, but demonstrating the beneficial impact on others of the highest standards of discipline and organisation in the immediate area.

However, supply problems were about to rear their head. In April the weather turned hot and dry and 'our blood was getting into a dreadful state for want of vegetables. We were covered in boils and sores…' They eventually got to their place for a promised 'long rest' near Bourlon Wood, just west of Cambrai. Corbett remembered that 'there was scarce a thorn amongst the roses. True, we always had to wear our tin hats, which in weather immoderately hot for North France was a nuisance'. The real issue was water and vegetables:

> There was none of the former in the Line and during each eight-day

> tour [of the trenches] we had to go without washing, which sounds disagreeable, but you get used to it after a day or two. The daily allowance was 10 petrol tins [14 or 15 pints to a tin] of water and 13 tins of tea per Company [200 men] – not enough for drinking and shaving… [Thus 270 pints of liquid per 200 men each day.]
>
> Everything had to be brought up cooked, for the essence of our position was secrecy, and we must not make fires. So well did we manage this that for two months the enemy never found out where we were… In all this long time we had only two killed and five wounded, one being killed was CSM Heydon, slain by a shell that burst 70 yards from him.

This was, presumably, a reflection of the hard, dry ground with shrapnel being deflected over a much wider area than in the winter mud. CSM John Heydon was 32 years old and hailed from Cherry Orchard in Worcester, was killed on 8th June and is now lying in the Louverval Military Cemetery in Doignies. Major HT Clarke, then commanding, wrote to his father:

> It is with the greatest sorrow that I have to inform you of the death of your son, CSM J Heydon. He was hit in the head by a shell splinter the day before yesterday, and died almost at once. The Chaplain came up and buried him the same night in a small cemetery by Battalion Headquarters. Your son was one of the smartest Warrant Officers it has been my pleasure to meet, and his loss will be deplored by all of us. He had recently been promoted, and showed great promise, which endorsed the previous good opinion we had of him.

Four graves along from Heydon is the other casualty: LCpl Martin, 23, from Barbourne, Worcester, killed some three weeks later.

Corbett then explained the vegetable issue:

> The want of vegetables was much more serious. We did not even get potatoes often, green stuff never at all – only dried vegetables – and the state of our blood became terrible. The slightest wound became

> dangerous – one man died of a mere scratch from shrapnel on the head [presumably LCpl Martin] – we were covered in sores and boils, even chat-bites [lice] festered and suppurated. We lost about 50 men, temporarily or for ever, from this cause, and it was a marvel that we did not develop scurvy … this was the duty of the Q side of the Divisional Staff and in that duty it sadly failed.

Bomford wrote to his father indicating it was a little different for the officers:

> The wood [Bourlon] is close to a chateau which must have been a top hole place but three or four mines have done their work very thoroughly … but the vegetable garden is useful still. We have some asparagus and a few lettuces.

Bomford described their summer near Bourlon Wood – 'our trenches are very quiet and cushy and quite nice. We have to be very quiet all day and do all our work by night'. Corbett added a little flesh to those bones: 'Lieut. Bomford, with a patrol drove an enemy patrol into their own wire there [Tadpole Copse], where they destructively bombed their own friends'. He also wrote of a visit by the Divisional Band to their camp to provide some Saturday-afternoon entertainment and of a less successful church parade as there was neither band nor hymn books.

The *History* recorded simply that 'at the beginning of July the 48th Division was relieved and ordered back into reserve. The 1/7th and 1/8th handed over the trenches … and marched westward to Achiet-le-Petit. The heat was overpowering. The troops were in poor physical condition after their long stay in the line; they suffered severely on the march, and many fell out'. Bomford and Corbett were more forthright, though not of their own men. Bomford added more detail to his father:

> We came out of the trenches the day before yesterday at about 1 o'clock in the morning and marched until it was light. Then we

> halted till 2 o'clock and marched on until seven, right through the hottest part of the day. Yesterday we started marching again at 7 a.m. and got here about 12 and spent the remainder of the day making shelters for ourselves. This morning we paraded at 8 and got back here at 11 hoping for a moment to rest and clean up. Now we have to move again to a nice place two miles away. Isn't that enough to make anyone bad tempered? Not only do we have to build all our shelters again, and it's not a short job to make a decent place, but we move two miles further from civilisation.

He went on to explain what was important to the men, although he ended by saying 'the men are a splendid lot, they couldn't be more cheerful, but I don't need to tell you that the infantryman's lot isn't all cream':

> Two miles from here is a village with roofs on its houses and most of the church is left and what interests us is the fact that we can buy fruit and vegetables, butter and all sorts of things. Most of the men haven't seen a civilian for about five months now and it means a lot to them to get a few luxuries and a little French beer. The men haven't had a change of underclothing for more than a fortnight of this weather with long marches into the bargain … and now we shall be four miles from civilisation … [and to] intensify the feelings you come back and see all sorts of peace soldiers riding past you in luxurious cars.

It is not clear if 'peace soldiers' was a reference to staff officers or to journalists or to visiting members of the government.

On 7th July the 1/8th Battalion received a large draft of NCOs and Other Ranks from the 7th (Service) Battalion, The Norfolk Regiment. They numbered 144 in all. The Battalion recorded the fate of these men over the remaining sixteen months of the War – 21 were killed or died of their wounds, 1 died and 59 were wounded, of whom 5 were wounded twice. This draft would have made a material difference in reducing the percentage of men from Worcestershire in the Battalion.

It showed also the casualty rate of an infantry battalion which served both at Passchendaele and in the latter part of the Last Hundred Days – some 59.7 per cent casualty rate for this draft.

Corbett entitled his paragraph 'The Terrible March' so it was obviously one that stuck firmly in the memory when writing some two years later. He estimated the overall march as being 15 miles on 'the hottest day of a blazing summer'. He described the equipment in addition to full-marching order which they carried: '… heavy scorching helmet and the respirators, Very pistols, wire-cutters, grenade-dischargers…' but overall he said the Battalion did better than the one in front and was 'rescued by the humanity of an Australian officer, who … borrowed a lorry and brought them (those who had fallen out) along'. Corbett then went on to confirm the extra moves described by Bomford:

> We reached Monchy and built ourselves a camp out of stakes and sheet iron. As soon as this was done we were marched to Adinfer, where we built another, and then marched back again. The Staff was getting into its stride. We then began to train. Everybody trained and economy went to the wall. It was very hard work for the Q[uartermaster] side, who had to get breakfast ready by 5 a.m., train all day, return about 5 p.m., and then begin the long day's work. It was equally hard on all of us that we should still be quartered in the desert (tantalisingly close to inhabited country) and still out of reach of vegetables.

One must assume that the generals and their staff had reasons for this seemingly unnecessary deprivation and for the hard training, of which one of Corbett's privates said 'we practiced this when Julius Caesar was a lance corporal!' Bomford was more understanding about the training, writing that 'it was nice to be able to get your platoon for a bit' – presumably meaning to be able to work them as a unit, even with their new intake including a couple of Cockneys 'to make up my numbers' – an indication, perhaps, that the county of Worcestershire was running out of men as well as officers. Bomford also mentioned that 'most of the Battalion have been inoculated this morning and are rather sorry for themselves', continuing that it was two years since his last one. This was likely to have been against smallpox, cholera and typhoid. The heading of Corbett's next chapter in bold black writing provided a degree of explanation for all this training – PASCHENDEALE, forbidding even with Corbett's misspelling.

PASSCHENDAELE

With Vimy Ridge still firmly in Canadian hands and with limited success in front of Arras, Haig's focus turned to the 'clearing' of the Belgium coast of U-boat bases. This was, in essence, to be fought in three phases: to capture the ridgeline to the south of Ypres as far as Messine; to push forward the British line in front of Ypres as far as the village of Passchendaele, giving commanding views to the east and to the north towards the coast; to advance up the Belgium coastline towards Ostend and Zeebrugge. The first phase, the Battle of Messine, fought in mid-June, was a significant success fought largely by General Hubert Gough's 5th Army; this convinced Haig that the German forces in this northern sector were weak. Phase Two was planned for 31st July after a ten-day barrage of 4.25 million shells and with the French First Army on their left. The rains started shortly after the first day's successful attacks, most especially to the north by the French and by the British XIV Corps under Lt General the Earl of Cavan.

We have to rely on Corbett for this next section because Bomford 'is down for a course lasting a month … at 18 Corps Infantry School, BEF … lasting until 12th August'. This was, presumably, a company commanders' course, although Bomford's letter referred to 'a good deal of bayonet fighting and obstacles courses, also Physical Drill. There was also much sport – athletics and football'. He lost the high jump 'by a couple of inches' but excelled at rifle shooting where he got 17/20 in 4-second snap shooting. The school was some six miles back from Amiens and the officers were billeted in local houses. This must have been a good break from the Front and Bomford hoped to be able to take his deferred home leave straight afterwards.

Back with the Battalion, Corbett recalled entraining at Saulte to head towards Ypres on 23rd July. He described the endless lines of tented hospitals beside the railway before 'hopping out at Hopout' and marching into Poperinghe, just over the Belgium border and four miles short of what was left of the town of Ypres. Poperinghe was the first town that the Battalion had visited in their 28 months at the Front. Corbett remembered that 'we revelled in the salads and green meat, spending every available penny on them at ruinous prices ... double, treble, quadruple that charged to a French soldier'. There were 'egg and potato shops for the men, all doing a roaring and piratical trade'. There were five Worcestershire battalions at the Ypres Front and an officers' dinner was hastily organised in Poperinghe. The 1/8th played the 4th Battalion at football and the 1/7th won the 48th Division football cup on 25th July – the day originally planned for the full offensive to begin. Instead, it was not until the 31st that Corbett could report hearing the first blows of the Third Battle of Ypres from their camp in a scrubby wood:

> Earth and air quivered with its appalling roar. Presently news came through: We had carried the front line, captured Calf Reserve, the Guards on the left were held up but would soon be through: the Belgiums were successful, all was going well. The troops were gaining their objectives easily, and a great success was almost for sure. And then came the rain. For three months the weather had been perfect, and now for three days fell an almost ceaseless downpour. Brooks were flooded, roads ruined, trenches filled, the battlefield turned into a quag of deep alluvial mud; and all those vast preparations, embattled hosts, monstrous machines (tanks), and invincible artillery, were brought to nought by three days of deluge.

Dramatic language but a fair assessment.

The *War Diary* for the next three days of the Battle said simply:

> Aug 1 – Heavy rain. Training impossible. Reconnaissance to KITCHENER line captured previous day.
> Aug 2 – Heavy rain. Training impossible.
> Aug 3 – Heavy rain. Training impossible. 2Lts HE PENNINGTON and JC HEMMING joined the Bn for duty...

What must it have been like for those engaged at the Front and in the advance?

The 3rd Battle of Ypres – (Passchendaele), July–November 1917

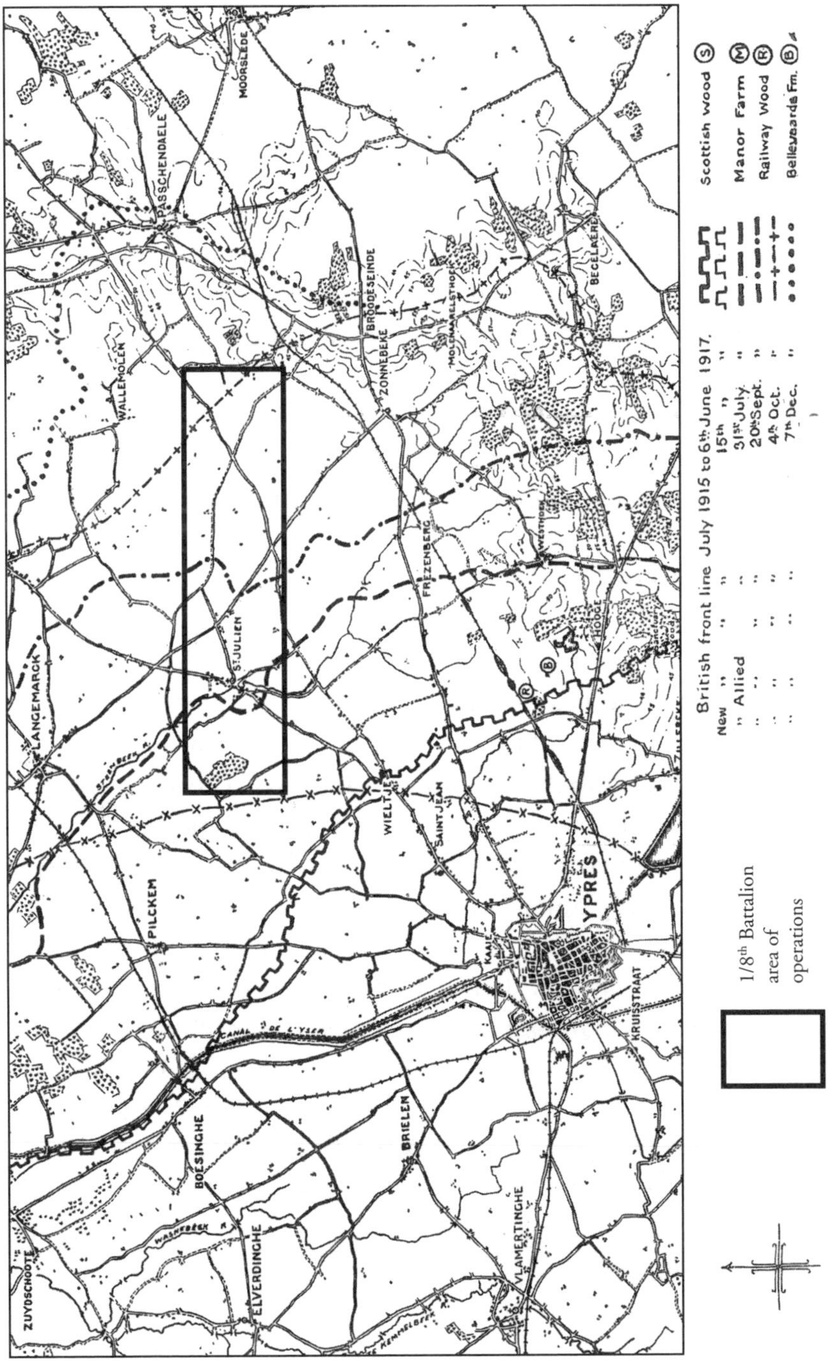

To give an idea of the intensity of the battle on that first day, 31st July, fourteen Victoria Crosses were awarded for acts of extraordinary heroism, often combined with inspirational leadership – or in the case of Captain Noel Chavasse VC, heroism over that and the next two days which earned him a Bar to his VC, the second of three ever to be awarded. A review of these fourteen awards provides a fascinating set of different examples of the ranks and deeds of their recipients. The awards were mostly gazetted on 6th September. Only eight of the recipients would have known of them, two being 'killed in action' and three 'dying of their wounds' the following day and one, a 40-year-old doctor, Captain Harold Ackroyd, killed on 11th August while tending to more of the wounded out in No Man's Land. Beyond Chavasse and Ackroyd who were captains in the Royal Army Medical Corps but attached to individual infantry battalions, there were four other officers to win VCs that day and eight Other Ranks. The officers included the first general to be awarded a VC in the War – Brigadier-General Clifford Coffin, commander of 25th Brigade, who, 'aware of the parlous state of the troops on the [Westhoek] ridge and with no thought for his own safety, walked in the open from shell hole to shell hole to encourage his men and organise defensive measures. He even carried up ammunition'. The next senior officer was the splendidly named Lt Colonel Bertram Best-Dunkley who, at Spree Farm (just south of St Julien and a half mile from Springfield), 'moved to rally his men and was seen to rush forward, cane in hand, to take command of the leading company, which had lost all its officers. The attack took several strongpoints including Spree Farm … in the evening he was mortally wounded … retaking the farm'. One of the notable awards to the Other Ranks was to New Zealander Corporal Leslie Andrew, who led his platoon twice on flanking attacks against the machine-gun posts holding up his company. Cpl Andrew was to win a DSO in Libya in the Second World War and retired as a brigadier in 1952. The actions of Sergeant Robert Bye of 1st Bn, the Welsh Guards, give an indication that once the orders are given and the advance started, it was, as with Cpl Andrew, down to the leaders at platoon, or even section, level to make the real difference:

> As the barrage moved on, 1st Welsh Gds were stopped by deadly fire from the ruined wood [Wood 15]. Sgt Bye, with his comrades pinned down, inched his way from shell hole to shell hole until able to put the garrison out of action with bombs. The advance continued, until again stopped, this time from the fire from several pillboxes in Wood 16 on the left. Some men on the right reached the Black Line [the objective] while others on the left, led by Sgt Bye, dealt with the boxes … Sgt Bye had accounted for 70 Germans dead, wounded or captured.

There were no awards for rescuing the wounded, all were for actions similar to that of Lt Col Best-Dunkley and Sgt Bye; even that of Private Thomas Whitham of the Coldstream Guards who was 27 days into a 56-day sentence from a court martial for 'disobeying a lawful command'. The whole of the ensuing three and a half months of Passchendaele was fought like this with company, platoon and section commands helping to gain ground, pillbox by shell hole. A further 46 VCs were won before the battle came to an end on 10th November; eight of the men were killed in the action in which they gained their VC and two were killed before the end of the battle. What is more remarkable is that many lived very long lives, with ten still alive in 1970 and three in the 1980s. Sgt Edward Cooper VC, MM (Fr) lived to be 99, and the Canadian Major-General George Pearkes who had earned five different gallantry medals – the VC, DSO, MC, Croix de Guerre (Fr), and Legion of Merit (US) – died in 1984 aged 96. Like Captain Pawsey MC*, he was an old boy of Berkhamsted School. Any formal invitation to him in his later life would be addressed to: the Honourable Major-General George Pearkes VC, CC, CB, DSO, MC, CD, PC, OD – having also being Lieutenant Governor of British Columbia from 1960-68. The main feature is that only Pearkes and two commanding officers were above the rank of captain which, again, confirms the importance of the low-level commanders.

Those in the 1/8th Battalion must have known that they would be taking their turn at the Front in due course. Arguments can be made about foreseeing the rains in the forecast but delaying the start would have given the generals no easier answers, as the ground would remain soaked for three months. If you have walked these fields now, you can tell by all the ponds and dykes that clay abounds. Arguments are equally plentiful as to whether the whole offensive should have been aborted at any stage but the prize was very great and had the Russians continued their fight on the Germans' Eastern Front beyond the early spring of 1918, the story may have been very different. It was to be a slog through the Belgium mud taking farms or pillboxes, one at a time. By 20th September, a little more than 1,000 yards had been gained across the whole of the Front.

Their sister battalion, the 1/7th, were called first to action in a Divisional attack on a series of little forts. The strongest was Maison du Hibou and this was selected for C Company of the 1/7th after the failure of the 145th Brigade. It was to be under the cover of darkness and without artillery support. They lost their two leading officers and were held 100 yards short of the fort and went to ground. At 2.30 a.m., B Company was ordered to attack, aided by shellfire. They reached the building but a counter-attack saved the day for the Germans, and the surviving Worcesters retreated back. The following day, 17th August, was one of both sides remaining static. The 1/7th were relieved by the 1/8th in an operation described by the former as 'an extraordinarily good relief … taking into consideration the amount of hostile shelling'. The operation had cost the 1/7th two officers and 12 men killed, six officers and 118 wounded with 12 missing. A Lt HB Bate won an MC for his actions that day with the 1/7th Battalion but I cannot see that he was related to Captain Jack Bate of the 1/8th – his brother being William and ten years younger.

Approach towards Maison du Hibou

Corbett described Maison du Hibou (owl's cote) as lying on rising ground to the left of the direction of Kerselaare, 'towards which we were working'. The axis of advance was the road heading almost due north out of St Julien, the village on the main road at the crossing of the infamous Steenbeck River. The attacks of 16th August had captured St Julien and Hillock Farm, leaving Maison du Hibou to dominate the open and flat country, into which C Company had hidden amongst the shell holes some 150 yards from the fort. Corbett noted that 'each side was employing such a weight of artillery as had never been dreamt of before'. Thinking back to CSM Heydon being killed by a shell landing on hard ground some 70 yards away, Corbett observed that 'had the ground been hard both armies would have been annihilated'. But, as it was, 'the bulk of the shells plunged into the mud, throwing up enormous fountains of it, but not scattering much, so that men passed unscathed through barrages in which it seemed nothing would live'. An important observation when considering those who have argued that Passchendaele would have been won without the rain and, given the rain-soaked ground, others believing the attacks should have been aborted long before November.

Steenbeck River – without the mud

Allied Advance in front of St Julien
15th–27th August 1917

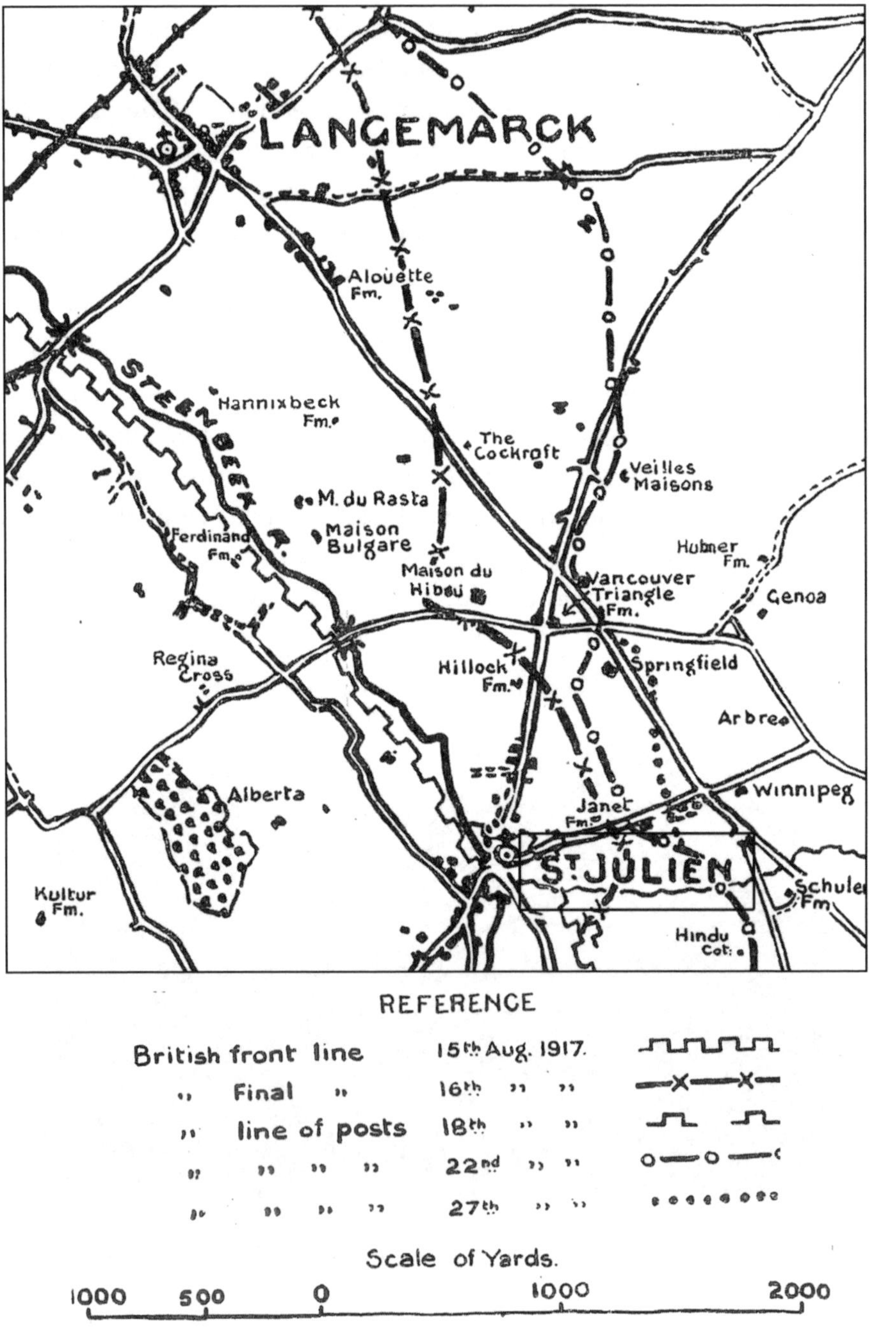

Maison du Hibou, despite being under attack for three days, was still in German hands. Shortly after midnight, in the early hours of 19th August, Captain SH Wilkes MC brought up B Company to join C and D Companies between the Steenbeck and the fort. It was almost daylight when D Company reached their deployment positions, having already taken casualties from German artillery at the river crossing points. The Battalion was to go into action with tanks in close support for the first time. Tanks had, until that time, made little serious impression on the battlefield. Under the intense British barrage launched as dawn broke, six tanks (from G Battalion Tank Corps) crossed the Steenbeck at the bridge in St Julien, passing Hillock Farm and the gun-pits at Triangle Farm before circling behind Maison du Hibou. The artillery laid smoke to shield their advance. There was no immediate coordination between the tank commanders and the company commanders on the ground. Each would have known what the other intended to do and no more. Corbett recorded that 'a tank rolled up through the mire to assist, opening heavy fire on the blockhouse, and (crucially) keeping its machine gun busy'. He went on to describe the infantry attack by B Company:

> Captain S Wilkes attacked at the head of B Company [at 6.30 a.m.] … [which] came up by sections, outflanked and exterminated the snipers, carried the house, killing over 40 men and taking 10 prisoners – at a total loss of 12 killed and wounded! When we got back to the camps it was pleasant to see in them great diagrams of this attack posted up for instructional purposes.

It is most likely that it was the use of tanks as gun platforms rather than Wilkes' tactics of launching the attack in section (8 men and an NCO) strength that would have been the new doctrine for taking out blockhouses. Still, Wilkes' leadership and gallantry were recognised with the award of a Bar to his MC. It is not clear if the losses were really as small as Carr recorded, but he noted in his description of the next action (27th August) that D Company were very weak due to shellfire on 17th and 18th when the *History* recorded 5 deaths on 17th and 1 on the 18th. It gives 8 more, including 2 dying of wounds, on the 19th, and another dying of wounds on the 20th. The *CWGC* website rarely records the company of the dead – of the 19 who died between 17th and 20th, only two are shown. Pte John Bayliss of B Coy died on the 19th – so in Wilkes' attack – and Pte James West of D Coy died on the same day – so of shellfire.

The *History* recorded casualties for the three days – 17th to 19th August – being 2 officers (2Lts J Guilding (on the 18th) and WM Jotcham in the barrage crossing the Steenbeck before the attack) and 19 Other Ranks killed, together with 47 NCOs and soldiers wounded. However, Lt Col Carr recorded that just 2Lt Jotcham was killed and 3 men wounded; but he had reason, as commanding officer, to show very modest losses. He concluded his report as:

> The garrison of Maison de Hibou were bombed out and shot as they emerged by No 5 Platoon under 2Lt Pennington. No 6 Platoon captured the machine gun position, killing the garrison, and capturing the Gun, and then pushed on to Triangle Farm (on the road junction); finding this a mass of mines the platoon pushed across the main road, and dug in under fire. No 7 Platoon passed through No 5 and 6, and, after taking another position and killing the garrison, dug in at the Cross Roads, forming a defensive flank on the left, to await the advance of units of the 11th Division. The position was consolidated and held for 48 hours, until the Battalion was relieved by the 1/7th Worcestershire Regiment.

Carr wrote of a surgical operation, capturing multiple targets, with only three men wounded (as 2Lt Jotcham was killed before the attack started). There is no doubt that the presence of tanks would have helped, but German machine guns were rarely captured without loss. The Roll to which Carr's report is attached, records the death on 19th August of Cpl F Shorthouse and ten privates, with Pte P Evans dying the following day of his wounds.

The three subalterns mentioned – 2Lts Jotcham, Guilding and Pennington – merit no record in the *History* beyond the deaths of the first two. They had, presumably, not been in the Battalion for long. Guilding's body was not recovered as his name is on one of the panels at the Tyne Cot Cemetery which looks back eastwards over this area of the battlefield. Walter Jotcham was 28 when he died and lies with 1,453 others in the New Irish Farm Cemetery. He was an accountant in Cheltenham before the War. There were five Jotchams killed in the First World War. Walter's brother Cyril died in June 1918 as a private in the 1/1st Royal Gloucestershire Hussars, both the children of Arthur and Eliza of Wotton-under-Edge. Two other Jotcham brothers were the sons of Frederick and Elizabeth of Haw Street, Wootton-under-Edge. Herbert, a private in the 1/2nd (North Midlands) Field Ambulance, was killed on 21st October 1917 aged 29, and Fred, a 2nd Lieutenant with the 4th Special Company, Royal Engineers, was killed on 27th September 1918, aged 25. The fifth Jotcham, William, was a LCpl in the 12th Battalion of the East Surrey Regiment when, aged 26, he was killed on 25th March 1918. His father also lived on Haw Street. The 1901 Census shows that Frederick and Elizabeth lived in 70 Gloster Street, Wootton-under-Edge with six children, the eldest three sons of which were Herbert, William and Fred – all of whom laid down their lives for their country. These five must all have been cousins, lost in a 13-month period. The handsome War Memorial in the centre of Wootton-under-Edge has 114 names from the three services. As all such memorials are listed alphabetically, with no precedence for service, regiment or rank, the cousins are listed one below the other on the northern aspect. On the west-facing side is what appear to be another group of five cousins, the Cornocks, two of whom served in the Royal Navy – a terrible loss for any family to sustain. Three were brothers, Archibald (aged 26), Sidney (32) and Ralph (44), whose mother, Ruth, was already widowed so bore these losses alone.

Since that research, I was reading Sarah Wearne's wonderful *Epitaphs of the Great War* – there are three editions of 100 epitaphs each. In that for Passchendaele, it features the inscription on Walter Jotcham's grave:

I Have Fought The Good Fight
I Have Finished My Course
I Have Kept The Faith

These chosen words are from the Second Epistle of Paul the Apostle to Timothy. Sarah, too, notes the Jotcham family sacrifices but also that Walter had left England in June 1914 to become a fruit-grower in Washington State in the western United States. He quickly enlisted in the Canadian Expeditionary Force and served in France from August 1915 to July 1916 before returning to England for a commissioning course. He joined the Battalion in the spring of 1917. Buried near to Jotcham in the New Irish Cemetery on the north side of Ypres is an Australian infantry corporal. Corporal Goodall's grave has one of the few controversial inscriptions and it was subject to review by the Imperial War Graves Commission. The initial application for 'He died the just for the unjust' was rejected but the following was allowed after another review:

I Am Here As The Result Of Uncivilised Nations

This was requested and paid for by his mother, Mrs C Goodall of Brisbane, Australia. His body was not recovered until April 1921 and was identified by his chevrons (corporal's stripes of rank) and his identity disc. The Commission reserved the right to censor inscriptions which it considered unsuitable or inflammatory, either to Germany or to Britain.

The Battalion was to be in action again very shortly, as were all other battalions on the Ypres Front. Lt Bomford had returned from his course 'in time for the second trip'. His memory was that 'we marched up a bit north of Ypres over endless duckboards. Rain and shelling had made the ground a quagmire, useless for tanks. The line was just rifle pits and very wet'. Clearly, he had not seen the instructional briefing boards of the attack on Maison du Hibou. Bomford's 'second trip' is described by Lt Col Carr under the heading:

Operation on August 27th 1917
Attack by Battalion on portion of German Langemarck-Gheluvelt Line
Capture of Springfield Farm.

Maison du Hibou and Springfield, September–October 1917

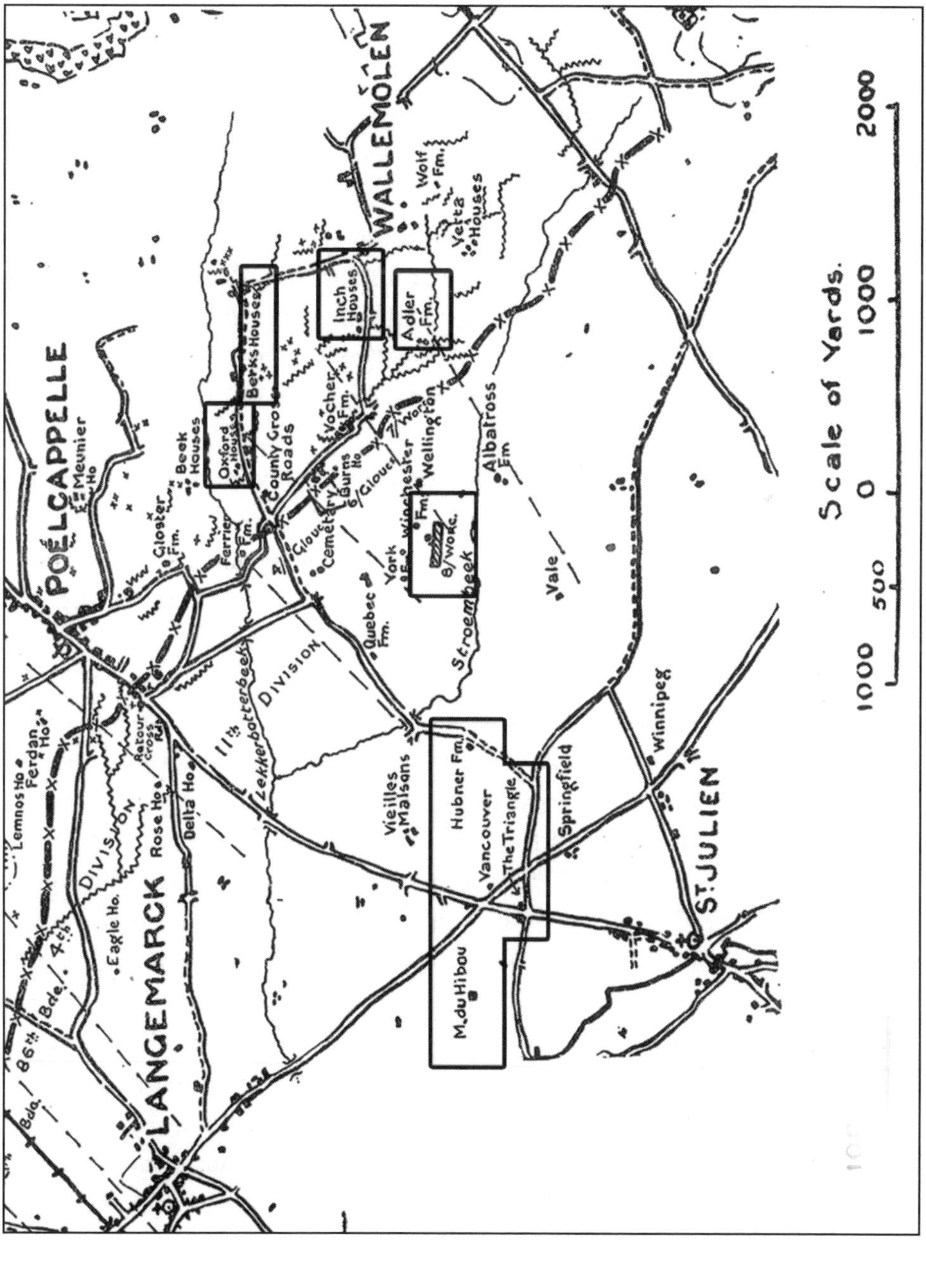

This was part of a general attack by the 2nd and 5th Armies. Springfield Farm was just some 200 yards from the crossroads position which they had established after capturing Maison du Hibou. These farms and houses were all rebuilt, as a visit to this area of the Front today shows. Bomford's subsequent memories provide a stark resume of the operation:

> D and A companies were detailed to attack a pill box about a mile across the mud and shell holes. Sanger [Bomford's runner] and I did a daylight reconnaissance. A German aeroplane repeatedly machine-gunned us. No cover, most unpleasant. The attack was in daylight. We soon lost the barrage because of [our] slow progress in the mud but we got near the pillbox and were badly shelled and shot up. It was a hopeless attack. After dark I took the remnants back to our line. I was the only surviving officer of the two Companies.

Corbett started his report on the operation in a very different tone:

> Springfield was an equally brilliant affair [as Maison du Hibou]. It was a tall upstanding farmhouse on the right, near Kerselaare [the crossroads] and the place which had once been St Julien.

However, he finished: 'Progress was slow and terribly costly … of all our battle experiences this was infinitely the grimmest and most dreadful' – thus, worse even than Gillemont Farm that April.

So, how did the commanding officer remember the action? He explained that his and the 1/7th Bn headquarters were co-located in the German bunker at Maison du Hibou but that it was cramped and the door opened towards the enemy – as would be expected as it had been a German stronghold a week before. As in previous actions, Carr's own role seemed to have been limited to giving the initial orders, although this time he is gracious enough to acknowledge that 'the Capture of Springfield Farm was a brilliant operation, requiring great power of leadership on the part of subordinate Commanders, and determination on the part of the men. Both qualities were conspicuously displayed'. The company commanders this day were: A – Captain BH

Tullidge; B – Lt SH Wilkes MC*; C – Captain CR Pawsey MC*; and D – Captain HR Ryan-Bell. We know Pawsey and Wilkes from previous actions and gallant leadership. The other two have no previous mention in the *History.* This was to become increasingly the case as the rotation of officers continued apace, in the main due to injuries and death.

All four of the Worcestershire Regiment's Territorial Battalions (1/7th, 2/7th, 1/8th, 2/8th) were involved in this action – the only such time. This assault on the Springfield Farm area was part of a coordinated attack across miles of the Front. Commanders are reliant on each battalion and brigade achieving their given objectives broadly at the time allotted. If one fell behind, it left German 'blockhouses' which could shoot into the flanks of those whose advances were still on schedule. This was very much the case on the morning of 27th August for the 1/8th Battalion – as it had been in their assault on Gillemont Farm some four months before. In almost all cases, the success of these assaults was dependent on the leadership of those at the very front – in the 1/8th's case, the company commanders because the commanding officer and his headquarters team were sheltered and reliant on runners to bring back information. Lt Col Carr was not alone in this regard. The commanding officers of the 2/8th (in 183rd Brigade) some 500 yards to their south (right), and of the 1/7th immediately to their left are not recorded as having taken any physical part in the battle. The 2/8th lost three officers that day, all Second Lieutenants, and the three company commanders were all wounded. Captain Lance Evers won a very good MC that day. The *History* recorded him as being:

> … conspicuous by his contempt for danger. Although wounded early in the attack he continued to lead his men onward, cheering and encouraging them throughout the day; but his soldiers were shot down all around him … 138 other ranks were killed or wounded. All the officers of A Company were killed or wounded. B Company came out of action with one subaltern and one sergeant … it was clear that success was impossible against the machine-guns of Aisne Farm.

There was no record of Lt Col Lionel Bilton (2/8th) being near the Front, likewise the new commanding officer of the 1/7th, Lt Col Francis Tomkinson. This may, of course, have been at the instruction of their brigade commanders. The 1/7th had one officer killed that day, 21-year-old Captain GR Wallace MC, and the account of his death helps to explain the sort of fighting required when advancing across the mud and shell holes:

> On the right flank … Captain GR Wallace led A Company forward most gallantly. The attack had passed the defences of Vancouver Farm [now the site of the Canadian Memorial] and was nearing a concrete fort beyond it when two German snipers rose from a shell hole close at hand. They shot Captain Wallace and a corporal who rushed to his assistance. Sergeant Marchant, endeavouring to assist the officer was wounded, but at the same moment Sergeant Cooper succeeded in shooting both the Germans.

Immediately to the right of the 1/7th, who did not retain Vancouver Farm that day, was the 1/8th Battalion. We need to revert to Lt Col Carr's post-War report to best understand what happened:

> The 1/7th and 1/8th Battalions the Worcestershire Regiment were detailed by the 144th Infantry Brigade to attack the hostile positions East of the St Julien-Poelcapelle Road, the final objective being Genoa Farm [an overall distance of about 1000 yards] … the weather, which was fine, broke as the Battalion moved off after dark from [Reigensberg] Camp, and heavy rain continued throughout the operation.
>
> Camouflaged trenches had been dug between the Steenbeck [river] and the St Julien-Poelcapelle Road in which the Battalion was to wait until Zero Hour, 1.55 p.m. These trenches were found 18 inches deep in mud and water, and, being very narrow, were most uncomfortable, but in spite of a heavy barrage, all units of the Battalion successfully occupied their allotted position, and remained hidden during the long period of waiting.

This is just as the images of World War One portray – the officer ready to be first over the top with the company sergeant major at the back to encourage and help every man to head off into the assault when the moment came and the whistles blew.

> Headquarters of both 1/7th and 1/8th were established in the converted Farmhouse at Maison de Hibou, captured by B Company on August 17th. This was very cramped, and, having its entrance on the exposed side, gave little cover, and several casualties occurred through shells bursting in the doorway.
>
> The Battalion was disposed as:
>
> Assaulting Companies: A on the right under Captain Tullidge [including Lt Bomford as commander of No 2 Platoon]; C on the left under Captain Pawsey MC*.
>
> In Reserve: D under Captain Ryan-Bell; B on the left [about Maison du Hibou] under Lieut. Wilkes MC*. D Company was very weak, having suffered severely from shell fire on August 17/18.
>
> Objectives: 1. German Position north of main road; 2. Genoa Farm. – with 1/7th Bn to our right and 143rd Brigade [all battalions from Royal Warwickshire Regiment]. The strong hostile position of Springfield farm on our right was one of the objectives of 143rd Brigade.
>
> At Zero Hour a terrific barrage was put down by our guns along the whole front, and was promptly replied to three minutes later by a hostile barrage, falling luckily behind our position which was evidently unknown to the enemy.
>
> In spite of the long hours of waiting and their cramped position and heavy loads, the assaulting companies formed up promptly and commenced their advance. The going was terrible, men could only move with difficulty, and it was impossible to keep up with the barrage which was too thin in places.

This comment about 'heavy loads' is disappointing. No lessons from the Somme seem to have been learnt. The generals by then must have been aware of the effectiveness of the German 'Sturmtruppen' (stormtroopers) who carried only spare ammunition and bombs (grenades). Given the known difficulties of the ground and the short distances of advance intended, it was surprising that the assaulting troops of the 1/8th and others were not similarly lightly equipped.

> Many hostile snipers posted in shell holes continued to be aggressive and the failure of the attack on Springfield by the Brigade on our right exposed A Company to heavy enfilade fire. Captain Tullidge and 2Lt RN Horsley were killed and 2Lt Myhill, the CSM and one Sergeant were wounded.

Confirming Bomford's memory that he was the only officer unscathed and thus in command that evening.

Reading of Captain Wallace's death and with the knowledge that officers went into the advance carrying only their pistols, it is easy to understand the snipers having such success in singling out the officers.

> With Springfield in hostile hands any further progress was impossible, and A Company's advance was held up. Meanwhile C Company [Captain Pawsey MC], in spite of all difficulties, pushed on and occupied the enemy's front line of organised shell holes, where they killed a number of the enemy. After advancing a further 200 yards, Captain Pawsey found himself under a very heavy and effective fire from the enemy's main position, while the 1/7th on the right and A Company on the left were checked. Captain Pawsey and C Company were, therefore, compelled to halt and hold the ground.
>
> An attempt made by 12 Platoon to attack a concrete strong point in advance of C Company was frustrated owing to one of our tanks opening fire, but a party of Germans who attempted to reinforce the garrison were wiped out by rifle and hand grenade fire.
>
> Meanwhile, measures were being taken to deal with Springfield. B Company, less one platoon, moved up in support of A Company, one platoon forming a defensive flank to our right and two platoons taking up a position to the West of Springfield and keeping it under heavy fire. Orders were sent from Battalion Headquarters to D Company to move up and capture Springfield, as no sign of an attack upon that position by the Brigade on our right could be detected.

Captain Ryan-Bell had, however, correctly appreciated the situation and had ordered two platoons under Lt JR Willis to attack the position. The attack was pressed home most gallantly in spite of the enemy's fire and the terrible going. Several advanced positions were taken and six prisoners captured, but when the leading wave arrived within 60 yards of the main position our casualties were so heavy that Captain Ryan-Bell decided to withdraw and reorganise prior to a fresh attack.

Having reorganised his Company and obtained help from B Company, Captain Ryan-Bell launched a fresh attack, which he led personally, and though himself mortally wounded 10 yards from Springfield, the position was captured, a large number of the garrison killed, one officer, one sergeant-major, 25 men and a Machine-Gun taken, and a position about 50 yards in advance was consolidated and held until the Battalion was relieved by the 145th Brigade the same night.

The map in the *History* shows that this attack by these three brigades captured a slice of the mud some 800 yards long to a depth of 300 yards. It merely straightened the front line in that section. The *History* recorded that the four Worcestershire battalions involved lost about a third of their fighting strength that day:

1/7th – 1 officer killed and 5 wounded, 99 Other Ranks killed or wounded;
1/8th – 4 officers killed and 3 wounded, 47 Other Ranks killed and 60 wounded;
2/8th – 3 officers killed and 5 wounded, 138 Other Ranks killed or wounded;
2/7th (in reserve but subject to shelling) – 'lost' 1 officer and 20 Other Ranks.

The three battalions in the assault had half the officers of the 'rifle' companies killed or wounded. To give an example of what being wounded meant to the officer and to the battalion, Captain Lance Evers was wounded in the abdomen by shrapnel from our own guns and a bullet in the thigh from the Germans. It took three men to lift him from the battlefield, 'Holliday [presumably a young officer], Corporal Coleman and one other soldier'. He did not leave England again to come to the Front until the following 23rd June, in time for him to win a Bar to his MC at the Passage of the Lys on 3rd September and be killed on 1st November. As such, his battalion was without one of their best and most experienced officers for ten months.

Lance Evers

Lt Col Carr concluded his report:

> Shortly after the news of this success reached Battalion Headquarters, an order was received [by] the Divisional Commander that Springfield must be captured at all costs. The Commanding Officer [Carr himself] had the satisfaction of replying that it was already in our hands. At dark the action died down. Both sides were glued to the ground, rifles and Machine-Guns alike were charged with mud. Orders were received … that the Oxs. and Bucks Light Infantry would relieve us during the night. Owing to the difficulty of communication, C Company (Pawsey) could not be relieved until the following night.

The capture of Springfield Farm was a brilliant operation, requiring great power of leadership on the part of the subordinate commanders and determination on the part of the men. Both qualities were conspicuously displayed.

Captain Ryan-Bell, had he lived, would have received a DSO for which he was recommended while still alive.

Hugh Ryan-Bell

This last sentence requires a little explanation. Firstly, the only medal which could be awarded posthumously at the time was the Victoria Cross. Secondly, it says that Captain Hugh Ryan-Bell was mortally wounded. His death is recorded as being two days later, on 29th August. He was 30 years old and married to Maude, living in Erdington in Birmingham. He is buried in the Dozinghem Military Cemetery with 3,308 others in the wooded area a mile or so to the north of Poperighe – the main hospital base for the Ypres battlefront. His mother was sent a notice by Gerard M Davidson CF, 4 CCS, BEF on a pre-print format with a black cross at the top:

30. viii. 17

My Dear Mrs Bell

It is with profound regret that I, the Church of England padre attached to No. 4 Casualty Clearing Station write to tell you of the death of your gallant son, 2/Lieut hr ryan bell, 1/8 worcesters at 8pm last night.

I officiated at his funeral this morning. The Place of Burial and the particulars of Grave may be obtained from the Graves Commissioners, The Base, B.E.F.

I am indeed sorry that I give you no particulars as to how he met his death, for I possess no further information that I can give you.

A man cannot do a nobler, or a more heroic, deed than to die fighting for his King and Country, and in the Cause of Honour, Freedom and all Christianity stands for.

There is a gap before the signature block into which Captain Davidson added in his own hand:

He received a shell wound in his right buttock & a fractured femur. All that skill, care, attention can do was done for him by our nurses & doctors who assurance that he was too ill to feel much pain. He sent no message but then these very severely wounded men hardly ever do.

He was admitted into this hospital on 28th august.

Yours truly

Gerard M Davidson, C.F.

4, C.C.S., B.E.F.

This letter remains with his family – they knew him as Jack. He was the only Ryan-Bell killed in the War. The 'recommended while still alive' shows how quickly the process of writing Battle Reports and making recommendations for gallantry awards was done and passed up the chain of command, in their case to the commander of 144th Brigade. He was buried as Lieutenant Hugh Ryan-Bell with the inscription UNTIL THE DAY BREAKS AND THE SHADOWS FLEE AWAY chosen by his wife, Maude Marie Chapman, whom he married on 18th

November 1916 when home on leave. He had been a pupil at King Edward's School in Birmingham, alma mater of the Old Gent and of Captain T Stinton. At the outbreak of the War he had enlisted with the 'Birmingham Pals' Battalion – the 14th Bn, The Royal Warwickshire Regiment – as a private. He was commissioned in August 1915 but, as was the custom, he was posted to another regiment and reported for duty with the 1/8th Battalion of The Worcestershire on 5th May 1916.

The casualties in that action were on the scale of Gillemont Farm with two company commanders, Captain BH Tullidge and Lt HR Ryan-Bell, and two platoon commanders, 2Lts Jesse Hemming and Ralph Horsley, killed with another company commander, Lt SH Wilkes, and two subalterns wounded, 2Lts J Myhill and J Clarke. There were 46 Other Ranks killed of which five were sergeants (one being Sgt John Sergeant) and five were corporals – so a high proportion of leaders. Being an English county battalion, it is perhaps not surprising that the Christian names of these 46 men are nearly all traditional, with five Ernests; four Harrys, Williams, Alberts and Fredericks; three Charleses and Georges; two Arthurs, Jameses, Thomases and Sidneys; and one each of Walter, Edwin, Leonard, Stanley, Frank, Ronald, John, Lawrence, Benjamin and Reginald. Hyman Welt was the sole exotic.

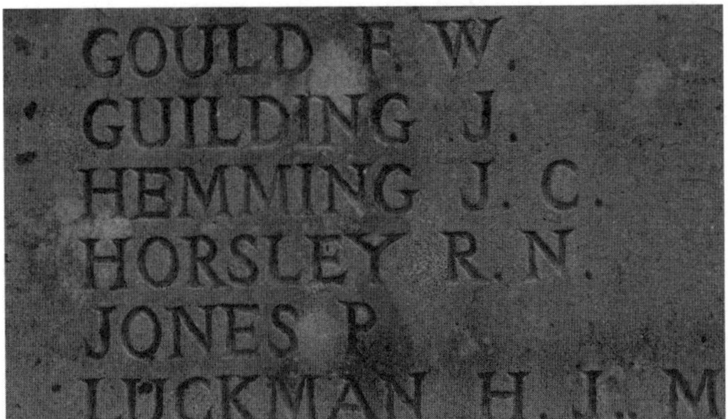

The Battalion would have known that they would be back at the Front before long, attacking across the Passchendaele mud shell hole by shell hole. Kathy Gee's second poem fits well with this narrative, if premature as this is now October, not yet Christmas:

Between The Lines

I'm not the man you think that you remember,
not the son you waved away to war.
I'm just a cog in somebody's machine –
a faceless part, a nameless number,
nothing more.
I touch your letter in my pocket,
search for words to tell you how it is.
You write that you are doing fine
and hope that I'm the same.
So, let us talk of hope:

I hope that I will be alive tomorrow night.
I hope that their bombardment will fall short,
that ours will cut the wire before we charge.
I hope for one more mug of hot sweet tea,
for dug outs dry enough to sleep in,
friends that live as long as I do.
Hope is safety in a shell hole,
someone else's helmet
when I've lost mine in the mud;
it's sheltering behind an old pal's body
as the shrapnel falls like hail.
Hope is getting up and moving forward,
ever forward. If I fall, I hope to hear
the sound of stretcher bearers
calling to the living, hope to stumble back
behind the line and fight another day.

We've got a night of nothingness ahead.
It could be worse. I think of home,
of my sweet Jeannie, sleeping like a dove
beneath this Christmas moon. And listen,
I can hear the Hun. They're singing carols.
Will it ever end?

Kathy Gee, *Suite for the Fallen Soldier*, 2016

BACK IN THE MUD NEAR THE OWL HOUSE

The battles of Passchendaele were a long way from complete. The names of Maison du Hibou and Springfield were to appear again on a number of occasions in the *War Diary* as the Battalion continued to take its place in the front-line trenches. The Battalion was sent back to School Camp near St Jan-ter-Biezen after the Springfield action. They needed officer reinforcements. Two previous adjutants were immediately available: Captain KM Mylne and Lt HGC Carter MC, both of whom had crossed with the Battalion back in March 1915. Also reporting for duty on 29th August for the first time were 2Lts CA Fletcher (B Coy), WG Bullock (C Coy), HG Higham (C Coy), A Aldrich and WS Gundry, to help replace the six officers killed over the previous two weeks, with 2Lt AR Watson transferring from the 2/7th Battalion. The *War Diary* gives one word for the work of the Battalion the following day – 'Reorganisation' – and for the 31st, 'Physical training, etc.' Training at a company level continued until after the church parade on Sunday 16th September. On the 8th, there was a Brigade parade at which the Divisional Commander, Major General Sir Robert Fanshawe KCB, DSO took the salute and at which all officers, warrant officers, non-commissioned officers and eight men per company were addressed and watched the General present the 1/7th with the Fanshawe Cup for winning the Divisional Football competition back in July. Fanshawe had been their Divisional Commander since June 1915.

The *War Diary* at this time was being signed off by JP Bate as 'Major Commanding'. It recorded on 20th September that Lt Col HA Carr DSO relinquished command to take over the 7th Bn, the Manchester Regiment and that their commanding officer, Lt Col AE Cronshaw TD, aged 44, would assume command of the 1/8th. This arrangement lasted for three weeks until Major HT Clarke returned for duty. The following day, the 13th, the *Diary* recorded: 'Major HT Clarke assumed command of the Bn. Lt Col AE Cronshaw TD having proceeded on leave'. It is not clear if this was always the plan or if the Brigade Commander, Brigadier HR Done DSO*, made the decision. The Battalion had to take part in a Brigade exercise the day after Cronshaw assumed command 'according to 48th Div. Scheme' which would have been a challenging start. This position is confused by a *War Diary* entry of 12th October: 'Lt Col AE Cronshaw TD look over command of the Bn. from Major JP Bate MC who had commanded the Bn. through operations'. Then, the following day the entry reads: 'Major HT Clarke assumed command of the Bn., Lt Col AE Cronshaw having proceeded on leave'. Interestingly, a narrative for the sale in 2001 of Cronshaw's medals by his family indicated that he was 'suffering from the effects of gas, the stress of command and the tribulations of the unsuccessful programme to "exchange" battalion COs within front-line regiments – in Cronshaw's case with the 1/8th Worcestershire Regiment – he was evacuated home in January 1918. Not, perhaps, surprisingly, given the strain of constant active employ [including the Boer War and Gallipoli] (and command) over a period safely in excess of two years, the Medics, quickly ruled that Colonel Arthur Cronshaw was "only fit for home service", so ending a remarkable operational career'. He was awarded a DSO in the New Year's Honours on 1st January 1918 for his service at Ypres. He died on 14th October 1924 aged 50 and was buried at Burnham-on-Crouch with a headstone which details his full military service but makes no mention of his wife, whom he had married in the spring of 1914.

Corbett reflected on the change of command as:

> While in Recques we lost Lieut. Colonel Carr, transferring to a battalion which required a master hand. After a brief interregnum Major HT Clarke succeeded to command to our great advantage and content. (This was written with the hindsight of the successes of 1918).

These operations, which Major Bate commanded, began with a march from their camp at Recques (Hazebrouck) to Audruick, before proceeding by company on a train to Vlamertinghe HQ. The British front line on 8th October was just 2,000 yards to the front of Springfield, which the Battalion had captured on 27th August – the advance had averaged 50 yards over each of the subsequent 42 days.

The task of 144th Brigade on 9th October was not going to affect that average. Corbett started his paragraphs on this action by saying that 'a fine month had far advanced the line'. Given the above statistics, it shows the modest expectations of the troops after three years of war. The *History*, in its telling of the action, did not reflect well on the generals who sent the Brigade into the attack, later to be known as the Battle of Poelcappelle. On 7th October, the Battalion had a four-mile march to their dugouts on the canal bank to the north of Ypres. It was another day of pouring rain so they could not move up to the area of the attack for reconnaissance and rest. In the hours of darkness, the Battalion started their march in full equipment to their position as Brigade reserve at Springfield. Corbett described the move to the Front that night:

> We were getting close to the coveted [Gravenstafel] ridge, but the enemy seemed in as good form as ever. We lay in caves [dugouts] by the Canal and waited till the rain had restored the battlefield to its familiar state. Then, in a furious gale of wind, a torrent of rain, and unbelievable darkness we moved up.

This may be an exaggeration but if it felt like this to a CQMS, it would have certainly done so to a private soldier under the burden of equipment, ammunition, rifle and bayonet.

> We went without orders and without an objective, for no-one knew quite where the fighting-line was or what was doing there. The weather surpassed itself. Men were blown off the [wooden] causeway into shell-holes, and a small but gallant warrior was nearly drowned.

In front of them were, from left to right, the 1/6th Glosters, 1/4th Glosters and the 1/7th Worcesters. The 1/4th Glosters only completed their trek to the Front as the barrage started to signify the attack was starting. The *History* recorded the now well-known problem of 'the heavily-equipped troops sink[ing] to their waists and to their armpits in the mud. Many such unfortunates were overlooked and were left to struggle helplessly in rain and darkness under the enemy's fire'. They all 'had to advance at once as best they could, having been more than fourteen hours under arms' – i.e. fully equipped and on the move. Did the generals really believe that these men could give a good account of themselves in such circumstances?

Herbert Benjamin

Two companies of 1/7th Battalion, 'after a prolonged struggle' captured their first objective, Adler Farm, killing 50 and capturing 70, together with nine machine guns. Their other two companies then moved forward to attack Inch Farm and Wallemolen but their attack was defied, German 'machine-guns swept away everything to their front'. As the attack started, the 1/8th Battalion, under Major Bate, moved forward 1,500 yards to Winchester Farm, so just 500 yards from the front line. The enemy artillery targeted the stream to their rear, the Stroembeek, killing one and wounding 20 of B Company, in reserve. Already by 7.50am, the 1/4th Glosters' attack on the right had ground to a halt. Major Bate sent D Company to support them, but in the maze of shell holes they could not find the Gloucesters'

HQ. Attempts at section-level infiltration of the enemy failed. At 11.30 a.m., the 1/7th Worcesters on the right needed support and B Company went to aid their advance but with the enemy fire 'unsubdued' and their own barrage close in front, they too could make no progress. A Company was sent forward to help D Company's attack on Oxford Farm on the left for an attack at 5 p.m. behind a dedicated artillery barrage. German machine guns from blockhouses to the Front and from shell holes on both flanks killed one of the two officers in D Company, Captain Herbert Benjamin, who was from London and who had joined the Battalion back in July 1915, and wounded the other, the recently arrived 2Lt HG Higham. Corbett described Benjamin's death as being 'first wounded, then killed in his stretcher when close to the safety of Alberta [Farm]'.

The *War Diary*, unusually, recorded only the orders for the relief at the end of that day as an appendix and provided no details as to the actions or outcome of the day. Bomford, who never wrote in letters about the actions in which he participated, said only:

> I've lost another Platoon Sgt. He got a bit of shell in the face but I think he will be all right. He was a nice chap, a dentist called [Walter Charles] Tolley [aged 38, who was to be discharged from the Army in March 1918 due to this wound], the men used to call him Father Tolley [He died in 1972 aged 92]. I've also lost my other Sgt, Sgt Fitzer. I think I've mentioned him to you. He was my servant all the first time I was out. Then he went to my platoon, took a stripe [Lance Corporal] and rose to be a Sgt. He was an awful nice chap and a very good NCO and he's missing poor chap. I feel very cut up about him, he's been with me so long. I've just been writing to his people, they work for cousin Frank. A month ago [27th August] I had to write to tell them of the death in action of his brother and in this letter, besides him missing, there is another brother wounded. At the last moment I took another platoon [in A Company] so I wasn't close to him.

Sgt George William Fitzer was never found and presumed killed that day, 9th October. He is commemorated on the walls of the Tyne

Cot Cemetery – the same wall panel as his brother Lance Corporal Arthur Fitzer, who was killed in the Springfield action on 27th August. The third brother survived the War. Being named on a memorial panel does not necessarily mean that their bodies were not found. If a body was found, there may have been no way to identify it. Such bodies lie in front of a headstone inscribed with 'A SOLDIER OF THE GREAT WAR, KNOWN ONLY UNTO GOD' or, if regimental badges on remaining pieces of uniform, it may say 'A SOLDIER OF THE WORCESTERSHIRE REGIMENT, KNOWN ONLY UNTO GOD', of which I found more than one in Tyne Cot. Captain Benjamin was buried in Poelcapelle Cemetery which is a 'concentration' cemetery with bodies gathered from eight smaller battlefield burial places. There are 7,479 bodies now in that cemetery but 6,230 of them could not be identified. This gives the scale of the destruction of these battles.

L.-Cpl. A. Fitzer.
Wor'ster. Killed.

The *History* continued the story of the Battalion's action that day, which was ultimately unsuccessful:

> D Company gained some 70 yards and had nearly reached a blockhouse when a fresh burst of machine-gun fire shot down most of the two leading platoons and forced the rest to cover in the surrounding shell-holes. The two surviving sergeants discussed the situation. They decided that the attack could succeed if only some covering fire could be brought to bear on the machine-guns which were enfilading their advance. A corporal and two runners volunteered to go

> back with this message, but they were shot down on their way back.
> The desperate situation was nearly retrieved by Private W[illiam] Chesterton who with a bomb in his hand crawled forward alone to attack the blockhouse. He got within a few yards of it and was on the point of throwing his bomb when he was seen and shot dead [he is with the Fitzers, remembered on the Tyne Cot wall]. His brave act so scared the enemy that they evacuated the blockhouse and ran back; but the flanking machine-gun stopped any attempt by D Company, and presently the Germans returned to their position. Then the enemy began to close round the remnants of D Company, working forward from shell-hole to shell-hole and eventually the two sergeants decided to fall back.
> Meanwhile A Company in support had drifted somewhat to the right and had come into line near the Cemetery. Messengers were sent out to right and left to gain touch with other troops; but no sure indication of the position could be obtained, the enemy's fire became heavier, and at last the commander of A Company decided to stop where he was and entrench … the remnants of A and D Company were ordered back to Springfield to act as Brigade reserve … hot cocoa and rum was brought up.

Major Bate, in his Battle Report, noted that in A Company 'only a few rifles would fire' – such were the muddy and wet conditions.

The Brigade lost (killed, wounded and missing) 800 of all ranks. The 1/8th had two officers killed – Captain Benjamin and 2Lt Cecil Beacham, also of D Company, who had been a private soldier in the Artists' Rifles before his commission. Beacham, like the Bomford brothers, had been at Wycliffe College. He was 34 and from Ipsley Mount, Redditch. Captain Benjamin is remembered in the *British Jewry Book of Honour 1914–1920.* A photograph on the IWM website shows a small, neat man with a full but trimmed moustache. He was born in Paddington and was a Metal Broker's Clerk in 1911, living in Paddington. He joined the Inns of Court OTC (Officer Training Corps) – 'The Devil's Own' – like so many who lived and worked in central London. Benjamin's army number was 2221 and he was commissioned on 23rd March 1915, reporting for duty at the 1/8th

Battalion on 16th July that year – the first, with Lt HG Newman and 2Lt HHG Bennett, also commissioned from the Inns of Court – to do so after the Battalion's move to France. Newman had graduated from Oxford in February 1914 with a BA First Class in Modern History.

The Inns of Court Officer Training Corps focused on the immediate demands of the Western Front rather than being based on the 'Sandhurst' model for their Gentleman Cadets, where time on the drill square and in the classroom was plentiful. Becoming 'hardy and self-reliant' was the focus, with the ability to march with full packs for eight to ten miles, undertake a military exercise, and then march back to camp. *The Inns of Court Officer Training Corps in The Great War* by Lt Col FHL Errington CB, VD – who commanded the Corps from March 1913 until September 1916 – provided a detailed history of The Devil's Own which numbered 213 men at Camp on Salisbury Plain on 2nd August 1914 but was to go on to provide full officer training for some 13,800 men, of whom between 11,000 and 12,000 received commissions in infantry battalions.

Errington's book lists every officer trained by the Inns of Court OTC with their commissioning date and regiment. Benjamin and Bennett can both be found on page 91 of this tome. Captain Alan Plaistowe, commissioned the same day as Bennett, and 2Lt Francis Potter – both killed at Gillemont Farm – were trained by The Devil's Own, as was 2Lt Ralph Horsley who was killed in the action at Springfield Farm at Passchendaele and 2Lt John Ibbs who died of shell wounds in March 1917. The Inns of Court OTC was one of the three sources of the Battalion's officers: those from the county of Worcestershire, who had generally enlisted before or at the outset of the War; those from the Inns of Court OTC and thus mainly working in the London area; and, in later years, those commissioned from the ranks of other battalions. The correspondence and diaries of those in the first category made little mention of those from the second and third categories. In the main, this is because those back at home in Worcestershire to whom the letters and for whom the diaries were written will not have known these men, nor their families.

Errington's work provided for every officer trained by the Inns of Court OTC the details of their counties of service, their awards gained and either a date of death or their permanent home address after the War. The other Battalion officers who came through the Inns of Court OTC were: TH Myhill from Saffron Waldon in Essex, who was to transfer to the Machine Gun Corps; CK Turner who hailed from Bournemouth; HJ Winter from Hampstead; JR Willis MC from Putney, who in 1918 transferred to the RAF; WR Baker from Bristol, who was to transfer to the Royal Flying Corps; RM Pittard MC from Cardiff; WOH Williams from Penarth in Glamorgan; and RJCW Hawtrey from central London. The only one who hailed from Worcestershire was John Taylor Hill, who lived at Cawney Hill House in Dudley; he was wounded and then sent to the Royal Sussex Regiment. There is no doubt that those officers who joined early, especially from southern England and London, will have had to work hard to impress the SNCOs and Other Ranks from Worcestershire, notably those with pre-War service.

Errington calculated that 11,485 men were commissioned from the Inns of Court OTC, of whom 35 died while serving in the Corps (most probably during training), and 2,147 were to be killed in action, died of wounds or of disease. Some 2,777 were wounded (1 five times, 6 four times, 50 three times, 366 twice). Between them, they earned 3 VCs, 88 DSOs and 1,248 MCs as well as almost every British and Foreign award available. In the Battalion's statistics were two who joined before they crossed to France – Plaistowe and Hawtrey – and eleven 'reported for duty' in France, of whom 4 were killed. Two MCs were won – by Lt James Willis and Lt Robert Pittard. The latter was announced as having retired from the Army and the 7th Battalion with the rank of Lieutenant on 28th November 1918 due to his wounds. He is not mentioned after Passchendaele in the *History* but one must assume that he returned to action but with the 7th Battalion, perhaps being wounded again.

Returning to Passchendaele, the *History* recorded 15 Other Ranks killed, 85 wounded and 9 missing in this action at Springfield Farm on 9th October. The Roll shows 24 as dying that day and over the next few days, 5 of their wounds. For those on these Tyne Cot panels, there is no detail as to age or parents. There was no room for family inscriptions so there was no need to find the next of kin. These narratives from

Corbett, Bomford and the *History* give a flavour of the extraordinary conditions in which young officers and their men were expected to operate. The adjutant, Lt E Gilbert, made a record of the day's actions – as Appendix A, the only occasion so far in the War when appendices were used – but it has not survived. His Appendix A1 was for the relief operation which followed and is clearly written. The October entry in the *War Diary* concluded with listing the six Other Ranks who were awarded MMs for their 'gallantry and devotion to duty' that day: Sgt Osborne JG, Pte Marchment EJ, Pte Styler HJ, Pte (A/Cpl) Wood H, Pte Weston AE, Pte Perry AW. Presumably Sgt Osborne was one of the two sergeants in the above narrative. The other must have been killed or, surely, he would have received recognition as well. Two sergeants died that day, Fitzer and Walters. We know from Bomford that Fitzer was in A Company so the other must have been Sgt Thomas Walters who had already earned a MM. He is with Fitzer, Chesterton and others at Tyne Cot. No officers received awards that day, perhaps a reflection of the lack of success but also of no officer taking control, though in the case of D Company, they were all dead or wounded.

1. A Company officers, 2/8th Battalion at Kandahar Barracks, Tidworth, May 1916.

2. The officers of 2/8th Battalion in Tidworth, May 1916.

3. Second Pl, A Company, 1/8th Bn in 1916. 2Lt LR Bomford is centre with Sgt E Wedgbury to his right and Sgt WE Edwards to his left.

4. Officers of B Company, 1/8th Battalion in Italy 1918 with the CO, Lt Col HT Clarke. Lt LR Bomford MC and Lt GL Watkinson in centre back row.

5. The Old Gent on horseback at Tidworth, May 1916.

6. Lance Evers looking very smart when training in England; 7. *Right*: washing at the Front.

8. The Battalion being trained in the fitting of early gas masks.

9. Battalion stretcher bearers at Hébuterne in 1916.

16. *Opposite: The Old Firm* newspaper: Christmas Edition 1917.

10–11. Battalion trenches at Ploegsteert, May 1915.

12–13. Trenches as inherited from the French Army at Hébuterne in 1915.

14. Captain Lionel Kerwood using a periscope in trenches at Ploegsteert, May 1915.

15. Alternative periscope design in use at the same time.

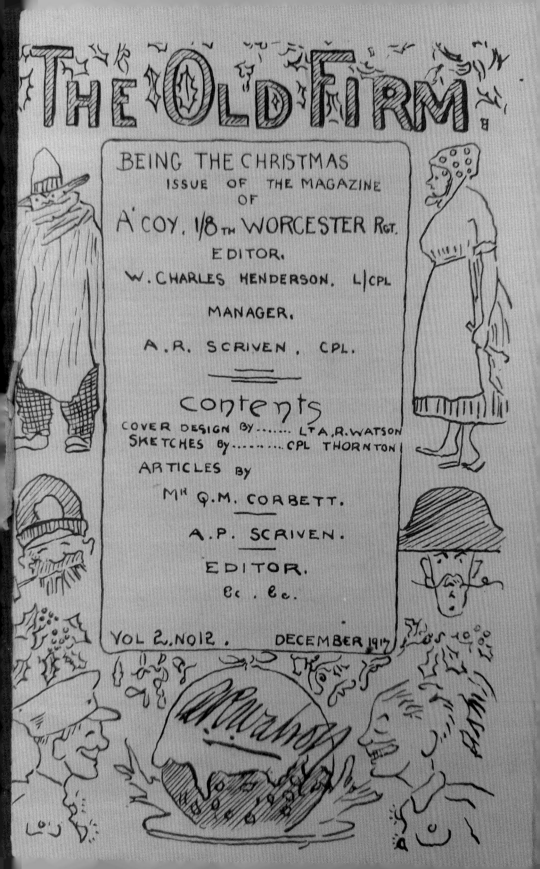

THE OLD FIRM

BEING THE CHRISTMAS
ISSUE OF THE MAGAZINE
OF
A COY. 1/8TH WORCESTER RGT.

EDITOR.
W. CHARLES HENDERSON. L/CPL

MANAGER.
A.R. SCRIVEN. CPL.

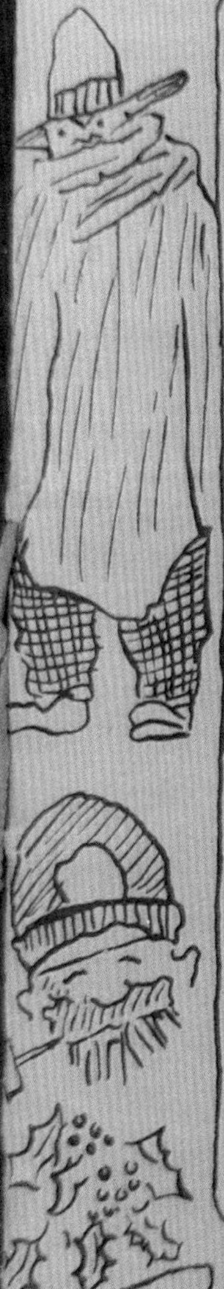

contents

VOL 2. NO 12. DECEMBER 1917

17. Soldiers in reserve and using local stream for company washing, 1916.

18. The devastation of the church at Hébuterne during the Battalion's eleven months in that area of the British trench line, 1915–16.

19. The Old Gent and his son, Scott Walford, when the latter was a Gentleman Cadet at Sandhurst in 1918.

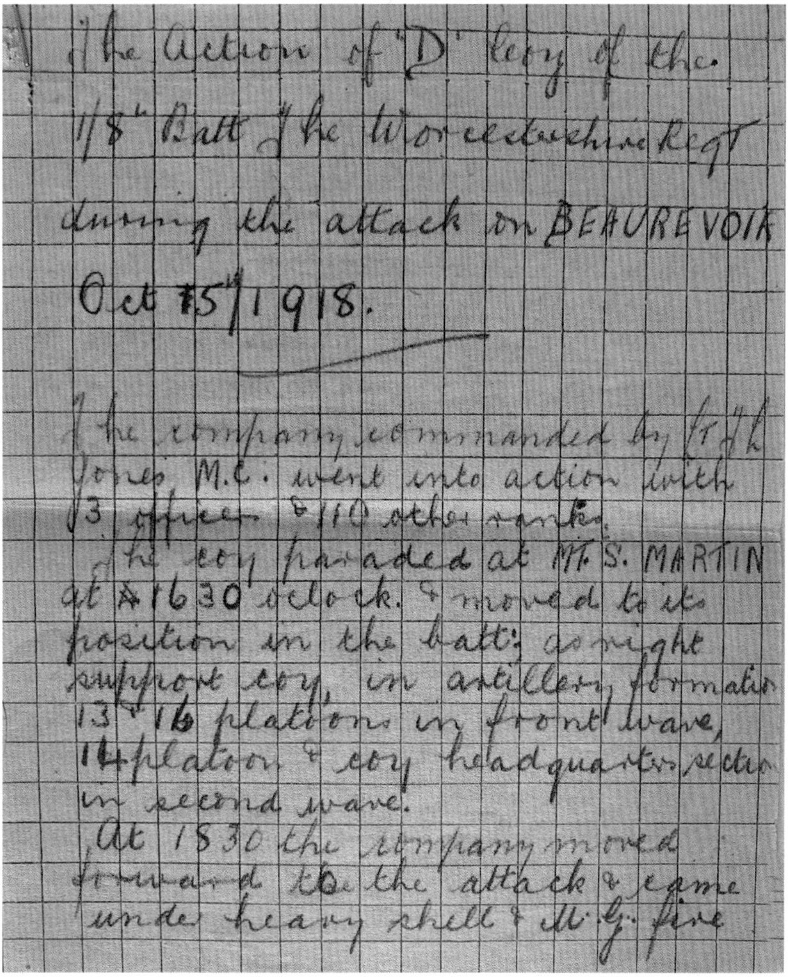

The Action of "D" Coy of the
1/8th Batt The Worcestershire Regt
during the attack on BEAUREVOIR
Oct 5th 1918.

The company commanded by Lt [illegible] Jones M.C. went into action with 3 officers & 110 other ranks.
The coy paraded at Mt S. MARTIN at 1630 o'clock & moved to its position in the batt: as right support coy, in artillery formation 13 & 16 platoons in front wave, 14 platoon & coy headquarters section in second wave.
At 1830 the company moved forward to the attack & came under heavy shell & M.G. fire

20. The D Company battle report written by 2Lt Edmund Wedgbury DCM, MM immediately after the Battle of Beaurevoir on 5th October 1918, still held by his family.

21. The only possessions of the Old Gent to be retained by his family – his medals and a pair of gold cufflinks.

22. The grave of the Old Gent, discovered with the help of the churchwarden, Judith Berman. St Mary's Churchyard, Hanbury.

23. Restored, with the Regiment's insign and his gallantry medals added.

24. The medals of 2Lt Edmund Wedgbury DSO, MC, DCM, MM, presently displayed in the Worcester City Museum.

25. The medals of Major Jack Bate DSO*, MC*, recently presented to the Regiment by his granddaughter, Ruth Wright.

THE IMPORTANCE OF RANK AND SENIORITY

Bomford's next memories provide an illustration that exercised the minds of young subalterns throughout the War:

> Our next attack was eventually cancelled and we were marched back to a camp ground, muddy and weary. While there [11th October] we had a batch of officer reinforcements including GL Watkinson [known as 'Kinson']. He was senior to all the subalterns in the Batt. I remember an indignation meeting in the latrines. He was posted to A Coy and was on parade before me when we moved. When I arrived I said 'You may be senior to me but I'm going to have the horse'. A Coy Commander (which I remained despite his seniority) had a horse, very nice on a long march.

It was not really the horse that was the issue but the seniority. Watkinson had been commissioned before Bomford but had remained in England. Bomford wrote shortly before this, on 2nd October, to his mother: 'I've got my two pips up and don't know how I have been antedated yet'. This tells us that he was a lieutenant when he had his discussion in the latrine as the company commander. More importantly, it showed the focus on one's actual seniority. This was for two reasons: the pecking order amongst one's peers for command and for pay. The former was perhaps less important as the company commander appointments were in the sole gift of the commanding officer, while the pay and substantive promotion was controlled by the administrative department of the Army. It must have been very confusing to the NCOs and soldiers as to who was actually commanding their company. It would normally be the officer wearing the King's Crown on his shoulder – or forearm in the Great War, signifying the rank of major and someone a few years older than the other officers. The company commanders in September 1917 included Pawsey who was 23, Bomford 20, Wilkes 21 and Bate 23, but age was no restriction to gallant leadership. By the time the War was over, these four young officers would gain nine MCs and three DSOs between them.

2Lt Sydney Herbert Wilkes was awarded his first MC in the King's Birthday Honours on 4th June 1917 for 'Somme, Winter 1916' for his constant patrolling and raiding at Le Sars, won the Bar to his MC at Springfield and was to gain a second Bar the following summer in the Italian campaign. Only two other officers in all 14 battalions of the Worcestershire Regiment achieved this feat in the War, both from another Territorial battalion, the 1/7th – Captain AO Lloyd and Captain WR Prescott. It is difficult to know how common this was throughout the Army but just four officers were awarded three bars. Wilkes was photographed in full uniform with a 'wounded/service' badge which is likely to have been after Passchendaele as he is noted as returning to the Battalion on 24th January 1918. Wilkes hailed from Dudley (which was then in Worcestershire) and was living with his family in 1911 as a schoolboy at 28 Prospect Row. His father, Herbert, was the secretary and manager of the local ironfounders, so again, not a member of a landed or professional family. Wilkes' MC at Springfield was gazetted as:

> For conspicuous gallantry and devotion to duty when in command during an attack on a strong enemy position. He showed able leadership in working his company forward to their assembly position through a heavy barrage with very slight casualties. At the critical moment he displayed correct initiative and a clear grasp of the situa-

> tion in ordering his company to advance, whereby all the objectives were captured and consolidated. Throughout the operation he showed a magnificent spirit of leadership and contempt for danger, which had the greatest moral effect on all under his command.

It is interesting to read the citation for his Italian Bar as some of the wording was familiar:

> For conspicuous gallantry and devotion to duty. During a raid on the enemy's lines, when the attack was held up by a large party of the enemy on the flank, this officer, without hesitating, led a platoon and dislodged them. He then returned and took command of two companies, the commanding officer being missing, and successfully carried out the operation. After the party had withdrawn he stayed behind to look for the missing officers, and was the last man to enter our trenches. He set a splendid example under difficult circumstances and displayed great gallantry in leading his men.

His award, according to the *History*, was an 'immediate' MC. Wilkes' leadership qualities were clearly understood from an early stage as he was mentioned in the *War Diary* four times in a two-week period in the beginning of December 1916 as the leader of patrols into No Man's Land. Normally a single or just two patrols were sent out on any one day or, more usually, night and there would be up to 16 platoon commanders in the Battalion. Wilkes and Norman Clutterbuck seem to have been chosen more often than all others, frequently operating together on the same night. These patrols were an opportunity for a subaltern to make a name for himself – but this did not guarantee that he would be equipped to lead a company of about 150 men into action with the same gallantry and effectiveness. It is interesting that Wilkes got no mention in Leslie Bomford's correspondence and only twice in Corbett's *War Story*. The reason was perhaps that he was not in A Company, like Bomford and Corbett, but more likely because he was not a man of rural Worcestershire. He would not have taken his leave in the county, therefore was not travelling home with the Bomfords, Walford, Davies, Evers, Symons, the Holcrofts or Stallard. Corbett's book was first published in instalments in the *Berrow's Worcester Journal*, so it would have featured those from the heart of the county in the first instance. Wilkes, as with Jack Bate, was not a schoolboy hero, but he had the chance to go to university, going up to Keble College, Oxford in 1914. 2Lt JR Willis went up to Balliol College at the same time and it was these two officers who were the only ones to receive MCs for their two August actions. Lt Victor Fox-Smith was still attached to the Brigade Trench Mortar Battery and was to earn his MC at this time.

2Lt Jesse Hemming was only with the Battalion for 24 days, reporting for duty on 3rd August and being killed on the 27th, aged just 20. He was posted to C Company under Captain Pawsey. He was not the shortest-lived young officer serving with the Battalion. At the point when Hemming died, that unfortunate record was held by 2Lt Stanley Clutterbuck who was killed on his eleventh day of service by shellfire – his elder brother and fellow subaltern, Norman, attending his funeral. The *War Diary* is the best, if only, place in which the service of young officers can be ascertained. It recorded when they reported for duty; when they went out on a 'useful' patrol; when they were wounded; when they received an award; (sometimes) when they were posted away from the Battalion (as to the 144th Brigade Machine Gun Company, in the case of 2Lts JJ Paskin (on 23rd January 1916) and HB Borlasse; both served with the MGC until the end of the War); and when they were killed or died of their wounds. Captain JJ Paskin was to gain an MC in April 1918. He was listed in the *Gazette* on 15th May 1916 as promoted to Temporary Lieutenant amongst a list of six of his fellow subalterns. This is a list of great importance to each as it gave the order of seniority as well as of pay for the rank:

KM Mylne	20th May 1915
HP Borlasse	25th June 1915
JJ Paskin	14th Oct 1915
CR Pawsey	17th Oct 1915
JR Blake	12th Nov 1915
RJCW Hawtrey	23rd Nov 1915

The *London Gazette* recorded that Paskin [spelt Pasken] and Pawsey were both 'absorbed in the establishment of the 8th Battalion' on 19th May 1915 – remarkable that both were to be knighted in later life. All those listed were to survive the War and were still serving at the Front, wounds permitting, excepting one who was to become a Prisoner of War. When seeing whose medals were held by the Regiment, I found that the list included Sir (Jesse) John Paskin KCMG MC – a fourth young officer who served with the 1/8th Battalion and who was to be knighted for services in World War Two and thereafter. On 1st January 1944 Paskin became a Companion of the Order of St Michael and St George (CMG) as Assistant Secretary in the Colonial Office and ten years later to the day he was raised to the rank of knight in the same order (KCMG) as the Assistant Under-Secretary of State in the Colonial Office. His ashes and those of his wife are in Great Wishford, Wiltshire. He died in Salisbury on 16th September 1972 and his gravestone records that he was awarded also the Croix de Guerre in the Great War. He must have married late as his wife died in 2009. In his memory, she made a gift to his alma mater, St John's College, Cambridge in 1999/2000:

> Lady Paskin MBE (widow of Sir Jesse John Paskin KCMG, MC, Croix de Guerre (BA 1918)) made a gift of £200,000 (£212,692.31 by Gift Aid). It was Lady Paskin's wish that a John Paskin Fund be established in memory of her late husband, to promote scholarship and research in the areas of archaeology and philosophy.

2Lt Kenneth Mylne was the son of the Bishop of Bombay, where he was born in May 1890. His father had taught at Merchiston School in Edinburgh and became a housemaster at Marlborough College where his six sons were educated. Two, Edward, a captain in the Irish Guards, and Ewan, who followed his brother into the Irish Guards, were to be killed in the War. Kenneth, like Wilkes, had attended Keble College, Oxford before the War. His father was Bishop of Alvechurch at the start of the War, no doubt the reason for his son joining the Worcestershire Regiment. Mylne survived and, in 1918, wrote the 32-page *The History of the Worcestershire: A Lecture to Recruits*, available for the price of one shilling (5p) – written initially for those of the 3/7th Battalion stationed in Catterick. In 1920 he became prep school headmaster at Merchiston Castle School. In 1925, he left to found Dalhousie Castle School in Bonnyrigg just south of Edinburgh. He moved it to Melville House near Cupar Fife in 1950 where it remains today. He was its headmaster until 1954 and its principal until 1960 when he sold the school. He died in Edinburgh in 1968.

It is rarely possible to work out exactly which officers were on Battalion duty at any one time. For instance, a number of subalterns were recorded as being out on patrol or in battle without, apparently, ever reporting for duty with the Battalion – including 2Lts CWH Franklin, CG Eaton, FG Potter, AG Richards, JT Ibbs, JE Rayer, RF Amphlett, WT Jotcham and WH Reynolds. This would have been an oversight by the adjutant, a role which Reynolds himself held in some of the Battalion's last battles, gaining himself an MC. Five of these subalterns were to lose their lives before otherwise being mentioned in the *War Diary*. 2Lt John Thomas Ibbs died of his wounds on 20th March 1917, although there is no record of when he was wounded. His family recorded that he was shot in the thigh when approaching German wire while leading a patrol from C Company on his 36th birthday. He was carried back under fire by Corporal Randolph Harris and taken to the 48th CCS at Bray-sur-Somme on 15th March 1917, succumbing to his wounds five days later. He had been a steward, one behind the matron in seniority, at the Greenwich Union Infirmary in 1911. RF Amphlett, aged 38, was killed at Templeux-le-Guérard on 5th April 1917. A solicitor from Wolverhampton, he was one of the ten Oxford graduates who served with the Battalion, in his case an Oriel man. FG Potter and AG Richards were killed on 24th April 1917 at Gillemont Farm, and WT Jotcham at Maison du Hibou on 19th August 1917. It is understood that the average lifespan of a young infantry officer at the Front was just six weeks – as so well described by John Lewis-Stempel in his work, *Six Weeks: The Short and Gallant Life of the Young British Officer in the First World War*. These 'reporting for duty' omissions have made it impossible to calculate whether the 1/8th Battalion reduced or increased that six-week average. Neither is it clear if the six weeks is just for those killed or also includes those, like Douglas Bomford, whose wounds were so bad that they were never able to return to the Front. One figure that startles from my research is that by the end of August 1917 – 28 months after the Battalion landed in France – some 94 officers are recorded as having either crossed to France with the Battalion, reported for duty with the Battalion, taken part in an action, or been killed. Given that the average number of officers on Battalion duty at any one time was thirty, it means that the whole Roll of officers had been completely turned over three times in that 28-month period. Obviously, there was not a single great change but a series of those being wounded, posted to other appointments, sent on leave, or killed – thus being replaced by subalterns new to the Front or by officers returning after posting, or having recovered from their wounds. It does, however, make the responsibility of the SNCOs so much the greater in maintaining a degree of continuity concerning both the command and the modus operandi of their company and the Battalion.

However, of those 30 officers who landed in France on 1st April 1915, only two seem to have taken part in the 'Springfield' action just under 28 months later – the gallant Captain CR Pawsey MC* and, most probably as the temporary commanding officer, the equally redoubtable Captain JP Bate MC*. Of the three other company commanders (other than Pawsey), Captain Bernard Tullidge joined on 3rd July 1916 so had a year's experience of command in battle; Captain Hugh Ryan-Bell joined two months earlier, on 5th May 1916; and Lt SH Wilkes between the two, on 5th June 1916. Tullidge and Ryan-Bell were to be killed in the action, meaning a cadre of four company commanders with a little over a year's experience at the Front, though mostly commanding only at platoon level, lost half their number in a single day. Tullidge had been commanding A Company; Bomford is recorded as being the only officer from A and D Company not to be killed or wounded that day. Bomford was, thus, in command of A Company at the age of just 20, with twenty months' experience at the Front.

This was the last major action of the Battalion in front of Ypres. In the *Divisional History,* Mitchinson reflects that 'the Division's involvement in Third Ypres was heavy but it did also have several periods of recuperation and training in the rear – which seems to be militarily sensible to ensure the best performance when they were called on to continue the attritional British advance'. Mitchinson continued in his 'Finally' chapter:

> [RQMS] Corbett later claimed that at Ypres, 1/8th Worcestershire 'always made our objective, and clung to it' which in the case of that battalion was probably correct. There were many other instances, however, when battalions were unsuccessful. Again, it is difficult to condemn individual units for a lack of drive or determination for their failures to gain their objectives because the weather, terrain and resolute defence were sufficient to frustrate the best of divisions.

The Battalion was the only one picked out for special mention in his concluding chapter. Twelve months later they were to figure equally prominently in the history of another Division, the 25th.

THE MISSING

The Battalion suffered a number of Other Ranks reported missing after the battle at Gillemont Farm. The various actions in the mud of Passchendaele meant that this became a common occurrence, though not according to the Appendix of the *Booklet* to the 1/8th Battalion. This is most unlikely to have been the case at the time of the battles, especially given the number of those killed whose bodies were never identified – the names of five officers of the eight killed are on the panels at Tyne Cot, so they were not found or could not be identified at the end of the War. In the Battalion's first action at Passchendaele, 26 Other Ranks died, six of their wounds so they have a grave. Of the other 20, 9 have graves and 11 are on the Tyne Cot panels. The battle a week later tells of a very different outcome: 48 Other Ranks died, only two having been wounded. Of the other 46, just 8 have graves. All three of the officers killed that day (Tullidge, Horsley, Hemming) are commemorated on the panel at Tyne Cot. Thus, very few of the badly wounded were retrieved from the battlefield and less than 20 per cent of the bodies – no doubt a reflection of the intensity of the bombardments across the battlefield and the effects of the incessant rain. It is interesting that the *Booklet*, published in 1919, does not record any of those on the Tyne Cot panels as being 'missing' – except that they had not been found in any Prisoner of War camp as the War ended. However, many of the families must have been told at the time that their loved one was missing unless, presumably, an officer or soldier had seen their body on the battlefield and reported it to Battalion HQ. The *War Diary* did record 3 Other Ranks as missing in the immediate aftermath of the battle, later known as Springfield Farm.

It is perhaps time to demonstrate the lengths to which the families of the missing were kept informed of any search for their loved one, either as a prisoner or to ascertain if they had really died. The family of Private Arthur Reginald Read of the 1/8th's sister battalion, the 2/8th (that of Captains Douglas Bomford, Osborn Walford, Hugh Davies, Dick Stallard, Noel Symons and Lance Evers) kept all the papers which they received over the anxious days and weeks after he was reported as missing on 3rd December 1917 at the Battle of Cambrai – an action notable for the gallant defence by the 2/8th Battalion at which a DSO, 5 MCs (including to Lt RH Stallard and Captain HW Davies) and 5 DCMs were earned. Pte Read's family have lodged all his letters and 'missing' papers with the Imperial War Museum (*IWM Document 14176*). They start with Read's last letter home which was one of the brown pre-written cards provided for the Army for those wishing to send something home when time was short or for those who were not confident of their own writing skills. Soldiers merely crossed out the sections or lines which were not appropriate and addressed the front of the card. Read did often write home so he must have been short of time as this battle approached. The text of his card (Form W1566) read as follows:

I am quite well.
I have been admitted into hospital
{sick } and am going on well
{wounded} and hope to be discharged soon.
I am being sent down to the base.
{letter dated ________
I have received your {telegram __________
{parcel __________
Letter follows at the first opportunity.
I have received no letter from you
{lately
{for a long time
Signature only ______REG______________
Date ____1/12/17______________________

The *History* recorded for that day, '1/12/17' that 'the battalions of the 183rd Brigade lay in Havrincourt Wood all day of the December 1st, listening to the roar of the battle in front. After dark came the orders to advance…'

The shaded lines are those which Read crossed out as not being appropriate that time. It must have been heart-breaking that this was his last letter. Most letters in his IWM file have a familiar start: 'Just a line hoping you and all at home are in the very best of health…' The letter which appears to be his last before that formal card concluded optimistically: 'Well then remember me to all the people I know, tell them I am all merry and bright none the worst for my little experience. Well Ma that is all just now so with love and kisses to all, I remain your loving son, Reg'. All his letters were to his mother. He asked in one that she tell his father that he has met someone who has worked with him. Perhaps Read's father was not able to read and write, so did not communicate directly with his son by letter.

The next document in the file and thus received by Read's father, Mr FW Read of 51 Bestwood Rd, Millbrook, Southampton was Army form W5490 stamped from Infantry Record Office No 7, Warwick. It read:

> Sir or Madam
> I regret to have to inform you that a report has been received from the War Office to the effect that (No.) 260266 (Rank) Pte (Regiment) WORCESTERSHIRE REGT
> was posted as 'missing' on the 3rd December 1917
>
> The report that he is missing does not necessarily mean that he has been killed, as he may be a prisoner of war or temporarily separated from his regiment.
>
> Official reports that men are prisoners of war take some time to reach this country, and if he has been captured by the enemy it is probable that unofficial news will reach you first. In that case, I am to ask you to forward any letter received at once to this Office, and it will be returned to you as soon as possible.
>
> Should any further official information be received it will be at once communicated to you.
> I am, Sir or Madam
> Your obedient Servant
>
> Officer in charge of Records

This was followed by two letters, one from his Company Commander and one from the padre. The first was dated 17th December 1917:

Dear Madam
By this time you no doubt have heard the unfortunate news concerning your son Reggie.
He was in the attack with me & all the company & what became of him is not at the present time known but you may be sure as soon as all the particulars come through, I will let you know but at present he is reported missing.
All his chums here are indeed very sorry. I hope to hear something concerning him soon. I may state he was a very willing chap & liked by all here.
A parcel was received here for your son & was given to the platoon as all the contents were eatables only.
I am enclosing the letters which were in the parcel.
Trusting you will cheer up & trust God for the best news.
Yours very sincerely
Albert A Hudd Cpl

The one from the padre was on a page from a notebook with cross line margins, written in blue crayon with Pte Read's details in pencil:

2/8 Worcester Regt
B.E.F.
13/12/17

Dear Mr Read
I regret to inform you that 260266 Pte AR Read was killed missing on Dec 2nd. The Germans attacked & after a valiant resistance our battalion had to fall back slightly & your son was left in enemy hands. Please don't give up hope as he may well be taken a prisoner.
Please accept my deepest sympathies in your great anxiety.
Yours sincerely
Ronald C Wainwright
(Chaplain)

It is perhaps understandable as to why the padre's letter was so formal and appeared to have been 'mass-produced'. The 2/8th Battalion suffered some very significant casualties in this action. The *History* recorded that 2 officers and 36 Other Ranks were missing in addition to 2 officers and 10 Other Ranks killed – thus some 50 letters for the padre to write. One of Read's fellow private soldiers in D Company, later 263005 Cpl AS Little (*IWM Document 16899*), wrote a memoir in June 1919. His description of this action gave a vivid picture of the horror of being subjected to a full German attack, something which the 1/8th were fortunate to avoid:

> I was detailed to march with the field kitchen and act as brakesman. We left Arras early in the morning and marched through Bapaume to Metz Wood, a distance of 40 kms, arriving at 3 o'clock the next morning dead beat, when we were rushed into the line straight away.
>
> When we got in, we found it one of the hottest shops we had ever struck, for the shelling was perfectly devilish. Fritz didn't give us a minute's rest, but shelled us incessantly. We found out that this was the place which had just been captured by the strategy of General Byng, and well we knew it, for Fritz tried to blow us sky-high to get the position back.
>
> On 3rd December, Fritz launched his counter attack, and well we knew it; we were ordered to man the trenches and he dropped a hellish barrage plump into our trench, which was full of men. In a few minutes the place was a perfect shambles, the trench literally flowing in blood and our dead and dying lying about in piles. Our brave fellows were absolutely massacred by the barrage, and when it lifted, the few of us left saw his attack coming along the trenches in the form of two huge bombing parties gradually closing in to cut us off.
>
> They were throwing their stick bombs over in clouds and we hadn't got a bomb in the place to reply with. The numbers with which he attacked was overwhelming and it looked like a grey field of figures coming over at us. We resisted as long as we could, firing at them until our rifles got red hot and so massed were they that you couldn't miss them with a rifle. His casualties were terrible, but he drove us

> back, gradually cutting us off, until at last I found myself with an open space of about 30 yards to get through to our reserve line.
>
> All the chaps around me were killed, so I threw myself down on my stomach and crawled that 30 yards in record time, with both parties of Fritz's were [*sic*] chucking bombs at me, and taking pot shots with their rifles. However they missed me and eventually I found myself dropping into the old British front line, from which the original advance had started.
>
> This was being held by fresh troops which had been rushed up and the survivors of our battalion which didn't number very many – about 200 all told – out of 800, the original number. Here we resisted all further attacks as it was a good strong line, and this once again became the front line.
>
> That was the end of General Byng's great advance [the Battle of Cambrai 1917], for which the joy bells were rung in Blighty. Our casualties in our battalion alone were 600, and goodness knows what other battalions suffered. That was one of the narrowest escapes I ever had from annihilation, and I didn't want any more like it.

The casualty figures quoted above by Cpl Little turn out to be a considerable exaggeration, although the numbers are still terrible. The 2/8th lost 4 officers and 24 men killed according to the Roll, although the *History* quotes, presumably from the *War Diary*, 2 officers and 10 men killed with 9 officers and 89 men wounded and 2 officers and 36 men missing – which would include Pte Read. One of the wounded officers died and one of the missing officers likewise with the other, presumably, being taken prisoner. The *History* concluded the footnote on the casualties for that day: '13 officers and 135 Other Ranks, according to the official [War] Diary; but that figure is said to be an underestimate'. Amongst the wounded officers was the Bomford brothers' friend, Captain Dick Stallard. This was only three months after the 2/8th had suffered 146 casualties at Aisne Farm near the Steenbeck next to the 1/7th and 1/8th Battalions.

Cpl Little concluded his memoir by apologising for:

> … my description of the horror of the campaign [being] very bald

> and conveys very little meaning to the average reader … the deeds of valour they performed (and I saw a good many) were not done for Victoria Crosses and Military Medals, but were done for pals, and the homes in old England they were fighting to protect. Many brave deeds I saw done would have earned a VC over and over again, but were never noticed. It was all done as part of a day's work. When going 'over the top', I never saw any go over with a joke on their lips, like the papers described, but with set, strained faces, for they knew only too well what a hell they would go through … they realised to the full, what they would have to face, in the hundreds of machine gun bullets, shrapnel bursts, and hand to hand fighting, and they didn't fancy the jobs, but all the same, they never thought of not facing them.
>
> I include this which I ask you to remember with each action of the 1/8th Battalion when they rose from their trenches or railway cuttings to go into the attack. Cpl Little knew what it was like.

It is difficult not to think of Pte Read's parents every time the postman called – in the hope of news that Read had been reported as being held as a Prisoner of War. There were two other Army documents with these papers which may well have accompanied the above letter. The first is a two-page notice entitled: *MISSING OFFICERS AND MEN* which detailed the actions that would be taken by the authorities and begins:

> The following are the steps taken by the War Office to ascertain whether officers and men who have been reported Missing are Prisoners of War, or, if not, whether any definite information is obtainable as to their fate:-
>
> The Commanding Officers
>
> The Officers Commanding the Unit, before making his return, ascertains as far as possible from the officers and men present with the Unit, whether any reliable evidence is forthcoming. If not, he reports the soldier Missing.
>
> The British Red Cross and Order of St. John.
>
> Lists of the missing are supplied by the War Office to the Enquiries

> Department of the Red Cross, 18, Carlton House Terrace.
>
> The representatives of this body are given facilities at the hospitals and camps at home and overseas to collect information from wounded soldiers.
>
> Information so collected, if likely to establish the fate of the officer or man, is passed to the War Office and in the case of the rank and file is taken up officially without request from the relatives.
>
> In the case of officers these reports if sufficiently definite are also investigated, but the initiative is as a rule left to the relatives, since the Red Cross reports are frequently numerous and conflicting, and it is found that the relatives have in many cases received reliable information direct from the officers of the unit.
>
> Enquiries addressed to 18, Carlton House Terrace, will also be answered direct, and all reliable information collected will be communicated. The enquiry should give the name, Christian name, regimental number, regiment, battalion, company or platoon, and date of casualty…
>
> Enquiries in Germany and other enemy countries.
>
> Full lists of the missing are prepared in the War Office, and a large number of copies are sent monthly to the Foreign Office for transmission through the good offices of the Netherlands Government to Germany and to other enemy countries…

The Netherlands were, of course, neutral in the First World War. This document was designed to give reassurance that there is a full organisation devoted to the search for the missing, including the Red Cross and the Netherlands Government. This document, when sent to a wife or dependent of the missing, was accompanied by Army Form W3268, entitled: *Notice to Wives and other Dependants of Soldiers reported missing.* The contents would have been of comfort for those who relied on their husband or father's wages:

> You are informed that the issue of Separation Allowance to the wife or other dependent of a soldier reported missing **ceases** after 30 weekly payments have been made from the date the payee was notified of the fact that the soldier is missing.

Pension (or gratuity in certain dependants' cases) then becomes issuable, but the change of payment must not be taken to mean that there is any proof of death or that the Army Council have yet accepted the soldier as dead.

No certificate of death can be issued and no steps taken for the disposal of any amount that may be due to him, or of any articles or personal property that may have been recovered, until the Army Council are able to accept the soldier as dead for official purposes. The Payee will be informed when this has been done.

It does make one wonder if wives would know the difference between the War Office and the Army Council in all these papers. Progress in following up Read's case was slow but that may well be due to the sheer numbers of the missing and the time taken to receive answers from Germany about Prisoners of War.

There is then a brief letter from the British Red Cross dated 15th May 1918:

Dear Mrs Read
We are very sorry to learn that your dear boy is missing. We shall enquire at once and let you know the result. It may be through God's mercy that he is a prisoner of War. If so, you will get news soon.

Meanwhile, there is one true Comforter who invites you and every sad heart to go to Him for consolation and wisdom – Jesus.

We pray for you. (in signatory's hand: God comfort your son. He can.)
Yours very sincerely
James C Cook Lieut. Colonel

The next correspondence appears to be a letter stamped on 12 June 1918 by the Warwick Office – so more than six months after Read went missing. It was written to Mrs ME Read at the same Millbrook address. The letter refers to 'son' so she must be Read's mother. It is not clear that his father had died in this interlude; it appears he died in 1922. Private Read was the second of five children, the son of a dockworker and just 19 when he went missing. The *CWGC* website provides no age or parental details for him. The letter came from the British Red Cross:

> Pte. Arthur Reginald Read. 260266 2/8 Worcester. D[ivision] XIII
> Dear Madam
> We have just received some news about your son and would warn you against attaching too much importance to the latter part of this information until further news is received. Had your son been taken prisoner alive, we fear that his name would have come through by now on the Prisoners' List from Germany. Pte L Rollason 263132, Worcesters 2/8, D 13, in hospital in France states:
> 'I saw him in the same dugout as Wilkinson at La Vacquerie – he was unwounded, but was helping the wounded. I think he must have been captured as the Germans were close to it when I left. They took the ground and dugout. Fair Hair, about 5'5", slim, about 22.'
> We are trying to obtain further news for you.
> Please accept our deep sympathy.
> Yours faithfully
> For The EARL OF LUCAN

Then, with no new news, and as the 30th week approached, Read's mother, Mary, received the promised letter from the Ministry of Pensions (Widows and Dependants Branch) dated 3rd July 1918 and headed: DEPENDANT'S PENSION:

> Madam
> I am directed by the Minister of Pensions to inform you that a [provisional – handwritten] pension of Seven Shillings and sixpence [handwritten] a week has been approved for you in respect of No 260266 Pte Arthur Reginald Read, 2/8th Worcester Regiment with effect from 6th August 1918 to the _______ [left blank] in the first instance.
> The enclosed Life Certificate should be completed and returned to this office in the enclosed envelope as quickly as possible, in order that the necessary instructions for payment may be issued.
> I am, Madam,

Your obedient Servant
EC Fournier d'Albe
for the Secretary

There was still no official notice that Read had died, although there was his death certificate in the file with the date of 3rd December 1917. Even after the War, the British Red Cross and the Order of St John were still trying to locate the missing. Mrs Read was to receive a final letter from them on 3rd June 1919, although a standard one with his details added by hand:

Dear Madam
We much regret to say that notwithstanding constant and careful enquiries, we have not succeeded in hearing anything of 'your son, Pte A.r.read 260266 – 2/8 worcesters, except the one unconfirmed report that he was a prisoner'.
His name was on our lists for months, and we asked all the men of his unit who we were able to see, both in English Hospitals and at the bases abroad, but none of them threw any light on his casualty. We have also questioned released prisoners but have learnt nothing. We can therefore only send you a General Account of the action in which he was last seen, with sincere regret at our inability to help you any further.
We wish at the same time to offer our sympathy to the family and friends.
Yours faithfully
DR
For The EARL OF LUCAN

<u>2/8 Worcesters Dec 2-3, 1917</u>
D Coy was in reserve holding a dug-out … they were in the dug-out in the front line. The Germans advanced and captured them before they had time to get out. This was in a part of the trench that had been taken from the Germans, and the Germans surrounded them, getting in from all sides.

The fate of a missing officer is thus described: 'I heard that he was in the hand to hand fighting at La Vacquerie, was severely wounded, and was last seen throwing bombs'.

There is no doubt that tremendous efforts were made to find the missing and to keep the families informed of any developments or the lack of any progress. Had the science of DNA been available in the years after the War, many of the bodies now in graves marked as 'A Soldier of the Great War' would have been identified. The result for Pte Read is that his name is on a panel at the Cambrai Memorial and his body may be either in a grave for the missing or still buried in the trench where he died, now under a ploughed field.

There was however the undated notice sent to the next of kin of all who died or were killed under the royal cipher:

> The King commands me to assure you of the true sympathy of His Majesty and The Queen in your sorrow.
>
> He whose loss you mourn died in the noblest of causes. His Country will be ever grateful to him for the sacrifice he has made for Freedom and Justice.
>
> Milner
> Secretary of State for War

This is followed by the Effects Form – No 45 from the War Office and dated 27th November 1918, so after the War had finished and six days short of the first anniversary of Read's death:

> Sir
> I am directed to acquaint you that the sum of five pounds ten shillings, & sixpence [handwritten and with a tick to show the amount was checked before posting] is due from Army Funds to the estate of the late no. 260266 Private Arthur Reginald Read, 2/8th Battalion Worcestershire Regiment being the balance of pay, &c, due to him.
>
> The Command Paymaster, Eastern Command, Science Museum, Exhibition Road, South Kensington, London, SW7 has accordingly been authorised to issue to you the above amount.
>
> Should no communication on this subject be received from the

Paymaster within the next few days, application for payment should be made to him by letter.

No further amount is due from Army Funds to the estate.

I am, Sir,

Your obedient Servant

C. Harris

Assistant Financial Secretary.

This amount would be his outstanding pay but does include the wording 'No further amount is due from Army Funds to the estate' which may well have gone unnoticed. Read's family could make no other claim if they received these 'five pounds, ten shillings and sixpence'.

There is one other document amongst Read's papers. It is on card with a seal duly stamped and an insignia of crossed Union Jacks with a Crown above a motto 'DULCE ET DECORUM EST PRO PATRIA MORI'. This was an official recognition by the County of Worcestershire of Read's sacrifice:

To Mrs ME Read, 51 Testwood Road, Millbrook, Southampton
The Territorial Force Association for the County of Worcester desires to express the warmest sympathy with you in the loss of your gallant Son, No. 260266, Private AR Read, 8th Worcestershire Regiment who gave his life for his Country, 3rd December, 1917.

England to-day perhaps more than at any time in her glorious history, expects every man to do his duty, and it must be some consolation to you to feel that, in making the ultimate sacrifice, your son justified, to the supreme point, his Country's trust in her Sons.

Coventry President

RC Temple Chairman

JM Reddie Secretary

Each had signed in his own hand. The Territorial Battalions of the Worcestershire Regiment lost in excess of a thousand soldiers so the completion and signing of these Presentation Cards was no small undertaking. There was also, perhaps from the same source, a two-sided card with a black line surrounding the text on the front:

1919
To: Mrs ME Read
Mother of No 260266
Private AR Read
8th Worcestershire Regiment
From **Sir Richard Temple**
Chairman of the Worcestershire County Territorial
Force Association
With Sincere Sympathy
And
In Grateful Respect to the Memory
of her Son

and on the reverse a poem:

KILLED IN ACTION

I

So he is dead, that clambered to my knee
And clutched with hands so soft, so very small
So warm with love for me, his all in all
In those far days when he was all to me.
So he is dead, that grew so fair to see,
So strong, so brave, so debonair and tall,
So good to me, his mother, and withal
Such comfort to my age that hoped to be,
And that was peace: that clanging of the bells
And shouting gladness in the crowded street;
For Victory has proudly raised her head
With conscious grandeur in her mien, that tells
Of vanquished Evil fallen at her feet.
But what are these to me, since he is dead?

II

Yes, mother, he is dead. But then he died
For you and me, and all the holy things
That Death by sacrifice in glory brings
To us, through them whom he hath sanctified.
Yes, he is dead. Our solace and our pride
Has joined the Army that the whole world sings
Is flown aloft, upborne on honour's wings,
Through Heaven's gates in welcome opened wide.
And, mother, he is dead, that knowledge be
To those that live regenerate and whole
Of heart, so they be better that he bled:
And this for memory to you and me –
That there is grace unto his living soul,
And peace unto his body that is dead.
21/11/18 R.C.T.

Sir Richard Temple's own composition. He lived at The Nash in Kempsey, Worcestershire and was made a Companion of the Most Honourable Order of the Bath (CB) for his wartime services to the Joint Committee of St John's Ambulance Service and the Red Cross. He had been a soldier and administrator in India and Chief Commissioner to the Andaman and Nicobar Islands. He was a writer and collector, a true polymath.

Overall, these letters and papers are a great insight into the workings of all the agencies which helped the families of those who served as well as those who lost their lives in the War. Read's elder brother by three years, Leonard, survived the War, dying in 1949. His remaining siblings were too young to serve.

On 3rd December 1917, the *History* recorded the actions of the 1/7th as:

> By daylight the relief was completed and the 2/5th R. Warwickshire had taken over the front line. An hour later a fresh attack began. Again came an intense bombardment followed by dense waves of

> infantry. After a hard won fight, the two Gloucestershire battalions were overwhelmed and the enemy pushed through the ruins of La Vacquerie [where Read was last seen]. Beyond that village their further progress was checked by fire from 'Corner Work'. A fierce and prolonged struggle followed around that redoubt. The garrison of 'Corner Work', Worcestershire and Warwickshire lads inter-mixed, maintained all day a most gallant resistance in the redoubt and in the trenches around…
>
> The German bombers worked up the communication trenches on either flank occupied 'Corner Support' and closed in on the garrison from the rear. Death or capture seemed certain and the officers burnt their maps and papers…

This was classic counter-attacking by the Germans, in strength and with heavy and well-coordinated artillery. The 1/8th Battalion experienced this at Gillemont Farm with similar losses and there was a considerable number reported as missing in the days after the action.

Read's name can be found on the Cambrai Memorial at Louverval, which is next to the Bapaume–Cambrai road, built to commemorate over 7,000 men from the Battle of Cambrai who have no known grave.

WALFORD JOINS THE BATTALION

The 1/8th Battalion had fought their last action in the Ypres area for that autumn and, indeed, for the War. On 12th October, now with Lt Col HT Clarke definitely in command, they retraced their steps back to School Camp at St Jan-ter-Biezen, two miles to the west of Poperinghe. Major JP Bate MC* was second-in-command. The 48th Division was moved from this Front, with the 1/7th and 1/8th Battalions marching to Hopoutre Siding's trains. The 1/8th had fought gallantly but to no great avail in the advance to Passchendaele. It may seem the same for all the battalions who fought in the Third Battle of Ypres but, in the bigger picture, the actions at Maison du Hibou and Springfield were important. Corbett reflected on their time in the Ypres Salient:

> We breakfasted at the station in a clear dawn, under the same sickle of an old moon as we had seen when we first came here, only three months ago. We had lost 112 killed and 202 wounded in that dreadful slough, but not in vain. The work was nearly done, Passchendaele was bound to fall, the Canadians were to have the honour of taking it, and we were off to Vimy to relieve them.

He related then an oft-told tale:

> We had added to our laurels. At the beginning of the battle a distinguished German general was captured who told which of our divisions the enemy considered the most dangerous. Their classification has often been garbled for local or journalistic reasons, but as reported at the time it was as follows:
> The 51st (Highland Territorials)
> A Canadian Division (believed from Winnipeg: in any case it included the Royal Canadians)
> The 1st Australians (The Anzacs)
> The 48th
> The Guards.

This puts the 48th (South Midland) Division in esteemed company.

The Battalion was now heading to one of the few areas of the Front on which it had not yet served – the Vimy Ridge. The Ridge had been famously captured in April 1917 by the Canadian Corps under Lt General Sir Julian Byng and is now the site of Walter Seymour Allward's wonderful seget limestone monument at the Canadian National Vimy Memorial. Six months later, the Front had been advanced some two miles eastwards towards the outskirts of Lens. Corbett remembered the train journey towards Vimy:

> On a lovely day the train took us through the Lys Valley, past Burbure and other familiar places, down to St Pol, a little beyond which we detrained at middle day in some huge railway sidings. For the rest of that day and all the next we marched parallel with the railway, and why we could not have trained the whole way is one of the mysteries of the war. But the ways of the R. O. D. [Railway Ordnance Department] pass understanding.

Bomford took a different view in a letter to his father on 15th October, but perhaps he was on a horse – if we remember back to his first meeting with Lt Watkinson:

> Yesterday and today, we have been marching through delightful country, we have been having delightful weather for a wonder and parts of Northern France with autumn colouring are very pretty. Nearly all the roads run very straight and have rows of very regular trees on each side. Often when we are marching you can see the road for a mile or two ahead.

It is remarkable how these young officers were able to block out the memories of a battle of only a few days before and convey home a picture of calm. His letter continued:

> Last night we stayed [in] a little out of the way village [Penin]. The Company went into barns and made themselves very comfortable. They were amongst straw and I was rather afraid they would set

> themselves alight but they didn't. I billeted with some charming old French people. We persuaded them to let us mess there and they were very good to us. They were both white haired and seemed not at all French. They even had cats as pets and seemed very fond of them. The walls of my bedroom were covered with quaint old prints and paintings in big gilt frames and I had a bed with sheets. Unfortunately I was so tired I only appreciated the bed for 30 seconds before it was time to get up.

It reads more like a letter from a son on his gap year!

Bomford was still in command of A Company:

> I don't know how long I shall have the Company for. It seems quite likely I shall be in command for another week. I have only two subalterns [Watkinson being one], both of them just out of England. In a Batt like this the NCOs do a lot of the work that is really an Officer's work simply because we are short of officers.

Having only two subalterns meant that two of the platoons would be under the command of sergeants. He completed his letter with an aside about the calibre of the new young officers: 'However we hope for some more soon. If only they can stick a bit of roughing we shall be much better off'. He made an observation about promotion opportunities shortly afterwards which is a reflection of a subaltern's lot in an infantry battalion at the Front:

> I'm still in charge of the Company but I don't suppose it will last a lot longer. We have had a good many senior officers turning up lately and they don't become casualties like the subalterns. Some of them do go sick and that gives us a chance [to command a company, a captain's appointment].

A little unfair: five company commanders in the Battalion had been killed in action by then: Capt FW Hemming, A/Capt A Plaistowe, A/Capt BH Tullidge, A/Capt HS Benjamin and Lt HR Ryan-Bell. Also, it was written by a young officer just approaching his 21st birthday.

Corbett described the approach to their new trench line:

> Here for two days we took stock of equipment lost in action, and then went on an admirable light railway to the neighbourhood of Neuville St. Vaast. We marched in the dark over Vimy Ridge, through the wreck of the village, and along an interminable trench to the firing line opposite a big village, with Lens to the left front and a landscape of mining-towns and mining-tips. In the rear was Vimy Ridge, looking very steep and imposing on this side … our trenches had been constructed by the Canadians, and most admirably they had done their work.

The Battalion took its turn in the rotation at the Front with the 1/4th Glosters and the 1/7th Worcesters. Incidents were few and Corbett remembered all the work undertaken to prepare the trenches for the winter season with improved drainage and more 'caves' or dugouts. The only incident of note during their tour was from 29th October to 2nd November. It was a time of bright moonlight. The *History* recorded that two subalterns went out in No Man's Land on the first of those nights and were wounded – 2Lt RW Stevens mortally so, and 2Lt A Whiston badly enough not to serve again overseas. The latter had joined the Battalion eighteen days previously and the day before Stevens. Stevens, however, had an MM so he had obviously served in the ranks. He was 24 years old and from Oxford; he had served previously with the 1/4th Oxford and Bucks Light Infantry before receiving his commission in August 1917. As explained earlier, it was the normal procedure that you did not receive a commission from your own regiment – Sgt Wedgbury was to be a valuable exception.

We have now assembled almost all those who were to so distinguish themselves at the head of the Battalion later in 1918: Major HT Clarke, Major JT Bate MC*, Lt LR Bomford, 2Lt GL Watkinson and 2Lt E Wedgbury DCM, MM were in the Battalion trenches before Vimy Ridge. Sgt Wedgbury had left the Battalion on 12 January 1917 to attend officer training and, in line with normal practice, had been commissioned into another regiment. In Wedgbury's case it was the 1/2nd Battalion, the Gloucestershire Regiment. He served with them from 21st August 1917. Notes indicate that he was posted back to his old Battalion on 21st October 1917 – no doubt at the behest of the commanding officer, Lt Col Clarke who had been his (A) company commander, but the *War Diary* stated only that 2Lt Blackler reported for duty that day. Wedgbury's identity card for Italy dated 5th January 1918 described him as:

Age	26 – 3 months
Height	5ft 8½ inches
Hair	Dark brown
Eyes	Blue
Nose	Straight
Moustache	None
Beard	None
Complexion	Fresh

There was no photograph attached, just Lt Col Clarke's initials. Formal photographs of the time show a very good-looking and dapper man.

The last to join was to be Captain JO Walford and we get a first mention of him being transferred from the 2/8th Worcesters in a letter by Lt LR Bomford to his father, dated only as 'Sunday' but likely to be 4th November:

> Capt Walford very nearly came to us, he got as far as our Transport the other day and then got a job in charge of some Camp some way from here. They came down to me for a servant for him and as we had no one we wanted to lose I suggested a most awful dud. Instead of going to another Coy for a suitable man as I expected them to do, they went and sent the dud. I'm afraid Capt. Walford will be rather fed up, but I don't suppose he'll know my share in it.

There had been mentions of a 'servant' in a few recent letters. These men were better known as a 'batman' or 'orderly' and they tended to an officer's needs and equipment when away from the Front and acted as his 'runner' when in action or at the Front. Often, as in the case of Bomford and Fitzer, a strong bond of mutual admiration and respect grew between the two men. For a company commander, it was important that his 'servant' was competent and able. By mid-November, Walford must have joined the Battalion as Bomford wrote: 'Capt Walford is here and doesn't fit in very well. He's a sort of supernumerary in charge of works [trench rebuilding]. It's hard luck on him because he is senior to all our Captains and is so to speak a stranger to the Bn. He hopes to get back to 2/8th shortly'. He did not, rather staying with the 1/8th for the remaining twelve months of the War.

The rotation in the trenches continued until mid-November which, except for 'raids', was quiet for most of the Battalion. Bomford wrote of a couple of instances which displayed that quietness:

> The last day in the trenches I spotted a covey of partridges in No-Mans-Land, it's a big no man's land just there or I shouldn't be potting at partridge. I took my orderly's rifle [as officers only had pistols] and sniped a brace before they flew. I had my sights up a little too much or I ought to have more than a brace as my first shots went high. I got one in the head, the other in the neck … the range was about 20 yards, they were beautiful fat birds and I sent them to

> Major Clarke who is commanding us now. [Adding in his memoir that 'I nipped over the top and got them. Only one German had a pot at me'.]

Giving them to the CO may have been prudent, not for his promotion prospects but because the best facilities to cook them were likely to have been at Headquarters. It is impressive that Bomford collected them himself and did not send his orderly. He told also of a measure of entertainment for those not in the lines:

> Tomorrow we are having a bit of a celebration, ourselves and six others are going to the Curios and then back here for dinner. It ought to be very bon. The Curios are having a new programme which will be a change. I've seen their present one about four times and although it is very good I think they ought to change it a bit more often.

Corbett wrote of the work being undertaken by the men when not in the trenches:

> All that is now required was brimming and riveting, a little draining, and more caves to fit them for winter … [also] road making, clearing away of mud, and other light tasks beguiled the short daylight hours… Neuville St Vaast was a very interesting place and full of souvenirs of the disastrous French battles and the great [Canadian] victory of the previous April. The enemy's old lines were well worth study, and there were some remarkably ingenious OP [observation posts] and sniping arrangements, notably a ruined tree made of hollow iron.

It is very likely that this is the same 'iron tree' which adorns the splendid Canadian Museum at Vimy Ridge to this day.

Times were changing for the Battalion, as noted by Corbett:

> Just as we were settling down for the winter back came the Canadians with the scalps of Passchendaele dangling from their belts, and

wanted their trenches back. We had done nothing but patrol and hold the Line, and our losses were two killed and five wounded. D Company had their usual luck, losing all their officers on the first day, though nobody else was hurt…

We went back past the topless towers of Mont St Eloy [which still stands as a ruin today] and thence made a prodigious long march to a place called Ostreville, near St Pol. Here we began to refit. It was rumoured that we were going to Italy…

TO ITALY

John Keegan's *The First World War: An Illustrated History* introduced the war in Italy:

> On the Italian front the defenders were heavily outnumbered by the attackers. On May 15, 1916, the Austrians unleashed their 'punishment expedition' between Lake Garda and the River Brenta, which leads towards the lagoons of Venice. The preliminary bombardment forewarned the [Italian] defenders and they fought with heroic self-sacrifice to hold the invaders at bay. The Rome Brigade was almost wiped out in its defence of Piazza. As a result, the Austrian nowhere advanced more than 10 miles...

Keegan applauded the Italian army's fortitude with its eleven attempts (Battles of Isonzo – a river to the north of Trieste) to open a new flank into the Central Powers' southern underside through Austria's mountain borderland. The eleven battles consisted of 'the incidence of an offensive every three months, between May 1915 and August 1917 ... higher than that demanded of the British or French Armies on the Western Front'. He continued that 'the contingencies were [more] wearing; shellfire in this rocky terrain caused 70 per cent more casualties per round expended than on the soft ground in France and Belgium'. In August 1917, the Austrian Emperor asked the Kaiser for support as he believed that he could achieve a breakthrough. Seven specialist German Divisions were sent, and:

> On 24th October 1917, a joint German-Austrian army containing a high proportion of mountain troops, broke through at Isonzo, captured nearly 300,000 prisoners and reversed all the [Italian] gains won in the previous two and a half years. Thereafter the Italian war was fought in the lowlands of the Piave River valley...

This action was known as the Battle of Caporetto and was notable also for the presence of a young German First Lieutenant 26-year-old battalion company commander. He and 150 men are reputed to have captured 81 artillery guns and 9,000 men. He was developing an infiltration tactic of attacking with small forces of agile soldiers, known by some as a blitzkrieg without tanks. Two weeks later, a similar force under his command captured Longarone and a further 10,000 Italian soldiers. He was to be awarded an old Prussian medal '*Pour le Merite*' to add to the Iron Cross Second Class awarded for his actions in France in September 1914. Perhaps fortunately for the newly-arrived Allied Expeditionary Force he was promoted to Captain and posted to the Western Front in the 64th Army Corps. He became better known in the Second World War, as Field Marshal Erwin Rommel.

The Germans and the Austrians advanced 80 miles to within striking distance of Venice, an action which Keegan described as 'one of the few clear victories of the First World War'. The Italians changed commander to General Armando Diaz, who was seen as more indulgent to the ordinary soldier regarding leave and other comforts such as rations. Mitchinson takes a less sympathetic approach to the Italians by quoting one of the senior staff colonels of the 48th Division, writing of the 'chaos', of the Italian authorities' 'quite deplorable ... lack of knowledge' and their 'complete failure to appreciate the importance of detail'. This seems to say more about the colonel than the Italians. They held the defensive line on the Piave river but had lost the services of some 700,000 of their soldiers – killed, wounded, captured or deserted, with some estimates putting the last category as the most numerous. The line was held chiefly by the Italian Third Army, commanded by the Duke of Aosta and undefeated in battle. Diaz quickly improved morale and this, and the arrival of the snow, brought proceedings to a winter standstill, which allowed the newly-arrived French and British troops to retrain and re-equip for their new Front.

Beyond these actions in Italy, the Third Battle of Ypres was coming to a conclusion. Russian participation in the War was ending after their Revolution, albeit without formally withdrawing until the Bolshevik regime negotiated the Treaty of Brest-Litovsk in March 1918; whilst the first American troops joined combat in France on 21st October 1917. The Allies decided that they needed a more coordinated approach to the War and the Supreme War Council was formed, based at Versailles, although its first meeting was in Italy, at Rapallo near the French border at the behest of King Victor Emmanuel III. The Allies agreed to send reinforcements and the redoubtable 48th Division was selected for the British Expeditionary Force along with the 5th, 7th, 23rd and 41st Divisions; in all some 60 battalions under the command of General Sir Herbert Plumer. Bomford wrote his last letter from France on 20th November to his father. There is much about inter-company football matches with his A Coy playing C Coy in the Brigade Final with a barrel of beer and medals for the winners. He detailed his daily programme during this 'rest' period:

> Called 7 (I don't get up), breakfast 8, parade with Company 8.45 to 12.45, 2-3 bombers (training the Bombers and Rifle Grenadiers), 3-4.30 see to football, 6 lecture, 7-8 Coy concert. It doesn't leave a great deal of time … [He concluded the letter with:] don't be alarmed if you don't hear from me for a day or so.

The rumours were yet to be confirmed but Lt LR Bomford must have known by then of the impending move to Italy. Corbett reported that the Battalion was 'ordered to get everything to complete equipment, and our Divisional Ordnance Stores were given preference over all others to enable them to get it for us. Of course, they did not take so much trouble, but merely let us have what few things they had in hand'. Dr Bill Mitchinson's *The 48th (South Midland) Division 1908–1919* – a disappointing tome from the Battalion's perspective (the index mentioning just two of its members: Lt Col Peake for being 47 years old and Cpl Gisbourne for shooting down a plane (while spelling him 'Goborne') – explained that a battalion took up two full trains and a brigade needed eleven trains. He said that each carriage held 24 men under the command of a corporal, 'with sergeants travelling four to a truck in Third Class Carriages'. He wrote nothing of the officers who, presumably, had their own mess carriage or two. We do better to turn to Corbett who explained some of the bureaucracy involved with the supply of reinforcements as well as describing the journey:

> The day before we moved some reinforcements turned up at day-break. They were transfers from the A.S.C. [the Army Service Corps] and were not pleased – first because they had left the amenities of the Base for the Line, and secondly because they had met an RTO [Railway Transport Officer], which was certainly the graver misfortune. They had reached St. Pol [two miles away] yesterday morning, and as it was the nearest station, naturally wished to detrain. But the RTO said that Tinques, eight miles further up the line was our railhead and they must go there. [As they had no officer with them, they had to obey.] At noon the train started on again and reached Tinques at 10p.m. They had seven miles to go by a cross-country road on a pitch-dark night and had wandered about till dawn before they could find us … next day we marched to [the same] Tinques and entrained. The last thing we saw here as the moon set was the Hanging Virgin of Albert.

General Plumer's force consisted of five Divisions – two from the Regular Army, the 5th and 7th, two New Army Divisions – 23rd and 41st – and one Territorial Division, our 48th. Mitchinson was unable to identify any reasons as to why each had been chosen but it was going to provide a welcome change of scene for the officers and men of the 1/8th, even if they could not speak Italian. Lt LR Bomford remembered the journey:

> … as taking a week. When the train stopped as it did frequently the troops would get out. They were badly crowded in their trucks. If there was a field, football would start. When the engine whistled we all sprinted back. We went along the Riviera coast and bought food on a beach near Cannes. At Sampierderena on the outskirts of Genoa on the Frontier there was an official reception party at about midnight, but no one called us and A Coy officers slept on and missed it.

Corbett, as ever, was more elaborate in his description of the journey through France:

Northern Italy

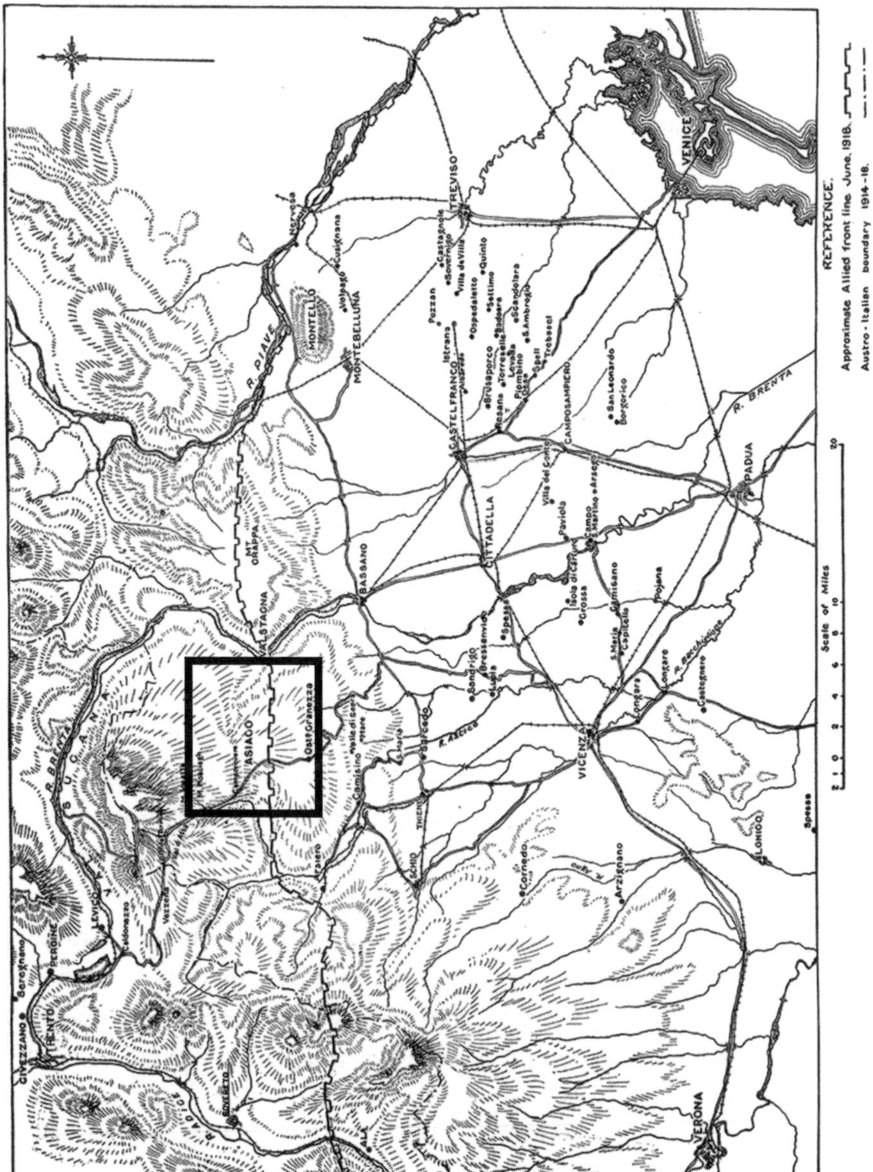

> Dawn found us at Longueval, not far from Paris, next dawn we were beside the great Soane in Beaujolais. The men were enraptured by the scenery. They had thought that all France was a bleak, rainy expanse of dreary downs, and never could be got to believe that she is really fair. The vast and glorious city of Lyon, with its castled hills, white streets, and two great rivers, and the monstrous impact of the blue Rhone against the bridge were a revelation: few had seen a large river or a large French town.

They reached the coast at Arles before turning east to Marseilles. Bomford's single sentence about the Riviera and Cannes was suitably embellished by Corbett:

> Out again (from Marseilles), up a lovely valley, past cheering villagers, through a mountain forest and a long tunnel to the loveliest scene of all – steep woods, white villages, a bay of the sea, a glorious cape, and the wide Mediterranean lit by a purple sunset. Dawn brought us to St Raphael, where we got down on the sea beach and bought fish and fruit and eggs for breakfast from stall-girls, one of whom dressed and spoke Catalan.

Corbett was probably the only man in the Battalion who could have made such a distinction. St Raphael is a few miles short of Cannes and the railway runs right beside the sea so perhaps Corbett's memory of St Raphael is more accurate than Bomford's of Cannes although the Battalion was split into two trains so they may both have been right.

Although it was November, this transformation from the mud and wire of Vimy Ridge to the beaches near Antibes must have been extraordinary. After their turn in front of Passchendaele, they deserved this change of luck but, then, perhaps every infantry battalion could make such a case. Corbett wrote of frosts and dense mist as they travelled on from Genoa through the historic towns of Parma, Modena and Bologna where:

> There were gay doings: our band played on the platform and, conducted by an Italian bandmaster, performed as never before. The

> Eighth is not musical. We danced with the ladies, shook hands with the gentlemen, and noted with pain that in Italy the embracing is done by the wrong sex.

They crossed the Po River and detrained at the village of Bovalone to the south of Verona. The marching now began. Corbett's men met with those from the other train at Albaredo on the northern bank of the Adige river. It was here that Major Bate 'achieved a feat which added indescribably to our comfort and well-being all the time we were in Italy: he stole an interpreter, an Italian soldier from London, Luigi Ciapancelli by name but Lulu on our tongues and in our hearts'.

Bomford was more expansive in the first letter to his parents to arrive from Italy, probably his longest of the War, dated 13th December:

> People talk of the boredom of an eight-hour journey; I wonder how they would like a week of it, in tight. We simply enjoyed it immensely. The scenery was lovely, we came through some of the finest parts of France and Italy… Meals were a difficulty and I think most of our drink was mild French bottled beer. I wish we could get it here, they drink rotten sour wine in this country.
>
> We attracted quite a lot of attention, especially in Southern France. We had a great time in some of the stations. The Italians, we usually call them Macaronies, seem very depressed… They are very glum, especially the soldiers, but I think we did them a lot of good.
>
> Now I come to think of it, this is my 21st birthday. It's not much of a place to have it.

This is a contrasting view to that of Corbett, who continued to wax lyrically for six more pages on the Euganean Hills, the marching on splendid roads in brilliant frosty weather and the lovely country. The *History* reported that by the end of the first week of December the 48th Division was in place to the south of the Bacchiglione river. The full Expeditionary Force was in place a week later and, with the Italian Army, held a line which ran along the western bank of the Piave river across the plain of Venetia to the high ground of the Montello, over Mt Grappa, across the Asiago Plateau and to the line of the old frontier near Lake Garda. There was little fighting for the first few weeks with much training and route marches.

For the fourth and last Christmas of the War, Corbett reported that 'we celebrated in better style than in '15 and '16 and had on the whole a jovial time, in spite of our bad lodgings'. The Battalion had been ordered to move on 23rd December to Bressanvido – the worst billet which Corbett remembered of the whole War. To make matters worse, they could not collect the chickens they had contracted to buy, nor could they carry the wine as they had no transport. They were able to sell it to their friends in the Royal Flying Corps and set about replacing everything with the invaluable aid of Lulu, although the French battalions had been through and the price of the remaining turkeys had risen threefold to 16 shillings (80p). The snow arrived shortly afterwards. Corbett described conditions for the soldiers:

> Our billets were open-fronted barns – half full of crops – airy and wholesome, no doubt, but after five o'clock when darkness fell, rather chilly, and lights could not be allowed because of the loose hay … the ration was two candles per company each six days (so of little use).

He continued with a narrative which showed not only the difficulty of providing food and warmth for the troops but also the life of the rural communities in northern Italy at that time:

> The fuel question in Italy was very difficult. The country produces no fuel [coal] except in Sardinia … in the War it was supplied by our Government at £3 a ton and was resold to the consumer at £30 a ton [some unpleasant profiteering which seems to happen in every war]. Timber is the obvious recourse, but these northern plains produce little or none. There are no woods, but nearly every field is divided by lines of trees, Virgilian elms chiefly, to support the vines, and these are all pollarded, not to provide hetherings [horizontal bindings for laying hedges] but firewood. These loppings, maize straw, and other waste provided scanty fuel for cooking. House-heating there was none: the people sit in the cow-house for warmth, and as

> soon as the cooking is done the embers are raked into earthenware pots and carried away to warm bedrooms … the cooking of meals was a daily and perplexing problem. But we managed that, and even occasional hot baths. Warming billets or drying clothes was, of course, impossible.
>
> Having neither fire nor light the obvious recourse was to sit and soak in taverns, but we were not paid for about three weeks so the men crowded into cowsheds for warmth … this was the only time pay failed us.

Bomford wrote home in mid-January describing the main training days as being from 9 until 4 with some 12 miles of marching with an attack in the middle. He told of the country being 'very flat and has such a lot of small trees that you can't see very far and get lost easily … especially crossing large streams'. He also mentioned the difficulties of keeping warm and trying to manufacture a stove for the mess, eventually with success but at the price of being smoked out quite regularly. Most officers had heavy colds due to going in and out of the warmth, whereas before the stove nobody had a cold.

Bomford's letters started to mention his brother officers again as things settled down. He had taken to Lt Watkinson:

> I've got a splendid 2nd in command. He is really senior to me (it still wrangled with him) but only came out from England in Sept 1917 [actually October] so I'm put over him. He has spent all his time instructing in England and has all his drills, etc, at his fingers ends. I'm going to put him on to instruct some of the junior NCOs and he ought to do them a lot of good. He's a very nice fellow and is our Mess President, a task that isn't light.

He turned then to Captain Walford, who he said in November was not fitting in very well. Two months later he was to write:

> Col. Clarke is now on leave in England and Captain Walford is in command. He will be Major Walford in a day or two and I expect he will keep this rank permanently. He is a nice old boy and keeps a

> fatherly eye on me. I suppose this is Doug's doing, it's a bit embarrassing but we get on well. He still has a lot to say and he's getting on much better now.

Douglas Bomford came to a similar conclusion in his letter on early September 1916, so about the same length of time after starting to soldier at the Front with Walford – a man much nearer to his father's age than his:

> He is such a figurehead in the battalion and has done a very great deal for me and several others of us. I don't know what you will think of him when you meet him after the war as he lives on whisky and is a type of man I had not struck before the war, but he has the kindest heart in the world and is a thorough English gentleman in the best sense of the word.

We have no evidence as to whether Walford took to whisky because of his experiences in the trenches or if he was a hard-drinking man beforehand, perhaps from his experiences in the bush of West Africa. The Bomford brothers had been sent to Wycliffe College, named after John Wycliffe. The College's website today explains that the founder, GW Sibly, choose this name due to Wycliffe's qualities of 'independence, a sturdy Protestant attitude towards life and a pioneering spirit'. Their father, Raymond, was a Baptist and he was believed to have been a teetotaller.

Bomford's reference to being junior to Watkinson and of Walford keeping his rank remained a recurring theme in his correspondence. His letter of 13th January explained more about this and many other junior officers' concerns:

> 1st Line people don't like having 2nd line people being put over their heads, not that there's bad feeling but it stops promotion and of course they are strange to the Bn… I'm so glad that Douglas is keeping his acting Captaincy. Its rotten going home and losing promotion earned in the field. My acting captaincy may be through any time. Waiting for it keeps you in suspense because you may

> always have a senior Capt that another Bn doesn't want shoved on you and then of course you not only don't get the promotion but have a stranger put in command. The 1/7th Worcs have got one or two spare Captains and it wouldn't be at all extraordinary to have one of them attached to us.

Bomford was able to report just four days later to his mother: 'My third pip is through all right … we've just had news of the increase in officer's pay. It's not at all a bad idea but in the case of young unmarried subalterns I can't see that it was urgently needed'. The Army had a tradition of having their pay defined on a 'by daily' basis. The rates for infantry officers at the start of the War were:

Lt Colonel	28s	(140p)	so £511.00 per annum
Major	16s	(80p)	so £292.00
Captain	12s 6d	(62.5p)	so £228.12
Lt	8s 6d	(42.5p)	so £155.12
2Lt	7s 6d	(37.5p)	so £136.87

Thus, Bomford's rise to Acting Captain gave him a 47 per cent rise in pay. However, as he wrote, to him the command position was more important. For an officer like Captain Walford, aged 48 in early 1918, with a wife and a son at Sandhurst, the rise in pay with the promotion from captain to major would have made a big difference. Extending this table to the Other Ranks is sobering:

CSM	5s 2d	(26p)	so £94.90 per annum
Sergeant	2s 6d	(12.5p)	so £45.62
Corporal	1s 9d	(8.75p)	so £31.94
Private	1s 1d	(5.08p)	so £18.55

In September 1917, the Government awarded extra pay for long service by adding one pence (1d) per day for each year served, but only since the start of the War – and not retrospective. For those who went to France in 1914, this might add 3d or £4.29 a year to a soldier's pay. All 'board and lodging' while serving abroad would be paid by the Government so, in the ranks, a single man was markedly better off than his married counterpart. By comparison, in 1914, a train driver received about £100 per annum, rising to £175 by 1919; a guard nearer £150 which changed little; and a docker some £11 per annum but this rose to £110 by the end of the War. Lastly, to give an idea of what a soldier's pay would afford when at the Front in Italy, Bomford wrote to his mother about them buying a barrel of beer and selling it a 5d a pint, which means a Private would be able to buy 2.5 pints a day. A cup of coffee cost 2d so a soldier could afford six cups each day.

At this time, various of the Companies were publishing their own version of *The Old Firm*. LR Bomford's copy of Vol 2, No 12 survives in extraordinary condition signed by Lt AR Watson, who designed the front cover, QM Corbert and by W Charles Henderson (LCpl) as the editor. It was the same Henderson who helped Corbett with his newspaper articles in the spring of 1919, which became Corbett's wonderful *War Story* on which I have leaned so heavily. It takes amusement from 'Algy' Bomford's pole-vaulting as well as poking fun at Lts Gilbert, Aldrich, Watkinson and 'Mustard' Keen. Henderson, writing his 'editorial' on 20 December 1917, is prophetic: 'I am confident that next Christmas will see the victory of the Allied Powers complete, and ourselves happy in the memories of a duty done, and in spite of hardship – a happy comradeship with each other.' In the Children's Rhymes section is a short poem about the above proposed pay increases:

> Sing a song of sixpence
> That's your rate of pay
> But Lloyd-George has promised
> Another bob a day
> But promises are pie-crusts
> He's made them oft before
> But if he fails we'll take good care
> We'll trust Lloyd-George no more.

At their new mountainous front, Corbett recalled climbing to the upper slopes of Monte Grappa – 'a fine mountain expedition in grand winter weather' – and watching the Battle of Bassano 'where the French drove back the enemy very neatly. We could not have done it better ourselves'. A compliment indeed, but it is difficult to find out anything more of that battle. Corbett then remembered that perhaps the same staff colonel, who thought so little of the Italian officers, waited until the thaw had set in before moving the Battalion down to the area of the Piave river:

> The ice-bound gravel roads (which are only constructed for light country traffic) were soft as mire … it was a long and awful march, along a route shaped like Z, passed the walled town of Cittadella to the village of Paviola. The light roads were churned by our monstrous lorries into loose gravel full of water. Wagons sank to their axles, lorries to their understructure, the roads were hopelessly blocked, and [our] Captain Rayer was the only T.O. [transport officer] in the Brigade who brought his train in. The men waded knee-deep along the ruined tracks: some even fainted with exhaustion.

Lieut. J. E. Rayer, Worcester. Mentioned in Despatches. Photo Elifle: W'ster.)

But the rains stopped and, due to taking detour routes on more major roads, better progress was made through Resana, S. Ambrigio,

Badoere, to Paese and Villa de Villa. Corbett continued on a more positive note:

> After the cold damp climate of the Western Front this was glorious. It was difficult to believe we were still in January and forty-six north. All night it froze hard, all day the sun blazed hot in a speckless sky.

The German air force was active on the moonlight nights, focusing on Venice, Padua and Treviso as well as the Battalion's medical base which had 'hospital' warning lighting on its roof. But the Italians had their revenge:

> Judgement awaited Gerry. Next night he had another shot at Treviso. The Italians were ready for him with their wonderful mobile artillery – great guns which move behind tractors at thirty miles an hour on the splendid roads – and a great barrage was raised. One machine passed it and fell in flames in the suburbs: seventeen more were brought down outside. One of our companies was quartered there at the time and saw it, a splendid spectacle. After this our troops were withdrawn from the town on account of the danger, and so were the aeroplanes; but later they had another try at Padua and lost five more.

Corbett and Bomford differ in the main focus of their correspondence and memoirs of the next few quiet months. Corbett and, indeed, Mitchinson focus on the finer things of life:

> What interested us more than the water was the wine. After the horrible beverages we had swallowed in France it was great to get good and cheap vintages of this admirable country. Of course they varied by localities: in clay areas they would be poor, but where limestone outcropped or on the brashy plains we would get it good again. We noticed these changes as we marched along, and many bold fellows became fair geologists… But some of the wines were uncommonly potent and could not be played with. The men were warned of too great a freedom in their use, but in spite of all they would drink them down like cider (at first) with occasional painful results.

This was a good time, when the winter conditions quietened the Front, to send young officers away for training. XI Corps must have been quick to set up training courses in the key disciplines, as the *War Diary* reported on 12th January that 2Lt AR Watson was sent on a 'sniping and scouting' course, 2Lt Nicholls on a 'bombing' course and Lt Pennington and 2Lt G Hales on 'general' courses. These courses were not to make individuals experts in specific skills in order for them to lead sniping or bombing patrols but, rather, to bring those skills back to the battalion in order to train the NCOs and soldiers to improve the fighting capabilities of the whole Battalion. An unfortunate example of this occurred on 20th January when the *War Diary* reported that 'whilst taking a squad loading with live cartridges a rifle fired accidently. Sgt AM Turner MM was wounded in the shoulder and spine and died before reaching hospital in Sandrigo'. A funeral was held the following day at which the whole of C Company, together with the commanding officer, the adjutant and the band was present. The commanding officer at the time was Major JO Walford, as Lt Col HT Clarke was away on three weeks' leave (although two of those would have been travelling to England and back). Walford was never to command the Battalion in action although he did command them on a Divisional exercise when they acted as enemy – seemingly his only such command.

Mitchinson's view was: 'While their officers enjoyed fine wines, the troops were treated to a strong black spirit, which "knocked them silly" and was consequently supposedly banned'. Corbett's reference to water was because the Division condemned the 'local water as dangerous and thought it to be the cause of an outbreak of diarrhoea in December' although only 854 out of a Division of 17,400 reported sick in January, with 549 of them needing evacuating further down the medical chain. Bomford, probably because of his upbringing, makes no mention of wine or spirits in his letters home. His focus is more on the football:

> This afternoon my Coy [A] won the final of the Brigade Inter-Coy Football Competition. We had to play A coy of the 1/7 Worcs on their ground. At the beginning things went against us a bit but our

> fellows soon got going and did them to the tune of 6-2… The prize was medals for the team and four small barrels of beer … the beer is so light there won't be any men the worse for wear…
>
> We had a sort of orgy the next night for the team. Old Corbett, my CQMS, arranged the food and gave us such a lot that Major Walford in the chair was absolutely stumped. After that we had a few speeches and a concert.

The first mention of the two Old Gents of the Battalion in the same letter, Walford being aged 48 and Corbett 47 that spring.

There was little action for the 48th Division but plenty of training, including for mountain warfare. Bomford wrote:

> We had a long Field Day today [17th January] and are all feeling comfortably tired. I was umpiring which meant all day on my horse. The poor animal was rather tired. I was out all the afternoon before on him, and in the morning before that, so he will be glad for a rest. He won't get it tomorrow as we have another Field Day.

And much movement of the Battalion to different places on the line:

> A day or two ago [13/14th February] we had a long march and now we've settled down. The billets weren't very good but I don't think we shall like leaving them now. That's the worst of always being on the move, you are continually having all the trouble of getting things straight. First you (as officers) have to get the troops into billets, then yourselves, then there are a lot of things to be seen to such as Coy. Stores, a Sgt's mess, recreation room, parade grounds, football fields, washing places and they aren't found in a moment.

This is all rather different from the Western Front where everything was organised on a Divisional scale and by 1918 on a relatively stable front line across the full length of the Front. Each battalion was replacing another in their training or reserve area. There was no need to negotiate with local farmers and village heads for accommodation, as Bomford and Corbett would have been doing for A Company in Italy. Some comments in Bomford's letters of early March give an indication of the difference between the two Fronts:

> Just now we are messing with B Coy and it makes an awful crowd but I've got quite a decent bedroom… I had a bathe in a river near here one day last week. I saw two Italians catching eels with long forks with barbs at the end. They stood in boats and jabbed in the mud till they got an eel. They caught quite a lot but I could only get one out of them…
>
> Primroses and little blue flowers very like violets are out all over the hills, and some of the hedges will be in bloom in a day or two…
>
> I had another bathe about a fortnight ago … with Watkinson, the others aren't sufficiently fond of cold water…
>
> At the last village we were in, the priest allowed one of the men to play the organ in the church…
>
> We had a game of football yesterday evening, Officers v Sergeants, and the Sergeants beat us 4-3. I was very disappointed as we are practicing for a match and we wanted to beat them.
>
> Three of us had leave in Rome … an Italian Countess … did all the showing round … the Colosseum, St Peter's and the Vatican, the Capitol and another church.

Corbett told the bathing incident with Watkinson slightly differently: 'a small canvas punt, embarked on a local river, which is about four yards wide. In this daring enterprise Captain Bomford and Lieut. Watkinson suffered a grievous shipwreck, a calamity which was attributed to the submarine activities of Private Sanger (MM and Bar)'. It is pleasing to see that awards to private soldiers were properly acknowledged as well as those of the officers. Sanger was Bomford's servant and runner.

The *History* recorded that the Battalion started to move in early April: 'The 1/7th and 1/8th Worcestershire marched with the Brigade through the city of Vicenza on April 3rd and had a great reception'. Corbett wrote: 'It was the first time we had ever marched through a big town, and the ovation was worthy of the city and us. Flowers rained down on us…' They had marched through big towns before – Albert and Ypres – but each had been flattened and few if any locals remained to do the cheering. There were no flowers to throw. On the 4th, Major Jack Bate MC* returned from a Senior Officer's Course at Aldershot, indicating that he must have been singled out, at the age of 23, for battalion command.

But all was about to change, as Bomford's letter of 21st April related: 'We are amongst the mountains here with snow on the ground … we have had quite a lot of hill-climbing lately so this mountain work isn't altogether fresh to us. Transport difficulties are the worst. It's no end of difficult to get things up here'. These difficulties are best shown by one of the only two deaths in the Battalion between Vimy Ridge in November and the summer battles in Italy, that of 2Lt Arnold Aldrich who, according to the *Divisional History*, 'died when he and his horse slipped over a cliff' on 2nd May. He was 34 so this was not the action of an impetuous young subaltern. He was a married man from Leckhampton near Cheltenham. Neither Bomford or Corbett mention the incident, nor indeed does the *History* but it gave some indication of operating in this terrain, which was:

> 4,000 feet up the mountain slopes to Granezza … good trenches cut or blasted out of solid rock [by the Italians]. The position on the Asiago Plateau was strange to troops accustomed to the close warfare of France and Flanders. The opposing trenches were separated by an expanse of open or wooded ground which in several places was a full mile wide. That broad No Man's Land was varied and undulating, affording good cover for scouts and patrols. Great vigilance was necessary and patrolling became an important feature of the routine.

Corbett described the difficulties of supply:

> Here we used pack mules to transport the rations. It was a very heavy task. To reach the remotest part of this sector – Poslen Gulley – from the Stores at Granezza and return involved a vertical ascent of 2,900, equivalent to the ascent of Cader Idris [in Snowdonia], and was a brisk top-up to the day's work, especially as it was usually done in

> deep snow or heavy rain and part of it along mountain tracks in the dense darkness of the fir woods by night … [this makes it easier to understand 2Lt Aldrich's accident] the whole train was of 19 mules and 30 men.

There was still no serious action as June approached. A marked difference from France where British and French forces had retreated up to 40 miles and the Germans had captured over 3,000 square kilometres of ground with Operation Michael. All the territory which the Battalion had been involved in taking in 1916 and 1917 was lost. In Italy a major Allied offensive was being planned for June – artillery targets had been registered and a 'great dump of shells was ready at a crossroads picturesquely named "Handley Cross"'. The *History* reported rumours of similar enemy activity but more so on the Piave plains. Corbett wrote that on 14th June a prisoner was captured who reported that the enemy was due to attack along the full length of the Front the next day. The *Divisional History* confirmed the story so Major General Fanshawe should have had his defences fully organised. There was the issue of 'mountain fever' which reduced some battalions by as much as a third. The 1/8th were the least affected with a strength of 617, but the 1/6th Warwickshire were down to 379. Corbett, perhaps with tongue in cheek, noted that the officers were the first to be affected and puts it down to them having the option of lightweight uniforms which were not advisable in the 'moist, windy and cloudy weather on the plateau'. He was critical of GHQ, particularly as they ordered the Battalion:

> in the first week of June … to the foot of the hill to receive our [drill wear], and a great storm blew so that we shivered round the fires. On the summit the 145th Brigade were tramping through six inches of snow. We went back again to high winds, bitter evenings, and wet days at Brusado Camp near the top of Sunio, and left a score of men in high fever at the hill foot.

Not ideal preparation for battle.

The resources of the 48th Division were very stretched as a major battle approached. The Division's AA & QMG, Lt Col GH Barnett CMG, DSO recorded the strength of each of the twelve battalions – remembering that the 1/8th crossed to France with a thousand men and thirty officers, thus at full strength. The overall infantry manning was a little over half strength:

1/5 Royal Warwickshire (Major EAM Blindloss)	436
1/6 Royal Warwickshire (Lieut. Colonel Pryor)	379
1/7 Royal Warwickshire (Lieut. Colonel JM Knox)	380
1/8 Royal Warwickshire (Major PH Whitehouse)	450
1/5 Gloucesters (Major NH Walker)	466
1/4 Oxford & Bucks (Lieut. Colonel AJN Bartlett)	552
1/4 Royal Berks (Lieut. Colonel AB Lloyd Baker)	497
1st Bucks (Major PA Hill)	566
1/4 Gloucesters (Major E Shellard)	466
1/6 Gloucesters (Lieut. Colonel H Schomberg)	538
1/7 Worcesters (Major JP Bate (of the 1/8th))	548
1/8 Worcesters (Lieut. Colonel HT Clarke)	617

This shows that the 1/8th was the best-manned battalion in the Division. The average number of officers and men in each of the battalions was 491. Thus, the Division was at half strength.

On 15th June, the 1/8th Battalion were in reserve some five miles from the Front with orders to hold the crest to their right. Breakfast was planned for 3.15 a.m. with reveille at three. The bugler was not needed, as precisely on time 'a gigantic shell burst in the camp'. Corbett continued:

> We turned out and stood to. Breakfast was eaten and dinner already cooked (for we had been at work all night, having got the warning [of the attack] at about 8 p.m.) was distributed. In Corriola great shells were falling and along the trench which in the last resort we must occupy they were bursting with beautiful precision. The Austrian guns (especially the howitzers) are perfect, and their gunnery past all praise. About the first thing hit was the great dump at Handley Cross which 'went up' with fearful effect… At six a.m. the fire slack-

ened … he could not fire blindly into the forest while his own men were there.

All day we stood to, having a meal occasionally, and late in the evening we moved up to Carrila. By this time we knew the battle was along the whole front. At midnight we learnt that the enemy really was through our front line and we were to go up and counter-attack.

Corbett, writing of course in 1919, reflected that the 48th Division 'was much blamed and derided for letting the enemy through' especially with all the warnings. He wrote that 'some battalion HQs in the Line were said to have actually been in bed when the enemy came upon them'. The 1/8th was in its reserve position, while the 1/7th was on the plain under the temporary command of Major JP Bate MC*. Lt Col FM Tomkinson DSO* was in temporary command of the Brigade. This was fighting just as hard as any on the Western Front, though without the mud. Two VCs were won that day, one by the commanding officer of the Sherwood Foresters, just 26 years old and already DSO & Bar, MC – Captain (T/Lt Col) Charles Hudson. His citation gives a flavour of the intensity of the fighting:

For most conspicuous bravery and devotion to duty when his battalion was holding the right front sector during an attack on the British front.

The shelling had been very heavy on the right, the trench destroyed, and considerable casualties had occurred, and all the officers on the spot were killed or wounded. This enabled the enemy to penetrate our front line.

The enemy pushed their advance as far as the support line which was the key to our right flank. The situation demanded immediate action. Lt. Col. Hudson, recognising its gravity, at once collected various headquarter details, such as orderlies, servants, runners, etc., and, together with some Allies, personally led them up the hill.

Driving the enemy down the hill towards our front line, he again led a party of about five up the trench, where there were about 200 enemy, in order to attack them from the flank. He then with two men got out of the trench and rushed the position, shouting to the enemy

> to surrender, some of whom did. He was then severely wounded by a bomb which exploded on his foot. Although in great pain, he gave directions for the counter-attack to be continued, and this was done successfully, about 100 prisoners and six machine-guns being taken.
>
> Without doubt the high courage and determination displayed by Lt.-Col. Hudson saved a serious situation, and had it not been for his quick determination in organising the counter-attack a large number of the enemy would have dribbled through, and counter-attack on a larger scale would have been necessary to restore the situation.

A reflection of the subsequent peacetime soldiering is that 'Lt-Col' Hudson was not to get battalion command again until 1938.

The *History* recorded that in the Brigade, the 1/5th Gloucestershire and the 1/5th Warwickshire 'had been overrun and almost wiped out', continuing 'their remnants had fallen back to the line of the Cesuna Switch. Further to the right the 1/4th Oxford and Bucks LI., although severely punished, were still holding on to part of the front line, to Hill 1021 and to the northern end of Lermerle Switch'. The 1/7th Worcestershire under Major Bate was the first of the sister battalions to be committed, for a counter-attack supported by the two remaining companies of the 1/6th Gloucestershire. Captain Stacke in the *History* is clear on the importance of this action: 'on that counter-attack depended the issue of the battle. If it failed, and if the enemy were to break through the line at that point, disaster must ensue'. By 7.15 p.m. all was ready. There was no artillery as observation in the woods was not possible to redirect fire – it would be rifles, machine guns and bayonets. The *History* described the action:

> About 7.30 p.m. the advance began. The 1/7th Worcestershire in their light khaki showed up conspicuously in the moonlight. The enemy's rifles spat venomously at them among the trees. Firing rapidly and rushing by alternative sections, the Worcestershire companies pushed on through the forest, driving the enemy's riflemen back on their supports. The Austrians brought machine guns into action, and burst after burst of rapid fire gradually brought the advance to a standstill. Then there ensued a fire fight of the most intense

> nature. 'Various officers in the Frontline' records the Divisional History, 'declared afterwards that for the sheer intensity of fire, they had never seen anything to equal this S.A.A. [small arms ammunition] duel during the war … afterwards on the ground over which the 1/7th Worcestershire fought more than 300 of the enemy was found dead' … Captain WRR Prescott, commanding A Company was hit through the arm but continued in command [winning his third MC]. Every one of his subalterns was wounded. Gradually the ground was won, three hundred yards by the left flank and almost as much by the right flank.

The 1/8th was then ordered to move from Carriola to the Lewerle Switch to conduct a converging attack at 4.30 the next morning. The move was through woodland at night which itself had been subject to the great bombardment of the previous day, with many of the tallest trees now lying across all the tracks. They just made the start line in time with B and D Companies in front. But, as the *History* recorded: 'the heart had been beaten out of the Austrian troops and before this new attack their resistance collapsed.' The two battalions swept on through the wood with the remainder of the Brigade in support. The old trench line was regained together with their artillery pieces lost the day before. The 1/7th checked to reorganise while the 1/8th sent parties across No Man's Land and into the Austrian trenches, led by two platoons under the leadership of Captain LR Bomford. They returned in triumph with three Austrian mountain guns. Bomford's memory was that he 'was told to cross No-Man's-Land to try to enter their lines, near Canove. We got into their outposts and were machine gunned. On the way back to our lines we found an Austrian mountain gun and pulled it back to our lines. A captured gun is a rarity'. As ever, his letters home made no mention of Battalion actions or his part in them.

Lt Col HT Clarke, as commanding officer, wrote:

> We moved off at 1 a.m. by the road from Carriola to Handley Cross, whence B and A Companies and Battalion Headquarters advanced by A Track to the right, and D and C Companies on B Track to the

left. Movement through the forest by these Tracks was exceptionally difficult, owing to the darkness and fallen trees, and B and A Companies only deployed just in time at 4.25 a.m. They found 1/4th Oxon and Bucks LI still holding out in front of their battalion headquarters, supported by some of the 1/4th Berks., with the Bucks battalion holding Lemerle Switch. B Company [Capt GH Smith MC] pushed forward with a screen of scouts, and when within 20 yards of our original frontline they came under machine-gun and rifle fire from in front of the wire. They pushed forward and occupied our original frontline at 5.25 a.m. Bombing parties were sent along the trench to the left, and touch was gained with the Division on the right. The enemy were seen to be holding the road to Roncalto and the latter village. Patrols were pushed forward to Roncalto and the hills to the west thereof. The enemy still holding these points were attacked and either killed or captured. These patrols came under heavy artillery and machine-gun fire, but succeeded in capturing two 15-pounder guns [thus, they fired 15lb shells], a machine-gun and 19 prisoners. The outpost line as formerly held was then re-occupied. A Company [Lt LR Bomford] acted as support to B Company until the latter had regained our original frontline. They then pushed forward and re-occupied the front line to the left of B Company at 5.45 a.m. At 6.30 a.m. a patrol was sent forward and cleared the ground in front of our wire, capturing one officer and 15 men unwounded.

On the left D Company [Capt HGC Carter MC] deployed at 4.10 a.m. with C Company [Capt EV Mitchell] in support. D Company moved forward at 4.30 a.m., gained touch with 1/7th Worcestershire on the left and passed through some post of 1/4th R. Berks. They met with hostile machine-gun and rifle fire, but pushed forward, driving small parties of the enemy before them. The left platoon became detached, having moved too far to the left, where they joined forces with 1/7th Worcestershire. The right platoon continued to advance and retook our frontline near Ghelpac Fork at 6.10 a.m. In the meantime, C Company and the remainder of D Company were formed up, with elements of the 1/7th R. Warwicks on the left, and at 7.30 a.m. the whole line advanced through the wood to our original front line, capturing several prisoners, most of them wounded,

Asiago Plateau Actions – June 1918

REFERENCE

British Front Line
Austrian " "
British trenches captured by Austrian attack 15·6·18. Ⓐ Ⓐ
Austrian advanced Troops 7pm., " " "
Front of 1/7th Worc. deployed for attack " " " " Ⓑ Ⓑ
Front " " " 4am 16·6·18. Ⓒ Ⓒ
Front " 1/8th " " " " Ⓓ Ⓓ

> on the way. By 9 a.m. the original frontline had been re-established and the patrols pushed through the wire. About 12 noon C and D Companies were relieved by the 1/6th Glosters, and by 2 p.m. we had re-established the whole of our dispositions as before the enemy attack.

A dispassionate and clinical account which belies the bravery of attacking in the face of machine-gun fire. It gives the impression of a well-coordinated attack with the various manoeuvres running to schedule. Unfortunately, it does not say where Lt Col Clarke actually was when organising these actions, the case in nearly all the Battalion's major actions. Clarke went on to describe Bomford's action that evening which was to win him a first MC:

> At 5.30 p.m. a patrol consisting of two officers and 25 other ranks of A Company, under Lieut. LR Bomford, went out from our left Company front and proceeded by Pesaventi and Bassastoc to ascertain if the enemy were still holding his line in front of Canove. They entered the enemy frontline south of Canove and pushed forward a scouting party towards the village. On reaching a point 50 yards from the village they encountered heavy machine-gun fire. Having gained valuable information and captured a 15-pounder gun and five prisoners, they withdrew to our lines.

Bomford added as Postscript to his letter to his father of 3rd July: 'They have given me an MC. It makes me feel very fed up because poor old Doug didn't get anything. He deserves it miles more than I do'. This stance contrasts with that of Siegfried Sassoon in his autobiographical novel, *Memoirs of an Infantry Officer*, where he wrote:

> Early in the afternoon the Doctor bustled up from Battalion Headquarters to tell me that my MC had come through. This gratifying little event increased my blindness to the blood-stained future. Homeliness and humanity beamed in Barton's congratulations; and the little doctor, who would soon be dressing the wounds of moaning men, unpicked his own faded medal-ribbon, produced

> a needle and thread, and sewed the white and purple portent to my tunic. For the rest of the day and, indeed, for the remainder of my military career, the left side of my chest was more often in my mind than the right – a habit which was common to a multitude of wearers of Military Cross ribbons.

Clearly Bomford was an exception. He was to write after the later award of the DSO: 'Douglas, my elder brother with the 2/8th battalion, was a much better fighting infantry officer than I was. He didn't get any decoration though he handsomely deserved one'. Sassoon continued his thoughts: 'Books about war psychology ought to contain a chapter on "medal-reflexes" and "decoration complexes". Much might be written, even here, about medals and their stimulating effect on those who really risked their lives for them'. It seems that Leslie Bomford was content with his gallantry awards but disappointed that his brother's bravery was never acknowledged – though a serious wound caused his war to be shortened to just over ten months. There is little in the correspondence of either the Bomford brothers or of Lance Evers or Captain RH Burlingham about the award of medals, although the latter did not receive any. There were celebrations when those like Lt NVH Symons gained his MC.

There was a desire that one's efforts were acknowledged, as Walford was to write in a letter during the Battalion's great battles in the last weeks of the War. Lance Evers was awarded two MCs. The first at Passchendaele for an action at Aisne Farm on 27th August 1917 during which he was severely wounded; neither his diary nor surviving letters make any mention of it. The second was for his leadership at the Passage of the Lys on 3rd September 1918. His only diary mention is on the following day: 'On my return (from a bath) find I have got a bar to my MC which is very nice. Dick (Stallard) comes in after dinner and we have a festive evening'. On the Monday evening, 'Dick, Franklin, James Bomford and I dined (on me) at Les Quatre Fils to celebrate current events and my bar'.

The 1/7th lost three of their second lieutenants and 25 men with 9 other officers and 57 Other Ranks wounded, which emphasises the intensity of their action and the battalion's importance to the battle as a whole. The 1/8th had just three soldiers wounded (also the figure given by Clarke in his report). These figures in the footnote in the *History* on the battle pages do not tally with the Roll, which noted five deaths between 15th and 18th June on the Asiago Plateau. They are all to be found on the *CGWC* website, including the Battalion's first holder of a DCM to be killed, 37-year-old Cpl Edward Donovan who died of his wounds on the 18th June, and Private AJ Cardin whose parents lived in Bristol. If five died, there are likely to be at least fifteen who were wounded.

The 1/7th officers and men received one DSO (Captain HGW Wood who was to be killed before it was gazetted), two MCs, a DCM and six MMs, while for the 1/8th, there was a first MC for Captain Bomford, a DCM and five MMs. A company sergeant major in each battalion was amongst the first Britons to be awarded an Italian medal for gallant actions – CSM F Mole of the 1/7th, a Croce di Guerra; and CSM ATJ Sherwood of the 1/8th, the Bronze Medal of Military Valor. The King of Italy, Victor Emmanuel III, inspected the Division on 4th July to convey his thanks for their support and awarded these medals. Such foreign decorations are worn to the left (nearest to one's left shoulder) of the recipient's British medals, both gallantry and campaign.

Despite the 48th Division recovering all its lost ground within a day, there were to be repercussions for the initial inability to hold off the Austrian attack. The main loser was the very popular Divisional Commander, Major General Sir Robert Fanshawe KCB DSO who was sacked by his Corps commander, Lt General the Lord Cavan, just four days after the battle. Many of his staff believed Fanshawe to have been harshly treated and campaigned on his behalf years after the War was ended. He made no fuss and quietly departed for England.

Corbett had little to add about the battle but he did record that 'the slaughter of the Austrians had been awful, and for days we were hard at work burying their dead … the full total we never ascertained, nor could we have found them all'. He continued more dramatically:

> On the second night came a great storm of rain, thunder and cold winds. One will not readily forget it. From Hill 1002 one could

> see the wooded mountains lit by the constant flashes of lightning, and between the gusts of wind could be heard the howling of some wounded man in the dark gulf below. Then came a monstrous thunderbolt with a glare of flame and a concussion that threw us all to the ground. In the thick of the wood the scattered dead were glowing with the bright light: from head to foot they glittered as brightly as a sea-wave in the Tropics brime…
>
> We went back to Carriola. It was Midsummer Day in Italy: a bitter wind blew and in the evening snow fell.

The Front was quiet. The Battalion spent some wet days near Rua, then went down to the plains at Cornedo and on to Arzignano for some well-earned light training. Corbett remembered the first half of July:

> We did our training in the morning, beginning about sunrise and ending at 10 o'clock. For the rest of the day we bathed in the river, played cricket, and had a highly successful sports meeting. The temperature at mid-day was about 100 degrees … after exactly a fortnight we were marched back to Granezza on the plateau.

The subject of leave started to appear again in Bomford's letters. On 3rd July: 'Leave goes on well and I'm hoping for mine in about a month. However, you mustn't be disappointed if it is a little longer'; on the 5th, 'I should like to get home before Dick [Stallard] and Evers go but there doesn't seem much hope', and on the 9th, 'Leave is going on as usual, perhaps it's hardly up to the mark but there's very little in it. Capt. Walford has just about finished his leave, I should think'. Bomford was not to see Evers again. Corbett indicated that home leave from Italy was not available for the Other Ranks but that did not seem to have bothered him:

> While in Italy, we had two great privileges. One was foreign leave – that is to say a few were allowed each week to visit certain Italian cities – a rare and valued privilege. It also gave occasion for the settlement of A.P.Ms [Assistant Provost Marshal], Town Majors and

> Police, and all the rest of it in such places as Rome, Florence, Naples and other agreeable theatres of war. Venice was always out of bounds, but it was something to see other places, and our hardy lads were not afraid of the Roman climate in July.
>
> The other privilege was the establishment of a rest camp at Sirmio on Garda Lake – three hotels had been taken over by our Military Authorities, and all the units could detail small parties for a week's holiday there.

Corbett told of problems of abuse of these privileges and that the normal reaction by the authorities was that one place after another was put out of bounds, but concluded: 'in the midst of our war it [Sirmio] was a blessed haven of peace, where the brutal and licentious soldier could forget for a while'.

***

With the 1/7th and 1/8th Battalions heading with the 48th Division – and five other Divisions – to assist the Italians, the village and ridge at Passchendaele were captured by the Canadians in early November. More importantly, on the Eastern Front the Russians, now under Bolshevik control, sued for peace and conceded some 750,000 square kilometres of ground with 4 million of their men prisoners of Germany or Austria. The Germans were free at last to transfer most of their best troops to the Western Front for their first full-scale attack since August 1914, Verdun excepting. For them time was of the essence. The British naval blockade was continuing to cause starvation at home but, more importantly, the United States had declared war on Germany on 6th April 1917 though, at the time, they had an army of just 128,000 men. Germany had a window in the spring of 1918 in which to launch its great attack. By March of that year, the United States had landed 318,000 men in France of which virtually none had been in battle. Another million were due by July, some 250,000 fresh troops each month.

Germany launched Operation Michael on 21st March with success very similar to that which they achieved in 1914. Within three weeks, the Germans were back on the river Marne in the French sector. To the north, Ypres, Vimy Ridge and Arras were held, but withdrawing in line with the French meant that all the ground on which the 'Somme' assault of 1st July 1916 had been fought was now back in German hands. However, their supply lines were heavily stretched and Ludendorff, now in charge on the Western Front, had to choose between attacking the French on the Marne and capturing Paris or placing full emphasis on the British sector and driving towards the Channel ports. He chose the former but the French anticipated his move and attacked first on 18th July in what became known as the Second Battle of the Marne. The Germans were suffering 200,000 casualties a month and had no source of replacements. On 8th August, the British, Canadian and Australian forces with 530 tanks launched their decisive attack in front of Amiens. By late morning the cavalry was, after four years of waiting, charging through the gaps in the German lines and the Front was moved forward by almost 7 miles in a single day. The Last Hundred Days had begun with what Ludendorff was to describe as the 'black day of the German army'. In mid-September, with the Germany army back to their Hindenburg Line defences, the 1/8th Battalion was marching past the scene of their battles of April 1917 at Templeux-le-Guérard and Gillemont Farm. The war of the Western Front was fought on ground that, at Verdun and Ypres, moved by no more than a few kilometres over four-and-a-half years. At its widest, the full battlefield covered and largely destroyed little more than sixty kilometres of ground.

***

Returning to Bomford's observation in his letter of 9th July that Captain Walford was in England on leave, we know that the following day he was signing and having witnessed his Will at his father's firm of solicitors, Messrs Cox & Walford, in Birmingham. He was days short of his 49th birthday and his only son was at Sandhurst undergoing gentleman cadet training. It is not clear what prompted him to write a Will, having already been at the Front since May 1916. He could not then have known that his war would not end in Italy but that he and the Battalion would be transferred back to France for thirty days of the most intense fighting. Did he have any premonition to ensure that all his affairs were in order? Interestingly, Captain Lance Evers, in a diary observation back in September 1916, wrote 'the Old Gent gets his leave – really, sick leave – but they won't give it him for that, so he gets it for "urgent private affairs" – the Old Gent who never has any business to do!' Evers was correct and Walford's Will is short and simple – and like all such legal documents, there is no punctuation:

> This is the last Will and Testament of me John Osborn Walford of Hanbury Mount, Bromsgrove in the County of Worcester a Captain in His Majesty's Army I give devise and bequeath all my property both real and personal of or to which I shall be beneficially possessed or entitled at the time of my decease to my wife Margaret for her sole use and benefit And I hereby appoint my said wife Margaret sole Executrix of this my Will I hereby revoke all former Wills I have made and declare this to be my last In witness whereof I have hereunto set my hand this tenth day of July One thousand nine hundred and eighteen – J Osborn Walford, Capt ________________ Signed by the said Testator John Osborn Walford as his last Will and Testament in the presence of us who at his request in his presence and in the presence of each other have hereunto subscribed our names as witnesses __________________ Stanley J Cox, 14 Melrose Ave, Woodfield Rd, Bham, Solicitor's Clerk ________________ Marie C Gilhooly, Queens Head Hotel, Steelhouse Lane, Bham, Solicitor's Clerk

It is difficult to imagine what any previous Wills might have said differently, although family legend tells of a difficult marriage. He left nothing to his son, their only child – not even a memento.

CAPTAIN PAWSEY GOES MISSING

The Battalion moved back to the Front, to Kaberlaba, where 'raiding' was the order of the day. The enemy was demoralised and it was necessary to keep up regular artillery barrages and support this with night-time raids to keep them on edge. The new Divisional Commander was Major General Sir Harold Walker DSO, who had been posted from France where he had been commanding the 1st Division. The whole Division was in reserve throughout July with training, rest and sports occupying daylight hours. The first of the Battalion's raids caused a degree of consternation. B and C Companies were ordered to undertake a raid on 2nd August, with Captain Bomford leading a small party out the previous night to 'mark out the route and bridge obstacles'. Bomford explained: 'I went out with Captain Pawsey of C Coy most of the way over, and on the way back picked up some rifles left by B Coy. Some of their rear had bolted. I telephoned Major Bate, temporarily in charge of the Bn, and got a considerable raspberry for being out of my front line'.

Captain Pawsey was to lead the two-company raid the following night. The enemy trenches were manned by Bosnians. Corbett recorded:

> Bosniaks, tall resolute men who were prepared for us and held their ground stubbornly, in spite of heavy losses from our short bombardment, and when we entered their trenches they fought desperately. They must have been told that we tortured prisoners for however cornered they would not surrender. Disarmed men fought with their fists, a large party surrounded fought to the end: by the best reckonings we killed in hand-to-hand fighting 108 men and only secured a half-dozen prisoners.

Bomford remembered the raid as a failure but that was because the raiding party returned without seven men including two of the officers – Captain Pawsey and 2Lt Granger:

> Bate came to my line a bit after dawn with an orderly and said that he was going to look for Pawsey. They were great friends. He didn't know the lie of the land so Pte Sanger [Bomford's servant] and I went with him. For much of the way dead ground could be used but we had to crawl through long grass across the dried-up course of the River Ghelpac in view of the Austrian trenches. This always makes you feel your backside is sticking up too much. We searched some caves in a big bluff, couldn't find anything and came home safely. We were relieved by the Glosters in the afternoon but in the evening the C Coy Sgt-Major and three or four of C Coy wanted to go out again and look for Pawsey, who was well liked, and asked if I could go with them. After dark we followed the track of the raiding party and got close to the enemy line when the SOS lights went up on both sides and barrages of shells came down. In the middle of No Man's Land we were all right. I decided to return by a post in No Man's Land that should have been held by the Glosters. We approached with care in case they were trigger-happy, but they had returned to their front line and the post was empty.

Captain Charles Pawsey MC* had crossed to France with the Battalion back in the spring of 1915 and had seen more action than any other officer with the possible exceptions of Bate and Wilkes. He and Granger had fallen into a railway cutting, were overpowered and captured unharmed. They were held as Prisoners of War for the remainder of the War. For all Bomford's efforts, he met with further disappointment when he returned to his billet to find his bed occupied by 'a very senior Captain Stinton … I had not only lost my bed but I had lost A Coy as he was well over thirty and vastly senior to me. I took a large dose of rum and lay down on a damp dugout floor'. Corbett wrote fondly of Pawsey:

> The loss of these two officers and their gallant companions spoiled the pleasure of this successful raid. Captain Pawsey [then aged 24] was especially missed – a most gallant and skilful officer, admired by the whole battalion and adored by C Company, in command of which he was succeeded by Captain Mitchell.

Then noting the peculiar circumstances which brought 2Lt Granger back to the Battalion:

> The loss of Mr Granger was a curious effect of Red Tape. He had left A Company some months before to undergo a course of training in the Air Force. This was completed, and in order to be transferred he must be sent from England to his Battalion in Italy – at least a ten day's journey – and then be sent back to England. He would only be with us for three or four days, but during this short and purely formal stay he found occasion to visit Austria [as a Prisoner of War]. The enemy treated them very well.

Awards were made for the action, notable amongst them being a second bar to Lt SH Wilkes' MC as well as an MM to Sgt Gisbourne. Wilkes' citation was fulsome:

> For conspicuous gallantry and devotion to duty. During a raid on the enemy's lines, when the attack was held up by a large party of enemy on the flank, this officer, without hesitating, led a platoon and dislodged them. He then returned and took command of the two companies, the commanding officer [Pawsey] being missing, and successfully carried out the operation. After the party had withdrawn he stayed behind and looked for the missing officers, and was the last man to enter our trenches. He set a splendid example under difficult circumstances, and displayed great gallantry in leading his men. [Gazetted: 4th December 1918.]

This is the last mention of Lt Wilkes by Corbett, Bomford or the *History.* He seems to have been sent on a course when the Battalion returned to France or he would have surely been commanding one of the companies in that month of near-continuous action. As with Pawsey, Wilkes had been in far more than his fair share of the action and was just 22 at the time of this third gallantry award.

Corbett and Bomford record a further raid just a week later – 9th August. This time it was A and D Companies' turn, with the newly-arrived Captain Stinton in command. It is fairer to start with Bomford's

Memoir as he was at the heart of the action, even if he still harboured some resentment over his loss of command:

> As a subaltern again, I was detailed to do a reconnaissance. Next day [9th], as soon as it was dark, I laid out white tapes for the assembly position. Stinton was in command of the raid and brought his two companies right over a brow. I thought that they must be seen and heard and shelled by the Austrians, but nothing happened. D Coy were to raid on the right. When the barrage started, we advanced. I remember tripping over some Austrian wire and falling into a shell hole. The troops behind me started firing over my head. Very inconvenient. We entered an empty line: they had just bolted. I took a party to the right and we took 40 prisoners and a machine gun. This was the only occasion when I used a bayonet in earnest and found how hard it is to get penetration. The whole raid got about fifty prisoners and was considered most successful. We had some casualties including Sgt Wall killed, a most promising NCO. They gave me a bar to my MC. Again it was the gun that did it.

Sgt Reginald Wall's action was detailed by Corbett:

> The enemy here were Hungarians and fought in a manner worthy of their great traditions. In this attack we lost Serjeant R. Wall, of [3 Edgar St], Worcester, commanding No 2 Platoon. His task was to hold the head of the communication trench. It was strongly held, but he attacked single-handed, killing three and dispersing the others: but in pursuing up the trench he was pistolled by an officer, who was immediately bayoneted by one of Wall's men. His body was brought back by his fellow serjeants and buried next day at Kaberlaba.

Had Wall survived, there would be little doubt that he would have won an MM with a citation to tell this tale of gallantry. Bomford's description of his use of a bayonet indicated that he had taken a rifle as well as his officer's pistol into the action. His son, Robert, recalls that this was the one aspect of the War which troubled him in later life and in his dreams.

Bomford recalled when addressing the Grasshoppers in 1971 some very sound advice which he received from the CO, Lt Col Clarke, whilst in Italy. It must have had a notable effect to be so clearly remembered 53 years later:

> The other happening was that my Company was detailed to go to a junction to unload railway trucks, which was bombed every night. We had a Company Commanders' Conference and I managed to wangle my way out of it. 'O' Company had to go and after we came out of the Conference I started chipping the Commander of 'O' Company. The Colonel came out behind me and gave me a good dressing down, and told me 'once you have got what you want, shut up': extremely good advice which I have applied ever since in business deals, arbitrations and various things of that sort.

A story which speaks well of both Clarke and Bomford.

Somehow, these 'raid' operations read more like Second World War actions than ones from the Great War. No mud and more space, though undoubtedly a demoralised enemy helped. We will see more such operations in the coming months back on the Western Front by these and other members of the Battalion. 2Lt Wedgbury would have been in D Company in these actions and may have been the other officer with Bomford in the operation above. It is a theme common to the accounts of the War that only the senior officer in each action, those officers who won awards, or those who were killed or wounded, received a mention in the War Diaries of each battalion. For the Other Ranks, it is mostly just the actions when a VC was awarded that are recorded with the soldier's name. The *History* of the Worcestershire Regiment does list all those who received DCMs or MMs in specific actions but neither the company to which they belonged nor, except very rarely, details of the operation which merited the award are mentioned in the main narrative. We have seen that Bomford's letters home are almost always silent on the details of any raids – the exception being when he was wounded. Soldiers' letters were all censored so certainly could not make reference to any specific operation. As such, we have very little information on such incidents or reflections of those of the Other Ranks who participated. Few wrote books afterwards – Edward Corbett being a rare exception, so fortunate for those with an interest in the Battalion's exploits over three and a half years of fighting.

After a week's rest, the Brigade was back on the front line with 'raiding' firmly on the agenda to ensure that the enemy got no rest and had to keep their own front-line trenches manned fully at all times. Again, only the officers received mention in the *History.* This time it was Lt WS Gundry:

> For conspicuous gallantry and ability as leader of an offensive patrol. He led his patrol forward with great dash and determination, completely frustrating the enemy's attempt at defence. Three prisoners were taken and valuable information obtained. He set a fine example to his men.

And Lt TL Jones:

> He was in charge of a party to block an enemy trench and take over prisoners. While waiting, he noticed that a party in front was not making much progress; so he rushed forward and led them 600 yards down the enemy trench and reached a point well beyond the objective. He personally killed one enemy and took three prisoners.

Both were to receive MCs for their actions. They had joined the Battalion the previous August and October respectively. Jones was to be killed in action leading his company before his MC was gazetted.

At this stage the Battalion returned to Granezza and there were two occurrences, neither of which merited mention in the *Divisional History* but which would have been of great import to the men. The first was the presentation of medals to 'our 1914 men' by the GOC – Maj-Gen Walker. Corbett recorded three names who 'were at Gheluvelt' – CSM Bankes, LCpl Shrimpton and LCpl Danks. Reference to Gheluvelt must mean that they were serving with the 2nd Battalion in 1914. Sadly, LCpl J Danks would be killed on 4th November 1918 in the rank of corporal after more than four years at the Front.

The second brought great cheer to the whole Battalion. Corbett described it:

> At G.H.Q. [at Praglia] a great competition in physical training and bayonet fighting, in which 168 companies of all services took part. A Company for physical training and D Company for bayonet fighting represented the Brigade, after a Brigade competition held at Arzignano. To the intense gratification of the Battalion and the whole Division we won both competitions and helped the Division to get more marks than either of the others. It was doubly creditable, as we not only had the highly-trained and professionally-coached Base Units against us, but had lost two of the original Physical Training Team wounded in action the week before.

The *History* makes mention of this as a footnote and gives the competition its full name – Lord Cavan's Cup.

BACK TO FRANCE AND THE HINDENBURG LINE

This was the time that the Allied forces in France were making solid progress towards the Hindenburg Line after the great advances of the Battle of Amiens launched on 8th August. To maintain momentum, Britain was bringing in battalions and brigades from England and Italy. The British had the American Army between it and the French to the south.

We need now to turn to a new history, that of *The 25th Division in France and Flanders* whose insignia was the Red Horseshoe. Part I of this history had already been written, by Lt Col M Kincaid-Smith, at Bapaume, dated 8th February 1918, and at Royon on 15th July 1918 as the remains of the Division returned to England. The first of these introductions recorded that to that date 270 officers and 3,683 Other Ranks had been killed; 44 officers and 2,337 Other Ranks were missing, presumed killed; and 858 officers and 17,947 Other Ranks had been wounded. Five months later, Kincaid-Smith wrote: 'Withdrawn from the line in the middle of June all ranks of the Division heard with feeling of the deepest regret that owing to the scarcity of reinforcements the regular battalions (3rd Worcesters, 1st Wilts, 2nd South Lancashires) would be transferred to other Divisions and the 9th Loyal North Lancs, 8th Borders, 10th Cheshires, 11th Cheshires, 4th South Staffords and 11th Lancashire Fusiliers would ultimately be disbanded to feed their sister battalions'. This gives a good indication of the predicament of the British Army after the devastating German advances of Operation Michael in the spring of 1918. If the above casualty numbers weren't awful enough, those last few months added another 102 officers and 942 Other Ranks killed; 187 officers and 7,320 Other Ranks missing; and 361 officers and 6,461 Other Ranks wounded. This was from a single Division of between 15,000 and 20,000 men. Both sets of casualties total 40,512 in just two years of fighting.

The 25th Division was ordered to reform once again:

> The middle of September the Divisional and Brigade Headquarters returned from England, and the 25th Division reformed at St Riquier, near Abbeville, with nine battalions from the British Divisions on the Italian Front. The Divisional troops [signals, engineers, artillery] who had been attached to other formations from time to time during July, August and September, also rejoined.
> Towards the end of the month the Division moved by rail and route march to the 4th Army area near Amiens, and joined the XIIIth Corps in time to take part, on the 3rd and 4th [and 5th] October, in the hard fighting connected with the capture of the Beaurevoir position [the last line of German defence on the Hindenburg Line].

Three battalions were selected, one each from the 143rd, 144th and 145th Brigades in Italy to head to France and the 25th Division, forming the infantry resource of the 75th Brigade. This would reduce each brigade in Italy from four to three infantry battalions. Mitchinson is uncertain as to why each battalion was chosen:

> It is likely 8/Warwickshire and 8/Worcestershire from 143 and 144 Brigades were selected on the ground of regimental seniority but it is far less clear why 5/Gloucestershire was the unit chosen from 145 Brigade. It may be that the geographical origin of the battalion was considered to be the least homogenous of the brigade's units and was selected for that reason.

Clearly Major General Walker did not record his reasons for releasing these three battalions. Corbett sheds no more light on the choices:

> We went back to Kaberlaba again, and there received a sudden order that we were to pack up and go back to France, toute suite. With us were to go the Fifth Glosters and Eighth Warwicks, each Brigade having to contribute one unit to form a new Brigade. We, of course, pointed out that the best battalions had been chosen, and the other fellows took it decently, cloaked with envy, and let it go at that. They sent their love to Gerry and we hoped they would have a jolly time in the snow which would soon be there. But short was the time for

> leave-taking. The next day we descended the hills and lorries, and two days later, one fine hot afternoon, entrained at Thiene for France.

The most likely reason that each was chosen was that they were the strongest numerically in each Brigade. Mitchinson reports that new drafts from England 'remained difficult to source' and if the Army in France required strengthening, there would have been little point in sending the least resourced battalions. The 1/8th had, according to Corbett, lost 12 killed, 51 wounded and 6 prisoners in their ten months in Italy. Stacke, in the *History,* gave his thoughts:

> The wholesale destruction of the battalions during the preceding months had left the British battalions in France with far fewer old soldiers and experienced officers than the battalions brought from Italy could muster. All the new units of the 25th Division (nine in total) had come from Italy, and all were well trained and experienced in war.

Bomford and Watkinson had managed to get some home leave: a very hot journey with the officers in carriage compartments – one to a seat, two on the floor and two in the corridor – and the men in 'goods vans labelled 8 horses or 40 men'. Bomford's only memory was: 'I recollect Watkinson and me in our underpants having a good wash under an engine filling hydrant on a Paris station to the disgust of some Paris ladies. Officers don't do that'. Bomford said nothing of the journey to France excepting: 'We arrived at Abbeville again and spent a fortnight training and organising, before taking another train up to the line. I remember a night in the open and then I was detailed to go on a Company Commanders' Course near St Omer'. This is rather against the policy, if indeed there was one, of taking experienced officers from within the front-line battalions. Bomford said that he was replaced as OC of A Company by Lt GL Watkinson, who at the time was the adjutant. Watkinson had been at the Front for less than a year. The other three company commanders were Captain GH Smith MC (B Coy), Captain JO Walford (C Coy) and Lt TL Jones MC (D Coy). It is not clear where Captain T Stinton had gone after his short command of A Coy. The most experienced of the company commanders, Captain CR Pawsey MC*, was now a Prisoner of War. Jones had joined the Battalion on 21st October 1917, so ten days after Watkinson, thus also with less than a year's experience at the Front. Captain GH Smith had reported for duty back in January 1916, the same day as Bomford. He had been awarded his MC in the June Birthday Honours in 1918 for his consistent gallant services in Italy, rather than for a specific action. Captain Walford had crossed to France with the 2/8th Battalion in May 1916 but with his sick leave, he does not appear to have taken part in any major action; however, he had been a company commander with two years' experience of raiding and being shelled. He had just celebrated his 49th birthday. Bomford was not to return to the Battalion until late October, in time for the last action and to resume his command of A Company. What was important also was that there were experienced officers ready to take over the various commands if any of the above company commanders became casualties. There were to be six major actions in thirty days when this command structure was to be put to the severest test.

The key experience in the Battalion was held by Lt Col HT Clarke and Major JP Bate MC* as commanding officer and second-in-command, both of whom had crossed with the Battalion back in March 1915. Bate had, additionally, commanded the 1/7th Battalion in battle, for which he was subsequently to receive a DSO in the 1st January 1919 New Year's Honours. Amongst the senior NCOs and warrant officers there was much experience and this was crucial. Corbett included a paragraph in his *War Story* at the outset of this new phase entitled OFFICERS AND GENTLEMEN:

> Indeed, we have never been more fighting fit. The long episode of Italy had done us unspeakable good: even when we first came out [to France] we were in no better condition than now, and added to that we were fully versed and deeply skilled in the practice of war. The Battalions that composed our Division – all from Italy – were particularly fortunate in possessing so many old soldiers. We actually counted more than two hundred of our original eleven hundred, and few there were among us who had not been in actions of all kinds

> over and over again. And now, as ever, we were particularly fortunate in our officers. If a little boasting may be allowed [and surely the events of the next five weeks may justify it] one would proclaim the praises of those skilful and gallant gentlemen who led year after year, ministered to our wants, shared our toils and hardships, our pleasures and our griefs, who trained us so thoroughly and wisely, and by their kindness and care made us so happy and therefore so dangerous a force.
>
> This last campaign was a captain's war, for the Company had now again become the Unit. In all these actions which followed, the Battalion was notified of its objective: Bn HQ apportioned the work among the Companies, whose duty it was by individual and concerted action, under their own arrangements and in accordance with the shifting conditions of the fight, to attain that objective.

Yes, this was written with the benefit of hindsight and the knowledge that the company commanders won two DSOs and four MCs for their fine and gallant leadership over the following thirty days. Perhaps what was more telling was that there was no need for anyone from Bn HQ – the commanding officer, second-in-command nor the adjutant – to become physically involved in any of the ensuing battles. Seven of the subaltern platoon commanders won MCs. Looking back over all the Battalion's previous actions, this is in keeping with its modus operandi and says much for the training regime organised over the three years at the Front by that same Battalion Headquarters. An example of this and the importance of the initiative in the advance being taken quickly by those in contact with the enemy is recorded in the *History*:

> Colonel Clarke then asked for an additional company from the Royal Warwickshire; with that reinforcement he intended to advance southward from Bazuel and take the obstinate enemy in the flank. But before that plan could be put into effect the desired advance had been made. Captain JO Walford of C Company after a personal reconnaissance [made on a captured horse] decided that a strong advance firing would have the required result…

Corbett, as ever, provided some lyrical prose to describe the first two weeks back in northern France:

> We were expected to stay a fairly long time around St Riquier, but the Division was very quickly mobilised and equipped, and entraining again we reached one night the familiar town of Albert. But how changed it was. Every house was roofless, most of them flattened out, the tall factories gone, and the huge church a shapeless pile of ruins. The Hanging Virgin was gone – beaten down with the steeple by our fire and carried away to a German munition works. And the prophecy was coming true: the Kaiser and his power were toppling to ruin. We marched to Warloy. It was like old times to see the dawn breaking behind the long ridge at Pozières, with the quick flashing of the guns between; and a low familiar rumbling came on the morning wind.
>
> After a night at Warloy we moved up country, dumping as we went our superfluous stores: for, as usual, we were short of transport. At Edge Hill, while we were unloading, a sapper was blown to pieces by a bomb in a trip wire in the very station. It had been there for months unremarked, but it found its victim at last. Poor fellow. He had only landed in France for the first time the day before. We camped again by Mametz Wood and on the 1st October, a heavenly

> summer's day, moved on to Lousy [Leuse] Wood. It is a curiosity that every 1st October during the five years of the War was a summer's day, and four times it was the last day of summer. Then on to Nurlu. All the time we could hear the trampling roar of the great guns by Cambrai, and the night was crimson with the burning of the town. The next night we reached St Emilie, which we had helped to take eighteen months before, the fire was out, and we thought the town was taken. Here we made a cold bivouac, and the next morning we marched away past Gillemont [Farm], the Buttes of Templeux, and Toine Wood, through Hargicourt, which the enemy still held when we were last here.

Corbett did not tell of the graves of his fallen comrades from these actions of April 1917. Perhaps they were marching past so many graves and graveyards that they had become immune to any sentimentality. Thus, the fact that a number of their officers and soldiers were in the Templeux area was not at the time special, even to the two hundred or so of their number who may have participated in those battles. It is noticeable that neither Bomford in his letters, nor Corbett in his reflections, make any reference to dread of any impending actions. It was perhaps indicative of the unwillingness of all those who fought on the front lines to talk afterwards of their fears and experiences. Corbett did tell of scenes from the aftermath of the battles of the Hindenburg Line, which began on 29th September. Unlike the strategy on 8th August at the Battle of Amiens, where the assault was launched without a prior artillery barrage, the more traditional devastating barrage was used here. Hew Strachan described it as a '56-hour bombardment, using 1,637 guns on a 10,000-yard front, twice the intensity of the Somme … in the last twenty-four hours the British fired a record 945,052 shells.' Corbett described part of the resultant scene:

> We came to the scene of a recent battle, where the ground was strewn with the corpses of American soldiers, who had been left (callously as it seemed) where they lay. [There is a great American cemetery just outside Bony where they now lie.] We topped the rise

above Bony, and settled down for the night in trenches in support. At Bony lay the advanced parts of our Division, and just ahead was the Hindenburg Line a-smoke under bombardment.

It was the evening of 3rd October and a most extraordinary month of fighting lay ahead for the men of the 1/8th Battalion. The 75th Brigade was in reserve under the command of the recently arrived Brigadier CW Frizell DSO MC. The Division was given orders that afternoon to continue the attack started by the 5th and 7th Australian Brigades on Beaurevoir and the high ground beyond it and to its immediate north. The 7th Brigade (20th Manchesters; 9th Devons; 21st Manchesters) relieved them at Quennemont Farm with the 74th Brigade (9th Yorks; 11th Notts & Derby; 13th Durham LI) moving to Mont St Martin in support. Reconnaissance was undertaken on the 4th October. The *Divisional History* recorded the German position as being 'very strong and well chosen, giving excellent command over the absolutely open and exposed ground with facilities for hiding large numbers of machine guns in farm buildings, houses and along the railway'. There was the small Canal des Torrents marking the southern Divisional boundary with more high ground to the south (right). The attack by the 7th Brigade on 4th October reached the village of Beaurevoir but German resistance and counter-attacks meant that no real progress was made. The *Divisional History* recorded that:

> during the day casualties were heavy especially on the left [9th Devons], but the difficulties of the task allotted to the Division and the importance of the position to the German defence made them inevitable. Orders were received to continue operations on the 5th October, as the early capture of Beaurevoir was essential to an attack on a very large scale which was contemplated for 7th October.

This was and would be the pattern of the Last Hundred Days as the Allied generals wanted to ensure that the Germans had no respite for reorganisation and replenishment. The 74th Brigade relieved the 7th Brigade as they themselves had relieved the Australians the night before. The 75th Brigade moved forward to join the 74th at

Quennemont Farm, behind a spur a mile to the west of Beaurevoir.

At 6 a.m. on 5th October, the two brigades moved forward with the 74th in front; 'the attack commenced well, especially on the flanks where good progress was made north of the village' but 'the Germans at once launched a strong counter-attack [in line with their long-held doctrine], supported by large numbers of machine guns, and succeeded in forcing back our troops once more to their original line, except in the centre at Bellevue Farm which was successfully held by men of A Company, 9th Yorkshire Regiment under Captain Blow. Two tanks gave some assistance in Beaurevoir village, which was entered by a party of men under Lt Redhead MC, 21st Manchesters, but who were eventually forced to withdraw to the railway cutting south of the village'. To the north, 1/8th R. Warwicks from the 75th Brigade were tasked with taking Guisancourt Farm on the plateau and, at 11 a.m., they advanced with A and C Companies supported by B and D. 'The attacking companies were at once met with heavy machine gun fire and were unable to get across the open ground where every movement was in full view of the enemy'.

For the 1/8th Battalion, it was at 3 o'clock that afternoon that orders came for action. After dark a second attack was to be made on Beaurevoir, this time by the 75th Brigade. Preparations were made, and at 4.30 p.m. the 1/8th Worcestershire moved forward. In 'artillery formation' the Battalion advanced up the slope and deployed for attack beyond captured trenches, just below the crestline of the ridge by Lormisset: A and B Companies in front, with C and D Companies in the second line. The 1/5th Gloucestershire formed up on the right, south of the canal. The other battalion of the 75th Brigade, the 1/8th Royal Warwickshire, had been detached to the left to attack Guisancourt Farm – about 1,200 yards to the north of Beaurevoir on the high ground. The *History* set the scene. This ground is almost unchanged to this day although the village of Beaurevoir has grown to the south of the old railway line and to the east, thus meaning the depth of the target was narrower at the time. As I walked towards the round tower some 400 yards in front of the village, a brace of grey (English) partridge rose from the young corn and curled out over the line of A Company's approach.

Beaurevoir, 5th October 1918

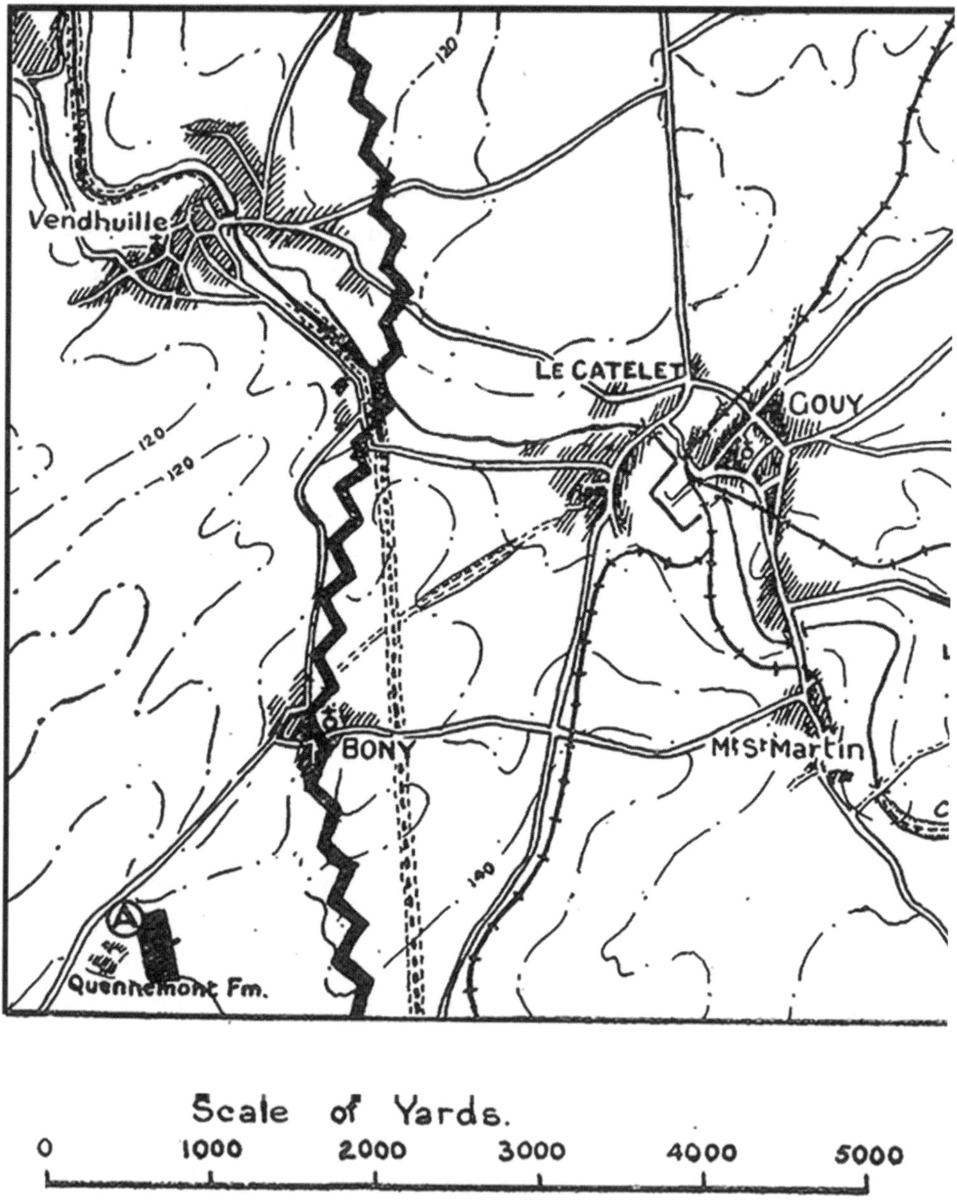

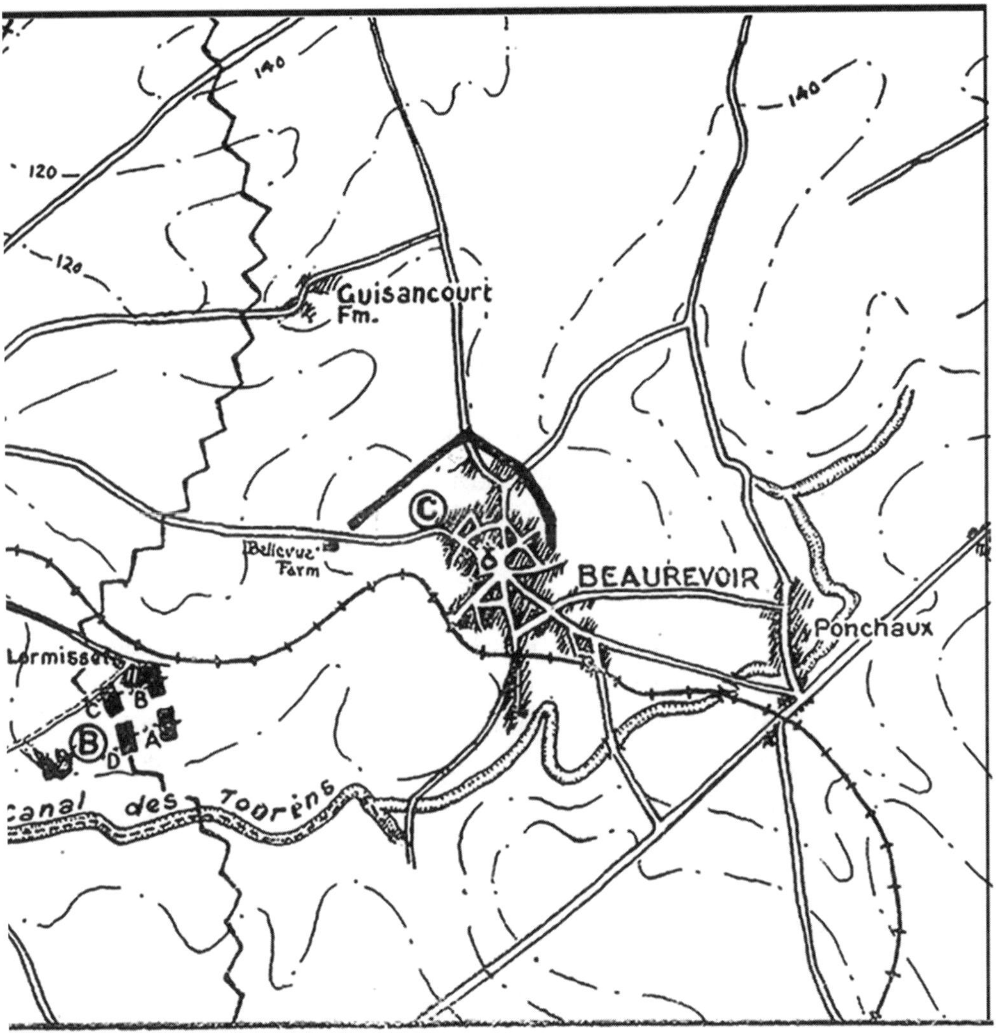

REFERENCE

Ⓐ 1/8th Worc. 4th Oct. 1918.

Ⓑ " " Assembly Position 5th Oct. 1918.

Ⓒ " " Midnight 5th/6th " "

Position of Hindenburg Line.

" " Beaurevoir "

The whole battlefield would have had enough ambient light in the darkness from the artillery bombardments and burning buildings to operate at platoon and company level, but battalion-level control would have been difficult even if the telephone lines being unrolled with the advancing companies had not been damaged by artillery fire. Thus, the key officers once orders had been given were the four company commanders: Lt GL Watkinson in command of A Company for the first time; Captain GH Smith MC commanding B Company; Captain JO Walford, perhaps commanding for the first time in a set-piece attack with C Company; and Lt TL Jones MC leading D Company. There were a number of seasoned platoon commanders and company sergeant majors who would prove invaluable through the remaining hours of darkness. An example was CSM Walter Wheeler from Bromsgrove, who when 26 had earned a DCM in the attack on Springfield Farm in front of Ypres the previous August as a platoon sergeant:

> For conspicuous gallantry and devotion to duty in an attack. When his platoon commander was killed, he at once took command, reorganised and consolidated the ground seized, and established touch with the troops on his flanks. He fearlessly exposed himself to machine-gun fire and snipers throughout, setting an example of coolness and indifference to danger.

Having such seasoned and brave SNCOs would have been a great comfort to the company and platoon commanders when the shelling and shooting started. Lt Col HT Clarke wrote from Cambrai in April 1919:

> At 6.15 [p.m.] the barrage opened and we advanced through the line of posts held by the 9th Yorkshire. The enemy immediately opened a very heavy counter-barrage, one shell mortally wounding Lt TL Jones [and another killing his CSM, Walter Wheeler DCM]. The enemy held machine-guns at the railway cutting and embankment, a high mound and some pits and houses on the west side of the village, and met the Companies with very heavy fire. Several of

these machine-guns were difficult to locate in the darkness, and although A and B Companies retaliated with Lewis gun and rifle fire, B Company suffered very heavy casualties while waiting for the barrage to lift, Capt Smith being wounded twice and a large number of NCOs and men killed and wounded.

CSM Wheeler when a lance corporal

The specific artillery orders in the Battalion's Operational Order No 91, dated 5th October 1918, help explain the difficulty in advancing:

> Artillery barrage will commence on railway cutting at 6.15 p.m. and will remain stationary until 6.40 p.m. when it will advance at a rate of 100yds in 6 minutes till it forms a protective screen in a semicircle 500yds to 600yds outside the village.
> Within the limits of the barrage, A Coy will establish posts forward.

It would appear that the speed of advance was set to that achievable by soldiers through the mud on the Somme or at Passchendaele – even in full kit, a soldier should be able to cover 100 yards in 30 seconds but if they were executing a section advance with each half dashing 20 yards before going to ground and giving covering fire for the other half of the section, it should take no more than two minutes. Initiative was needed with the two leading companies taking heavy casualties. Two second lieutenants from D Company, on the right behind A

Company, rose to the challenge:

> Sec. Lieut Wedgbury DCM, MM commanding 13 Platoon, D Company, seeing that A Company was held up by the machine guns in the railway cutting, took his platoon round by the right flank and attacked the enemy from the rear, capturing a machine gun and 36 prisoners. Sec. Lieut. GH Barber, commanding No 3 Platoon, A Company, then pushed up the village street, putting out of action a machine-gun in the Square, and consolidated on the high ground to the east of the village, also gaining touch with the 1/5th Glocesters on the right [who had had a very successful advance round the village and towards the same high ground].
>
> Lieut. Watkinson, with the remainder of A Company followed through the village, mopping up houses and cellars on the way, and extending the line to the left. About 7.20 p.m. Lieut. Redhead, of the 21st Manchesters, who had already made one attack on Beaurevoir that day, reported to Lieut. Watkinson with about 20 men, and rendered valuable assistance in consolidating the line NE of the village.

If accurate, this gives a good indication of the time taken to complete an attack – 65 minutes from the start of the barrage. Nobody remarked that this was the Battalion's first operation which involved capturing a village and clearing it house by house and cellar by cellar. This would be a complex act of war in daylight, let alone after dark. The D Company report on the action was written that night by 2Lt Wedgbury as Lt Jones, the company commander, had been wounded (mortally):

> The company commanded by Lt TL Jones MC went into action with 3 officers & 110 other ranks. The Coy paraded at Mt S. MARTIN at 16.30 o'clock & moved to its position in the Batt, as right support coy, in artillery formation. 13 & 16 platoons in front wave, 14 platoon and coy headquarters section in second wave [so the company was already a platoon short].
>
> At 1830 the company moved forward to the attack & came under

heavy shell & MG fire. Shortly after the action commenced a shell fell near the headquarters section severely wounding Mr Jones, killing the CSM & wounding several other ranks.

The leading coys being held up by MG fire the officer commanding A Coy (Lt. Watkinson) ordered 13 platoon to endeavour to push forward down the sunken road & turn the enemy's left flank.

13 platoon [2Lt Wedgbury] then moved forward down this road & found that the S end of the village in possession of 5th Glosters, it then made its way past the church to the gulley behind the railway embankment & came upon an enemy MG in action, the Lewis Gun was turned upon this post & the enemy ran away leaving the gun behind, the platoon [moved] to the railway cutting where it captured 36 of the enemy who were holding the western edge.

The position being secure, the platoon returned to the village & reported to A Coy headquarters who gave it orders to proceed to the N end of the village & assist in forming a defence line.

14 platoon working through the village captured several prisoners.

16 platoon worked up the Western side of the village & the railway cutting, finding itself isolated & no signs of the enemy, it returned to the village & was then ordered to support the front line.

The Coy dug itself in & stayed in their position till 3 AM on the morning of the 8th when it was relieved by the Surreys.

During the time the Coy was in the front line it was under continuous & heavy MG & shell fire but the men were determined & cheerful despite this & the very cold weather.

The Coy's losses during this action were:

1 officer wounded	[Lt TL Jones MC]
CSM killed	[CSM W Wheeler DCM]
1 Sgt killed	[Sgt AM Gisbourne MM]
16 OR wounded	

E. Wedgbury 2Lt

From this we learn that the Company went into action with just three officers and lost the most senior in the initial shelling. We learn also that Lt Watkinson selected 2Lt Wedgbury's platoon which conflicts slightly with the citation of Wedgbury's MC: 'when the leading platoon was held up by machine-gun fire he displayed great coolness and initiative in bringing forward his platoon, and assisting to outflank the enemy's position'. Given Wedgbury's nature, it is likely that he played down his own leadership and initiative.

Lt Watkinson was to write a rather intemperate letter to his friend Captain LR Bomford whose company he was commanding in Bomford's absence on a company commanders course – dated 26th October:

> Dear Old Bomf,
> Thanks awfully for your letter and the baccy. I was short of baccy when it arrived and I fairly whooped with joy.
>
> Well. Old son, we've had a mighty lot of fighting since we left you. The battalion has done jolly good work and has got a reputation of being easily the best fighting unit in the Division. As for A Company, well, you know they'd do well. In three attacks they did the show. In the first on an important village [Beaurevoir] which we had to capture they got the village an hour before anybody else (except Wedgbury and his platoon by the way) of the other Coys arrived at all…
>
> Of course, all this is very much in confidence and I wouldn't write like this to anyone else. It has been pretty wonderful good fighting, Bonf. I'm feeling quite cheery but a bit tired…

There is probably a degree of exaggeration here but the exhilaration of being under fire, operating well in front of those you command, and being part of a very successful battalion is clear from his tone. After all, since Bomford had gone on his course, Watkinson had won two MCs before writing this letter. This is the only letter from Watkinson which survives and can be compared with that of Captain Walford, perhaps written to his cousin, Colonel Matthew Dixon, the text of which was sent to me some five years ago by his family. Walford's is one of only two which we have of his from the War. The two men were from a different generation – Walford was 49 and Watkinson 22 at the time of these actions. To introduce Walford's letter, we must revert to Clarke's report and the actions on the Battalion's left flank at the time of Wedgbury and Watkinson's actions:

In the meantime, C Company, whose role was to form a defensive flank on the left, advanced to the right [and below] Bellevue Farm, where they were met by very heavy machine-gun fire, Lieuts. RJC Hawtrey [who crossed to France back in April 1915] and WS Gundry MC being wounded and the leading Platoons suffering heavy casualties. Capt. Walford, however, pushed on with his third Platoon and commenced to build up a defensive flank facing north.

Beaurevoir: line of attack of Walford and C Company

The north-east flank was of concern and CSM Leighton of A Company assisted the CO in this regard as the citation of his DCM acknowledged:

> He acted with great coolness and disregard of personal danger. On one occasion he moved for 200 yards along an exposed ridge swept by a storm of machinegun fire in order to gain information as to the situation on the flank, thus contributing materially to the success of

the operation. It was largely due to his indefatigable efforts that the organisation of the defence of the village was carried out.

Beaurevoir village edge from tower between D and C Companies

It is a piece of ground that remains exposed to this day.

Walford wrote some five days later of this experience – a rare first-hand report on a significant action fought by the Battalion:

> We left camp on the 5th at 7.30 am and marched about 6 miles, where we stayed for lunch. At 3.30 pm the CO sent for the Coy Comds and told us that we must move at 4.30 pm and at 6.30 pm attack Beaurevoir. Perhaps you have seen in the papers that there is a Beaurevoir line. This is about 2 miles before you reach the town and was taken by the Australians after the Americans having [failed] to do so. It appears two other brigades in our division had likewise failed to capture it separately, making afterwards a combined attack with the same luck. We who were in divisional reserve were then brought up! The barrage started at 6.15 pm and lasted till 6.40 pm when we got really right up and rushed the village on the centre and right. On the left, where I was, we ran into a nest of machine guns and had heavy casualties. However we also got through at last and took

150 prisoners. I don't know what the 5th Gloucesters' bag was. The people on our left (another division [actually the 1/8th Bn, The Royal Warwickshires from their own brigade]) who really seemed to have a very simple job didn't manage to get up and all night our left flank was in the air. It was part of my job to make it good and I can assure you it was a very anxious time: pitch dark, in a village I did not know anything about; Hun Verey lights [flares] going up in all directions and we didn't know which was our line and which the Huns! In fact we ran into one of their patrols and took them prisoners. However we got it done about midnight, and then retired into a cellar, as they were shelling us and shooting with machine guns all the time. I got a little sleep on the brick floor of the cellar, getting up next morning to improve the position. Fortunately the people on our left [74th Brigade] did manage to get up in the early morning [by 6.30 a.m.] as the Hun finding we had turned his flank had to retire and let them through. So I was able to join up the line again and push our outposts forward a little to a better position. But we could not move in the daytime [of Sunday 6th] as we were in full view and no cover at all. However that night we dug in and again all the time they shelled us and hit the house I was in the cellar of 3 times, smothering us in brick dust: we had to bolt each time to a ditch about 50 yds away, but found it so cold there we came back as soon as possible.

The last night at Beaurevoir [Monday 7th] I spent in a deep Bosche dugout, but we were quite safe from shells, but as they sent over a lot of gas we spent at least 4 hours with our mask on – altogether a most unpleasant time. On Tuesday morning at 3.30 am, we were taken 3 miles to our left rear where we arrived about 5am to find nothing but an open trench and it had started raining. About midday they moved us forward again as the big battle had commenced. It started from Beaurevoir that is. Why we wanted the place so badly: it was to be the centre of the attack on Le Cateau which you know by now we have taken. We followed up that night and had to wait in a field from 5pm until 9pm when we got into a village about 200 yds away. It was bitterly cold waiting and we might really have gone in straight away and had some sleep…

The Battle Report recorded the following casualties, prisoners and captured machine guns:

	OFFICERS		OTHER RANKS		CAPTURED	
COMPANY	Killed	Wounded	Killed	Wounded	Prisoners	MGs
A		1	6	17	100	2
B		1	13	32	50	
C		2	7	32	3	
D		1	2	22	50	3
Bn HQ				5	2	
TOTAL		5	28	108	205	5

These numbers were increased by the time of the *History* in part because of an incident in the transport lines over the following days, referred to in Captain Walford's letter and because the wounded officer in D Company (Lt TL Jones MC) died of his wounds on 10th October. Corbett recorded the final tally as 37 killed and 125 wounded and explained the incident:

Grave of Albert Wanklin

> Among the dead was another veteran of the Battalion, Serjt. Wanklin DCM., of Bromsgrove and C Company, best and most-beloved of NCOs. And many other valued friends went Home. Meanwhile the Transport Lines, which had been unadvisedly pitched on a registered spot, had been shelled by a very long-range gun, causing many casualties among the transport and the dumps of the Brigade. Captain Carter MC, commanding D Company [seemingly not at the time but the Transport Officer], and Lt King, a veteran of '14, were among the killed, and Transport serjeant wounded, other men killed or hurt, and many animals, among which was Dick Hook, our famous fat cob.

Captain Harvey Carter crossed to France with the Battalion in 1915 and won his MC when patrolling in May 1916. His parents, William and Ellen, from Maidsmere, Bromsgrove had FEW WORDS, FAIR FAITH inscribed on his headstone. He was 23 years old. His brother, Captain EPQ Carter MC of the Royal Warwickshire Regiment, was released as a PoW in Austria in late November 1918. His old school, Bromsgrove, published an obituary in their *Old Bromsgrovian* which was included in Philip Bowen's *Bromsgrove School at War 1914–1919: A history of life at School and the deeds of Old Bromsgrovians during the Great War*:

> Coming first as a day boy, he afterwards entered the School House, in which his high character and modest charm won for him a position of influence and esteem. Naturally of a retiring disposition, he hated prominence; his monitorship and cricket captaincy were both undertaken from a sense of duty which was conspicuous in all he did, and which led him, for he had no love of soldiering, to take a commission in the 8th Battalion of the Worcestershire Regiment as soon as possible after the outbreak of war. He reached France in the spring of 1915, was severely wounded shortly after and returned the following spring to the Front again, becoming Lieutenant in April. In May 1916 he was again severely wounded – in the leg – but, in spite of loss of blood, managed to crawl to the posts on his right and his left and ordered rapid fire, which drove off the enemy. For

this “conspicuous devotion to duty” he received the Military Cross. The effort had been great, and his wound was severe. so that his recovery was long and he did not return to France until the Spring of 1917. Later he was transferred to Italy where the beauty of the surroundings and their rich associations were a constant pleasure to his delicate mind; he always secretly cherished literary ambitions – not without hope, as his letters showed – and his imagination was stimulated by the Italian campaign. He devoted himself to the well-being of his men; and delighted in the success of his Company in a bayonet competition between 100 teams in the autumn of this year. He was killed instantaneously by a shell in his tent: in him there passed one of those gentle yet brave spirits who sweeten life for others and lend them unconsciously a great strength.

One can only imagine the pride of his parents in such an obituary, beyond that both their sons who served had been awarded a Military Cross. Carter was one of the few 1/8th Battalion officers who was a schoolboy hero. The book shows a photograph of the 1st XI of 1913 which included Carter. It says simply: ‘The remarkable 1st XI of 1913 – all fought and six died.’ 2Lt HD King is buried beside Carter but the *CWGC* website gives no more details, except that he was ‘attached' to the Battalion. Harold Dudley King had been a sergeant in C Company before being commissioned into B Company on 6th January 1918 – he left a widow, Martha Jane, and £80 in his estate; one of a number of junior officers upon whom the Battalion was increasingly to depend and who had been commissioned from the ranks. One other death needs mention, that of Sgt AM Gisbourne MM – an MM earned that August in the same action in which Captain Pawsey was captured. Sadly, his body was not identified so his name adorns the Vis-en-Artois Memorial, halfway between Cambrai and Arras.

A year later in the *Journal* was an *In Memoriam*:

> HUNT – In ever-loving memory of our dearly-beloved Lance Corporal F Hunt, 1/8th Worcesters, killed in action October 5th, 1918 in France.
>
> We who loved sadly miss him as it dawns another year, in our lonely hours of thinking, thoughts of him are very dear.
>
> We think we see his smiling face, as he bade his last goodbye, and left his home forever, in a foreign land to die.
>
> No father or mother to see him die, no brother or sister to say good-bye. No loving friends to clasp his hand, but we hope to meet in a better land.
>
> Lovingly remembered by his Mother and Dad, Brothers and Sisters.
> Mr & Mrs T Hunt, Smithend Green, Leigh, near Malvern.

The astute amongst you will notice in the photograph of his grave that his initial shows as 'T', yet the above gave it as 'F'. The *CWGC* has a document marked 'Exhumation' which explains that he was moved from a trench (mass) grave of sixteen on 24th August 1924. Hunt is recorded as having fair hair and being about 5 feet 8 inches tall. His identity disc was with him and was marked as:

> 242413 F. Hunt 1/8 Worcestershire Regiment

I have informed the Commonwealth War Graves Commission.

The ground to the north of the village and referred to by Captain

Walford as Guisancourt Farm was not captured until the following morning with an attack at 4.10 a.m. by two companies of the $1/8^{th}$ Royal Warwickshires and two from the 11th Sherwood Foresters who must have been part of the Corps Reserve. The *Divisional History* records that:

> Brig.-Gen. Craigie Halkett personally directed the attack until his men were finally established in possession of the Farm, and secure against any counter-attack. Posts were soon established north and east of the Farm, and at the same time the line was straightened out, and parties pushed forward into the valley between Beaurevoir and the Farm.

Grave of
Pte F Hunt

Overall, the 25th Division had advanced 3,000 yards in three days which: 'had been in face of great difficulties, considerably increased by the lack of time for previous reconnaissance of the ground by the regimental officers which proved a serious handicap in organising the attack. The German position was extremely strong and well-chosen, and had also been strongly wired'. It is not clear why the two reserve brigades (74th and 75th) could not undertake some reconnaissance when another brigade was launching the Division's initial assault on Beaurevoir. Having a second and third wave was always part of the plan if the first wave should fail. This ground had been fought over before, the maps accurate and the Royal Air Force, as it had become on 1st April 1918, had taken many photographs. Fighting amongst buildings and rubble may well have been new to these battalions. What had not yet been fully learnt, perhaps until well into the Second World War, was that capturing built-up areas, especially when they had been bombed or bombarded, was a slow process. It is not clear why the 25th Division needed any excuses as it had captured all its objectives, though 24 hours later than was intended.

We can conclude this chapter on the Battle of Beaurevoir with the entry for that day in the 25th Division's *War Diary*. It reported for 5th October: 'Combined attack but little progress made. 75/Bde moved up in the evening, attacked and took the village of BEAUREVOIR. GUISANCOURT FM and high ground about it taken'. Not much for the historian to get their teeth into!

2nd Battle of Le Cateau, 8th–11th October 1918 and Battle of Selle 17st–25th October 1918

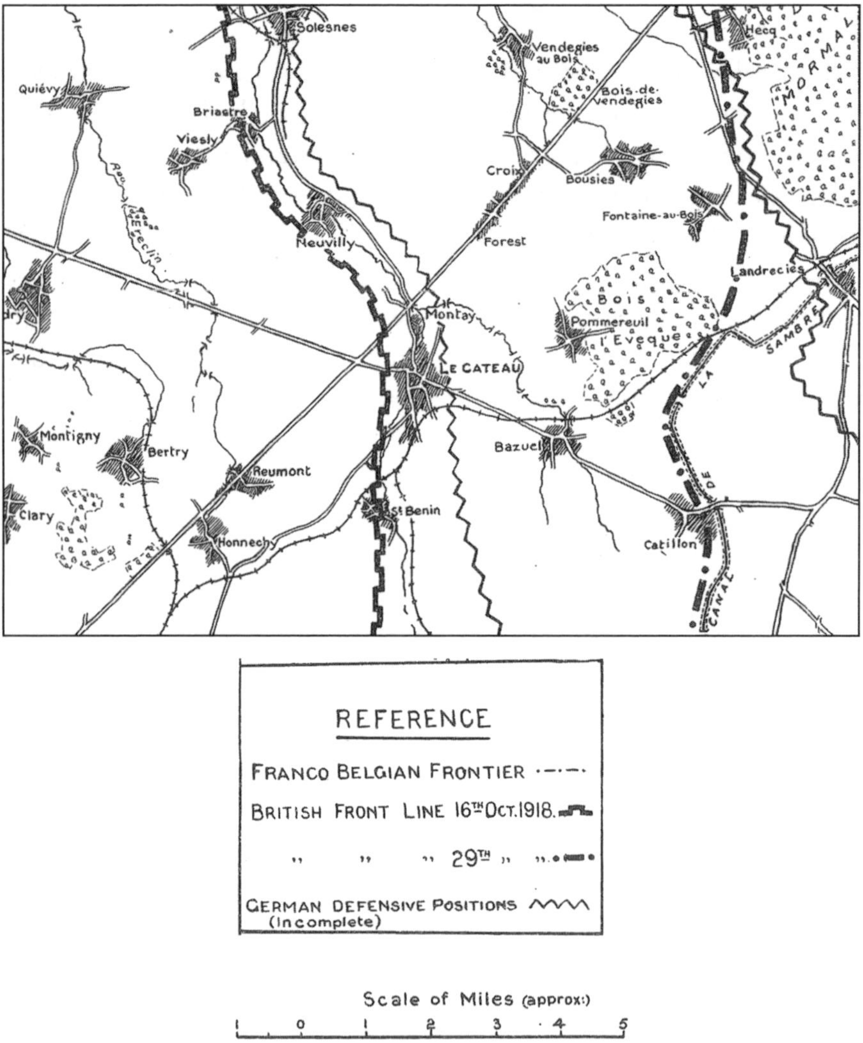

THE OLD GENT TAKES TO HORSEBACK

The Battalion needed a degree of reorganisation, having lost the services of seven officers and some 130 men. It was crucial that new company commanders were put in place. 2Lt E Wedgbury DCM, MM (and soon to be awarded an MC for his actions at Beaurevoir) was given command of D Company in place of Lt TL Jones MC – an appointment that Wedgbury was to hold until the last major action on 4th November. In B Company, Captain EV Mitchell replaced the wounded Captain GH Smith MC who would not return to the Battalion before the War ended. Watkinson and Walford retained their commands of A and C Companies.

Operation Order No 92 was issued for 9th October and began by explaining that: 'The 25th Division is continuing the attack this morning with American troops to the right and the 66th Division to the left'. The axis of the attack was the Roman Road which runs just to the south of Beaurevoir and heads in a north-easterly direction, passing just to the north of Le Cateau. This would be their first action as part of the Battle of Cambrai 1918. The Battalion assembled on the road at Ponchaux at 3 a.m., where it had been subject to heavy German artillery and aerial bombardment over the previous 24 hours. It marched for three miles and formed up to the right of the road between Serain and Premont, close behind the 1/5th Gloucesters whose task it was to take Maretz, some two and a half miles further up the road. There was little resistance as the Germans had decided to withdraw from the village to keep their line straight. Thus, the 1/8th Battalion was formed up on the north-east edge of Maretz by 8.30 a.m. and set off to the south of the road in the direction of their objective Honnechy, some three miles across undulating chalk farmland. The artillery had to lift their fire until the new German positions could be ascertained as well as the speed of progress of the British advance. The enemy had been waiting with machine-gun posts both in the Bois de Cartigny to the left and on the railway embankment to the right. The Battalion was checked, went to ground and returned fire. It is interesting to compare two summaries of the action which ensued. Firstly, there is Lt Col Clarke's report which gives the impression of an orderly operation:

> One Platoon of C Company under Lt AR Watson attacked and drove off the machine-guns on the railway, but the others continued to give trouble, and were holding up the 66th Division to the left. However, by skilful use of cover afforded by the undulating ground the advance was continued up to a quarry and wood about 400 yards short of the first objective [the railway cutting some 400 yds before the village], where more heavy machine-gun fire from a railway cutting was encountered.
>
> Large numbers of our cavalry then deployed from behind Maretz and moved forward, causing the enemy to shell the whole area rather heavily, shortly afterwards several enemy aeroplanes swooped down from the clouds and used machine-guns with considerable effect.
>
> A concerted attack, with a barrage, was then organised, and at 2 p.m. the whole line advanced, A and B Companies capturing the first objective, and C and D Companies passing through the village and consolidating on the high ground to the east of it, C Company arriving just in time to prevent the enemy blowing up a railway bridge, and capturing a large quantity of rolling stock and other valuable material.

Captain Walford's letter, half of which we have read, described his part and that of C Company in the battle:

> I had had only 4 hours sleep since Saturday morning [this was Tuesday evening]. At 9pm I had to see the CO; left him at 9.40 pm, had some cold meat and lay down at 10 pm. At 1.30 am [Wednesday] we had a cup of tea and a very small bit of tinned salmon. Started at 2.30 am and marched 6 kilometres, having to be continually putting on our gas masks as the enemy kept sending gas over all the time. We had been badly bombed too during the night by aeroplanes. We got to the jumping off point and started behind our own barrage at 5.10 a.m. The first part was quite easy for us all. We advanced about 2

1/2 miles with two battalions in front of us and had quite a pleasant country walk until it was our turn to go ahead. We passed through them, and then ran straight into it. However we pushed on and by means of our own Lewis guns and rifle fire and flanking movements gradually drove them back for about one more mile, when things got very sticky. Again the line was held up and shelling was very hot but we pushed on until we had no one on either flank as the divisions on our right and left hadn't got on as well as we did. I was getting rather anxious as the Colonel was at his Headquarters more than a mile back and I was Senior Officer. All of a sudden I saw the most magnificent sight I have ever seen, squadrons of cavalry galloping up from behind. A whole brigade of cavalry came up galloping over the skyline in squadrons right through the shelling and machinegun fire. They lost very few men considering, and we all went forward together. However we got hung up again by a railway cutting full of machineguns and had a big scrap.

The CO came up and we arranged for an artillery barrage at 2pm (we'd been on the go since 2am). I got a bit of bread and cheese, and the CO went back leaving everything to me – if we won the cutting I must decide whether to go on or not. Well, we kept fighting and before the time came for the barrage the Hun decided that he'd had enough and evacuated the cutting. We found several dead and judging from the equipment left, their casualties had been considerable. I decided to keep on. They were still shelling heavily which meant many wounded – crossing the next field my servant and I were knocked down by a shell bursting about 3 yds in front of us but we weren't touched and soon got up again though my legs were a bit shaky for the next 20 yds! But we went on and could see the Huns running but by then we hadn't a run in us especially over such rough country. They were only 400 yds in front, if only we'd had the cavalry! But they'd gone in another direction. We marched at 3/4 mile more, still under heavy fire, but we got our objective. I don't think I was ever so done in my life! I carried my pack, my loaded revolver, another one which I won in a Hun dugout, my box respirator, field glasses, spare revolver ammunition, and two Mills bombs, from 2.30am until 4pm on a cup of tea, a bit of tinned salmon and a small bit of bread and cheese! I then had to get into communication with those on our right and left. The left hadn't come up and I filled in on that flank with odd people I found:

1. Queens Bays (cavalry) Hotchkiss gun
2. Armoured cars.

I had no right to these people but they kindly said they would stay for a bit to help. Ultimately the battn on my right came up and Archie Watson who is now one of my subalterns, and at that time the only one, as two were wounded at Beaurevoir and the other the same day later on. Watson was splendid. I then sent word back to the CO, he was awfully bucked and so were the Brigadier and Divisional Gen. [Charles]. They had the Corps Commander down; it appears they never thought we could get the 2nd objective, so were proportionately delighted!

I finally stopped at 8.30 p.m. had some cold bully and went to sleep about 10pm after visiting my sentries. A pretty good day for an old man!

The next morning we were up at 5.30am: this time in Brigade support. We continued the attack but couldn't get far as the whole line was held up and again badly shelled. We had no breakfast as they couldn't get the rations up to us as we were so near the machine guns etc. So about 9am I told the men to eat their rations, which we all did, and the CO brought Watson and me some whiskey, the first we had for two days. Sleeping out in the open and then only for short times, for you can't sleep long in that cold, one wants whiskey or something badly and we'd had no rum ration for some time.

Now you can't say I don't tell you all I can! I wonder if Harry and Matt Dixon would like to see this letter…

We went in 107 strong and after the first effort [Beaurevoir] they sent me 18 reinforcements fresh from England – all young lads – that made 125 but we came out with 54 so you may gather we had a hot time. Battn orders came out with a list of mentions for good work, mine heads the list as you'll see but only because of seniority and I don't suppose I will get anything as there were no senior officers present and after all I only did my job. Still it's better than nothing to be mentioned in battalion orders.

I must stop.

The *Divisional History* said simply that 'Lt Col HT Clarke of the 1/8th Worcesters organised and carried through the attack on Honnechy with the greatest ability'. It did acknowledge that 'fortunately the railway bridge was reached by the Worcesters [C Company] in time to prevent its destruction, and a great deal of rolling stock and railway material was captured'. So Clarke, Walford and Watson all had a good day.

There is much else of interest in Walford's account, perhaps the most important aspect of which is the scale of C Company's casualties – 57 per cent – over the four days of Beaurevoir and Honnechy with the shelling in between – leaving Walford with just one subaltern for the attack on Honnechy. The second is the reference in both halves of the letter to the amount of time in Beaurevoir and on the march that they had to wear their gas masks. Neither the Battalion or Divisional diaries made any reference to it, presumably because it was now just part of operating on the Western Front. The third is his wonderful description of the cavalry 'galloping up' – a rare sight throughout the War, though nothing about Lt Col Clarke's German aircraft. In this case the Divisional *War Diary* reported that the cavalry captured 'the villages of REUMONT and ESCAUFORT'.

The cavalry which Walford witnessed was one of very few days in the whole War when they charged across the fields of Flanders – the 1st Cavalry Division at the Somme on 14th July 1916; the 5th Cavalry Division at the retreat to the Hindenburg Line between 23rd & 28th March 1917; the 8th Brigade at Cambrai on 20th November 1917; most notably the 3rd Cavalry Division on 8th August 1918, the first day of the Battle of Amiens, including the 5th Dragoon Guards' charge at Harbonnieres; and lastly, on 8th (1st Cavalry Division) & 9th October 1918 (3rd Cavalry Division) in the Second Battle of Le Cateau. It was the latter operation which Walford was to witness and which is celebrated by the 3rd Dragoon Guards with the painting by Lionel Edwards of their charge at Honnechy. David Kenyon, in his excellent *Horsemen in No Man's Land* described this action from a cavalry standpoint:

Honnechy, 9th October 1918

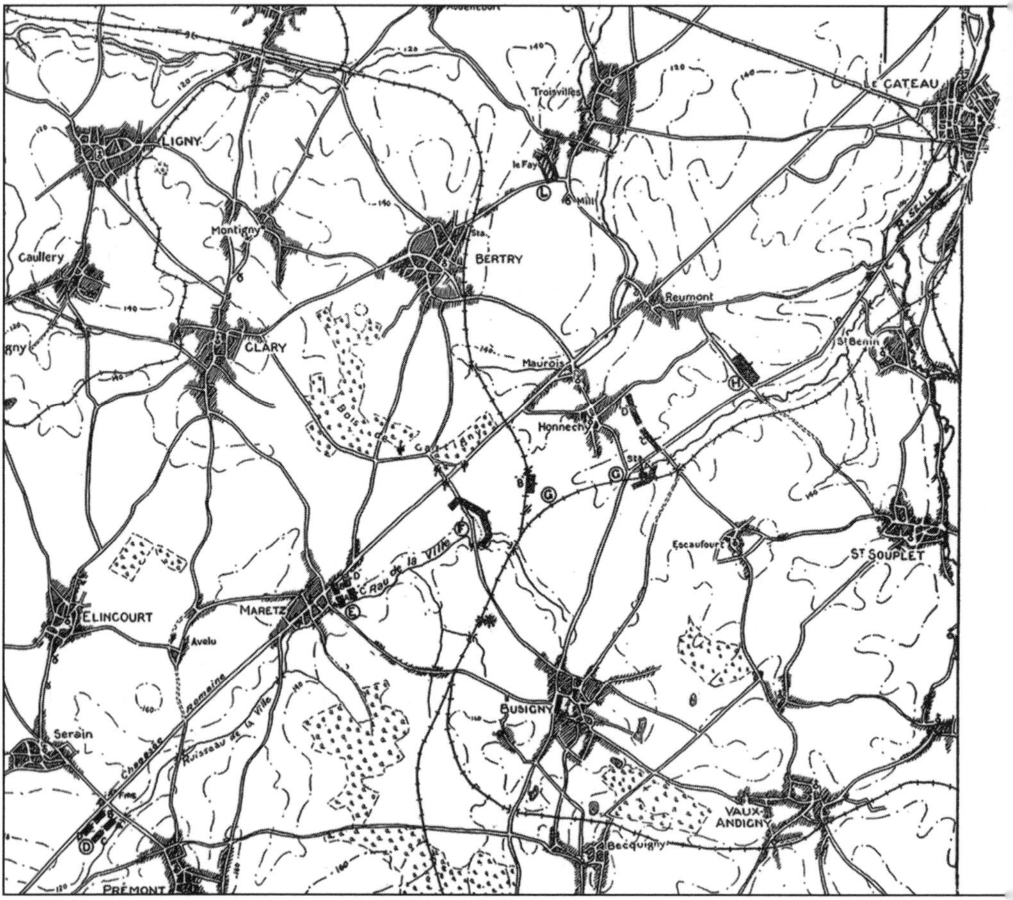

REFERENCE

Ⓓ " " Assembly Position 9th " "

Ⓔ " " Deployment 8-30am. " " "

German Machine Guns " " " " " "

Position of German M.G. Captured by "C." Coy.

Ⓕ 1/8th Worc. Midday 9th Oct. 1918.

Ⓖ " " Final Position " " "

Ⓗ " " in reserve 10th-11th " "

Ⓙ 2nd Worc. Morning 9th " "

Ⓚ " " Nightfall " " "

Ⓛ " " Night 10th/11th " "

Position of Hindenburg Line.

" " Beaurevoir "

Scale of Yards.

1000 500 0 1000 2000 3000 4000 5000

To the south of the main road the 6th Cavalry Brigade had joined the leading infantry on a line close to the railway south-west of (and short of) Honnechy, but heavy fire was encountered from the village and the infantry attack stalled at about 11.00am… The brigade commander, [Brigadier] Ewing Paterson made his own reconnaissance at about 11.30am., and was told that the infantry 'were so exhausted and resistance so strong that it was not intended to advance further that day' [written in the 1930s but tallying with Walford's description of the action – though he said nothing of not advancing further that day]. At about 11.50am. a conference was held of all the senior cavalry commanders … it was decided that 'a vigorous attempt should be made to capture Honnechy and Reumont or the whole advance would peter out'. The plan called for a frontal assault on Honnechy by the Royal Dragoon Guards and 10th Hussars, while the 3rd Dragoon Guards [Lionel Edwards' painting below] circled the village to the south and the Fort Garry Horse [Canadian] attacked from the north… The attack was timed for 2.00pm., at which time the infantry attack would be renewed.

It is not clear that Walford was informed of this by Clarke as he referred only to a supporting artillery barrage which would not have been sensible if a cavalry charge was due – also the 3rd Dragoon Guards started to the south of the railway with the Inniskillings providing flank protection. This meant that Walford is unlikely to have seen them as they passed under the railway bridge to his front right. It must be remembered that cavalry charges were so rare in the War that each received a whole chapter and with, in Kenyon's words, their lack of success on the previous day (8th October), it made the concentration on, and possible embellishment of, the actions around Honnechy and Reumont more understandable.

Along the main road, the Germans had few troops in Maurois, such that two troops of the Fort Garry Horse (FGH) captured the village, allowing the Royal Dragoons to push on towards Reumont. The FGH encircled to the north and the Germans quickly retreated from the village. Meanwhile:

> To the south the 3rd Dragoon Guards moved around Honnechy to attack the village from the south-east. They were under heavy fire from their flank and rear (despite the efforts of the [6th] Inniskillings [Dragoons] to provide flank protection) and had to close up to pass under the railway line via a bridge over the Honnechy-Busigny road [by the railway station]. They soon opened out again and approached the village at a gallop. The attack was a rapid success. Honnechy was occupied by 2.40pm., and the infantry of XIII Corps [a grand title for C and D Companies of the 1/8th Battalion!] followed the Dragoons in and were able to complete the clearance of the village shortly after.

Wedgbury, in his D company commander's report, wrote:

> At 0200[pm] the coy moving in artillery formation supported B coy in its attack on the railway cutting.

Passing through B coy the coy moved to its objective, the road E of HONNECHY which it reached at 1510 – which meant they were on the far side of the village just 30 minutes after the cavalry claimed to have captured the village on their own.

Walford and Wedgbury made no reference to the cavalry after the 2.00 p.m. assault so it does not seem to be as well coordinated as Kenyon believes but, then, the cavalry had so few opportunities for successes in the War, one must give them credit here for easing C and D Companies' capture of Honnechy and for Watson's capture of the railway bridge – before it was blown – and the 'rolling stock'.

This discussion of the work of the cavalry on 9th October is very important in a military context and much of the reason for the writing of his PhD by David Kenyon. The British Official Historian and Royal Engineer Officer, Sir James Edmonds, famously wrote about this day: 'the cavalry had done nothing that the infantry, with artillery support and cyclists, could not have done for itself at less cost' – a damning statement which Kenyon does much to rebut. As a retired officer of the Inniskillings' successor regiment, my immediate thoughts are to support Kenyon. However, he is not convincing on the 'at less cost' section. He acknowledges that the 3rd Cavalry Division lost 369 'human casualties' that day – 'human' as he does not give the number of horses lost, an important aspect given all the fodder demands required to keep them at the Front over the months. He continued that 'no detailed infantry loss figures … have been identified'. The 1/8th Battalion lost 5 killed and 71 wounded that day and they were in the thick of the fighting, the morning attacks being almost unopposed. The claim that the 3rd Dragoon Guards (The Carbineers) captured Honnechy was more important to the cavalry than to the 25th Division and the 1/8th Battalion. It ignores the capture of all the German rolling stock and the taking of the railway bridge is not mentioned by Kenyon; yet Lt Col HT Clarke concluded his report with: 'Captures –

a large amount of railway stock and other material at HONNECHY railway station' – to him the most important aspect of their work that day. It also ignores Walford's comment as he advanced on the village:

> But we went on and could see the Huns running but by then we hadn't a run in us especially over such rough country. They were only 400 yds in front, if only we'd had the cavalry! But they'd gone in another direction.

The historian of the 25th Division, a staff officer in France at the time and brother of the Division's Commander Royal Artillery, did not mention the cavalry's role but he did record: 'The enemy offered considerable resistance at first, but as our troops pressed on his resistance suddenly broke, and the line retired rapidly before becoming engaged at close quarters'. Perhaps the appearance of the cavalry coming under the railway bridge and heading behind them caused panic in the German lines. Thus, just as General Rawlinson would have wished, combined arms operations won the day.

The last aspect of his letter is the Old Gent's keenness for recognition for his efforts. He was obviously pleased with how he had performed, though in more modest language than that of Watkinson in his 'Dear Old Bomf' letter. Lt Col Clarke finished his report on the two actions – Beaurevoir and Honnechy – to say that he had been awarded a DSO and Lt Watkinson and 2Lts Wedgbury and Barber got MCs with one DCM (to CSM R Atkinson) and twelve MMs also awarded – one to Cpl AJ Wood: 'after his platoon commander [Lt FW Wiles or 2Lt G Hales] was wounded, and heavy casualties suffered, he reorganised the platoon, and by his skilful leadership under heavy artillery and machine gun fire he finally achieved his objective'. Wood had crossed with the Battalion in March 1915, been gassed in July 1916 and wounded in October 1917. He had a brother in the Battalion, both sons of Mr & Mrs D Wood of 72 Chestnut Terrace, Worcester. But there was nothing for Walford or Lt Watson for their work in either battle. The award of a DSO for the commanding officer was gazetted as:

> For fine leadership and gallantry during the period 5th/10th October 1918. He was called upon suddenly to organise and carry out the attack on Beaurevoir. This he did with the greatest skill, his battalion, in face of heavy opposition, finally gaining all their objectives, and thereby making the next big attack possible. Later, he captured Honnechy, showing skill and ability in doing so. Throughout these operations his grasp of the situation was clear and concise.

Lt Col Clarke was a bright commander who was able to show clarity of thought under the most severe pressure. He was not afraid to delegate responsibility to his senior officers who, after a year in command, he had trained well. He was commanding 21- and 49-year-old company commanders so his personal skills must have been of the highest quality – although his supply of whisky was also well received! He had the advantage of having as his second-in-command Major Bate, an officer who had already commanded another battalion in action. The casualties that day were three officers wounded, five Other Ranks killed and 68 wounded – so another 76 Battalion casualties, on top of the 141 from Beaurevoir.

The Battalion was due some rest after the capture of Honnechy, but not quite yet. Corbett takes up the story:

> Next day we went on again and came up a deep valley of the river Selle. Ahead, on our left, was the town of Le Cateau, in front was the railway station and great factories and warehouses, to our right the village of St Benin. This was taken by our 74th Brigade after a stiff fight. We could go no further until the guns came up. This battle – or rather, series of battles – was over, and that of Le Cateau [later known as the Selle] was about to begin. Another Division [7th Wilts of 50th Division] relieved us, and went back to Serain, where we were reinforced and reformed. We were working now with three companies, for B Company had been so badly mauled at Beaurevoir that for the present its survivors were reinforcing the other Companies.

The *War Diary* confirmed that each of these three companies were split into just three platoons. Thus the Battalion had an effective fighting strength of about 300 officers and men. It was not further reinforced in time for the next three actions but it was better off than an American battalion on their right which, according to Corbett, was down to just 90 men under the command of a captain. The Allies might have had the Germans in full retreat but they were suffering almost as much on the casualty front. It is at times like this that it is so crucial that the supply and administrative chain worked well. Corbett provided us with a timely appreciation of the 25th Division supply system and, by deduction, we can establish that Corbett was now the RQMS and the RSM (H Heath MC – who is to be shown as Lt H Heath, Quartermaster of 8th Battalion at Summer Camp 1924 at Swanage) has been promoted to Acting Quartermaster:

> At this time we had the opportunity of seeing and admiring the splendid Staff work of this Division and Corps, for though we may be some 30 miles from the Railhead there was no failure of rations, ammunition, or other stores. Along the great Roman Road which leads to [Le Cateau and onto] Mons poured a ceaseless stream of traffic which supplied the least of our wants. The Twenty-Fifth [Division] had always prided itself on its interior economy, and it was said that even in the tremendous fighting round Bapaume and the horrible disaster on the Aisne the fighting men had their rations regularly. We now saw that this honest pride was honourably justified, and did our part in justifying it. In this connection due praise must be given to Serjt.-Major H Heath, acting Quartermaster, the Company Quartermaster-Serjeants, and to Serjeant A. Pritchard, our Master Cook and his merry men, who even when left miles behind by the rapid advance continued to supply the Battalion with cooked food and hot drinks by night and day, and never let them go fasting into the fight. Whenever the Commanding Officer ordered a meal [for the battalion] it was at once produced. And the work of the Transport was, as ever, far better than one has a right to expect of mortal men and mules.

No reinforcements arrived and the Battalion was ordered back to Honnechy to await orders to support the 50th Division in their attack on the high ground to the south-east of Le Cateau on the 17th October. Captain E Gilbert, as adjutant, wrote the orders for the march:

Order of March:	A Coy, HQ, Drums, C Coy, D Coy, section of TMBs, Transport, B Echelon
Starting point:	Orderly Room
Time:	15.25
Distances:	100 yards between Coy's and between sections of 6 vehicles
Dress:	Fighting Order (Picks instead of haversacks)
Billeting party:	2Lt Bateman and 4 Runners (with cycles) report to Staff Captain.

HONNECHY CHURCH 15.30
Blankets, Officers Kit (Surplus), Greatcoats, and mess boxes, less ONE per company to be dumped at Billet No. 12 by 1400. Valises and Mess Boxes at Stores by 14.15

They moved up to the Selle river the following morning. Corbett described crossing it by 'fallen trees, pontoons and rafts'. He noted a change to the countryside, comparing the Selle valley to that of the Salwarpe back in Worcestershire, and that 'the weary plains of chalk and clay gave place to a dark sandstone with deep valleys, brooks, much pasturage, and many hedges: it was more like England, and a village instead of being a glacis-girt fortress, would be a tangle of closer hedges, lanes, and buildings'. This would remain the case for the remainder of the ground over which the Battalion were to advance and, in the main, offered greater cover for those attacking. The *War Diary* recorded simply that on the 18th October the Battalion was 'still in the Sunken Road awaiting orders'. These came at 2.30 the following morning.

The 75th Brigade was to advance through the 50th Division after the 1/5th Gloucesters on the left were to capture the line of a road starting at 2.45 a.m. The 1/8th had A Coy on the left, D Coy in the middle and C Coy on the right with D Coy 1/8th Royal Warwickshire in reserve. This meant that the Battalion was laid out with Lt Watkinson on the left, 2Lt Wedgbury in the middle and Captain Walford on the right. The objective was the village of Bazuel to the south-east of

Le Cateau with the 1/5th Gloucesters tasked with capturing the road embankment over the railway between Le Cateau and Bazuel on their left flank. C Company were the right-hand company of the British forces, with the 54th American Brigade to their right. Due to the rate of attrition of subaltern platoon commanders, most platoons were led by sergeants. The *Divisional History* reports that 'Sergt. Turner MM, Sergt Faulkner, Sergt Jones and Sergt Hodgetts led their platoons with great courage and dash, the latter going forward alone to locate a German machine gun which was causing trouble'. Captain Walford had just one subaltern, Lt AR Watson who had done so well at Honnechy. He was to be wounded in this attack. There was an enormous amount of experience amongst the key command structure of the Battalion from Lt Col Clarke and Major Bate in Bn HQ with Captain Gilbert, the adjutant joining on Christmas Eve back in 1915. After Watkinson's and Wedgbury's inspired leadership at Beaurevoir, this was to be Walford's time. His letter describing his role and leadership at Beaurevoir and Honnechy gives the impression of a confident man who had proved himself both to those in his Company and to those above.

As the 50th Division moved forward at 5.30 a.m., the accompanying barrage brought about retaliatory salvos on the railway cutting in the low ground where the Battalion was waiting. To give an idea of the impact of a shell, Lt Col Clarke's later report stated that 'one shell inflicted 18 casualties on No 4 Platoon, A Company – thus rendering it almost inoperative for the impending attack'. If one considers the requirement of those without wounds to help those who were wounded, it can be presumed that very few if any of the men of the platoon were available to strengthen a sister platoon in the attack. The fog and mist persisted well after the Battalion was given the order to advance through the 50th Division which had been held up by machine-gun fire from the right flank and which was also to check C and D Companies when they took the lead. The ground is open rolling farmland, presently with no hedges except from the base of the final hill before the village. Those in the village would have had a good view, mist permitting, over which to correct artillery fire and direct their machine-gun fire. There are few new houses since the attack just over one hundred years ago to change the landscape. I last viewed the ground on a cold spring day and was thrilled to watch a pair of marsh harriers quartering the ground along the line of C Company's attack.

Area of Walford's horseback reconnaissance with Bazuel in background

Clarke's account continued:

> A Company, however, pushed on on the left and reached the outskirts of the village, where they were met by enfilade machine-gun fire and direct fire from a 77mm gun at a 400 yards range. Lt WH Reynolds [another old hand who had been with the Battalion for over two years] replied with his Lewis guns and drove the enemy gunners away. [Reynolds was awarded an MC for his efforts] … D Company of the Warwicks [from reserve] then moved forward and gained touch with A Company, and by protecting their right flank, enabled them to make a further advance and gain touch with the Glosters who had reached their objective on the left flank, a railway embankment N.W. of the village.

Corbett best described the actions on the Battalion's right flank:

> Captain Walford did great service here. He captured a horse and galloped it about the field, surveyed the enemy, directed his men, cheered on the Yankees, damned the Durhams, and generally had the time of his life. We had come on so fast that we captured not only the enemy's guns, but their ammunition train, which jogged up straight into our hands [not realising that their battery had been captured], giving us four and twenty horses and we knocked out another train with LG [Lewis Gun] fire. Our prisoners were numerous, and the enemy's loss in killed and wounded very heavy.

Corbett's comment about Walford 'having the time of his life' may well be close to the mark. He had some more notable performances over the next two and a half weeks but this earned him his first MC. He was the twentieth officer in the Battalion to win that award, and the oldest by more than a decade – and probably one of the very few infantry officers to win an MC whilst operating on horseback. The citation read:

> Capt. John Osborn Walford, 1/8th Bn, Worc. R., T.F.
> In the attack on Bazuel on 18th October 1918, he commanded a company in the leading wave with conspicuous courage and skill. When the advance was held up by heavy machine-gun fire, he made a personal reconnaissance, and gaining touch with a company of the left, he gave orders to the remainder of the line to advance, gaining the objective with few casualties. His company captured a complete battery of 4.2-inch howitzers.

The context of his reconnaissance on the horse needs to be explained as it showed that the initiative of his young comrades was rubbing off on him. The *History* recorded:

> On the right, however, D and C Companies were still held up by the machine guns firing through the mist along the ridge. Colonel Clarke then asked for an additional company from the Royal Warwickshire; with that reinforcement he intended to advance southward from Bazuel and take the enemy in the flank [led by A Company].

But before the plan could be put into effect the desired advance had been made, Captain JO Walford of C Company, after a personal reconnaissance [made on a captured horse], decided that a strong advance firing would have the required result; for the enemy's morale was believed to be low. After forming a strong front line he gave the word to advance, and his men moved forward through the mist rapidly firing their rifles and Lewis-guns from the hip. That method of attack would have been folly in broad daylight; but in the general obscurity that oncoming blaze of musketry frightened the enemy machine-gunners from their position; and the advance continued unchecked past the southern (furthest) outskirts of the village.

Site of captured German gun battery

In the valley below four [artillery] guns were suddenly sighted looming up in the mist. They were rushed and captured by C Company, and proved to be a complete battery of 4.2 inch howitzers. The German battery commander was taken, as well as eighteen horses. Later in the day two ammunition limbers, ignorant of the battery's fate, drove up to the battery position in the fog and likewise fell into our hands.

The Battalion was ordered to hold the village over the following two days as the mist rose. The shelling was persistent as a second great battle to the north of Le Cateau was opened.

1/8th Bn Actions at the Battle of the Selle

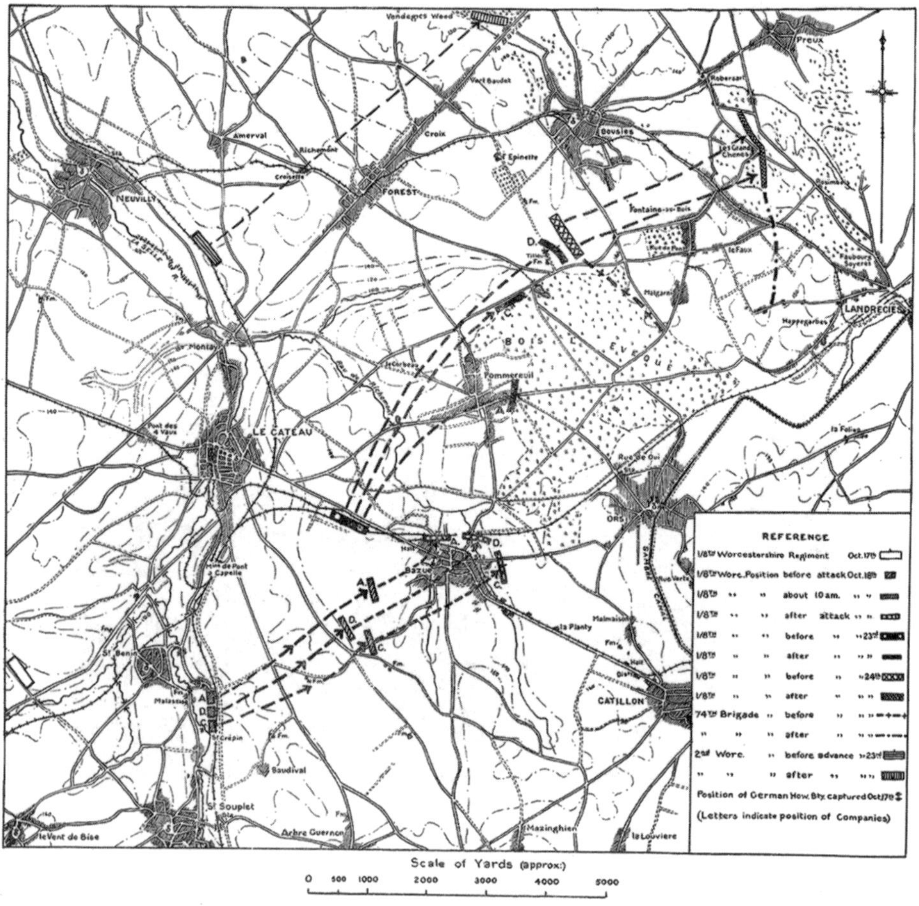

THE WEDGE OF WORCESTER

The Battalion was ordered back to St Benin for a short rest next to where they had begun their advance to capture Bazuel. Their rest lasted two days before they were ordered back to the railway embankment between Le Cateau and Bazuel to take part in the 75th Brigade attack on the next village, Pommereuil, and the north side of Bois l'Évêque. They left St Benin at 10 p.m. on 22nd October. The three companies, A, C and D, remained under command of the three Ws – Watkinson, Walford and Wedgbury – but Lt Col Clarke was given some rest and Major Bate took command. Already much decorated, Bate had commanded the 1/7th Battalion with distinction in Italy, earning a DSO to add to his MC and bar. His command was to be for just three days but extraordinary gains were made during thirty-six hours of almost continuous action and Major Bate was to add a bar to his DSO, thus ending the War in which he started as 2Lt JP Bate as Major JP Bate DSO & bar, MC & bar. He was later to struggle from his wartime experiences and, perhaps, these successes. A fine description of these actions was later written under the title of:

> Narratives of some of the Operations carried out by the Battalion under the command of Major JP Bate DSO, MC: (1) BOIS L'EVEQUE, 23rd OCTOBER, 1918
>
> At 11 p.m on the 22nd the Battalion moved forward to a railway cutting [North-]West of Bazuel, and at 1.30 a.m. on the 23rd, Lieut RS Miller and eight scouts were sent to get in touch with the 7th Brigade, who were attacking Pommereuil, and to act as guides to the Battalion, who were to go through the 7th Brigade and form a defensive flank to the 18th Division [on the left] along the North edge of the Bois l'Évêque. Lieut. Miller and five of the scouts were hit shortly after moving out.

Corbett expanded on this incident:

> Lieutenant Miller received a bullet wound and was left behind with

two stretcher-bearers. We were never able to find him again, and he had not been admitted to any hospital, so we sadly gave him up for dead. But when the British entered Cologne he was found in hospital. The Germans, in the retreat, had found him, and through all the hurry and panic of what was practically a flight had had the humanity to take him with them and care for him.

This provided some evidence of the difference between an officer or soldier being killed outright and one being wounded. The two stretcher bearers are an obvious resource being used. There would have then been much staff work by the adjutant and his clerks to locate the missing within the medical system. Bate continued:

The Company Commanders were then ordered to find their own way to the 'jump-off point' (the NW Corner of the Wood), and to endeavour to do so without becoming involved in the fighting to reach that point.

C Company were to form the first part of the defensive flank, from the NW corner of the Wood to Flaquet Brifaut and D Company to capture Tilleuls Farm and a mound beyond. A Company was to be in Battalion Reserve just north of Pommereuil.

C and D Companies moved forward at 1.35 a.m., ignored several enemy posts which, in the dark and fog, were still holding against the 7th Brigade, and, moving through close country by compass, stars and natural features, reached the jump-off point at 3.55 a.m. They came under machine-gun fire on the way, and rushed two posts, capturing five machine-guns. C Company also passed through Pommereuil from South to North, engaging and putting to flight about 150 Germans at the North end. At 4.20 a.m., the barrage lifted and the advance continued, D Company going forward towards Tilleuls Farm. By this time, owing to the darkness, fog, enclosed country, and casualties, 2Lt Wedgbury only had one corporal and 17 men still with him.

We will come back to the conclusion of that action after noting the following exploits of A Company:

> A Company moved forward from the railway cutting at 1.45 a.m. and soon came under machine-gun fire. They sent forward scouts to find a way through the enemy posts and over the Richemont Stream, which was crossed at Jean Jacques Mill, where an enemy post of ten was captured. They then pushed on towards Pommereuil, coming under fire twice on the way: the first time they changed direction slightly to avoid being checked, but on the second occasion they sent a patrol forward, which killed an enemy post of 10 men in a house. At 4 a.m. the mist lifted and the Company occupied its position as ordered, just to the north of Pommereuil. Captain Watkinson then came to the conclusion that the village was still in the hands of the enemy, and that they were not aware of A Company's position. He and his CSM met two German officers, one of high rank, and their orderlies. They killed both officers and one of the orderlies after a heated encounter, but he did not make an immediate attack on the villages because (1) he might be required to support C and D Companies and (2) he had very few men, and there was every indication that the village was strongly held. However, about 6 a.m. a tank came along and A Company then cleared the village in conjunction with it, and afterwards consolidated on the objective given.

Corbett explained that the fleeing Germans were pushed into the hands of C Company 'who gave them a very hot time', presumably as they approached the edge of the wood, Bois l'Évêque (the Wood of the Bishops).

However, it was the actions of the small group of D Company under 2Lt Wedgbury which not only put the icing on the cake for the Battalion that night but was, in its own right, a remarkable feat of arms. It is perhaps best to start with the words of Wedgbury himself: 'The action of D Coy, 1/8th Batt, The Worcestershire Regt in the attack on TILLEULS FARM, 23rd Oct 1918'. As with the *War Diary* and the orders and Battle Reports, these are written by hand and it is one of the great privileges of undertaking the research for this book that I was able to read the reports in the handwriting of the main protagonists themselves. In Wedgbury's case, these two and a half pages are written in his notebook with square lines and then torn out along the perforations. It is signed *E. Wedgbury OC D Coy. 2Lt* and was his report to Battalion HQ of the actions of his (D) Company that night:

> The coy paraded with the battalion at 10 PM at S. BENIN Oct 22/18 & moved to Railway Cutting W of BASUEL.
>
> At 1.35 AM Oct 23/18 the coy followed C Coy out of the cutting and came under heavy artillery & MG fire, owing to the difficulty of getting out of the cutting connection was lost with C Coy but after some little distance connection was again made with a platoon of C Coy who were sheltering under a bank, about this time a platoon of C Coy came saying that they could not get forward.
>
> These platoons were reformed and went forward followed by one platoon of Coy HQ of D Coy. No British troops were met with till the stream about L25 c9.0 was reached, where we came up with a company of the R.W.Kents, who informed us that they had reached their objective & were consolidating. I enquired how far the leading troops were ahead & was informed that there were no British troops in front.
>
> We crossed the stream pushed forward for our starting point & came under heavy MG fire from edge of orchard in L25d, this position was rushed & enemy retired leaving 4 MGs behind, we continued to advance again & again came up with enemy MG in trenches at L26a, these people also retired leaving one gun behind.
>
> At 3.55AM we arrived at our starting point & waited for barrage to lift. During this wait I got into touch with a platoon of R W Kents who had come up behind us & were about 300 [yards] to our left rear, the enemy were still in POMMEREUIL.
>
> At 4.22AM I asked Mr Bateman who had roughly two platoons to move forward in 2 waves extended, the third wave consisting of 1 platoon & HQ D Coy.
>
> We moved forward without opposition & Mr Bateman took up his position.
>
> D Coy moved forward & after advancing about 300 yards observed two guns [artillery] fire from behind a hedge about L16 a3.3. Lewis guns & rifle fire were brought to bear upon them & they stopped firing immediately. Immediately afterwards MG & rifle fire was

> opened upon us, we advanced & captured our objective, TILLEULS FARM, also 3-4.2 Long How[itzers]: killing or capturing all the team at 5.57 AM.
>
> Nothing has been seen of the rest of the battalion or of other British troops.
>
> It seemed as if we had pushed right through the enemy because his SOS [flare] was being sent up from our rear.
>
> At dawn large parties of the enemy were observed returning from our left flank & rifle and Lewis gun fire was opened with them.
>
> We captured about 100 prisoners including several [7] officers.
>
> About 7 AM British troops were seen advancing from the left rear & about 7.45 AM a batt of East Surreys passed our left flank.
>
> At 8.20 AM, 4 tanks passed through our line but soon returned.
>
> About 10.30 AM, 13 & 14 platoons [Bateman] came up & were at once sent forward to take and hold second objective, the high ground in L16b & this was done at 12.20 PM.
>
> In this action we lost 3 killed and 28 wounded.
>
> E. Wedgbury
> OC D Coy. 2Lt

A modest but factual account of the action. It is extraordinary to hold and read the report written, presumably in the field later that day, in blue crayon by 2Lt Wedgbury in his notebook and torn out along the perforations. Remembering also that this action was conducted in the dark, yet his map references are accurate. Corbett provided a little detail:

> At our furthest objective Lieut. Wedgbury captured with the bayonet a whole battery of guns which were busily in action. To show the quality of our shooting, four men, the only survivors of the battery, running away, were brought down by four of our men with one shot each. He went on still further and captured the farm of Les Tilleuls with a garrison of 150 men and five machine-guns. He was nearly two miles past the village [of Pommereuil], and his total force had been one corporal [LCpl AP Owers who was awarded an MM for his actions that night] and 16 men of whom he did not lose one.

Top: Site of Wedgbury's bayonet attack on German Battery
Bottom: German WW2 bunker at Les Tilleuls Farm

Whichever of these reports one reads, or the words of Major Bate, the *History* or the *Divisional History*, this was an extraordinary feat of arms. 2Lt Wedgbury won a DSO, the only second lieutenant in the whole Worcestershire Regiment to gain such an award. Of the 82 other DSOs, only one was awarded to a subaltern, to Lt J Mould for a solitary action involving initiative and bravery but not leadership. A Victoria Cross would not have been awarded because his actions were not witnessed by anybody more senior than himself. It was dark and misty. Captain Walford was the nearest senior officer but he was at the edge of the wood some hundreds of yards from most of these actions. A Victoria Cross was awarded that night just a mile from Wedgbury, to Pte FG Miles, 1/5th Gloucestershire Regiment. He was not in command of other men but showed extraordinary initiative and bravery, as his citation testifies:

> For conspicuous gallantry and splendid initiative in attack. On the 23rd October 1918, during an advance against the Bois l'Évêque, his company was held up by a line of machine guns in the sunken road near the Moulin L Jacques. Pte Miles alone, and on his own initiative, made his way forward for a distance of 150 yards under exceptionally heavy fire, located one machine gun and shot the man firing it. He then rushed the gun, and kicked it over, thereby putting it out of action. He then observed another gun firing from 100 yards further forward; he then advanced alone, shot the machine-gunner, rushed the gun and captured the team of eight. Finally, he stood up and beckoned his Company, who, following his signals, were enabled to work round the rear of the line, and captured 16 machine guns, one officer and 50 other ranks.
>
> The courage, initiative and entire disregard of personal safety shown by this very gallant private soldier, was entirely instrumental in enabling his Company to advance at a time when any delay would have seriously jeopardised the whole operation in which it was engaged.

There can be little doubt that Pte Miles' actions were worthy of a VC; there was no expectation that a private soldier should show such initiative nor drive home attacks on two machine gun positions single-handedly.

It seems there was also no doubt in the mind of the Battalion as to what award should be given to Wedgbury for his actions, as a letter to him from his commanding officer shortly after the Armistice reveals that the Battalion proposed that he should be awarded a DSO – telling also of the fate of Lt RS Miller, for whom the *Journal* of 14th December announced: 'Previously reported killed, now reported wounded and missing'.

Wedgbury, as a company commander, even if as a second lieutenant, would have been expected to take the initiative which he did at the front of his small team – that being the main difference between their two actions. Without either man, there is little doubt that their company objective would not have been achieved. Wedgbury's award of a DSO meant that he was to end the War as Second Lieutenant E Wedgbury DSO, MC, DCM, MM, the only British soldier ever to win those four gallantry medals. His medals can be found in the Worcester Museum in the case with the Victoria Crosses won by members of the Worcestershire Regiment and other Worcester men. Looking at them, it is difficult to comprehend the consistently gallant, effective and decisive actions of Wedgbury over a period of some three years which was required to merit such a medal collection. We read of Watkinson and Walford's reactions to such performances and the self-esteem each generated. Lt Dennis Gordon, who served in D Company under Wedgbury in these few weeks in 1918, wrote in 1972:

> I was sent out again to France and joined the 1/8th being posted to D Company, Lieut Wedgbury being in charge of the Company and the only other officer being 2nd Lieut Coleman. I was in action several times but the most outstanding battle of all was at Ferme de Tilleul. We were emerging from the Bois l'Évêque when we came under heavy machine gun and rifle fire.
>
> Lieut Wedgbury attacked one of these posts and in doing so got shot in the arm, he sent a runner to let me know what had happened, so I took charge of both platoons [13 & 14] and attacked both machine posts capturing 2 officers and twenty men.
>
> Lieut Wedgbury was a quiet sort of chap dedicated to his job and quite fearless. I never saw him again although he wrote to me several times.

This letter raises one or two questions as Wedgbury was shot in the arm twelve days later, on the Sambre Canal and was sent home on sick leave – hence Gordon not seeing him again. Wedgbury's report of the Tilleuls Farm action made no mention of any officer in the Company being wounded. However, Lt Gordon was awarded an MC for his work at the Battle of the Selle as this action became known – described in Wedgbury's company Battle Report as: 'It was arranged that Mr Gordon & 14 Platoon should move forward at 1.30PM, this he did & gained objective at 1.45PM'. Gordon, like Wedgbury, was commissioned from the ranks so another experienced soldier to rely upon. He was born on Christmas Day 1896 and was a blacksmith's assistant at the Bucket Factory in Wollescote at the age of 14 when the 1911 Census was held. Both his parents worked there, his father as an ironplate worker and his mother as a galvanizer assistant. They must have been so proud that their eldest son achieved so much in the War – a commission and an MC – from such a humble background. Dennis Gordon himself returned to heavy industry and was recorded as being a steel furnaceman in 1939. The only other officer platoon commander in D Company was 2Lt ST Bateman MM – his Military Medal indicating that he too had been given a temporary commission from the ranks and, like Wedgbury, had managed to return to his own battalion when commissioned. Bateman crossed to France with the 1/7th Battalion on 31st March 1915 and the announcement of his MM in the *London Gazette* was on 11th November 1916, the same edition as the MMs for both Corbett and Wedgbury.

The Battalion had very few young subalterns of the type with which the First World War was so synonymous. This was at the time when Captain Walford's only child was at Sandhurst as Gentleman Cadet JES Walford, passing out only in December, so too late to take his place beside his father at the Front. He was to be posted to the 3rd Battalion, eventually heading with it to India in 1920. Another example of the geographic scope from where the Battalion's junior officers were gathered can be found in the CWGC Cemetery at Pommereuil. The *History* noted that amongst those wounded in this action was Lt CA Connor. He must have died at the Front because there is a grave for him giving the date of death as 23rd October. His only other mention in the *History* is when he reported for duty to the 9th Battalion of the Regiment in Mesopotamia on 4th July 1916. The *CWGC* website provides other details – that he was born in the USA, had spent many years resident in China, had married Mabel Zilpha Clay of Hong Kong; plus the address of his widow in England – Ibstone Cottage, Haddenham, Buckinghamshire. He was 26 when he died and inscription on his grave tells of a son:

Fondest Love Daddy
Till We Meet Again
Widow And Sonny

Lt Connor left just £181 16s 2d. Mabel was born in Mitcham in 1890 and was living with her sister, Florrie Giles, in Aylesbury in 1911 as a schoolteacher. She sailed from Liverpool for Vancouver, Canada with her 5½-year-old son, named after his father, in 1923, returning from Adelaide, Australia to the Port of London on 7th August 1928. Young Cleveland [Sonny] was born in Aylesbury on 13th September 1917, so his father should have met him. He and his mother were living together in Yeovil in 1939. He died there in 1980. Mabel's life never seemed to have recovered from the death of her husband.

The citation of Wedgbury's DSO was not published in the *London Gazette* until 9th December 1919 and read:

> T/2nd Lt. Edmund WEDGBURY, M.C., D.C.M., M.M., Glou R., attd 1/8th Bn., Worc. R. (T.F.)
> For conspicuous gallantry and leadership in command of a company forming a defensive flank along north-west edge of Eveque Wood, on 25th October, 1918. He advanced three miles through country held by the enemy, picking up two platoons, which had lost direction, and reached Tilleuls Farm, two miles in rear of the enemy's main line of resistance. Here, with only 17 men, he charged and captured three 4.2 howitzers, killing the battery commander himself and capturing three other officers and the crews. Thanks to his determination and coolness, the defensive flank was successfully formed, with a total capture of five officers and 156 men.

As with Lt Gordon's letter, the confusion of the night and other battles means that even these official announcements may not be devoid of error. The date should have read the 23rd October. The number of guns and machine guns would vary with each telling of Edmund (Ted) Wedgbury's wonderful military service. The obituary in *FIRM*, the Worcestershire Regiment's magazine, in October 1956 stated:

> On July 1st, at his home in Worcester, Captain E. Wedgbury, DSO, MC, DCM, MM. Captain Wedgbury served with the 8th Battalion in the 1914–18 war and was commissioned into the Gloucestershire Regiment.
>
> As a Serjeant in the 8th Battalion, Captain Wedgbury won the Military Medal in November, 1916, and the Distinguished Conduct Medal in 1917. Though commissioned into the Gloucestershire Regiment he continued to serve with the 1/8th Battalion. He was awarded the Military Cross for gallantry in leading a Platoon of D Company at Beaurevoir in 1918 and the Distinguished Service Order for conspicuous gallantry at the battle of the Selle in 1918, in which the 1/8th Battalion captured 11 guns, 13 machine guns,

25 horses and several hundred prisoners. Living in Worcester, his unassuming modesty was such that the general public and indeed most of the Regiment were unaware of his great distinction. Captain EAJ Perry and RSM A Foden MSM represented the Regiment at the funeral.

After the War, Wedgbury's report on 15th January 1919 by Major Bate as commanding officer described him as 'a very gallant officer, looks after his men well & is invaluable in action' to which the Brigade Commander, Brigadier Frizell DSO, MC added 'I quite agree: this officer had done extraordinarily well for the time he was under my command'. This is high praise from a highly-decorated senior officer who also led from the front. Wedgbury was to be Mentioned in Field Marshal Haig's last Despatch, thus his work was recognised as notable across the whole of the British Army in France. Its text also explains why he was associated with the Gloucestershire Regiment, which held his commission. This is despite all the gallantry awards he attained when serving with the 1/8th Battalion, the Worcestershire Regiment:

The War of 1914–1918
Gloucestershire Regiment
T./Lt. E. Wedgbury, D.S.O., M.C., D.C.M., M.M., attd. Worc. R. (T.F.)
was mentioned in a Despatch from
Field Marshal Sir Douglas Haig, K.T., G.C.B., O.M., G.C.V.O., K.C.I.E.
dated 16th March 1919
for gallant and distinguished services in the Field.
I have it in command from the King to record His Majesty's high appreciation of the services rendered.

War Office
Whitehall S.W.
1st July 1919

Winston S. Churchill
Secretary of State for War

It is when reading this notice, which is still held by his family, that one begins to understand the achievement of being Mentioned in Despatches. What is not possible to show on the oak leaf on your ribbon is the level of command at which the Despatch occurred. For Wedgbury, it could not be a higher command, nor signed by a greater political war leader. Robert Bomford retains a similar one for his father from the same Despatch.

The importance of the Battalion's achievements that night was that they allowed the 18th Division to advance, secure in the knowledge that its right flank was protected along the whole northern wood line of the Bois l'Évêque. Indeed, such was D Company's progress that it was several hours before the 18th Division's right flank was able to protect Wedgbury's left flank. The *Divisional History* introduced the task of the 25th Division that night as being 'somewhat ambitious', requiring it to make:

> an advance of about 8,000 yards on a 2,000 yard front, including the capture of the village of Pommereuil and the clearing of the Bois l'Évêque and the countryside beyond to a line east of the villages of Fontaine and Malgarni on the edge of the forest of Mormal, a tract of country much intersected by thick hedges and covered by orchards.

The advance of D Company and the capture of Tilleuls Farm was only the first 5,000 yards of the 8,000 planned. The commander of 74th Brigade was a man who liked to be in the thick of the action, as we have seen when he led the capture of Guisancourt Farm to the north of Beaurevoir. The *Divisional Diary* recorded that night:

> a good many pockets and isolated groups of Germans were overrun in the dark. Brig-Gen Hickie, riding with his groom into the village of Pommereuil before dawn, himself captured several Germans. Two tanks gave assistance to the Infantry clearing the village. As soon as it became daylight, local commanders were able to organise 'mopping-up' parties which soon overcame all resistance, and the battalions were established by 11.55am along the line of their first objective east of Pommereuil.

This is a second mention of tanks which had been operating at the Front for well over a year. They are not included in battalion orders as they remained a Divisional asset. The Battalion would have known of the Divisional and Brigade tasks and the timings of when the tanks would have advanced independently of local command, making themselves useful as gun platforms, mobile shelters and ammunition carriers for the infantry. Commanding officers would have known from Brigade orders if any tanks had been allotted to their line of advance and a section of Battalion Orders devoted to tanks first appears on 22nd October:

> One section of 4 tanks will follow the Battalion assisting to establish posts and to capture the Farm LES TILLEULS. Each tank will carry 5 boxes S.A.A [small arms ammunition] available for infantry.

None of these tanks took part in D Company's capture of the battery or Les Tilleuls but their use as a resupply vehicle would have allowed the infantry to travel lighter into battle – a useful innovation after the problems at the Somme of full-laden soldiers attacking uphill. The full Operation Order for the attack, No 99, has a section on 'Pack Animals' which were to 'move in the rear of A Coy [reserve] with one carrying signals equipment [wire], three carrying SAA and two carrying TM [trench mortar] ammunition', thus in this instance the tanks were really there to support D Company alone. Company and platoon commanders could speak with tank commanders on the ground to identify targets or buildings on their line of advance which may be harbouring the enemy and needed softening up. We will hear more on the subject from Captain LR Bomford once he had returned to Battalion duty.

With the Division now secure in their first objective by midday on 23rd October, with the 18th Division on their left having reached the line of Wedgbury's D Company, orders came through for the second phase before any of the Battalion had rested. Major Bate, still commanding, recorded that the Battalion was 'concentrated about Flaquet Brifaut, expecting to be withdrawn for a rest. However, at 11 p.m., orders were received that the Battalion was to be attached to the 74th Brigade for a further attack early the next morning [the 24th]'. They were formed up to the north-east of Les Tilleuls Farm at 4 a.m.

and C Company [Walford] were advancing as the left flank of 74th Brigade at 4.30 a.m.

Corbett described the ground and the action in his normal ebullient fashion:

> La Fontaine was a maze of lanes and hedges, very thick still, but the wood had largely been felled by the enemy who had worked its great timber on a great scale… Once more we were completely successful in a very hot action, turning every formation of the enemy and beating down his machine-gun fire by our rifles and Lewis guns, whose mobility in thick country like this gives them a great superiority over the heavy emplaced machine-gun. The whole village and some fields beyond fell into our hands, and we were able to assist the unit [18th Division] on our left flank which was being held up.
>
> We had taken La Fontaine and were hoping for a rest, as we had now been fighting for nearly forty hours, when we got orders to attack the hamlet of Les Grands Chenes (Big Oaks) close by, to straighten our lines. There was very short notice – indeed our barrage fell on our outposts before we had time to withdraw them, wounding five men, but we carried the affair with our usual good fortune, taking several prisoners, besides guns. This was another great day for Captain Walford, and for more others than one can enumerate.
>
> In the three actions [over almost 45 hours] we had 24 killed and 76 wounded, a loss serious in itself, but slight in comparison with that which we had inflicted. In La Fontaine were a good many civilians who gave us a delighted welcome. They should not be pictured as waving handkerchiefs at ivy-clad cottage doors: on the contrary they were crouched in cellars, drinking their oppressors' brandy. It was another great day for us – a double event: our Derby and the Oaks.

Corbett's prose fits well with the reports at both Battalion and Divisional level. Major Bate added that Lt Watkinson's A Company moved forward from reserve to assist in the capture of La Fontaine by 7.45 a.m. 'with 400 to 500 Germans being driven out, and retiring to their next line of resistance and about 30 were killed'. 2Lt Wedgbury in his D Company report identified that 'Mr Gordon and 14 Platoon should move forward at 1.30 PM, this he did & gained objective at 1.45 PM'. He also confirmed the story of the five men wounded by their own artillery: 'Owing to alteration of ZERO time this platoon (14) was caught in our own barrage & suffered five casualties. The platoon was withdrawn & moved forward again at 2.30 PM & gained touch with the Sherwood Foresters on the right'. The Queens on the left did not come into line with C Company until 8.00 p.m. This concluded the Battle of the Selle.

The Battle Report recorded the capture of 25 cycles, 1 GA wagon, 3 MGs and 3 prisoners at a cost of 1 officer wounded (2Lt Bateman), 9 Other Ranks killed, 44 wounded and 2 missing. This was on top of 1 officer killed (Lt Connor), 2 wounded, 3 Other Ranks killed and 41 wounded from the previous day. In all, a total of 103 men of a depleted Battalion unavailable for the next action. The Roll records the death of 22 Other Ranks who were killed or died of their wounds in these two actions described as 'Bois l'Évêque', showing the initial casualty figures should be treated as a first estimate at best. The awards for the two days of action were a DSO for Major JP Bate MC*, a bar to his MC for Lt GL Watkinson, MCs to 2Lt D Gordon and 2Lt ST Bateman MM, a bar to his DCM for A Company's CSM, Sergeant ATJ Sherwood, and 12 MMs including to D Company's LCpl AP Owers for his work with 2Lt Wedgbury at Les Tilleuls and C Company's CSM Atkinson, a DCM to add to his MM and bar.

The *Journal* of 28th December 1918 celebrated CSM Robert Atkinson's war service:

> Company Sergeant Major Robert Atkinson, of the 1/8th Worcesters, who has been awarded the Distinguished Conduct Medal for bravery and devotion to duty was already the proud holder of the Military Medal and bar for his gallant deeds on previous occasions. He is one of four sons of Mr and Mrs William Atkinson, of 1, Nursery Road, St John's Worcester. He joined the 1/8th in 1914, and went with them [to France] in April 1915. He served in both France and Italy since and has risen from private to a warrant officer. Though he has been in every hard fight in which the 1/8th have been engaged, he has happily suffered no hurt. His three brothers are all on active service. Walter, who went to France in 1916, is now an instructor in signalling; Harold, in the Engineers, has been in Italy for twelve months; Arthur, in the 13th Berks, has been in France for two and a half years.

The *Journal* of 25th January 1919 announced the citation of the bar to CSM Atkinson's MM:

> In the attack on Honnechy on 9/10/18 he did conspicuous good work as acting CSM under heavy shell and machine gun fire. When his company was temporarily checked with both flanks in the air [unsupported by neighbouring formations], he immediately volunteered to establish communication, which he succeeded in doing, regardless of danger, and thus materially contributed to the success of the attack. When the objective was gained he rendered valuable assistance in the work of consolidation and gaining touch on both flanks.

The only slight confusion is that the *History* recorded his award at Honnechy as being his DCM. His first MM was gained the night that Captain Pawsey was captured in Italy on 8th August 1918, presumably placing him in C Company and, thus, to come under Captain Walford's command when back in France. Atkinson and Walford seem to have made a formidable team. This confusion seems to be confirmed by the *Journal*'s entry on 1st February 1919 when it announced the citation to his DCM:

During the operations 23-24 October, 1918 [Wedgbury's great night], his conduct was beyond all praise. He continued to search the houses during the advance from Pommereul, he helped to maintain fire on numerous enemy parties who impeded our advance and especially one party of about 150, which he drove out of the village without loss. He assisted to reorganise the Company and to form posts in face of numbers of the enemy. On October 24 [in the attack on Great Oaks] he again displayed great initiative and leadership, and in the final advance when our left was held up by the enemy he established his post according to orders after a stiff fight. During both days his conduct and leadership were marked. He was worth a platoon.

He is a son of Mr Wm Atkinson, 1 Nursery Road, St John's. He was recently awarded a bar to the Military Medal.

ACROSS THE CANAL

Relief was to come in the form of Operation Order 101 of 24th October:

INFORMATION	1.	The Battalion will be relieved by 2 Coys of the 20th MANCHESTERS.
INTENTION	2.	On relief, Companies will march back to billets at POMMEREUIL.
INSTRUCTIONS	3.	GUIDES will be at X Roads in L20 central to guide Coys to billets. GUIDES for incoming units will be at GARAGE CORNER.
REPORTS	4.	Relief complete to be sent to Bn. HQs by runner when moving.

E. Gilbert Capt/Adjt
$1/8^{th}$ The Worcestershire Regt.

It might be 'relief', but there was still a four-mile march to accommodation at Pommereuil described by Corbett as 'the well-furnished, but very verminous billets of the enemy'. He continued: 'We were covered in glory and received the warmest compliments from all sides … in the 25th [Division] our Brigade [75th] was mostly highly prized, and a large share of these continued and unbroken successes most generously attributed to us'. There is some proof that this was not an over-flattering view, both in writing at the time and the fact that the Brigade was given the toughest assignment within the Division the following week, and that the Battalion was assigned its most challenging task. They rested for six days in Pommereuil during which some of the 'warm compliments' were received, first from the gallant brigade commander of the neighbouring 74th, Brig-Gen Hugh Craigie Halkett DSO:

From the time that the $1/8^{th}$ WORCESTERSHIRE Regt. came

under my orders on the 24th October to support the attack of the 74th Infantry Brigade on the FINAL OBJECTIVE, the Battalion under the command of Major JP Bate MC did everything that was asked of them.

The advance was carried out in close and difficult country against stubborn resistance, the Battalion showing great courage and determination throughout.

During this operation Major JP BATE MC showed the utmost coolness and skill in handling his Battalion and sent in excellent reports.

I wish to take this opportunity of thanking Major JP BATE MC and all ranks of the 1/8th Bn. The WORCESTERSHIRE Regt for the assistance they rendered the Brigade in carrying out the operation.

HM CRAIGIE HALKETT Brig. General
Commanding 74th Inf Bde
Oct. 26th 1918

This was a report submitted to the commander of 75th Brigade who ordered that it be forwarded to Major Bate:

OC 1/8th Bn. The WORCESTERSHIRE Regt

The Brigadier General Commanding is highly gratified with this report and wishes to communicate it to all ranks at the first opportunity.

F. Teacher Captain
Staff Captain. 75th Infantry Brigade
27/10/18

As with all such reports in this book, these are the actual, if formal, words used at the time as well as a good facsimile of the layout each time. The last comment on this acknowledgement of the Battalion's achievements can be found in the *War Diary* on 26th October after its return to Pommereuil, stating simply:

The Divisional General [Major General JRE Charles CB, DSO]

addressed the Bn. and said how pleased he was with the excellent work the Battalion had done.

The downside to such accolades was the human cost of this series of successful actions – successful in terms of ground gained, men and equipment captured. The *War Diary* concluded October 1918 with what might be described as a scorecard:

Total casualties for the month of October 1918

	Killed	Wounded	Missing
Officers	3	12	
O.R.	51	313	4

Total Captures

Prisoners	M.G.	Guns	Horses	Material etc.
16 officers 657 O.R.	13	11 including two batteries of 4.2"	25	40 R'way trucks 4 Limbers 2 Baggage wagons 1 Signal wagon with equipment 25 cycles

Total of drafts received:

8 Officers 436 O.R.

The page was signed by Lt Col HT Clarke who had returned to command the Battalion. In fact the officers killed total should have been two (Lt CA Connor and Lt E Stainton) with Lt RS Miller having been wounded and captured. Ernest Stainton died of his wounds in London a month later, 25th November and is buried in the Hanwell Cemetery in Ealing with 51 other casualties of the Great War – almost half of whom had died after the Armistice, with the last dying on 19th June 1921. Stainton was 41 when he perished but he was a long way from being the oldest of the soldiers, sailors and airmen buried there. Of those with known ages, seven were older than Stainton with the Army chaplain, the Rev Somerset Pennefather from Dublin, dying in August 1917 aged 69. He was born on 1st March 1848. Seemingly the oldest recorded soldier to die in the Great War is buried in the Norwich Cemetery, Captain George Clements of the 1st (Royal) Dragoons. His medal collection would have included the Crimean War and he was 85 when he died on 3rd March 1916.

The *War Diary* is not its normal complete self in October, perhaps unsurprisingly given the number of orders to write, Battle Reports to complete and that two men had commanded the Battalion over the hectic four weeks. This was particularly with regard to the drafts of new officers and men who joined the Battalion each day, if any. Lt Col Clarke provided a total for the month of October but the entries in the *War Diary* do not add up to that total. It was clear as to the numbers who joined after these actions when they were billeted at Pommereuil: 28th – 14 ORs; 30th – 2 officers, 238 ORs. This leaves us 6 officers and 188 ORs short. Corbett, as ever, provided some background:

> All through these operations reinforcements had come in – they arrived, were posted to companies, their names and next of kin were taken, and before we knew them or their qualities they disappeared. But still there were plenty of the Old Firm left [those who had crossed to France in March 1915], and as one after another fell out their ranks were taken by others who did as well. Indeed, we could not have had better material than the great drafts which reached us here [Pommereuil]. The last reinforcements had been miners in the North – fine fellows, but with their short training somewhat out of place in this incongruous employ. But there were men of Somerset and Devon, rustics fresh from the plough. They had only been enlisted twelve weeks, the last of the indispensables, but they were of the right stuff and the right spirit. There was no running about to push these into place, no bunching or ducking, no obstinacy nor bewilderment: they did not know what to do, but they did whatever they were told, and did it at once and with a will. They took to war as their natural heritage, and seeing how they shaped one could understand Sedgemoor and Waterloo and the Frenchman's saying that the English never fight better than in their first battle. We went into our last [on 4th November] with 270 men who had been shot over and 300 who had not, and never did better.

This is a fascinating insight into the state of the manpower available from Britain to the generals in France and, also, of the importance of having the enormous influx of raw recruits from America to bolster Britain and France over these last months of the War. It told that as they approached the Sambre Canal, more than half the Battalion would be fighting their first action – extraordinary after 51 months of war. Also, that being so the Battalion strength was only about sixty per cent of that which had crossed the Channel some 43 months before. Any such battalion would have to lean heavily on its senior officers and seasoned Other Ranks, some of whom had been commissioned – like Wedgbury, Gordon and Bateman as well as 2Lt Arthur Coe who was to command the reserve company – 'B' – at Landrecies and who was to win the last MC in the pursuit that afternoon, and 2Lt DA Franks who was wounded that day having been commissioned from the Royal Warwickshire Regiment. They were all now 'temporary' officers – seeming the significant majority of the subaltern platoon commanders in those last weeks. Captain LR Bomford returned to the Battalion on 31st October, his course complete – a most valuable extra resource. As an example of the devastation wrought on the fighting platoons, there is a photograph of Bomford with his platoon, the 2nd in A Company, in 1916. It records underneath that only 13 of the 32 men in the photograph were 'still alive at the end of the War' – Bomford and Wedgbury being two.

Corbett explained that the 'rest' at Pommereuil was not without incident: 'We were shelled daily and suffered many casualties. In the Transport lines, a mile behind, many men and horses were hit, and all together we had two men killed and 24 wounded, some on the very day they joined'. Lt Col Clarke recorded in the *War Diary* on the 31st October that: 'Battalion was reconstructed into 4 companies of 3 platoons. The Commanding Officer addressed the battalion in the afternoon' – presumably with more than half of the men seeing their commanding officer for the first time. It is interesting to note that the level of losses suffered by the 1/8th was very similar to those of the other two battalions in the 75th Brigade, being 470 for the seven weeks in France until the Armistice (so including the forthcoming Battle of Sambre), as compared with 406 for the 1/8th R. Warwicks and

385 for the 1/5th Glosters. They are also a demonstration that these last weeks when German morale was weakening, casualty rates were still extremely high and battles and awards were hard-won. Within the Division, the 13th Durham Light Infantry – those 'damned' by Walford at Bazuel – suffered the worst with 740 killed, wounded or missing, in effect the whole battalion strength, including 27 officers – probably their full cadre.

The wonderful esprit de corps of the 1/8th Battalion was built on the base of the six senior officers, their commissioned sergeants, RSM Heath and RQMS Corbett and their 'original' sergeants at the head of many platoons. This may seem to be the reason for the strength and fighting expertise of many of the front-line British infantry battalions in France, but that was not always the case. Captain Lance Evers MC had returned to the 2/8th after his wounds from Passchendaele to find a new commanding officer taking the opposite stance as to experienced officers – in his diary note of 28th July 1918:

> Distressing news that Peary is going as 2nd in Command of the 1/5th Lincolns. I am really sorry. Apart from personal grounds he is the only 2/8th in any authority and it is so obviously the intention of the CO [Lt Col Bernard Barton] to destroy the old 2/8th feeling and keep us old originals under and apart, and after all it is largely this esprit de corps for which we had fought, got wounded and worked our way out [to France] again.

Lt Col Barton was a lance corporal in the 8th Battalion at the start of the War, received a commission in December 1914 and crossed to France with the 11th Battalion in September 1915. He took command of the 2/8th Bn on 5th July 1918, although Evers describes him as CO on 1st July when he returned to the 2/8th: '...then meet our new CO Major Barton – by chance. I don't know him and he doesn't know who I am at all', before returning to him in the following day's entry: 'The Colonel seems neither interested nor pleased to see me and he doesn't seem a bit popular and they all dislike him'. His entry of 11th August relates that Barton's command was short-lived: 'I have a wash and shave and write up this book and the CO comes round to see me.

About half an hour after, he treads on a bomb and is killed which is rather a shock'. He was a married man from Bushey in Hertfordshire, the son of the Reverend Haycroft Barton, the rector of Malton in Yorkshire. It is sad to reflect that his death may have been a blessing for the 2/8th. He was succeeded in command by Lt Colonel Delme Davies-Evans, a seasoned Territorial from the 1st Pembroke Volunteer Battalion who had already had a few months in command of the 5th Battalion of the Lincoln Regiment. Evers' diary entries for later that month were in a different vein: 'The new CO makes a very happy start'. In his second week, he put Evers in command of an assault by C and D Companies in the Passage of the Lys outside Ypres on 3rd September. Evers was to gain a bar to his MC that day:

> During the crossing of a river and subsequent operations, this Officer behaved with great courage and dash, and on two occasions led out-flanking attacks on machine-gun positions. His inspiring example greatly contributed to the success of the operations.

Sadly, Evers would become the only 'original' 2/8th officer to be killed in the War when, on 1st November 1918, he was undertaking a reconnaissance for a battalion attack the following day. He pushed through a hedgerow and was shot in the chest by a German sniper. He was 37. His name can be found on the Memorial in the centre of Stourbridge. Lt Col LL Bilton CMG, his commanding officer from June 1916 to June 1918, wrote:

> I never had a braver or more reliable Officer. When he was wounded at Ypres in 1917, we were all depressed and felt his loss tremendously. His magnificent courage, enthusiasm and leadership made all the men love and trust him and, consequently, he always had a first-class company, ready, under him, to do anything. I consider it a real privilege to have called him a friend. Men such as he make one very proud of this old Country.

There can be no officer who has served his country who would not wish to have such an epitaph. His family continued to be supported after the War by 'Sym [Captain Noel Symons MC], Douglas [Captain Douglas Bomford] and the Old Gent [Walford]' in the best Worcestershire tradition.

Captain Leslie Bomford, just returned to Battalion duty from his course, and the Old Gent would not have known of this sad news as they prepared for their last battle. The *Divisional History* set the scene, explaining the reason for the pause after four weeks of relentless attacking from the start of their assault on the Hindenburg Line on 29th September until the 1/8th's retirement back to Pommereuil on 25th October. The last major feature which the Germans could use as a defensive line lay across the path of the British advance, the Sambre Canal. It linked the river Seine on the western edge of Paris with Charleroi in Belgium, which in turn linked Mons and Brussels with the North Sea. The canal was a substantial obstacle and being November, the water temperature would have been very cold. The advance in these four weeks had been of the order of 12 miles:

> Railways [needed to be] repaired, bridges re-built, and the railheads gradually advanced close up to the fighting troops. Thousands of prisoners and men from the Labour Coys, were employed on this work, which became the main factor governing the advance of the armies.

An indication of the replenishment requirements was the number of reinforcements needed by the 1/8th Battalion alone – and they lost fewer than other battalions in the 25th Division. The British lined up with 13 Divisions on a front of some twenty miles with over 1,000 artillery guns and some 70 tanks. Derek Clayton's *Decisive Victory: The Battle of The Sambre, 4 November 1918* is the complete work on this battle, based on the doctoral thesis for which he was awarded his PhD. Each Division would have had nine battalions so a total of 121 battalions needing reinforcement and resupply, let alone the movement of all the artillery batteries to be near the battlefront, together with the supply of all their ammunition requirements.

Germany had lost its two key allies: the Hapsburg Empire after the Battle of Vittorio Veneto in Italy; and the Ottoman Empire after

General Allenby's victory at Megiddo and the fall of Damascus and Beirut. Each had negotiated separately with the Allied victors in their theatre. The new German Chancellor, Max von Baden, had already made approaches to President Wilson but that was not known by the German front-line troops who were making a phased withdrawal to each pre-planned defensive line, nor to the British forces opposing them. The Sambre Canal was the next challenge and the 1/8th Battalion would return to the area of La Fontaine and Bois l'Évêque from where they would be part of the 25th Division's assault of the Landrecies area of the canal. Indeed, they were given the honour of leading across the canal and assaulting the town, the only one in the 25th Division's path.

We can return to Captain LR Bomford's *Memoir*:

> I got back in time for the attack on Landrecies [on 4th November]. We had a morning reconnaissance and then assembly that evening. The night was bad. Tanks were moving about in the dark; it wasn't only their noise but fear of being run over.

His mention of the tank noise must have acted as a warning to the Germans that an attack was imminent so they would have been alert as dawn broke. The orders were very different from the earlier ones, those of the assaults at the Somme and Passchendaele, and would be more familiar to those organising such an attack a hundred years later, aside from mules no longer being in use. They were written out by the new adjutant, Captain GL Watkinson MC* who had passed command of A Company back to his friend Captain Bomford. Watkinson had won his spurs and deserved his time in Battalion Headquarters but then Walford and Wedgbury had also fought all these autumn battles, yet they remained in command of C and D Companies respectively. B Company had been reformed and command was given to 2Lt JA Bullock who had won an MC in Italy on the night that Captain Pawsey and 2Lt Granger were taken prisoner. They were held in reserve.

It is worth providing the full Instruction (No 1) which was issued on 2nd November:

Secret — 1/8th Bn. The Worcestershire Regt. — Copy: No. 1
Ref. 57A NW — Instructions No 1 — 2/11/18

1/20,000

1. The following instructions are a resume of points gone over at the recent CO's conferences with the addition of such information as has been received since the last conference.
2. On Zero day the 75th Brigade will cross the SAMBRE CANAL & establish a bridge head on the high ground east of LANDRECIES. The 50th Division is attacking on the left (49th Brigade on the right) & 32nd Division on the right (96th Brigade on the left). The 74th Brigade will go through the 75th Brigade at Z+7 hours & the 7th Brigade is in Divisional Reserve.
3. The 1/8th Royal Warwicks (left) and the 1/5th Gloucester Regt (right) will carry on the attack as far as the canal, arranging crossings on rafts NW and SW of LANDRECIES respectively, & pushing over small covering parties. The 1/8th Worcesters will cross the Canal & occupy the Red Line, (tracing [map] being passed round) establishing an outpost line on the dotted red line; when they have been reinforced in the Red Line with a Company of Gloucesters & of Warwicks.
4. At dusk on Y/Z night [3rd November] the 1/8th Worcesters will move up to MALGARNI, halting in the fields NW of that village. Coys will move from there so that they are in the following positions (shown on trace) by Z-2 hours.

   A Coy – Green lane from G14C 3.4. to G14C 8.7.
   B Coy – On road from G14A 2.1. to G14 a 8.1.
   C Coy – On lane N. of LEFAUX from G14a59 to G8c90
   D Coy – On road from G14c 4.2. to G20a 8.7.
   Bn HQ – House G13d 81

   Lewis Gun Limbers will accompany battalion to junction of MALGARNI road and New Track (about G17a 5.9.). C Coy limber will carry on as far as OC Coy wishes & will then return to G19a 5.9. Tool limber and TM limber will bring up clothing, food & rum. SAA &

Signals mules will accompany Bn HQ & stay in a field about G19b6.9. As soon as road line is gained, mules will take ammunition up to A Coy, (OC A Coy will send back a guide) & dump it. On return they will be used to carry up clothes, food & rum from limbers.

5. At Z+4 hours Coys will commence the advance in rear of the Gloucesters & Warwicks, who should be allowed to gain at least 700 yards (NB. Coys on road. The barrage goes at 100 yards in 6 minutes). C & D Coys will move down the roads they are on towards LANDRECIES. A Coy with B Coy in touch in rear by connecting files, will move up to road [triangle] in G14C and strike across country, Bearing 112 true. Before Zero, OC D Coy will get in touch with his 20 rafts at their assembly point, and later at their forming up point & see that when the advance is commenced they follow his company.
6. The crossing of the SAMBRE CANAL:

   D Coy cross stream in G22a. & b. on Gloucester rafts, & canal on their own as well.

   C Coy cross on Warwicks rafts.

   A&B Coys cross either on main town bridge, if not blown up, or bridges over locks, if Sappers, who advance with Gloucesters have made them; or failing this on rafts of first Coy across.
7. When across C & D Coys go straight for their objectives on the red line (Boundaries D Coy G23c02 to road junction G23d3.8 inclusive; C Coy road junction to Canal at G17b7.0)

   A Coy will mop up town & form an inner line of defence on its eastern outskirts.

   B Coy will settle down in practice trenches about G23c3.8 until the Warwicks & Gloucesters are up, when they will go forward & make good the outpost (dotted red) line. Each Coy will have two platoons in the line & one in support.
8. Artillery. On Divisional Front. Four Brigades Field Artillery, one Brigade of Heavies, & some Corps Heavies. Barrage creeps at 100 yards in 6 minutes from AB on trace at Z+4 hours, halting at CD (300 yards E of Canal) from Z + 3 hours, 18 minutes to Z+4 hours, 18 minutes, then carrying on to EF where it forms a protective barrage for

consolidation of Red Line, carrying on at Z+5 ½ hours for advance to Outpost Line. At Zero barrage selected targets (48 guns).

9. Machine Guns. At Zero barrage selected targets (48 guns). During crossing of canal, 8 guns take up commanding positions in houses & railway cutting, engaging any target which appears. Also protect troops crossing, from counterattack. B Coy MGC less 1 Section help in consolidating Red Line, with one gun on each flank & one in the centre.
10. Tanks. Will assist leading battalions to Canal & then cruise about railway to assist crossing.
11. R.A.F. Keep a smoke cloud on high ground E of LANDRECIES (enclosed by 160 contour) while crossing going on, Call for flares at Zero+5 hours & Zero+6 hours from Red Line. Counter attack patrols will indicate counter attacks by dropping a white parachute right over the enemy centre.

Distribution:
1 CO.
2 – 5 Coys.
6 QM.
7 T.O.
8 RSM
9 File
10 War Diary

G.L.Watkinson
Capt & A/Adjt
1/8th Bn. The Worcestershire Regt.

These orders raise a number of interesting historical points which show the development of the 'all-arms' warfare of General Sir Henry Rawlinson, in particular, with the inclusion of tanks and the RAF down to battalion-level instructions. From a tactical perspective, this represented a continuation of the British 'bite and hold' operations with a clear but limited 'red-line' objective for each Brigade. The company commanders have clear goals and boundaries but all depended on the progress of the neighbouring battalions achieving the advance to the canal bank on time and close to the progress of the creeping barrage. There was an assumption that the two leading battalions would clear up all enemy pockets during their own advance as the 1/8th Battalion had no orders to engage any enemy in their advance behind the Warwicks and Gloucesters, nor in the handling of prisoners. This was understandable as each company would need to be at full strength for the crossing of the canal itself – which for the 1/8th Battalion would be in full view of any enemy in the buildings in Landrecies set back from the canal bank. As ever, the leadership of the three principal company commanders appeared to be crucial, most especially at the actual crossings themselves, be they on rafts or across lock gates or bridges. Overall, the 25th Division was to advance on a 2,000-yard front with the capture of Landrecies as its main objective. The canal was some one and a half miles from the start line. The *Divisional History* recorded this country as 'very intricate and enclosed' which remains the case to this day – though many of the orchards on their maps have now been felled. It noted the canal as being 55 feet wide (16.75m) and 6 to 7 feet deep (2m). Between the lock gates on the main axis into Landrecies and the intended crossing point of C Company the width was about double that, as it was a harbouring and unloading area for the barges.

The *War Diary of the 25th Division CRE* states that the practice crossing area on the 'Selle River was about 32ft wide, but served for our purpose'. The CRE [Commander Royal Engineers] confirmed some of Corbett's doubts:

> A platoon of infantry [D Company, 1/8th Battalion, Worcestershire Regiment, so 2Lt Wedgbury to the fore again] made a demonstration attack on it followed by Sappers carrying rafts and superstructures. On reaching the River, the Sappers duly paddled across, the platoon of Infantry was ferried across and the rafts were made into a bridge. The realistic nature of the operation was somewhat marred by the enormous crowd of spectators, who found amusement in the efforts of one or two of the Infantry to balance themselves on the rafts. There was some general feeling of doubt, I think, as to whether the operation would be feasible under fire. One CO gave it as his opinion, that it would be a 'Sporting Event'.

Sambre Canal at Landrecies with C Company crossing point towards top right

Bomford has already mentioned his uneasy night with the noise of the tank movements, let alone the worry of the canal crossing which, as at the Canal de Saint-Quentin in September, was very likely to cause heavy casualties. Corbett, with a degree of hindsight, summed up the situation:

> We received orders at last, and learned that our part was to take the town of Landrecies, famous for the Guards' [4th Brigade] great street fight in '14. The 75th Brigade was to lead the way. The scheme was to advance from a place beyond the Big Oaks, called Malgarni, to which the Line was now advanced, fight our way through thick country for about two miles, carry a suburb on this side of the great Sambre Canal, cross the canal somehow, and establish a bridgehead on the further side. We were to go into action rather curiously equipped – with lifebelts and light lines – and should not take haversacks and entrenching tools. They would only be a hindrance in crossing the canal, and in any case, as it was rather grimly hinted, we should not be likely to want them again. The enterprise was regarded as rather a forlorn hope.

On the evening of [Sunday] the 3rd November we moved out from Pommereuil and established ourselves in orchards near the hamlet. The night was dark and warm, and very quiet, save for occasional rush and roar of a great shell, and there was a good deal of gas in the air [but no mention of Bomford's tanks].

Here again, there was evidence of the progress in British tactics. The men had the basic fighting equipment only, not the great burden of equipment of those who rose from the trenches at the Somme on 1st July 1916. When one reads the full Instruction, there is no indication that the generals believed that this operation was a 'forlorn hope' with heavy casualties expected. However, Corbett alluded to the Battalion having to fight its way to the canal, rather than leaving that aspect to the leading battalions of the Brigade.

The Battalion issued an Operational Order on 3rd November to confirm the final details for the following day:

Secret

1/8th Bn. The Worcestershire Regt.
Operational Order No. 103

Ref: 57A NW
Forest 1/20,000

Nov. 3rd 1918

1, INTRODUCTION

The Battalion will move forward to Assembly Position tonight.

2. INSTRUCTIONS

a. Starting Point: junction of BAZUEL and LE CATEAU road.

Time: 22.00hrs

Dress: As detailed to Company Commanders

Order of Companies: C, A, B, D, HQ

Formation: 100 yards between platoons.

b. Lewis Gun Limbers will follow their Coys. Pack animals follow Bn HQ. T.M. limbers will follow A Coy.

c. Guides for A, B, D, and Bn HQ will be at L24a.48 in charge of 2/Lieut. EF BLACKLER. If the road is heavily shelled they will meet Battalion earlier and guide by an alternative route.
d. Officers' valises at QM Stores by 18.00. Packs and blankets left outside each Company HQ under guard before moving off.
e. Men dumped will report to RSM H Heath for orders tomorrow morning at 09.00.
f. Each CQMS will go with his company so he will know the place where cookers will be brought for tea at 0230 tomorrow.
g. Coys will arrange for men to have soup before moving off tonight.
3. REPORTS
(1) When Companies are in Assembly Position to L24a48.
(2) When Companies are in Forming Up Position to House at G13d91.

G.L.Watkinson
Capt & A/Adjt
1/8th Bn. the Worcestershire Regt

Distribution

Copy No 1	C.O.	
	2-6	Coys
	7	T.O.
	8	QM
	9	RSM
	10	File
	11	War Diary
	12	M.O.

This was in a different hand to that of the original Instruction with the ensuing Operational Order 104 being in a third hand. There were a number of clerks in each battalion headquarters, selected in part for the quality, speed and accuracy of their handwriting. As the 'Distribution' list above shows, there were up to twelve copies of each order to be produced neatly, accurately and in haste. Accuracy would have been crucial, most especially with the map references – even though the use of full-stops seemed to vary. The last order was, presumably, issued on the evening of 3rd November and is interesting mainly for its narrative of the movements of Battalion Headquarters during the operation. As there has been no mention of any commanding officer of the Battalion during the War being involved in the action of any operation of the Battalion, it is of interest to see how close they kept themselves to the action. They, I am sure, would say that the extraordinary leadership of a number of the company commanders since their action at Templeux in April 1917 meant that there was no need for them to take to the front line to rally their battalions like Lt Cols Roland Bradford, Adrian de Wiart, Dudley Johnson and James Marshall. We have read of Bradford and de Wiart's exploits. Marshall's and Johnson's actions were to take place on the banks and locks of the Sambre Canal on that same morning. It is doubtful that, if either Lt Col Harry Carr at Gillemont Farm or Lt Col Hubert Clarke at Springfield Farm in front of Ypres had raced to the front line, they would have changed the course of either battle or secured more ground for longer. Had they done so successfully, they would have, most possibly, earned themselves a Victoria Cross as did the other four.

This last order, again under the signature of Captain Watkinson, was the 104th of the War for the Battalion and was issued shortly before midnight:

SECRET Copy No. 6

1/8th Bn. The Worcestershire Regt.
Operations Order No. 104

Nov. 3. 1918

1. INTENTION.
The Battalion will attack (LANDRECIES [written in by Watkinson, presumably at the time of his signing of this copy of the Order]) tomorrow morning.
2. INSTRUCTIONS.
Zero: 0615
Objectives: Boundaries as detailed in Instructions & Amendments

The Right Flank Brigades will attack at 05.45
3. REPORTS.
Bn. HQ at House G.13d 8.0 moving forward by bounds along the road running Shrines G.20 through G.21 a&b on to LANDRECIES. A sentry will stop all runners passing Bn HQ.

GL Watkinson
Capt & A/Adjt
1/8 Bn, the Worcestershire Regt.

DISTRIBUTION
No. 1-4 Coys
No. 5 File
Issued to Coy. Cmdrs at 23.15

It was possible that these were given personally by Captain Watkinson to each company commander. This order is shown as being issued at 23.15 hrs and we know from the previous order that tea has been organised for 02.30 hours, indicating that Bomford, Walford and Wedgbury would have had three hours' sleep at most – probably a lot less.

Capture of Landrecies, 4th November 1918

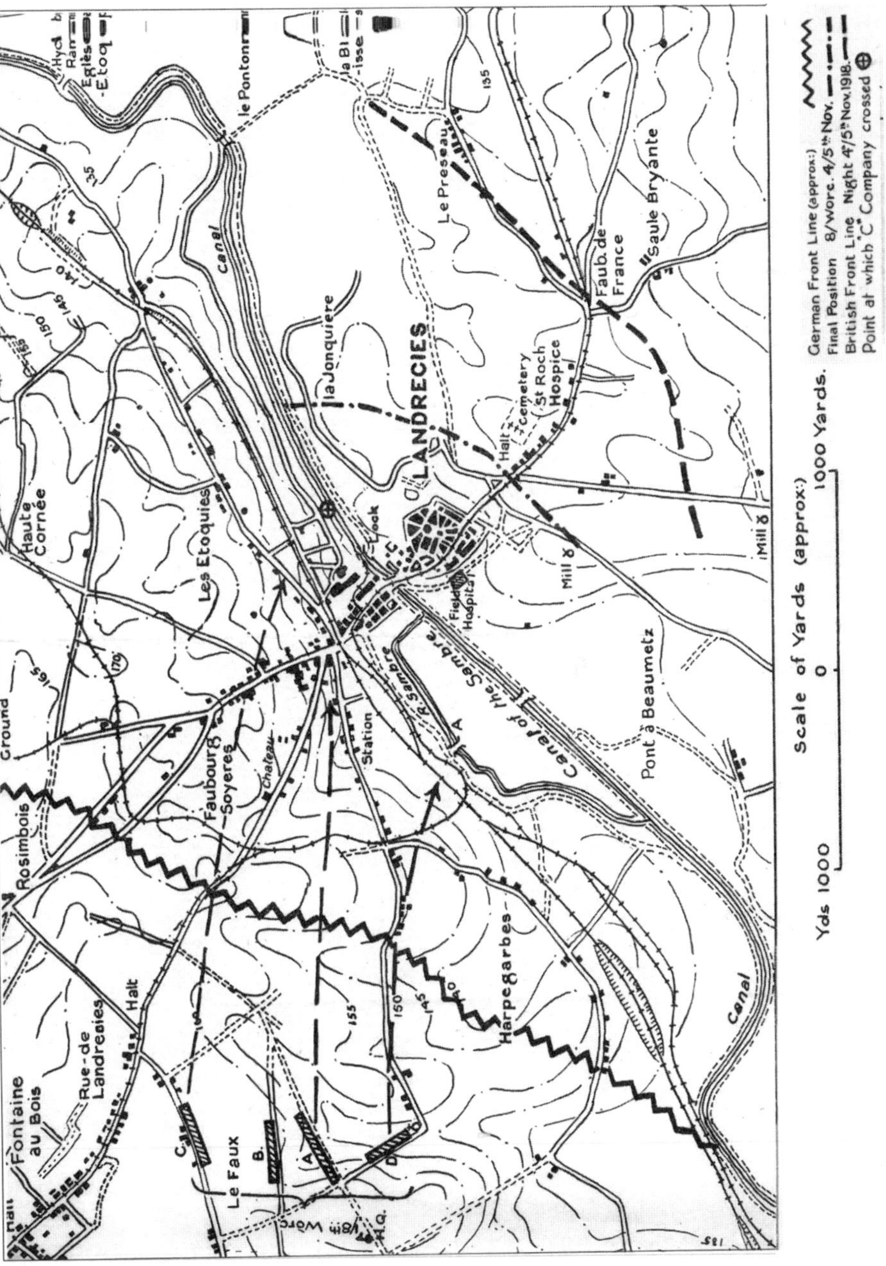

THEIR LAST BATTLE

The Battalion was up well before dawn on Monday 4th November 1918. Tea was issued, there was no mention of food but perhaps few would have had the stomach for anything, knowing what lay ahead. Not even Corbett as RQMS referred to food being offered. Instead, he started his narrative:

> The battle was to open at six o'clock. The first greyness began: one could see the courses of the bricks in a wall and the trees began to take shape. In the south-east the sky opened, great stars showed, and a primrose bar opened and spread [thus, unlike other great British assaults, the Battle of Sambre was not to be dogged by rain and wind].
>
> Then a gun sounded in the stillness, and the next moment all the world was ablaze. The ground trembled and the air was full of the howling passage of uncounted shells, and the glare of their explosion and crash of their impact dazzled and deafened the dawn – the last dawn of so many thousand men.
>
> For once the enemy seemed taken by surprise: perhaps he scarcely knew where to direct his fire: but soon he was busily at work, and the rattle of musketry and machine-guns added to the din…

We need to think back to the details of the huge drafts of reinforcements which arrived at the Battalion for this attack, with Corbett noting that more than half the Battalion would be going into action for the first time. Only two of this new draft were officers and their names are not shown in the *War Diary* for that day, Wednesday 30th October. They would, no doubt, have been allocated to platoons with very experienced sergeants. The old hands would have been used to the trembling ground and explosions but the hearts of those in action for the first time would have been racing. The steadiness of the seasoned platoon sergeants and section corporals would have been invaluable. In this respect the Battalion was very well served.

The *War Diary* included a 'Narrative of Operations: 4th November

1918', dated Wednesday, 6th November after they were replaced on the front line:

> The battalion formed up behind the Gloucesters & Warwicks in G14 at 0420 on 4.11.18. D Coy, right, A coy, centre, C Coy, left, B, reserve.
>
> The canal being 53 feet wide & 6 feet, 6 Ins. deep, and it being anticipated that the enemy would blow the bridges, the CRE had constructed 80 rafts, each capable of supporting one man. Parties of RE & men of the Pioneer Bn. were detailed to carry rafts to the canal, & by means of ropes affixed to each end, to ferry the infantry across, the raft in the first instance being paddled across by a sapper.
>
> Our barrage opened at 0615 hours, & the leading battalions moved forward. There was a thick mist, & we had to move behind them in order to keep in touch.
>
> At 0624 hours OC D Coy (2Lt WEDGBURY DCM, MM) was wounded by one of our MG bullets, & 2Lt COLEMAN took over command of the Coy…

And so ended the War for the Battalion's outstanding soldier, one of the British Army's outstanding soldiers: the only foot soldier to be awarded four different gallantry awards – DSO, MC, DCM, MM. Wedgbury had been hit in the arm – a bullet which was to stay with him for years to come – and, by the above reports, fired by his own side.

The ground has changed little over the last hundred years. It slopes steadily down to the railway line which lay across the path of the Battalion. The hedges are largely still there. There are a few extra houses and barns. The 'thick mist' might have been seen as a significant advantage for the attacker as the hedges and orchards made sure that there were not the long uninterrupted views over which the Somme's defenders used their machine-guns to such devastating effect. However, command and control of advancing troops was infinitely more difficult in such country, as was maintaining the direction of attack. Yes, it was safe to be heading always downhill but tracking across the slope would have brought sections and platoons across the path of others from the Battalion, or even of neighbouring battalions. Shapes in the mist would have been difficult to identify as friend or foe – as Wedgbury had been quick to find to his cost. The orders gave a compass bearing – 112 degrees, or east-south-east – which, on initial reading, seemed superfluous but would have been invaluable to commanders of all levels from section upwards if those in command had the steadiness to stop and check their compasses under fire or bombardment. The one constant would have been the wall of the British artillery barrage which crept along gradually in front of them. It was not made clear in any report exactly when the mist lifted but it certainly did not seem to aid the two leading battalions as all three Worcestershire companies were quickly in action. Again, relying on the *War Diary's Narrative*:

> The Gloucesters were held up at the light railway in G15d by machine-gun fire from a chateau at G16a11. A Coy pushed a platoon through the Gloucesters to attack this, & with the assistance of a tank & with the support of the two platoons, it was captured together with 4 officers & 35 men.

Bomford as A Company commander remembered the action:

> After advancing some way we came under machine gun fire from a chateau and the Germans surrendered a battalion HQ. I walked behind a tank in the gap between the tracks in comparative safety. You could hear the bullets smacking off the tank, it didn't mind us at all. The tank helped us with occasional use of its gun along the house-lined road to Landrecies…

Immediately to their left were the 1/8th Royal Warwickshires, with Walford's C Company in their wake – at the start at least. There was a network of machine-gun posts holding up the Warwicks, particularly in the area of another chateau at Faubourg Soyers. This and Bomford's chateaus are now little more than manor houses close to the roads leading down to Landrecies. At Faubourg Soyers, a 37-year-old lance corporal of the Warwicks took measures into his own hands and earned the ultimate accolade for his achievements. The citation of his VC gives a good indication of the challenges which lay in front of these battalions of the 75th Brigade:

> For conspicuous and outstanding gallantry on November 4th, 1918, during the attack on Landrecies.
>
> The attack commenced in the fog resulting in many hostile machine-gun nests not being 'mopped up' by the leading troops. The NCO with his Section, having lost touch with his Company, attached himself to another Company which was held up by heavy machine-gun fire, and carried out the following deeds of gallantry:
>
> On his own initiative, he led his Section to attack a machine-gun nest in the face of heavy fire. With great bravery, he forced the garrison to retire to a neighbouring farm, finally causing them to capitulate, and capturing about 50 prisoners and several machine-guns.
>
> Later, single handed, he attacked a hostile machine-gun post situated in a farm-house. Exposed to heavy fire, he advanced unhesitatingly, killed two of the garrison and drove the remainder into a cellar until assistance arrived.
>
> Again later and unaided, he attacked a Chateau at Faubourg Soyers which was strongly held, and holding up the line of advance. With determination and disregard to personal safety, he rushed the Chateau, killing two Germans and holding up the remainder until reinforced.
>
> The gallant act was instrumental in the capturing of a further 20 prisoners, and cleared away the last of the opposition in this Sector. Throughout the day, the conduct of Lance-Corporal Amey, in the face of such opposition and danger, was of the highest type and beyond all praise. The work done by him not only resulted in clearing up a critical situation, but was instrumental in saving many lives.

Amey, who had already won an MM, died in 1940 and is buried in the cemetery at Leamington Spa where his grave has recently been renovated to ensure his achievements continue to be remembered.

It might seem strange that LCpl William Amey had to undertake much of this work alone. The Warwicks did suffer more casualties that day than either of the other two battalions of the 75th Brigade – 1 officer killed and 2 wounded; 21 Other Ranks killed and 108 wounded – almost as many as the other two battalions combined. The *History* recorded that Walford's C Company's:

> … advance was difficult, for there was sharp fighting around the ruined cottages of Faubourg Soyers and there were many casualties. The two subalterns of the leading platoons were hit; but Sergeant H Faulkner took command of both platoons and led them resolutely forward. A German machine-gun post opened fire at short range in the mist, but Sergeant Faulkner led forward a Lewis-gun section to a flank, opened a sharp burst of enfilade fire, scattered the enemy and cleared the way from the remainder of the company. After a series of such fights, C Company eventually reached the canal bank…

Lce.-Cpl. H. Faulkner,
Bromsgrove.
"Mentioned."

Sergeant Faulkner won a DCM for these actions, to add to his MM, Italian Medal of Military Valor, and Mention in Despatches. The *War Diary's Narrative* explained that C Company lost touch with the Warwicks and, in their keenness to progress to the canal, suffered some casualties by getting too close to their own barrage. These were, presumably, the platoon commanders, one of whom was a young officer – perhaps one of the two new ones who was too keen to show his bravado in this, his first action.

In all, C Company encountered and extinguished four machine-gun posts or nests, the latter with the aid of a tank, down near the main railway line some 400 yards from the canal – in the same way as A Company had been helped earlier. How the Battalion would have benefitted from similar tank support at Gillemont Farm. C Company, attacking down almost the same line of advance as the 1/8th Warwickshires, was to suffer 47 of the Battalion's total of 61 casualties that day. It is not clear if it was in these actions against machine guns where the heaviest toll was suffered or in their crossing of the canal. The *Narrative* recorded that C Company passed through the Warwicks down by the railway so contact must have been rejoined at some stage. They reached the canal bank at about 10.15 hrs.

Lock gate at Landrecies

In the meantime, on the right, there were only reports of a single enemy machine-gun post with D Company making a rapid advance towards a footbridge over the stream beyond the main railway. They were quick enough to capture it before the mine below it was exploded. They were well ahead of the Gloucesters and the RE (Royal Engineer) rafting party. A patrol was sent forward to the canal which located a further footbridge and, as their barrage lifted and with skilful use of their Lewis guns, they stormed across the bridge under enemy machine-gun fire, with their leading troops gaining the far bank by 09.50 hrs. They did not have enough support to advance further until the Gloucesters were able to follow them across the canal, so no move towards the town from this right flank was made before 10.33 hrs. D Company's casualties were just 2Lt Wedgbury and 7 Other Ranks, of whom just one was killed. The benefit of the broad front of the attack was being seen as the Germans had concentrated their defence along the two roads leading to the main bridge in Landrecies as well as in the town itself. It was Bomford's A Company's task, with the support of B Company, to attempt to seize this bridge or, at least, the lock gates just beside it.

Bomford's account made their progress sound a little more challenging than that of D Company:

> The tank helped us with occasional use of its gun along the house-lined road to Landrecies where there was a bridge over the canal. It was sure to be mined and when it blew up I was never more grateful. Trying to rush a mined bridge is no joke. We crossed the canal at some locks a bit to our right.

The citation of his DSO told of greater action and leadership:

> In the attack on Landrecies on 4.11.18 he led his Company with most extraordinary bravery, skill and initiative. During the early stage of the advance machine gun fire was encountered coming from a house on the flank, and Capt. Bomford, summoned a tank, led it personally to attack the house, supported by his Company, and captured there four officers and thirty men. Later he went forward to make a personal reconnaissance of the bridge over the canal, under heavy rifle fire and machine gun fire at close range, and himself shot three of the enemy post which was covering it. The bridge then blew up, so he brought forward the R.E. bridging party and bridged the lock, led his Company across and captured the town. During the whole of the operations Captain Bomford displayed brilliant leadership and remarkable courage.

There are a number of claimants as to who 'captured the town'. Undoubtedly, it was achieved by the combined efforts of all companies of the Battalion but, as with many 'trophy' captures in wartime, a number claim to have been the first. The *Narrative* gave the time of this crossing at the lock gates being secure and crossed as 12.45 hrs. Corbett told of a most dashing blowing of the bridge as well as a considerable exchange of machine-gun fire throughout this phase of the operations:

Lock gate at Landrecies in 1914

> Meanwhile Captain Bomford led A Company into the suburb [in the area around the railway and before the canal], where they were galled by fire of a machine-gun from a window. They took shelter behind some stacks of bricks, which a gun began to batter at about 300 yard range. One shot missed the bricks and hit the machine-gun. The suburb was carried, but was under the fire of no less than 14 guns at point blank range, so men were put under covert while the bridge was reconnoitred. It was a fine steel bridge spanning the canal, which is about 20 yards broad and 7 feet deep, and just

> beside the bridge is a lock. Heavy musketry and machine-gun fire came from the big houses across the bridge. As the word of advance was about to be given the sound of hoofs was heard, and round a curving boulevard came a black horse, driven at full gallop by a German officer, who lay along its back, spurring hard. Opposite the bridge he reined up, rolled off, and touched something on the pavement, and with a huge explosion the bridge was cut in two. At that moment he was shot by Captain Bomford, whose own arm was broken by a bullet later on. His inimitable batman, Pte Sanger (MM and bar), who loved to lead the Company into action, was already wounded. The Company now beat down the fire from the houses, which were hotly shelled by the field guns close behind, and crossed the canal. The journals gave a glowing account of how we swam it, the expert swimmers supporting their comrades. No such thing: we swaggered across the lock-gates and nobody got wet, which might be dangerous on a raw November day.

It is clear from these accounts that Bomford was deserving of his award – as was Captain Walford of his MC although he did get wet. Corbett provided a marvellous picture of C Company's crossing:

> But to the left C Company crossed on rafts which had been provided for the purpose. They were made of 8 petrol cans, each under light frames, and would carry a man of about 11 stone. Captain Walford, who weighed 15 stone, was the first to embark, and made a full load for his vessel, but it bore him up, albeit waist-deep in the water. A smart race across ensued and was won by Serjeant Roberts. Half a mile to the left the Warwicks captured a military bridge before the enemy could destroy it, and crossed comfortably.

The *History* continued:

> It was clear that the crossing would be a perilous business, for bullets were hitting all along the bank and were splashing into the surface of the water; but Captain Walford dashed forward to the top of the canal bank, his men hurried after him, the petrol-tin rafts were set

afloat and the first ones were paddled over to the far bank. Corporal W Roberts actually won the race across, with Captain Walford close behind; then the corporal organised the first arrivals as a covering party while Captain Walford arranged ropes and tackle to pull the tin rafts to and fro. As soon as his platoon was assembled Corporal Roberts led them forward, and the rest of C Company followed on their heels. The enemy gave way before the advance and abandoned the canal banks.

Lock bridge at Landrecies after Bomford's action there

The *War Diary* gave the time of this advance as 10.45 hrs. C Company's high casualties on this day were mentioned earlier. It is possible that the machine guns spraying their fire across the water took a heavy toll. When filming for *Walford's War* on a cold late October day in 2017, I went with my aunt, Walford's granddaughter, into the town square for some warming sustenance. When asked why we were in the town, Pam Brooking explained the story of her grandfather. An elderly customer in the café was summoned, the local expert in such matters. He explained that this section of the canal is still known locally as 'the Red Sea', due to the blood of those who undertook the crossing that day.

Clayton, in his *Decisive Battle,* is aware of the competing claims for being first into Landrecies. His detailed research led him to the following conclusion:

> The race to the canal had, it seems, many winners: the identity of those first arriving at its banks varies depending on which account you read. On the left flank, to the north-east of Landrecies, No. 3 Bridging Party RE was reported to have reached the canal bank at 1010[hrs], the party under Second Lieutenant Petty … these, according to the 25th Division CRE War Diary were 'the first troops to reach the canal bank'…
>
> If Stacke is to be believed, the first men across the canal at this point were from the 1/8th Worcestershire … and 'Corporal W Roberts (C Company) actually won the race across', with Captain Walford close behind. In any case, within 10 minutes, 'about a company' were ferried over, this being a mixture of a few Warwicks and a large number of Worcesters. The time was 1045hrs…
>
> As soon as a company of Worcesters was over the canal, they continued their advance 'against desultory MG fire' and captured the hospital at G23a8.2 along with five officers, 40 men, three ambulances, two limbers and six horses, before pushing on to the final Red Line objective. On the right, south-west of Landrecies, D Company, 1/8th Worcestershire 'rushed for the [intact] footbridge [over the canal], crossed it and seized the further bank' … and moved on again behind the artillery barrage at 1033[hrs], 'meeting with little enemy resistance'. A strongpoint at G22d7.5 was overrun, capturing over 50 prisoners 'before they could man their weapons'. They had reached the Red Line by 1115.

Corporal William Roberts was awarded a DCM for his exploits that day. However, we must return to Corbett for the final word in this great action:

> The town was carried. It was but a little place, laid out like a wheel. There was some hot work in the streets, but we captured the whole place with 14 fine guns, over 14 machine-guns, the Commandant and his Adjutant, the Hospital Staff, and the sick-parade, 13 officers and about 860 rank and file, and booty beyond tale, including a warehouse full of bacon, of which we happened to be short. The civilian population was present (we were not expected so soon). We

advanced some distance beyond the town, and here lost Captains Walford and Bomford, both wounded in some smart skirmishing at a cross-roads.

The Brigade lay round the town that night, expecting a counter-attack but none came. The Sambre was passed and the enemy in full retreat.

Neither the *History*, the *Narrative*, nor Corbett mentioned that the Germans set fire to the old town hall as they withdrew – a great sore in the eyes of the townspeople of Landrecies. It is now a museum to the town's glorious history at a crossroads of Europe but outside are displayed the 'before and after' photographs to show the damage wreaked by the Germans that morning – just the outside walls remained. The Germans used it as a headquarters so, perhaps, burning the whole building was the quickest way to destroy all the evidence of occupation as their resistance in the town collapsed.

Bomford expanded in his *Memoir* on the wounding of these fine officers:

> We were lucky to get it [the Red Line objective] with very few casualties. Sanger got a bullet in his wrist. Capt Walford of C Coy got a bullet through his buttocks. C Coy crossed the canal on rafts, a good show.
>
> I was standing on our objective watching the next wave of troops going through when a bullet hit my right upper arm smashing the bone. This was just a week before the Armistice, and I was probably the last casualty in the Battalion. I had to walk back three miles to the Battalion Dressing Station with my hand shoved into my tunic and the arm dangling. They put a splint on my arm and gave me a large tetanus injection in the other arm, making it almost useless. A horse ambulance took me on a stretcher to the Field Dressing Station. When they carried me in my right arm slipped and my elbow caught the jamb of the door. A motor ambulance took me to the Casualty Clearing Station where the stretchers were in rows on the ground in a marquee. I was in the outside row and the fly[sheet] kept blowing in and I got soaked by rain. Finally my turn came. My clothes were cut off and I was carried into a big operating tent. I remember hearing a saw working before gulping down anaesthetic to get oblivion. I must have been very near to losing my arm. They put it in a Thomas splint, stretched and slung straight by my side. At the Base Hospital they pulled the packing down from the wounds. There were bits of bone in it, the most painful experience of my life. I got to a hospital at Epsom early on November 11th [seven days later].

By the evening of 4th November the four companies of the Battalion were all commanded by second lieutenants (A – 2Lt LR Cooper; B – 2Lt A Coe; C – 2Lt Elford; D – 2Lt Coleman) which gives a clear view as to how stretched these battalions had become after thirty days of continual action. The *History*'s only mention of any of these subalterns is of Coe and Coleman in this action; neither Cooper or Elford merit a reference, nor did the *War Diary* record their arrival, perhaps only days before.

The *Booklet* provided a summary of the numbers who served (they use the expression 'passed through') with the Battalion when in France and Italy, so from 1st April 1915 to 4th November 1918. Bearing in mind that at full strength the Battalion was 30 officers and 1,000 Other Ranks (though mostly between 600 and 800 men in total), the actual numbers are staggering – 171 officers and 3,246 Other Ranks served the Battalion for days or months over 43 months – indicating that the officers were changed completely six times and the men four times. We know that the only officers who crossed to France in April 1915 and who fought the last action were Lt Col HT Clarke and Major JP Bate, though Wedgbury crossed as a sergeant and was 2Lt Wedgbury at Landrecies. The *Booklet* recorded that there were 71 officer casualties including 31 deaths, and 2,041 Other Rank casualties including 408 deaths. A number of the wounded counted in both categories, including those like Leslie Bomford who was wounded three times, so he represented three of the 71 'officer casualties' himself. Regardless, and remembering that actual deaths rose by the time of the *History* (when all those 'missing' were accounted for) from 394 to 439, these numbers give a haunting picture of the devastation which the War wrought to those serving in infantry battalions.

An analysis of the 439 men of the Battalion who died during the War, 336 – just over three quarters (76.5 per cent) – were Killed in Action; 89 Died of their Wounds (20.3 per cent), 10 Died at Home (of wounds or gassing), 2 died as Prisoners of War, and 3 died (2Lt Aldrich in an accident in the Italian mountains, Pte C Preece of illness and 2Lt FM Walton in February 1919 at Cherbourg, presumably of illness). Does this mean that most men who were killed died instantaneously – it is what the letters to the families said whenever possible so as to soften the blow of losing their loved one? Probably not. In the main battles of Gillemont Farm and those at Passchendaele, the ground was either not held or not in sufficient strength to recover some of the seriously wounded. We will never know.

The *Journal* announced on 16th November under the headline 'Captain Leslie Bomford Wounded again' that 'Captain Leslie Bomford MC, son of Mr and Mrs Raymond Bomford of Bevington Hall near Evesham, is in hospital at Epsom, having been wounded in France on Thursday [in fact, Monday] week. A bullet fractured his right arm. He has twice before been wounded'. This wound was to change Leslie Bomford's life. He has provided a very helpful explanation of the various stages through which the wounded were taken until, ultimately, he arrived back in England. Depending on the severity of their wounds, others got part-way through this process before, if they were lucky, they healed sufficiently to return to the Front. Some died of their wounds as they were taken through this process. An example is Lt Col WRA Dawson DSO*** of the 6th Bn, the Queen's Own (Royal West Kent) Regiment. He was 25 when he was given command of his battalion and 27 when he was wounded by shellfire on 23rd October 1918. He was taken through the medical system as far as the Base Hospital at Camiers in the dunes near Etaples. After the Armistice, he was visited by his parents from Kent before succumbing to his wounds on 3rd December 1918. His fourth DSO was gazetted after his death. He had been wounded some seven times and was one of five officers of the Great War to be awarded the DSO on four occasions; one, Brigadier Frederick Lumsden VC, CB, DSO*** was to earn a VC as well before being killed in June 1918.

Bomford was not correct about being the last casualty of the Battalion. He was on his way through the medical system when, in Corbett's words: 'the last shell fired at us inflicted a grievous wound on CQMS Walter Carey, of Barbourne, than whom no man had done better work for the Battalion'. He was 36 at the time, married Harriet Whitaker the following year and was just 48 when he died in 1931.

There was time for one more Military Cross to be won, by 2Lt A Coe of B Company who, seeing two German batteries still firing defiantly from the high ground to the south of Landrecies, 'led the platoons of B Company forward to the attack. Sending a Lewis-gun section to distract the enemy on the far side, he worked forward into an enfilade position, surprised the gunners and captured both batteries with some forty prisoners'. The *History* recorded the overall losses on 4th November as 4 officers wounded, 4 Other Ranks killed and 61 men wounded. However, the Roll records ten were killed that day and my search of the local cemeteries found eleven who died that day: Cpl J Danks; Ptes A Clark, C Faulkes, A Lucas, TA Freeman, F Rhodes and RA Philpott in the Landrecies Military Cemetery; Pte Bert Baker in the Landrecies Communal Cemetery; Pte JE Watkins [missing from the Roll] and AE Spencer in the Crossroads Cemetery; and Pte G Pryke in Le Cateau Military Cemetery. The sight of Cpl James Danks led me on a search of the *Ancestry* website to establish if the Battalion's second casualty, Pte Alfred Danks, back on 2nd May 1915 was a brother of Cpl Danks but it appears not. It would have been a terrible blow to a single family. Intriguingly, Cpl J Danks 9476 was awarded a Medal of St George, a Russian medal, gazetted on 25th August 1915. He was one of ten men from across the whole Regiment to receive the award on that day.

Beyond the award of the DCM to Cpl Roberts, Sgt Faulkner (like Roberts, a member of Walford's C Company) was awarded a DCM. These men, Roberts and Faulkner, were having their last battles after 36 months at the Front. Bromsgrove celebrated Sgt Faulkner as their most decorated soldier in the *Journal* of 8th February:

> Sergt Harry Faulkner, 1/8th Battalion Worcestershire Regiment (T.F.) of 17 Hanover Street, Bromsgrove, has been awarded the Distinguished Conduct medal for gallantry and devotion to duty in the field. Last summer, while serving in Italy, Sergeant Faulkner gained the Italian Bronze Medal for Valour, and in October he was awarded the Military Medal for 'conspicuous skill and fearless leadership' while commanding his platoon in the course of the final offensive in France. The DCM, the decoration most coveted by soldiers in the ranks next to the Victoria Cross, now follows for distinguished bravery in one of the last great battles in the world war. In gaining these triple honours, we believe, Sergt. Faulkner sets up a record for soldiers from Bromsgrove and a wide district around. Mobilising with the Bromsgrove Territorials in August 1914, he has been serving on the Belgium, French and Italian fronts since the spring of 1915, and has been gassed twice. Sergt Faulkner is 23 years of age, and is the son of an old Bromsgrove soldier, Pte Edward Faulkner, of the Rifle Brigade, who rejoined the army when war broke out and is still on service in India, at 55 years of age. Two of his brothers also joined the forces.

These last months of the War were a period when there were few experienced platoon commanders, excepting those like Wedgbury, Bateman, Coe and Gordon who had all served extensively in the ranks before receiving a commission. Success depended so much on these senior NCOs with years of experience to come to the fore, often taking control where new young subalterns were faltering or wounded. The action on the Sambre Canal was no exception for the Battalion.

There has been no mention of Major Jack Bate in this battle. He had been given leave after his triumphant leadership of the Battalion for the Selle battles of 22nd to 25th October 1918. As an expression of his confidence in the future he was in St Augustine's Church in Edgbaston on Friday 1st November to marry his bride, Dorothy Muriel Player. He was just 24 and had survived the War without a scratch, earning four gallantry awards and having commanded two different battalions in action.

THE ARMISTICE

The Battalion's fighting in the Great War was, mercifully, over. This thirty-day period had taken a heavy toll on the Battalion. The *War Diary* recorded that one officer had died, Lt GH Barber MC, and three officers had been killed, Captain HGC Carter MC, 2Lt HD King and 2Lt CA Connor, with 20 of the other officers being wounded, of whom Lt TL Jones MC, Lt E Stainton and 2Lt C Brown died of their wounds. The *War Diary* stated that there were 59 Other Ranks 'Killed in Action' and 405 wounded. From research just of the Sambre Canal action, the numbers who died may well be an underestimate. The Roll recorded 78 Other Ranks as being killed or dying of their wounds, with at least Private Watkins to add. Although many of the Other Ranks' losses had been covered by the late October drafts, only two officer replacements seem to have arrived during this period.

The *War Diary* noted the Battalion's movements over the following days:

5 Nov	In the early morning the 74th Bde continued the Advance to the GREEN LINE. The battalion with the rest of the Bde, formed a defensive flank facing S.E. as the 32nd Div had not come up. Later in the day the Bn. went into billets S of MAROILLES [almost where they have bivouacked on the night of the 3rd/4th]. Reinforcements 51 O.R.
6 Nov	Stayed at MAROILLES
7 Nov	The 7th and 74th Bdes advanced to just E of MARBAIX and the 75th Bde went through them towards AVESNES. The battalion formed part of the main body and did not deploy. The Bde was relieved at night by the 66th Division and moved back into billets at MARBAIX.
8 Nov	The Battalion marched to billets at PREUX – en route passing through LANDRECIES where they were given a magnificent reception by the inhabitants who had

discovered that the 1/8 WORCESTERS had captured the town. Flags & flowers were given to the men and bouquets to the Divisional Commander (who led the Battalion) and to the C.O.

Memorial to Major General Ronald Charles and 25th Division by Canal at Landrecies

9 Nov	Inspections and refitting
10 Nov	Inspection and refitting. Reinforcements 51 O.R.
11 Nov	Training of specialists, and company training.
12 Nov	Training as above
13 Nov	Training as above
14 Nov	The Battalion moved to LE CATEAU
15 Nov	Company training
16 Nov	Parade Church Service
17 Nov	The Battalion went on a route march. Route BASUEL – POMMEREUIL – FOREST – MONTAY.
18 Nov	All Coys on training
19 Nov	A&B Coys on salvage parties, C&D Coys on training. Reinforcements 16 officers.

These were all signed off by Major JP Bate as Commanding 1/8th Bn Worcestershire Regt. All the entries appear to have been written in the same hand and in pencil. The 'Armistice' seemed to have slipped his memory by the time he came to write up the entry for 11th November. This excerpt ends on the 19th because it was then that the officer manning was increased to something akin to a full complement. Corbett wrote that these men were referred to as the 'Cease-fire Draft'. They were 'charming fellows and very willing to impart instructions'. Corbett concluded his *War Story* with 'Our Aristeia' – from *The Iliad,* for the section in which the heroes' greatest exploits are recorded:

> So gloriously ended our war-record with our greatest exploit. More than 30 years ago R.L. Stevenson had prophesied that Landrecies might again be involved in war and take a place among strong towns. He was doubly right, but while one does not remember a more successful attack on a strong place so difficult to access, it must be admitted that in the end it fell cheaply. One does not know what the losses of the Fifth Glosters and Eight Royal Warwicks were, but the assault cost us in casualties 18 killed and 69 wounded [another estimate in both cases]. In 30 days Lieut. Colonel HT Clarke commanded us in four battles and Major JP Bate in two. In each case we were completely successful. The first was an assault on a place which had already repulsed two determined attacks, but which had to fall regardless of the cost. In the last our portion was a forlorn hope, but the result was this decisive victory. Our total losses in these six engagements were 96 killed and 397 wounded [again, his estimate] – far less than often occurred to a battalion in a single day during the senseless and ill-considered adventures of the early part of the war. The DSO for Beaurevoir and the Bar for his subsequent achievements which rewarded Colonel Clarke and the Bar added to the DSO which Major Bate won in Italy were applauded and esteemed as a personal honour by every man who had the privilege of serving under those gallant and skilful commanders.
>
> Our total losses in the field were as follows [as known in March 1919]:

	Officers	Other Ranks
Killed	26	399
Wounded	43	1623

Prisoners	3	37
Missing	1	5
Accidental Death	1	2
Deaths by Disease	1	13

> The low totals of prisoners and missing are owing to the fact that save at Gillemont Farm we never had to give ground which once we had occupied. Nineteen of the prisoners and ten of the missing are due to that action, and there and at Fonquevillers all the prisoners were wounded. One is not aware of a single case of surrender in the Battalion. The scarcity of deaths by disease in all the thousands of men who served with us goes to prove that war can be a healthy occupation, but credit is claimed for the great care of the men, and for the skill and devotion of our incomparable Medical Officers, their NCOs and Orderlies, to whom a special tribute is justly due.

Indeed, the last medical officer, Captain GA Moore MC was wounded during these last thirty days.

The official *Narrative* of the 13th Corps of which the 1/8th Battalion, the 75th Brigade and the 25th Division were part included:

> The complete failure of so serious an obstacle (the Canal) to check the advance of our troops doubtless exercised a demoralising effect on the defenders at Landrecies. Attacked on three sides and threatened with being cut off, the resistance lacked both cohesion and energy, and the garrison was quickly killed or taken prisoners. The capture of Landrecies was an operation beset with many difficulties which might well have absorbed the resources of a whole Division to accomplish. Success was achieved with a single Brigade, and was due to the spirited leading of the officers, the bravery of the troops, and that element of good fortune which any well planned and boldly executed operation deserves.

General Sir Henry Rawlinson, commander 4th Army, sent the following telegram:

> Please convey to the 25th Division my congratulations and warm thanks for their gallantry and determination in forcing the passage of the canal and capturing Landrecies. It was a very difficult operation requiring great skill and dash. The success of their efforts is most creditable to all ranks.

Perhaps the citation of Lt Col Clarke's DSO for this action best sums up the view of the Brigade and the Division on the Battalion's achievements that day:

> For gallant leadership and good work during the attack on Landrecies on 4th Nov. 18. His Batt. was allotted the very difficult task of crossing the canal, taking the town & establishing themselves on the high ground beyond. All of this they did, in spite of the fact that they had to help the 2 leading battalions in their fight up to the canal. This Batt. took nearly 300 prisoners and several guns.

In Captain Bomford's papers is a wonderful colour document, also under the name of General Rawlinson, their Army Commander, and headed:

> **ARMY ORDERS**
> By
> **GENERAL SIR HS RAWLINSON, Bart. GCVO, KCB, KCMG, Commanding FOURTH ARMY**
> MILITARY SECRETARY'S BRANCH
> ***IMMEDIATE REWARDS***
> Section a) details a Victory Cross awarded to Lieutenant John Cridland BARRETT of the Leicestershire Regiment, awarded for an action on 24th September 1918. It gave the full citation.
> Section b) begins with an explanation of an 'Immediate' award: 'Under authority delegated by His Majesty the King, the Field Marshal Commander-in-Chief (Haig) had made the following awards for gallantry and devotion to duty in action'. These were awards where no doubt existed in the minds of senior officers as to their merit. Lance Evers's first MC was such an award as were the

Bars to their MCs of Bate and Pawsey at Templeux in April 1917. There were just fourteen such awards for the 4th Army for the last actions of the War and four were to officers of the 1/8th Battalion:

BAR TO THE DISTINGUISHED SERVICE ORDER

Major (a/Lieutenant-Colonel) HT CLARKE, DSO, Worcestershire Regiment

THE DISTINGUISHED SERVICE ORDER

Captain (a/Major) JP BATE, MC, Worcestershire Regiment
Lieutenant (a/Captain) LR BOMFORD, MC, Worcestershire Regiment

BAR TO THE MILITARY CROSS

Captain JO WALFORD, MC, Worcestershire Regiment

Perhaps this is the document which best signified the achievement of the remarkable Territorial Battalion.

Much is made, perhaps in modesty, of the ease of success and lack of casualties in the crossing of the Sambre Canal at this site of one of the key town crossings. Most of the German defence appeared to have been sited to the north of the canal, with the numerous references to machine-gun posts and nests encountered by the Battalion and by the Warwicks to the left of C Company. It is worth considering the exploits of the neighbouring 32nd Division immediately to the south-east of the 25th Division whose Front before the dawn of the 4th November was at the edge of the Bois L'Évêque, just 500 yards from the canal, some two miles east of Landrecies. It was here, at Ors, that the 2nd Bn the Manchester Regt had to cross the same railway and then the flooded fields beside the canal. There was no room for any German defence before the canal so their machine-guns were sited on their own bank covering these fields and the embankment on the British side. The embankment was in British hands by 07.00 hrs. The Manchesters were lined up with the 16th Bn Lancashire Fusiliers and were commanded by Lt Col JN Marshall MC*, late of the Irish Guards. Within an hour, four VCs had been gained but the losses had been so great that all attempts to complete the crossing had to be abandoned. Also lost in the action, shot whilst on a raft in mid-canal, was Captain Wilfred Owen MC. The plan was not individual rafts as Walford and his C Company had used but that the infantry would cross the canal on a pontoon-style bridge resting on cork floats put in place at 06.00 hrs by Royal Engineers with the protection of a barrage and smoke. The bridge was ready in 30 minutes but was broken by a shell before it could be used. Lt Col Marshall came forward to organise volunteer parties to effect repairs. The citation of his and three other winners of the VC over the next hour tell a story of gallant failure:

> On 4 November 1918 near Ors France, Major Waters [later, Sir Arnold Waters VC, CBE, DSO, MC], with his Field Company, was bridging the Oise-Sambre Canal under artillery and machine-gun fire at close range, the bridge being damaged and the building party suffering severe casualties. All Major Waters' officers had been killed or wounded and he at once went forward and personally supervised the completion of the bridge, working on cork floats while under such intense fire that it seemed impossible that he could survive. The success of the operation was entirely due to his valour and example.
>
> On 4 November 1918 near Ors, France, Sapper [Adam] Archibald was with a party building a floating bridge across the canal. He was foremost in the work under a very heavy artillery barrage and machine-gun fire. The latter was directed at him from a few yards distant while he was working on the cork floats. Nevertheless, he persevered in his task and his example and efforts were such that the bridge which was essential to the success of the operations was very quickly completed. Immediately afterwards Sapper Archibald collapsed from gas poisoning. [Archibald was 39 at the time of this action, though still holding the rank of sapper. He survived the gas, dying in 1957.]
>
> For most conspicuous bravery, determination and leadership in the attack on the Sambre-Oise Canal, near Catillon, on the 4th November, 1918, when a partly constructed bridge came under concentrated fire and was broken before the advanced troops of his battalion could cross. Lt. Col. Marshall at once went forward and organised parties to repair the bridge. The first party were soon killed or wounded, but by personal example he inspired his command, and volunteers were instantly forthcoming. Under intense fire and with complete disregard of his own safety, he stood on the bank

encouraging his men and assisting on the work, and when the bridge was repaired, attempted to rush across at the head of his battalion and was killed while so doing. The passage of the canal was of vital importance, and the gallantry displayed by all ranks was largely due to the inspiring example set by Lt. Col. Marshall. [He is buried in the Ors Communal Cemetery though set aside from other graves, showing him as Lieutenant Colonel James Neville Marshall VC, MC & bar, Irish Guards.]

For most conspicuous bravery and devotion to duty North of Ors on 4 Nov., 1918, whilst attempting to bridge the Oise Canal. To cover the bridging of the canal he [Lt James Kirk] took a Lewis gun, and, under intense machine-gun fire, paddled across the canal on a raft, and at a range of ten yards expended all his ammunition. Further ammunition was paddled across to him and he continuously maintained a covering fire for the bridging party from a most exposed position till killed at his gun. The supreme contempt of danger and magnificent self-sacrifice displayed by this gallant officer prevented many casualties and enabled two platoons to cross the bridge before it was destroyed. [James Kirk joined the Manchester Regiment as a private soldier in June 1915 and was commissioned in June 1918. He is buried with his commanding officer and with his fellow officer, Captain Wilfred Owen MC at Ors.]

This crossing point was not dissimilar to that of C Company although the setting up of the cork bridge was both lengthier in time as well as indicating to the Germans exactly where the British crossing in that zone of the canal would be. As has been demonstrated in so many of the 1/8th Battalion's actions, it was operating in small teams of up to company strength that brought their regular successes. From Beaurevoir onwards, their company and platoon leadership flourished. It became increasingly a real team effort with no need for either commanding officer to have to take command of any action from their company commanders. The three DSOs gained by Lt Col Clarke and Major Bate were awards in part for the whole Battalion and it is likely that each would have said as much.

Lt Col Marshall's VC as commanding officer was not the only one that day. Just a further two miles south-east from Marshall's action, Lt Col Dudley Johnson DSO*, MC was earning a VC at the lock gate, the next to the west of Landrecies, in an action not dissimilar to that of Captain Bomford and his A Company. As at Ors, it required the commanding officer, this time of the 2nd Bn the Royal Sussex Regiment, to step up, reorganise his leading troops and drive them forwards. This is not to decry the extraordinarily gallant actions of Lt Col Marshall and Lt Col Johnson, but rather to demonstrate the quality of the leadership of the four company commanders of the 1/8th Battalion – Bomford, Walford, Watkinson and Wedgbury – that neither Clarke nor Bate had to come forward to inject urgency or leadership into any action over those last thirty days. Sassoon made an interesting observation about such leadership when you give orders, bid your officers good luck and watch them set off in the advance. At the beginning of 'the raid' Sassoon asked if he might go into No Man's Land with the raiders:

> 'Certainly not' said the Colonel, 'your job is to stop in your trench and count the men as they come back'. He spoke with emphasis and he was not a man who expected to have to say a thing twice. We stared at one another for a moment; some freak of my brain made me remember that in peace time he had been an enthusiastic rose-grower – had won prizes with his roses, in fact; for he was a married man and had lived in a little house near the barracks.

And after the raid, in which Sassoon had become a key participant, although it failed to meet any of its objectives with over half the men becoming casualties:

> Nothing now remained for me to do except to see [Colonel] Kinjack on my way back. Entering the dug-out I looked at him with less diffidence than I'd ever done before. He was sitting on his plank bed, wearing a brown woollen cap with a tuft on the top. His blond face was haggard; the last few hours had been no fun for him either. This was a Kinjack I'd never met before, and it was the first time I had ever shared any humanity with him. He spoke kindly to me in his

> rough way, and in doing so made me very thankful that I had done what I could to tidy up the mess in no-man's-land.

Leadership came in many forms. Respect was not just gained by those leading from the front with pistol or cane in their hand. Clarke and Bate must have had the full confidence of their Brigade Commander as it was their Battalion which was so often given the key roles in this great advance. But, as Sassoon made clear, it was these same commanders who suffered with the implications and results of the execution of their orders.

GALLANT MEN

Gallant has been an oft-used word in this tome to describe many of the officers and men of the 1/8th Battalion – a word that I have used for their brave and heroic actions and behaviour at the Front. 'Gallant' alone does not do justice to the extraordinary bravery and leadership, some of which has been recorded above. Lord Moran, best known as Churchill's personal physician during the Second World War, wrote of a 'bank balance' of courage after his experiences in the First War:

> Even prodigal youth had to husband its resources. Likewise in the trenches a man's willpower was his capital, and he was always spending, so that wise and thrifty company officers watched the expenditure of every penny lest their men went bankrupt. When their capital was done they were finished.

General Sir Peter de la Billière KBE, KCB, DSO, MC* expanded on this in *Supreme Courage,* his 2004 book on holders of the Victoria Cross:

> Each of us has a bank of courage. Some have a significant credit balance, others little or nothing; but in war we are able to make the balance last longer if we have training, discipline, patriotism and faith. We can enhance these through managing our fear, while always remembering that on the battlefield unfairness [bad luck] rules.

Field Marshal Lord Slim KG, GCB, GCMG, GCVO, GBE, DSO, MC – all his honours and awards are shown but just the two at the end are those where bravery in front of the enemy was involved. The remaining awards were for displaying outstanding ability at every level of command. Slim believed that there were two types of courage – physical and moral:

> Physical courage is an emotional state which urges a man to risk injury or death … [moral courage being] a more reasoning attitude, which enables [a man] coolly to stake career, happiness, his whole future, on his judgement of what he thinks either right or worthwhile.

General de la Billière closed his book by listing the various qualities which he believed to be important to the thirteen VC winners on which his book focused. Of those thirteen, two have been mentioned already in this book: Roland Bradford VC, MC and Noel Chavasse VC*, MC. To Bradford he attributed 'Outstanding leadership. Religious faith. Modesty' and to Chavasse 'Compassion. Strong religious faith. Love of his men'. There are three others of the thirteen who served in the Great War – Albert Ball VC, DSO**, MC and William Barker VC, DSO*, MC** who were both airmen; and Albert Jacka VC, MC*, an Australian infantry NCO when he won his VC at Gallipoli before being commissioned and gaining two MCs on the Western Front. To Jacka, de la Billière attributed 'Independence. Resentment of authority. Single-mindedness'. While to Ball, he ascribed: 'Intense patriotism. Dogged determination' and to the Canadian, Barker: 'Ambition. Patriotism'.

This gives me a selection of attributes which I can use as a basis to analyse the performances of the leading bemedalled officers of the 1/8th Battalion. Perhaps it is easier to start with those attributes to which it is hard to give to any of the Worcesters: independence; resentment of authority; dogged determination; ambition; and single-mindedness. There is no doubt that a number of our officers had ambition but not the ambition of airmen like Barker whose ambition was to outscore their renowned colleagues in the league table of 'kills'. Barker wrote in October 1918: 'I have got thirty-seven Huns down and Major Richotfen [*sic* – Richthofen] the German who is now dead claims eighty. I am going to try and break this record if only my health will hold out'. These airmen lived and flew on their wits in a very solitary world. They hold many of the medal records of the Great War, including Major Mike Maddock VC, DSO**, MC* and Major Byford McCudden VC, DSO*, MC*, MM who were both killed before the War was over. You will notice that McCudden gained four different British gallantry medals, like Wedgbury – hence my description of Wedgbury as the only British 'soldier' so to do.

This leaves patriotism; outstanding leadership; religious belief; compassion; and modesty as attributes for the Worcester heroes – together with ambition, but ambition to do well both for one's family and in front of one's peers and men. A body of men could not have achieved so much in their forty-three months at the Front without being very well led. It is safe to say that all were driven by patriotism and by a firm belief in the cause for which they were fighting.

Lt Col Clarke was a compassionate, modest and effective leader and coordinator of the Battalion, seen as dependable and efficient by the brigade commanders under whom he served. He was never called upon to lead from the front but that was a measure of his training and leadership of the Battalion, not of missing an opportunity of turning a battle in the style of Bradford or de Wiart. Major Bate was only called to lead his own Battalion on two occasions and the 1/7th once in battle. That he should have been awarded a DSO for two of these three battles is a measure of Bate as a leader. Perhaps more telling was his leadership at the company and platoon level where his MCs were earned. Bate's business life after the War showed a man with ambitions but no letters or diaries mention him as being keen on self-promotion. Without doubt, he must have been cool under fire as well as in his dealings with the commanders above him. The actions of Bate and Pawsey at their first main battle as company commanders, that of Templeux-le-Guérard, show two men able to make and carry out a plan in the heat of battle – cool and effective leaders. Their MCs in this action gained each an 'Immediate' award of a Bar to their MCs.

An attribute which de la Billière does not use in his list is confidence, confidence in one's own abilities gained from previous success. While this must be balanced against the use of part of one's credit balance of nerve and willpower, Bate – like Wedgbury – must have gained great confidence that he could operate under fire and under pressure in successes acknowledged by his two MCs. With that confidence would have come an increased respect from those in his commands, and a virtuous circle would result.

A test that none of these gallant officers were subjected to, except for Bate, was to be appointed to command in battle men who knew nothing of his coolness and confidence, seeing only the white and purple ribbon of an MC on his chest, supplemented with a small cross to note his second award. This came when, in June 1918, Bate was placed in temporary command of the 1/7th Battalion at the time of the Battle of Piave. To add to his challenge, the CO of the 1/7th Bn, Lt Col FM Tomkinson DSO* was himself in temporary command of the Brigade, so he was Bate's immediate boss. This was a battle which started badly and by nightfall not all the ground had been recovered, just 150 yards when the Divisional advance had stalled. The 1/7th Bn was committed at 20.00 hrs and a further 300 yards was soon recovered. It was a short but violent battle with the *History* recording that 'various officers in the front line declared afterwards that for sheer intensity of fire, they had never seen anything to equal this S.A.A. duel in the war'. The 1/7th lost three officers killed and five wounded with 25 Other Ranks killed and 57 wounded. Despite this, 'firing rapidly by alternate sections, the Worcestershire companies pushed on through the forest, driving the enemy's riflemen back on their supports' – thus, under Bate's command momentum was resumed and maintained throughout their part in the battle. Bate was just 24 years old when he was appointed to this challenging command. He was a Catholic but we have nothing to tell us if his calm demeanour under fire was a result of his faith. He did not get his DSO for this command until the New Year's List, 1919, but the Italians acknowledged his work with a Croce di Guerra, which was gazetted on 29th November 1918. The recommendation for his DSO would have come from his Brigade commander, thus the man he was temporarily replacing at the head of the 1/7th Battalion. One of his company commanders received a DSO for the same battle, which was gazetted on 24th September – though by then he had been killed. Had Bate been given such an immediate award, he would have been able to wear a DSO ribbon for those last battles. Indeed, it is unlikely that he ever wore such a ribbon on his uniform, except perhaps in the Quadrangle of Buckingham Palace.

Bate was a tall man, rather in contrast to Sidney Wilkes who was earning his third MC that same night. Wilkes' formal photograph at the time shows a small bespectacled man who we might consider nowadays to be a 'geek'. Without physical presence, he would have had a greater challenge in gaining the trust and respect of his men. Had he not been posted on a well-earned promotion course in the autumn of 1918, there is little doubt that he would have joined Bate and Wedgbury with a fourth award. An Oxford graduate, he was clearly bright and, doubtless, able to express himself clearly in training and when under fire. His only brother died aged just twelve in 1912 so perhaps he considered he was fighting for the two of them. Speaking with a recent head of Army officer selection, he explained that men will follow their officers if they have conviction that the officer will make correct and decisive decisions in the heat of battle. Wilkes must have passed this test with flying colours, indeed all these bemedalled officers seem to be of a mould of being quiet, effective leaders. Walford may be the exception who was not to be properly tested until October 1918. His escapade on horseback at Bazuel might have put him into the category, somewhat mockingly, of being followed out of 'curiosity'. His work at Great Oaks and Landrecies would have undoubtedly upgraded this to deep respect.

Leslie Bomford, the youngest of these 'gallant' men, came from a family with a strong Baptist faith. The tone of his letters and his need to obtain his father's permission to leave Edinburgh University in his first year to join up indicate both a great respect for his parents and, no doubt, a desire to impress them. He was just twenty when he first commanded A Company in the Passchendaele offensive. His first major action was at Gillemont Farm where he was lucky to survive with just a head wound from a glancing shot hitting his helmet and it was from the CCS that he wrote to his parents with a degree of bravado at still being alive. His letters home, as with all others which I have read from the Battalion, give no hint of anything other than full support for the cause for which they were fighting and risking their lives – some may call it patriotism, others a desire to do one's duty and to do it well. His brigadier wrote on his Officer Report in January 1919: 'A very good officer who is quite fitted for advancement. Very gallant in the field.'

The image of Watkinson is influenced by his letter to Bomford after his success at Beaurevoir. He appears to be a man of great ambition as well as confidence. By then he had been at the Front for a year and was without an award – not a reflection of his performance; as a platoon commander and as an adjutant an opportunity for demonstrating his bravery or leadership under fire may not have come his way. He lost little time when back in France to demonstrate his abilities and coolness under fire.

What of Wedgbury? Clarke recorded him as being 'invaluable in action' and his Brigadier as 'doing extraordinarily well when under his command'. His platoon photograph when he was the platoon sergeant shows a man wearing his cap at a jaunty angle, yet that when he was commissioned shows an immaculate officer with a steely glare. If we refer back to General de la Billière, we need to look at those with VCs from the Second World War and to the most extraordinary fighter of them all, Captain Charles Upham VC*. I am concerned that this puts Wedgbury in too exalted company but de la Billière starts: 'A loving father, a dedicated farmer who put his animals before himself, a born leader and a fearsome soldier … his two leading characteristics were his modesty and his ability to focus on the task in hand with the greatest intensity'. And 'he was an extremely good-looking man, about 5' 9" tall and of medium build, with extraordinarily clear, ice-blue eyes' – as Wedgbury. Upham was a corporal when in training and promoted to sergeant just before heading to the Front – much as Wedgbury. De la Billière summed up Upham's military performance as: 'Apart from his bravery, which stretches belief, two qualities stand out in his war service: his complete focus, and his total disregard for his personal welfare or safety. When he was engaged in operations, nothing stood between him and the need to kill Germans and win his local battle.' There is nobody still left to ask how much of this applied to Wedgbury. Let us take out 'which stretches belief' – Upham deserves that epithet all to himself. However, much of the rest describes Wedgbury's actions at Les Tilleuls, let alone in the actions in which he earned his earlier awards. Upham shunned the limelight after his War; Wedgbury never sought it in a land of heroes after his War.

Lastly, Walford. His commitment and belief in the cause of his country is not in doubt, emphasised by his speeches at the recruitment rallies of 1914. However, Evers had written him off as a soldier fit enough for the Front back in the autumn of 1916 when gout and malaria or trench fever had got the better of him. As with all the other senior officers of both battalions at the time of their crossing to France, there was plenty of opportunity to get staff appointments in France or for commands within the training establishments back in England. We have no correspondence from Walford or his family to understand why he did not seek out one of these routes – perhaps he did not have the qualities required for a staff job which were themselves much sought-after, particularly by pre-War regular officers such as Lt Bernard Montgomery DSO, who had been badly wounded in October 1914. Evers, Symons and Douglas Bomford visited Walford at The Holmwood, a shell-shock hospital, on 2nd December 1916 and reported 'He is getting better but is very thin and cannot walk much.'

Walford and his son, Gentleman Cadet Scott Walford

Walford must have been a patriot who was determined to do his bit as he returned to the Front in July 1917, but to the 1/8th Battalion. He does not appear to have been given a company to command, rather staff jobs within Battalion Headquarters, including that of second-in-command when in Italy, from where he was raised to temporary command when Clarke was given leave in February 1918. It appears that it was the loss of Pawsey as a Prisoner of War which gave Walford the opportunity again to command a company (C) when he returned from his leave in late July 1918. He was not due any more leave or, indeed, courses in the ensuing months and, as such, did not miss a day's action in those glorious thirty days until his wounding at the close of the battle for Landrecies. He had just rewritten his Will and his only child was due to be commissioned from Sandhurst that December. He was 49 years old. Beaurevoir was his first proper battle when in command of a company. His letter told his story. His company suffered many casualties from shelling and machine-gun fire as they waited for their time to advance. Walford was spared then and in that advance. He had with him two of the most experienced platoon commanders, Lt RJCW Hawtrey who had crossed back in March 1915 and Lt WS Gundry MC, but both were quickly wounded. Walford carried out his orders and advanced with his remaining men – as he had been trained and as he had seen his predecessors do as company commanders over the previous years. Was he being heroic – certainly not in his eyes. His description of the next action, the capture of Honnechy, in the same letter shows a man now confident in his actions and decision-making under fire. He emphasised the confidence placed in him by his commanding officer – there is no reference to their 16-year age gap. Thereafter, I have no doubt that his performances in the remaining four major actions came from this confidence and a renewed belief that he was worthy of his command – rather like scoring your first century and from then on having belief that you are deserving of your place in a winning team.

This was a group of very competent men – as shown by their post-War civilian achievements – each confident that their fellow officers would perform their separate orders with coolness and bravery, so important when each company, platoon and section is in the advance in the noise and brutality of battle. To these men must be added the

Rupert Hawtrey

seeming calmness and discipline of the three senior professionals – Captain Daniel Sallis OBE, TD, the Quartermaster; the RSM, Harry Heath MC and the RQMS, Edward Corbett MM. They were very much part of the Battalion's first eleven. Heath was not to retire from the Army until 1938 with the announcement in the *London Gazette* referring to him as: Major (Qr.-Mr.) H. Heath MBE, MC, TD – an extraordinary military career.

These men survived, which undoubtedly required a considerable degree of good fortune, as shown by Bomford being wounded three times and gassed once. We know that Hugh Ryan-Bell was to be awarded a DSO should he have survived his Passchendaele wounds, just as Francis Hemming and Alan Plaistowe would have been if they had survived Gillemont Farm. Who knows what they would have gone on to achieve, or the Kerwood or Clutterbuck brothers or Hugh Wilson, Gilbert Slater, Harvey Carter MC or young Gordon Barber MC? They are all still in France and Flanders. Hemming's family inscription on his grave perhaps best sums up why all who fought with the 1/8th Battalion did so with such loyalty:

I, And My Comrades, Fought That Wars May Cease.
Let It Be So, O Lord And All The World Have Peace.

DENOUEMENT

The War might have been over for the Battalion but there was to be no quick return to England, except for the wounded, like Wedgbury, Walford and Bomford. Although from the *War Diary*, it seems that Bate was commanding, a letter which Lt Col Clarke wrote to 2Lt Wedgbury on 1st December – the text of which has found its way into the Bomfords' *Brothers in War* – would indicate that he was still in France with the Battalion:

My dear Wedgbury,
I am very pleased to hear that you are better and have been given a month's leave, and hope to see you again at the end of that time.

We are allowed to send home for our Colours and I should very much like you to be one of the Colour Party, if you are fit enough. We have not decided on a date but it will probably be in a fortnight's time.

You have probably heard that you have been awarded the MC for the Beaurevoir attack, my heartiest congratulations. Watkinson also, and poor Barber. I have the DSO for the show & Honnechy combined. Leighton has a DCM, and we have 33 MMs up to date. There are some more of the higher awards yet to come but I think that is all the MMs.

The GOC [General Officer Commanding] Div. went to meet the King today at Landrecies, to tell him how we captured the place and got across the canal.

Walford is better, and will be staying at The Elbows, Tardebigge in a few days. Bomford is at Manor House Hospital, Epsom.

We have been in Le Cateau for some time, and are now at Carnieres, about 7 miles east of Cambrai, doing training and salvage work.

Cheer jolly old ho! My love to all old friends.

Yours ever
Hubert Clarke

En mai 1922, le roi George V du Royaume-Uni fait une visite officielle sur les lieux de combats dans le nord de la France. Landrecies fait partie de l'une de ses étapes. Au premier rang de gauche à droite: Sir Henry Rawlinson, le général Marie-Eugène Debeney, le général Ferdiand Foch, le roi George V, Sir Douglas Haig, le maréchal Philippe Pétain et le général Marie-Emile Fayolle/ In May 1922, King George V of the United Kingdom mades an official visit to the scenes of fighting in northern France. Landrecies is a part of one of its steps. First row from left to right: Sir Henry Rawlinson, General Marie-Eugène Debeney, General Foch Ferdiand, King George V, Sir Douglas Haig, Marshal Philippe Petain and General Marie- Emile Fayolle – © AssociationHistorique de Landrecies

The news that the King had been to Landrecies on his battlefield tour only added to the lustre of its capture and the importance attributed to it.

A second letter followed a week later, a photograph of which is held in the Bomford archive:

> My dear Wedge,
>
> I find that this Div. does not give people who are decorated typewritten copies of the recommendation, so I am sending you a MS (manuscript) copy – [for his MC at Beaurevoir]. I am afraid it will be some time before you get anything for Tilleuls Farm. We put you in for a DSO, Div. altered it to Bar to MC, now [4th] Army has sent it back to be altered to DSO again, so I hope you will get it in time.
>
> I have decided to come home for the Colours about Jan 2nd. You and Walford will receive them from Mr Willis Bund and carry them down Silver Street – that is if your wound is quite healed, as I hope it is. I will let you know the exact date later.
>
> The Brigadier told me to tell you to look sharp and come out again, so that we can have a fitting celebration. We had a <u>great</u> time last night, Watkinson and I gave a dinner to which we invited the Brigadier and Brigade Major.
>
> We have just heard that Miller is a prisoner at Cologne, wounded

in both legs. How the Huns got him away we don't know yet.
Best wishes for Christmas
Yours ever
Hubert Clarke

This letter has particular importance as it clarified that the award recommended by the Battalion for 2Lt Wedgbury for his actions at Les Tilleuls was a DSO. It showed also that there was a checking system as such recommendations worked their way up the Army's hierarchy. Even after the War was over, there were down-gradings of proposed awards, rather than the over-generosity which some historians have suggested was the case.

The letter seems typical of a very caring commanding officer. There was pride at the various gallantry awards but he was keeping in touch with his officers and NCOs who were wounded in their last battles. Bomford's son, Robert, told me that his father's most prized possession was a Hardy's salmon fishing reel which was given to him by Lt Col Clarke on a visit to him in hospital to cheer Bomford up and to tell him of his confidence that his arm would recover and that a normal life would be possible. Bomford was to be cared for in various hospitals over the next two years. To his amusement, both Epsom and Horton Hall were, in his own words, 'ex asylums'. Only Walford was to make it back to the continent, though not to the Battalion.

'Poor Barber' was 2Lt G Barber who joined the Battalion on 12th March 1918, aged 19, and won himself an MC at Beaurevoir when commanding a support platoon under Watkinson. When a machine-gun held up the leading troops, he 'led his men swiftly forward, engaged and silenced the machine gun, and then headed the advance on to the further side of the village'. He was not marked down as wounded there or at Honnechy but he died in hospital at Rouen two weeks later on 20th October. He was a student at Birmingham University and the son of Alexander and Rebecca Barber of 8 Evesham Street in Stratford-upon-Avon. Barber's medal card records that he died overseas of disease and that his father was Rev A Barber. Gordon Barber was born in Wymondham in Leicestershire, the eldest of four children and the only one to serve.

Wedgbury's wound healed but they did not take the bullet out of his arm. His family papers record that it was to cause him trouble many years later. It did not affect his choice of career, unlike Captain Bomford who wrote afterwards:

> In common with most bad wounds my arm was treated with fomentation above and below. I suppose it was septic. Unless someone held the two ends of my arm when the splint was undone it sagged at the break and gave me hours of pain. Some of the nurses were the old asylum staff and callous, at Horton Hall, where I had an operation to join the muscular spiral nerve which had been severed. The Major who did it made a marvellous job of it and I was told the operation had been written up in the Lancet. [There is certainly a letter in the 11th January 1919 edition by Major RH Jocelyn Swan RAMC entitled Advances in the Treatment of Fractures and referring to the work of a Major M Sinclair.] He took bits of my thigh to make up the arm. When they took the stitches out of my leg the slit gaped and took a long time to heal. The ulnar nerve was damaged but not completely cut.
>
> Then came months of electrical treatment on my arm muscles and joint bending while the nerve fibres grew along the nerve sheaths down from the join. They had a chart of my hand and pricked it with a needle to record the return of sensation.

Leslie Bomford with arm in a sling

Bomford was well enough in May 1919 to attend an Investiture at Buckingham Palace where King George V awarded him not only his DSO but also his MC and Bar. He would not be alone amongst 1/8th Battalion officers on that parade.

Returning to the Battalion, it might have been thought that, having been at the Front since 1st April 1915 and with the level of casualties over the previous weeks, it would be withdrawn to England at an early opportunity. Paradoxically, those casualties may have counted against it, as the huge new drafts of reinforcements in the last days of October meant that half the Battalion was either new to the Front or had been away recovering from wounds for many months. This did not stop individuals being discharged from the Army over the next few months, but it would not be until the summer of 1919 that the Battalion as a whole was posted back to England. As the DSO certificates of Clarke, Bate, Bomford and Wedgbury show, the Minister of War from 10th January 1919 until 13th February 1921 was Winston Churchill. It was he who was responsible for the demobilisation of the Armed Forces. One of his first tasks was to redraft the scheme to increase its fairness. It had been the work of Lord Derby in 1917 and was based on the principle that those most needed in vital industries back in Britain were to be released first – but it was those who, for the same reason, had been amongst the last to arrive at the Front. Churchill instituted a scheme which was based on a man's age, length of service and the number of times he had been wounded. This should have ensured that the 'Old Gents' of the Battalion were at the front of the queue. The Army numbered 3.8 million men at the Armistice, just under 900,000 within twelve months and 230,000 by 1922 – and a little over 70,000 as I write.

The first matter to be resolved was that of Battalion's Colours. The *History* explained that the old battalions would take responsibility for their Colours which had been left in the safekeeping of the Church. 'Very few of the officers and men who were serving at the end of the War had ever seen the Colours of the Regiment; but from such old soldiers as were left small parties were selected by each Battalion and dispatched to England to fetch the Colours'. They were handed out by the Dean on the steps of the Cathedral, 'and carried back to France those beautiful symbols of everything a soldier holds dear'. The party for the 1/8th Battalion sent back from France was: 2Lt JA Bullock, 2Lt ST Bateman MC MM, CSM J Leighton DCM, CSM WH Griffin MM, and CSM GJ Osbourne MM. They left Carnieres on 20th December and received their Colours on Friday, 27th December with Captain JO Walford MC* representing the commanding officer. He was joined at the Ceremony by his cousin, old Colonel Matt Dixon but not by his wife, Margaret. The Colours arrived back with the Battalion on 29th December and were Trooped in a parade on 2nd January. The absence of Wedgbury would indicate that he was not sufficiently recovered to join the party as wished by Lt Col Clarke. It is not clear if Walford accompanied the Colour to France but he was certainly to serve on that side of the Channel in 1919.

The Battalion was not to leave France until 1st July. The *History* recorded:

> A month's work by the 75th Brigade had by that time effectively cleaned up the country round Carnieres, and on December 16th the battalions of the Brigade marched into Cambrai; where the 1/8th Worcestershire were billeted in half-ruined streets, which were slowly filling with a returning populace.
>
> The weather before Christmas was miserable, but Christmas Day itself was fine and sunny. The Battalions spent their last Christmas Day on Active Service in great happiness. Peace was assured, and already the demobilisation of the armies had begun. [The first men recorded to have been demobilised in the Battalions of the regiment were coal miners who left in the middle of December – thus before Churchill's changes had been instituted.] … Educational classes were organised to train those who were not qualified in a trade. Those classes and every possible form of recreation were the principal preoccupation of all ranks during the winter months. Week by week the strength of the battalion dwindled.
>
> The 1/8th Battalion was almost the last unit of the [Worcestershire] Regiment to leave the Theatre of War. Throughout the Spring months the units of the 48th Division remained in Cambrai, engaged on general salvage work in and around the shattered city. Gradually

> their numbers were reduced; and on 25th February a strong draft [7 officers and 198 Other Ranks] of retainable men were sent from the 1/8th Worcestershire to join the 2nd Battalion of the Regiment – leaving the 1/8th with only about 100 all ranks. The strength gradually dwindled until the end of June, when orders came for the cadre to leave for home. The 1/8th Worcestershire marched to Cambrai station and entrained; and on the 1st July the cadre of the Battalion, with their Colours, embarked at Boulogne for England.

The next occasion in Worcester was the visit of General Sir William Robertson, the Chief of the Imperial General Staff from December 1915 until February 1918, when finally he fell foul of Mr Lloyd George, then Prime Minister. Robertson was the only man ever to rise from the ranks to become a field marshal. He came to Worcester to lay the foundation stone for the Homes for Disabled Sailors and Soldiers which was to form the city's war memorial. Captain Walford was present at the official launch, but again without his wife. It is believed that they had been estranged for some time before the War and her absence at these great occasions in Worcester seem to confirm that this remained the case after the War. However, an announcement in the *Journal* in August 1919 conflicts with this:

> The engagement is announced between Mr John Erskine Scott Walford, the Worcestershire Regiment, only son of Captain and Mrs JO Walford of Hanbury Mount, Bromsgrove, and Miss Catharine Walker of Chad House, Egbaston.

Walford's son, known from his Sandhurst days as Ben, did not marry Catharine. However, this announcement confirmed that Walford and his wife were still residing at Hanbury Mount, the address from his Will in July 1918. This was also the address used for their brother-in-law, Colonel Edward Sydenham DSO's, war pension. As such, it seems that their wives, sisters Margaret and Gertrude Scott, lived together while their husbands were away at war.

The big parade for the Regiment was not held until the Treaty of

Versailles had been signed. Initially there was a thanksgiving service at the Cathedral on the following Sunday, 8th July. It was a county-wide assembly of all who had contributed to the final victory both at the Front but, more importantly, all those who had been in the support arms, the medical staff and all who worked so hard on the home front. Lt Col HT Clarke DSO* was one of the officers representing the Regiment. The Lord Lieutenant, the Earl of Coventry, decided that a full parade should be organised and set 23rd August as the date. Detachments from the eight battalions and from the service battalions were gathered with the 1/8th and 2/8th marching as one – the 8th Battalion. A number of officers who had not served with the 1/8th since the early months in France were amongst those on parade: Lt Col HT Clarke DSO*, Major FAW How, Major SH Clark TD, Captain LR Bomford DSO MC*, Captain RH Burlingham, Captain GH Smith MC, Lt ST Bateman MC MM and Lt GL Watkinson MC* carrying the Colour, together with 850 Other Ranks. Bomford's brother Douglas was also marching with the 8th Battalion which must have given their parents much pride; the parade made its way from Pitchcroft to the Cathedral with the Lord Lieutenant taking the Salute at the Shirehall. The total on parade was 10,522 (including 374 women) so the aging Earl of Coventry would have been quite tired having saluted each battalion's Colour. Two other officers who had served with the 1/8th Battalion but had later commanded other Worcestershire battalions were also on parade: Lt Col HA Carr DSO with the 2nd Battalion and Lt Col PR Whalley DSO with the 4th.

There was a special ceremony to notable Other Ranks as part of the day, reported on as 'Presentation of Awards' by General Sir Francis Davies. First, he was presented to the three living Worcestershire-born VC winners – Lt John Crowe VC (who won his at the Battle of Lys when aged 41), Sgt George Wyatt VC (Worcester-born but serving with the Coldstream Guards. He won his VC at Landrecies when it was lost in August 1914) and Pte Thomas Turrall VC (who won his on the Somme, serving with the 10th Battalion). This was followed by individual presentations, including to a number of members of the 1/8th Battalion:

Hon Major and QMR Sallis	– Territorial Decoration
CSM A Sherwood	– DCM and Bar
CSM J Leighton	– DCM and Territorial Efficiency Medal
CSM R Atkinson	– DCM, MM and Bar
RQMS EC Corbett	– MM
Sgt E Turner	– MM and Bar

53-year-old Daniel Sallis, Quartermaster

Edward Corbett

The *Journal* reported that 'All were heartily cheered, Col Coventry, Major D Sallis and RQMS EC Corbett being especially cordially received – they were all so well-known among those assembled to witness the ceremony'. Major Sallis lived until 1938, dying, aged 73, when registered at Apsley House, Cutnall Green near Elmbridge where he had been a 'smallholder' farmer – though spending his final days with his daughter, Elizabeth Hinton, in Droitwich. He left a widow, Sarah. Edward Corbett lived until October 1952, leaving a widow, Edith, a son and two daughters – all born before his Great War service. CSM Arthur Sherwood DCM* was to lose a hand in an industrial accident in 1924, before establishing a successful news agency business. 'His courage was further tested in 1968 when one of his legs were amputated'. He died aged 79 in 1972. CSM John Leighton was married in 1906 to Mary Spilsbury and their golden wedding anniversary was celebrated in the Regimental magazine, *FIRM*, in the same edition as that in which Captain Wedgbury's obituary appeared.

The *Journal's* reports each week illustrated a somewhat forgotten factor of the War, by many historians at least. Page 7 each week had recorded the deaths, the wounded and the missing of the War, as well as those who had won awards for gallantry or for notable service. Now that the War was over this page in January 1919 had a different order. Taking 18th January as an example, the sections were:

OFFICERS

PRISONERS RELEASED

RANK AND FILE

KILLED – Previously reported wounded and missing, now reported killed

KILLED OR DIED OF WOUND – Previous missing, now reported by the German Government killed or died of wounds

DIED – died from influenza and pneumonia in a hospital in Salonika

DEATH OF A PRISONER OF WAR – through the Geneva Red Cross … died … while a prisoner of war

PRISONER WHO WEIGHED 60lb. – Private John H Pearce, Worcestershire Regt. who through starvation in Germany was reduced to a skeleton, weighing only 60lbs was buried in St Ives, Cornwall with military honours.

MISSING

PRISONER RELEASED

MORE LOCAL HONOURS

BAR TO THE MILITARY CROSS

CAPT. H. L. EVERS, MC, 2/8TH Bn. Worc R., T.F.

> During the crossing of a river [Lys], and subsequent operations, this officer behaved with great courage and dash, and on two occasions led outflanking attacks on machine-gun positions. His inspired example greatly contributed to the success of this operation.
>
> The fact that Captain Evers had been awarded the bar to his MC has already been announced. He was killed in action on Nov. 1st, 1918.

It is sad to discover that Pte John Pearce's name is not recorded in either the Roll or on the *CWGC* website, meaning that despite dying of the War and within two months of its end, he has not been formally honoured – other than being buried 'with military honours'. There are, however, two John Pearces on the St Ives War Memorial so let us hope that one of them is our man. For many families the Armistice did not mean that the war was over. For them it ended when their loved one(s) returned home, be it from the Front or from the Prisoner of War camps across the European and Ottoman territories. This was an especially testing time for those who had received a telegram that a family member had been posted as 'missing' – like Lt RS Miller during the operations on the night of 23rd/24th October 1918 or Private AR Read at the Battle of Cambrai in November 1917 when serving with the 2/8th Battalion. All would have been hoping that in some German or other enemy prison camp or hospital may be their man. There was unexpectedly good news for Miller's family but not so for Read's. These agonies would have been felt up and down the country each time there was a knock on the door over these three, or so, months.

The *Journal* of 22nd February 1919 recorded 'Worcestershire Casualties: Officers: Died: Worc R. – Granger, 2nd Lieut. AG'. His death is not mentioned on the Roll, in the *History* nor on the *CWGC* website. He was the subaltern who was captured with Captain Pawsey in Italy in August 1918. To add to the mystery, the *Journal* of 22nd March announced Granger's promotion to Lieutenant on 1st February and then again in the *Gazette* in December 1921 when the War Office announced a wholesale reduction in the Territorial Force with effect from 30th September of that year. I cannot find any correction of Granger's *Journal* announcement, presumably to the concern of him and his family.

An example of Lt Col Hubert Clarke's generosity can be found in the 29th March edition of the *Journal* in the bottom right-hand corner of page 4 under the title of: '1/8th Active Service Souvenir'. Seemingly at Clarke's own initiative and expense, he offered:

> All officers and other ranks who have served with the 1/8th Batt. of the Worcestershire Regt. on active service may obtain a souvenir card

by sending a postcard stating rank, name, decorations, and period of active service with the Battalion, to the CO, 1/8th Worcestershire Regiment, B.E.F. [British Expeditionary Force, thus he was still in France. The card bears the proud regimental motto, the star and the crown with the significant date, 1st June 1794, above the latter. And it bears also the following long list of engagements with the significant emblem of crossed swords against those marked with an asterisk.]

1915 – Ploegsteert, Hubeterne.
1916 – Fonquevillers, Auchonvillers, Le Sars.
1917 – La Maisonette, St Emelie, *Templeux-le-Guérard, *Gillemont Farm, Louverval, Ypres, *Maison du Hibou, *Springfield Farm, *Stroombeek Valley, Vimy.
1918 – Asiago Plateau, *Canove, *Gaiga, *Edelweiss Spur, *Beaurevoir, *Honnechy, *Bazuel, Bois l'Évêque, *Fontaine-au-Bois, *Les GrandChenes, *Landrecies.

I know from the card lent to me by Robert Wedgbury that there is then space for the rank, name and decorations of the individual, followed by:

Served with the 1/8th Battalion The Worcestershire Regiment on Active Service
From ……………………….. To …………………
………………………………………Lieut. Colonel

The Lieut. Colonel is each signed as *H.T.Clarke.*
The card in my hand shows: 2/Lt E. WEDGBURY, DSO, MC, DCM, MM

From: 31-3-1915 To: 4-XI-1918. (Wounded)

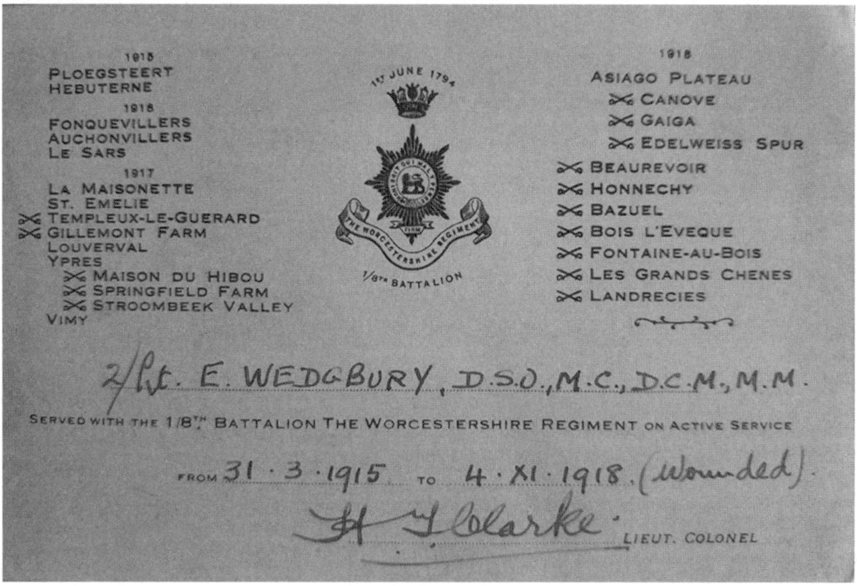
1915
PLOEGSTEERT
HEBUTERNE
1916
FONQUEVILLERS
AUCHONVILLERS
LE SARS
1917
LA MAISONETTE
ST. EMELIE
TEMPLEUX-LE-GUERARD
GILLEMONT FARM
LOUVERVAL
YPRES
MAISON DU HIBOU
SPRINGFIELD FARM
STROOMBEEK VALLEY
VIMY

1st JUNE 1794
FIRM
THE WORCESTERSHIRE REGIMENT
1/8th BATTALION

1918
ASIAGO PLATEAU
CANOVE
GAIGA
EDELWEISS SPUR
BEAUREVOIR
HONNECHY
BAZUEL
BOIS L'EVEQUE
FONTAINE-AU-BOIS
LES GRANDS CHENES
LANDRECIES

2/Lt. E. WEDGBURY, D.S.O., M.C., D.C.M., M.M.
SERVED WITH THE 1/8th BATTALION THE WORCESTERSHIRE REGIMENT ON ACTIVE SERVICE
FROM 31 · 3 · 1915 TO 4 · XI · 1918. (Wounded).
H G Clarke. LIEUT. COLONEL

The Card is printed in regimental green with gold edging. Beyond anything, it would have served as a reminder of places where each served. It was a most thoughtful souvenir of their service, as has been shown by it remaining today in the Wedgbury family papers. Walford would have been serving in Cologne by this time. I wonder if he ever applied for one – if so, it does not survive.

That of Captain Leslie Bomford still survives in his papers, together with a cutting from *The Times* dated 17th May 1919. It is the *Court Circular*. The day was preceded by a telegram to Bomford:

Buckingham Palace 10th May 1919
Capt. Leslie Bomford, Horton War Hospital Epsom
Your attendance is required at Buckingham Palace on saturday the seventeenth inst at ten thirty oclock in service dress please
Telegram acknowledgement
Lord Chamberlain London

Returning to *The Times*, it recorded:

His Majesty held an Investiture in the Quadrangle of the Palace at 11 o'clock.

The following Officers were severally introduced into the presence of The King, when His Majesty invested them with the Insignia of the respective Divisions of the Orders into which they have been admitted:

THE MOST DISTINGUISHED ORDER OF SAINT MICHAEL AND SAINT GEORGE

Knight Commanders.- Lieutenant-General Sir Claud JACOB…

The Regiment's *History*'s Foreword is written by the then Field Marshal Sir Claud William Jacob, GCB, KCSI, KCMG as the Colonel of the Regiment since 2nd February 1927. One can imagine his pride that a number of officers from his Regiment were on parade at that Investiture, including four from the 1/8th Battalion and one from the 2/8th:

THE DISTINGUISHED SERVICE ORDER AND BAR
Lieutenant-Colonel Hubert CLARKE, Worcestershire Regiment

THE DISTINGUISHED SERVICE ORDER AND THE MILITARY CROSS AND BAR
Captain Leslie BOMFORD, Worcestershire Regiment

THE DISTINGUISHED SERVICE ORDER AND THE MILITARY CROSS
Second-Lieutenant Edmund WEDGBURY, Gloucestershire Regiment, attached Worcestershire Regiment.

THE MILITARY CROSS AND BAR
Captain George WATKINSON, Worcestershire Regiment, …

THE MILITARY CROSS
Captain James BOMFORD, late Worcestershire Regiment, …

Leslie Bomford wearing DSO and MC ribbons

Clearly a great day for the Bomford family although, no doubt, Leslie would have been thinking that Douglas also deserved to be there. Watkinson was given his first name, although he used his second, Laurence. Wedgbury is correctly shown as being a Gloucester who held his commission despite his brief time in 1917 serving with them before transferring to the Worcesters. Walford had returned to the Continent and was helping to keep the peace in Cologne so missed this Investiture.

The battalions were back home, the parades had been organised, the medals awarded. It might seem that the War was over, except perhaps for those like Captain LR Bomford, who were still recovering in hospital from their wounds, but the Battalion would lose more men, not in battle but because of the battles they had fought.

Many of the surviving officers remained in the 8th Battalion until 30th September 1921 when, 'under AO/116/21 as amended by AO 332/32' there was a wholesale relinquishing of commissions from the 8th Battalion, in common with the 7th Bn, as well as many other

Territorial battalions. At the time forty pairs of Territorial battalions were amalgamated – thus the 7th and 8th Battalions for the Worcestershire Regiment. The 8th included a number who had crossed to France in March 1915: Captain HG Newman (granted the rank of major), Captain CC Davis, Captain KM Mylne, Captain HP Borlasse (granted the rank of major) as well as several who have featured in this story from the 1/8th and 2/8th: Captain RH Stallard MC*, Captain ES Mitchell MC, Captain JF Bomford MC, Captain RJCW Hawtrey, Lt WHS Chance, Lt RT Keen MC, Lt NVH Symons MC, Lt RS Miller, Lt SH Wilkes MC**, Lt JR Willis MC. No more major wars were expected and the country was very short of money.

SURVIVING THE PEACE

There is nothing in the *History* nor from Corbett nor in the *War Dairies* to record that Captain Osborn Walford had returned to service on the continent. It can be found in an article in the *Worcester Herald* in late February 1922 under the headline:

> TRAGIC DEATH OF TERRITORIAL OFFICER
> Capt. J.O.Walford Found Shot
> Captain J.O.Walford, of Dunstall Court, Feckenham, was found dead on Tuesday with a wound in his head. He was 52 years of age and had lived at Dunstall Court about 11 months. He was a keen sportsman, well known in the hunting field, and a follower of the Worcestershire Hunt. He served in the 8th Battalion of the Worcestershire Regiment in the war, and was wounded and awarded the Military Cross.
>
> He appeared in his usual health early yesterday morning and talked cheerfully and rationally to a workman on the estate named Ernest Reeve who, shortly afterwards found him lying dead in the orchard adjoining the Court with a six-chambered revolver in his right hand, one of the cartridges having been discharged through his mouth. He leaves a widow and son who is presently serving with the 3rd Battalion of the Worcestershire Regiment in India.
>
> Captain Walford was a candidate for the coming County Council election for the Feckenham Division.
>
> On Monday evening Capt. Walford addressed a well-attended meeting at Crabbs Cross in connection with the campaign. He then appeared to be in good spirits and went home quite satisfied with his election prospects.

The article then detailed his two MCs and their citations and a synopsis of his War service made by his brother-in-law, Colonel EV Sydenham DSO (Walford's wife Margaret (née Scott)'s sister's husband) before returning to the doctor's report:

Dr E. P. Davies said he saw the deceased in his surgery at 9 a.m. on Tuesday, and during the conversation witness said he could not take the chair at a meeting he was holding in connection with the county council election. That seemed to upset him. Witness heard no more from him until he was called to the orchard, and found him dead with a bullet wound in the head. The bullet had entered the brain and caused instantaneous death. He agreed that shell-shock sometimes left a man in a state of mental derangement. He thought that deceased had felt one of these attacks coming on though he might not have shown it, and was suffering from one when he killed himself.

PC Dudfield said there was one live cartridge and one empty case in the revolver when he examined it.

A verdict was returned, as stated.

A second report in another local newspaper under the headline FECKENHAM TRAGEDY. DEATH OF CAPTAIN J. O. WALFORD, MC. provided more detail of Walford the man as well as his struggles with shell shock during and immediately after the War:

The deceased, who was the son of the late Mr John Walford, solicitor, Birmingham, was born at Edgbaston, and educated at King Edward's School, Birmingham. He was 52 years of age and prior to coming to Dunstall Court about 11 months ago he lived at The Mount, Hanbury and before then at Salwarpe. When a young man he was a member of the Birmingham Volunteers (Warwickshire Territorials). On the outbreak of war he received a commission in the 2/8th Battalion Worcestershire Regiment, and went out to France in the spring (May) of 1916, serving through the war with distinction. He was invalided home with trench fever in 1916. On recovery he rejoined his regiment, and later on served in Italy with the 1/8th Worcesters. In his new battalion he succeeded Captain Pawsey in command of 'C' Company which had been formed by a merging of the old Bromsgrove and King's Norton Companies. In 1918 he returned with his battalion to France, and was wounded at the capture of Landrecies in November, 1918, and was awarded the Military Cross and Bar…

> On his discharge from hospital Capt. Walford was sent out to the Army of Occupation, and in Cologne contracted a severe attack of [Spanish] influenza, which, after the long strain of war, brought on shell shock. He was invalided home, and after some time in the Kensington Shell Shock Hospital, was discharged from the army as medically unfit.

Walford's widow and family were represented by Major Hugh Davies DSO MC, perhaps the Old Gent's best friend from his service with the 2/8th Battalion. He had been captured on 21st March 1918 at the Battle of St Quentin, at which the 2/8th Battalion lost nine officers killed and twelve officers captured as the Germans advanced as part of Operation Michael. Davies received his DSO for his leadership that day. The *Journal* announced his release on 14th December 1918.

Professor Edgar Jones of King's College, London believes the 'Kensington Shell Shock Hospital' to be the Special Hospital for Officers, 10 and 11 Palace Green, Kensington that was opened in 1915 and continued to treat officer patients until 1923. It was relatively small-scale and latterly funded by the Ministry of Pensions, providing care for officers suffering from post-traumatic illnesses. No 10 still survives as the Norwegian Embassy.

Another local newspaper report noted:

> After the Armistice he went to Cologne in the Army of Occupation, and while there he suffered a complete breakdown, so much so that he had to be put under restraint on account of showing suicidal tendencies. He was sent home under escort of an officer and doctor, and remained for some months in a shell shock hospital in Surrey. Previous to the war he was for some years on the Gold Coast where he suffered from … malaria. Apart from that he was a thoroughly healthy man as far as the witness [Col. Sydenham] knew. At the time of his death he was still drawing a wounds' pension for the wounds he received in France.

Perhaps the most devastating sentence in the above reports is 'discharged from the army as medically unfit'. It would seem that the

Army and thus the Government were washing their hands of men like Walford who had served both so gallantly. The *London Gazette* supplement for 16th July 1920 recorded for the 8th Bn, Worcestershire Regt:

> Capt. H.G. Newman is seconded for service with the Fettes College Contingent, OTC. 20th July 1920.
>
> Capt. J.O. Walford MC relinquishes his commission on account of ill-health, 2nd Jan. 1920, and retains the rank of Capt. (substituted for that which appeared in this Gazette, 1st Jan. 1920).

The announcement dated 30th December 1919 said exactly the same thing. Walford was a substantive captain so that rank could not be taken away. It is interesting to note the appointment of Captain HG Newman to a school OTC in Edinburgh. It showed what sort of appointment was available to a senior experienced captain. Such an appointment would have allowed Walford to feel wanted and valued, in an organisation in which he had experienced more success and camaraderie than in any other part of his life.

Walford's medal card provides three points of interest. It records, in small writing in one corner, '*Died suicide: Unsound mind: 22.2.22*' – it was actually the 21st; it shows his rank as 'major'; and that his widow, Margaret Walford, applied for his medals after he died – on 31st July 1923. The latter explains why the miniatures of his MCs and war medals are correctly mounted; he may have worn them at formal dinners. His MC and bar was still in its leather case. The Victory Medal and British War Medal came down the generations unmounted and with one ribbon missing, only coming to light in 2018. Walford was never able to parade with his medals. The fact that his suicide is recorded, as opposed to just his death – either would have ensured that his wife (of 24 years) received her widow's pension – meant that there must have been some interest in the Army that he committed suicide shortly after the War ended. However, the medal card is not a system for recording the scale of suicides amongst those who served. Professor Edgar Jones says he doesn't 'think any patient records survived for this hospital. Indeed, there are very few case notes for officer patients who suffered from mental illness. The vast majority were destroyed because of stigma to protect their identity. Data for suicide was not collected by the War Office to the best of my knowledge, in part to save the feelings of relatives'. This is a reflection of social norms at the time but it difficult to believe that it was a help to either the patients or to their families. Mrs Margaret Walford would have had to endure the inquest and the application for a widow's pension. At the time, their only child, then-Lieutenant JES (Ben) Walford, was serving on the borders of empire in Waziristan, having transferred to the Indian Signals Corps when the 3rd Battalion of the Worcestershire Regiment was disbanded. He was to be awarded an MBE for his services there that year, although as is the case with such awards, there is no citation. He was later to play cricket seven times for Worcestershire, for the Army and for Egypt in 1938. His daughter says that he never spoke about his father, neither of his suicide nor of his gallant war service.

What was shell shock? How was it treated at the time? Did the treatment carry on after the War was over? It is perhaps best to turn to the leading expert at the time, Lt Col Charles S Myers MD, Sc.D, FRS of the RAMC (Royal Army Medical Corps) who had a paper published in *The Lancet* on 11th January 1919 under the title: *A Final Contribution to The Study of Shell Shock being a Consideration of the Unsettled Points needing Investigation.* I do not intend to provide a full history of the discovery and development of the various treatments tried or considered for shell shock, rather to explain where the understanding of the illness had reached as the War ended. There has been little mention of shell shock in this story of the 1/8th Battalion thus far. In view of the destruction of the medical records of all officers who were treated in 'shell shock' hospitals, it is understandable that the *History* did not mention any cases across the whole Worcestershire Regiment.

The *War Diary* mentioned 2Lt Stuart Lewis who reported for duty on 7th July 1916 and was 'evacuated to hospital suffering from shell shock' the following day. Correspondence of the time told of another case, that of Captain RH Burlingham, whose letters to his wife, Ursula, we considered back in May 1915. This correspondence continued on an almost daily basis until June 1916 and included:

8.6.15 – A roasting day, not a breath of air in the trenches, thermometer over 100 in the shade and a thunderstorm brewing.

I am a bit seedy, so am going tonight to the first field Ambulance for a couple of days rest. It will be glorious to get out of one's clothes and have a bath; don't think I am very bad because I am not.

9.6.15 – I came down here (1st South Midland Field Ambulance) last night, and am lying in a little room. I am better and it is only for a short rest. The CO thought it better for me to come… Everybody is very good to me here. I was awakened at 3.30am by Davies (CC) walking in, he had been shot through the arm just above the elbow. They dressed his arm and put him to bed, he is in no pain and has left for England this afternoon, lucky man, I wish I was him.

Burlingham did not return to the trenches until 16th June and got leave from 20–24th June.

10.8.15 – Colonel Peake left yesterday for England, he has to undergo an operation, [Captain CC] Davies is also rather bad, and has had to go into Hospital.

Burlingham was sent on a course at 3rd Army School, Flexicourt from 13th February to 12th March 1916. He then spent time as second-in-command of the Battalion at the end of March, indicated by him signing off the *War Diary*. He did well on his course as his report made clear:

'A very good type, keen and interested in everything which has been shown him, conscientious and practical' – Major E Nairne, with General Kentish writing 'I have personally noticed this officer, and agree with all that Major Nairne has said of him, he is bound to do well'. [Burlingham quoted all this to his wife in that day's letter.]

7.4.16 – Last night was rather an eventful night, as there was an awful bombardment of the Frontline. As I was in command of the Battalion, I had to issue orders and get it ready for a Counter Attack etc. All this is in the dark, however, the thing passed off after an hour, but I felt responsibility to be very heavy.

13.4.16 – We are due to go out tomorrow (of the trenches), this will make 21 days without taking off my clothes, or rather 21 days sleeping in my clothes, as I have had them off once for a bath.

15.4.16 – It was very good of [2Lt TL] Jones to come over and see you [i.e while Jones was on leave].

29.4.16 – I wish I could hear of a job in England for a bit.

20.5.16 – My name has been sent in by the Brigade for a Staff appointment. I don't think there is the slightest chance of getting it but it is nice to be even suggested; as I can't have been said to have been suggested through influence.

27.5.16 [His first letter for a week] Am just off to hospital with CO's recommendation with six weeks in England.

28.5.16 – I am now writing in No 9 casualty clearing station after a varying experience. I was packed off first to the South Midland Field Hospital, where I stopped one night. It was a lovely chateau, next morning I was sent here.

I have been marked for Base, where I don't know. This is a lovely hospital with English nurses, who are very good to us.

30.5.16 – I am still here, and having a very quiet time, which is just what I like. I went with a Major from the East Lancs, who is also here, into Doullens this morning.

1.6.16 – No 8 General Hospital, Rouen

Here we are at the Base. We came down in No 3 Hospital train, a beautifully appointed train with every luxury … we are in wooden huts, 16 beds to a hut. The whole hospital is capable of holding about 1000, so you see it is a big place, but absolutely not a place to rest.

I hear they wire you directly you go to hospital so hope you got my letter first, written from the CCS. If I don't get sent home, I shall have to go to hospital in England, probably in London for a time. Don't worry, I can write but I can't talk. I am officially suffering from shell-shock. I am afraid this writing is rather shaky.

2.6.16 – I am up this afternoon and dressed, and am hoping I shall be marked 'B' in a day or two, which means 'boat'. It is a big job to get to England from this hospital, as the Doctor here is very stiff about it, but I hope my long service (they are mostly short service men here, 5 and 6 months), will help me.

3.6.16 – There is no news to tell you. I have not yet been told about leave. I expect you will see my name in the papers, as 'wounded, shell-shock'.

The *Journal* announced the following Saturday that: 'Capt RH Burlingham from Evesham is in a London hospital suffering from shell shock. Mrs Burlingham went to London on Thursday to see him'. These announcements were written as if to confirm that such 'wounds' were to be expected. Captain Burlingham must have recovered eventually and was found a staff job back in England. The *London Gazette* confirmed his promotion on 21st April in an announcement on 4th August 1916. By the following May he had his wish:

(Graded for purposes as a Staff Capt. whilst comdg. as CO., Officer Cadet Unit). – Captain RH Burlingham, Worc. R. TF.. and to be secd. 19th May 1917.

His only other mention in the *History* is as marching with the 8th Battalion at the Parade in August 1919 although the *Journal* noted his relinquishing that command, on 12th January 1919 – so he never returned to the Front. There seemed to be no stigma that he had been evacuated from the Front with shell shock. After all, he had served for a year there as a company commander. Burlingham's letters display a growing focus on either getting leave or being posted back to England. In June 1916, his commanding officer was Lt Col WK Peake who had himself been evacuated from the Front on two occasions, so he may well have been sympathetic to Burlingham's difficulties. Peake, himself, was 'transferred to England (sick)' on 8th September that year for the final time.

The only possible physical aspect that Burlingham seemed to show of shell shock is being able to 'write but I can't talk'. This may well mean that he could not physically talk – mutism – rather than that he did not want to. Myers was the first to use the term 'shell shock' in a paper in *The Lancet* in 1915. In 1916 he was appointed consultant psychologist at the hospital at Le Touquet – often used to describe an area of hospitals which included Etaples where the CWGC Cemetery now stands. It is possible that Burlingham was an early patient of Myers. His paper of January 1919 in *The Lancet* explained what his initial views were:

> In my early experience of shell shock I came to lay great stress on disturbances of personality, and I regarded the amnesia and the bodily disorder, mutism, tremor, incoordination, or spasmodic movement, so commonly observed in cases soon after their onset, as the expression of this change of personality due, like it was some functional disassociation. Accordingly, I adopted the therapeutic principal of restoring the amnesia with or without the aid of hypnosis; and with the restoration of the amnesia came a restoration of the speech and a resumed control of the bodily movement.

This treatment, as with others, was designed in the main to get the patients – officer or soldier – back to the Front in 'short order'. It is interesting to consider whether this short-term therapy was less important than the fact that the patient was retained within the military family and given the camaraderie and support on which these individuals had come to depend. Burlingham attained an appointment which he so clearly wanted – an opportunity for treatment that was denied to Walford in 1919/1920 and that may well have saved his life.

Perhaps the crucial short section is found in the third paragraph of Myers' paper:

> Many neurologists hold that the effects of suggestion and of functional disturbance are limited to phenomena which can be imitated voluntarily by the patient; they accordingly limit functional disturbances to those which can as well be produced by malingering.

The use of the word 'malingering' was all that many senior generals required. There was worse to come in many of the witness statements made to the Committee producing the *Report of the War Office Committee of Enquiry into 'Shell-Shock'* in 1922:

Sqn Ldr W Tyrrell DSO MC, Royal Air Force Medical

Services: "'Shell-shock' is born of fear. Its grandparents are fear and self-preservation."

Brevet Lt Col Viscount Gort VC, DSO, MVO, MC, Grenadier Guards: 'You must distinguish between shell-shock and nervous breakdown. Shell-shock is a word which has crept into public vocabulary for use on all occasions whereas most of the cases to which this term is applied are not shell-shock at all, in my opinion, but nervous breakdown caused through the soldier's nerves gradually wearing out. Among regular battalions with a good class of men the circumstances are rather different from those in the New Army units, and there are few cases of real shell-shock.'

Lt Col Myers was not called as a witness. The Committee's Recommendation was delivered under the headings of: Classification of Casualties; Prevention; Treatment; Forms of Treatment; Return to the Fighting Line; Cowardice, Desertion and Neurosis; and Recruiting. There was no discussion as to treatment once war had been concluded and it made no recommendations as to the closure or otherwise of existing 'shell shock' hospitals, many of which were already closed.

Herbert Adams

There is a telling entry in the diaries of Captain Herbert Adams MC who crossed with 2/8th Battalion as an older subaltern and graduate of Trinity College, Cambridge. He wrote on 14th August 1917 from the Ypres Front – when Walford had returned to Flanders, but to the 1/8th Battalion without a company to command:

> When I got back Capt. Walford, 8th Worcesters, walked in about 7 p.m. and seemed inclined to stay the night. Stallard also came in again, and the Old Gent started off on a long series of stories about different Worcestershire people he knew, but as no one else knew them, or cared, he became rather tedious. It was raining slightly: however by repeatedly pressing on him offers of Burberry's, ground sheets etc. etc. and giving explicit directions of the way to [Captain Lance] Evers' billet we managed to get him off about 8 o'clock.

Walford was clearly a lonely man who needed companionship and, at this stage of the War, the chance to prove himself. Adams later referred to other happy lunches with Walford and often Evers. The great battles of Passchendaele were underway so perhaps nerves were fraying.

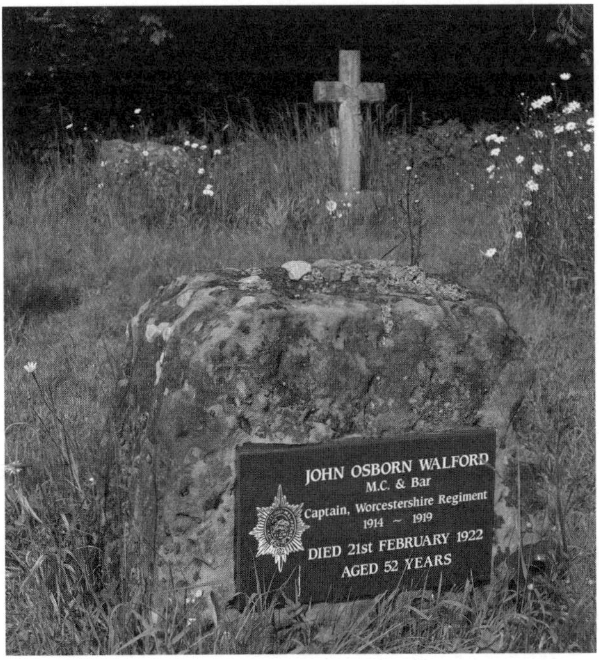

Walford's two gallantry awards meant that he had experienced battle with all its horrors on multiple occasions and he had been emboldened to perform his duty with increasing confidence. He had spent weeks in front-line trenches, being subjected to constant shelling and sniping. He had ventured on patrols into No Man's Land but, perhaps, less often than the young subaltern officers under his charge. With a measure of good fortune, he had survived. He did not survive the peace. As a friend of the local vicar, the Rev Gervase Blois, Walford was fortunate to have a service and be committed to the ground at St Mary's, Hanbury in late February 1922, ground which has since become sacred. A new slate plaque on his grave helps to tell his story and heroism, if not his difficulties.

The medals of Major JP Bate DSO*, MC* – still unmounted

There were seven other officers in this tale who also survived and who were entitled to wear at least two gallantry medals on the various

Remembrance Sundays of the 1920s and 1930s and beyond – Captain Charles Pawsey MC*; Captain Sydney Wilkes MC**; Captain Leslie Bomford DSO, MC*; 2Lt Edmund Wedgbury DSO, MC, DCM, MM; Major Jack Bate DSO*, MC*; Lt Col Hubert Clarke DSO*; Captain Laurence Watkinson MC*. We have already noted that Captain Hugh Chance – who became High Sheriff of Worcestershire in 1942 – and Major John Paskin MC were knighted for their service to the country before, during and after the Second World War. Two of these were also to be knighted, but others found their lives after their military service was not without troubles. Another was to die by his own hand.

An announcement in the *Journal* of 5th April 1919 recorded that Captain JP Bate DSO*, MC* relinquished the rank of major 'on ceasing to be employed'. However, he was promoted to major on 26th October 1920 so he was still serving in the Territorial Forces and the 8th Battalion at that date. When the Italian Croce di Guerra and twice being Mentioned in Despatches are taken into account, he was the most decorated of the Battalion's officers and men. His business career after the War resulted from a conversation allegedly in the trenches, but more probably on a course (perhaps the Senior Officer's Course at Aldershot) with the then Lt Col Lord Henry Lascelles DSO* who was to become the 6th Earl of Harewood KG, GCVO, DSO*, TD, JP, DL and who married Mary, the Princess Royal, in 1922. Their conversation was about manufacturing high quality British-made typewriters, which led to the creation of the Conqueror Typewriter Manufacturing Company. It raised £500,000 and built a state-of-the art factory in Stourton on the edge of Leeds. The *Leeds Mercury* recorded that the 'designer of the works and the general manager was Major JP Bate DSO, an experienced Birmingham engineer, who had become associated with Lord Lascelles in France in the latter stages of the War'. Economic slowdown and cheaper imports from the United States meant that no typewriters were ever sold. Lascelles is said to have invested £300,000 in the project (£17m in 2023 values). The site was sold to Messrs John Waddington, the printers, and subsequently makers of board games such as Monopoly.

Bate married Dorothy Muriel Player on 1 November 1918, on leave after his last battles and as the Battalion prepared to cross the Sambre Canal. They had two children: (John) Roger William Bate, born in 1920, and a daughter, Rosemary – seemingly the only daughter born to any of these gallant men. In 1926 Bate and Dorothy were living at the Laburnums in Stroud. His Probate recorded that in 1932 he was living at Langley Way, West Wickham, Kent but that he died at the Cotswold Sanatorium in Cranham near Stroud in Gloucestershire. His grave can be found in Woodchester near Stroud and is marked with a simple stone cross with the inscription:

Major
John Perceval Bate DSO, MC
Late 8th Battalion
The Worcestershire Regiment
Died 21st April 1932. Aged 38
R.I.P.

He lies in the churchyard of Woodchester Priory, the Church of the Annunciation, meaning he must have been a practising Catholic. There is no mention of his wife or children. At the time of Bate's death, he is recorded as being a 'Commercial Clerk and Army Pensioner', thus not at the director-level work of his immediate post-War working life. His widow moved to 28 York Road, Edgbaston, living next to her sister in 1935, and the same in 1940. He left £693 4s 4d to Dorothy so one must assume that he was still married to her in 1932. She survived him by almost fifty years, dying in Shardend, Birmingham in September 1981, still with Bate as her surname, so she never remarried. The Regimental magazine, *FIRM*, recorded in the July 1932 edition:

> We also regret to record the death of Major JP Bate who died in May at Woodchester, Stroud, at the comparatively early age of thirty-eight, as a result of being gassed during the War.
>
> Major Bate was on the Territorial Army Reserve of Officers.

No mention of his four gallantry awards which is surprising for a military publication. It stated that he died as a result of 'being gassed during the War'. We know that he was the officer leading the work party on the night of 19th/20th July 1916 when the Battalion was shelled with phosgene, from whose effects some 500 men suffered over the following months, including the then 2Lt LR Bomford and Lt CR Pawsey MC. The announcement of Bate's first MC in the *Journal* in January 1917 referred to him having 'twice been gassed' and being the son of Mr William Bate of New Street, Birmingham and himself residing at Lifford Grove, King's Norton. His death certificate provides clarity. Dr MG Harrison, the medical officer at Cotswold Sanatorium, Cranham recorded that Bate died as a result of 'Pulmonary Tuberculosis' at the age of just 38. The Cotswold Sanatorium gained fame in 1949 when Eric Blair, better known as George Orwell, became a patient and where he is said to have put the final touches to *Nineteen Eighty-Four*. It was established in 1898 for the specific purpose of treating tuberculosis and was for the most part run by the Hoffman family before closing in 1956. The only remaining evidence of its existence is that the road running west from the village below the ridgeline is called Sanatorium Road. Photographs show a series of chalets in extensive gardens which allowed plentiful fresh air, then the main therapy for tuberculosis. Orwell described the chalets as being 15 foot by 12 foot with glass doors and a glass-roofed verandah. Each had 'hot water pipes and a basin'. The Sanatorium was a private hospital and the photograph was found amongst a collection of wartime hospitals. Pulmonary Tuberculosis is a bacterial infection of the lungs and those with damaged lungs struggle to make a successful recovery. Bate was exposed to phosgene in July 1916, which includes amongst its many potential ill-effects 'fluid in the lungs (pulmonary edema)'.

Captain Leslie Bomford DSO MC* was photographed with his platoon (2nd in A Company) in early May 1916. It appears in *Brothers in War* with a note underneath saying that 'of the thirty-two men in this photograph only thirteen were still alive at the end of the war'. Beyond his gallantry medals, this one sentence is the best indication of what Bomford endured and witnessed during his 33 months at the Front. He was promoted to captain in the 8th Battalion on 15th April

1921 and was not amongst those who relinquished their commissions later that year. He wrote a 66-page *Memoir* from which I have already quoted. It covers three aspects of his life, two in detail and one in passing. It would be a fascinating read for anyone interested in either the development of agricultural machinery from the War until the 1950s as well as for those investigating the development of arable farming on the chalk downlands of Hampshire from 1931 until the 1970s.

Leslie Bomford spent the 1920s developing his own ideas on agricultural machinery, initially for his father's business and, when that faded, in order to sell such equipment in both Kenya and South Africa from 1925 until 1929. He returned to England and took a tenancy on 666 acres of farmland from Lord Portsmouth at Tufton Warren outside Whitchurch in Hampshire. His landlord described him in 1965 as:

> a gentle man whose machines do the shouting for him. He was a leader in the agricultural revolution and he still leads. Much of the chalk country's farming regeneration stemmed from his like. From the war years (1939–1945) onward he voluntarily doubled his own rent to me. I sometimes wonder if he is unique.

His nephew, Nicholas Bomford, in his *Brothers in War,* recalled Leslie as 'an enthusiastic collector of antique clocks … a keen fisherman and a very fine shot. Twice married, he had one son, Robert and two adopted daughters'. He died on 12 April 1981. In his *Memoir,* Leslie said very little of this third aspect of his life – limited to just four sentences:

> In 1937 I planned to start a pig unit and had a Danish Pig house all planned. Then I got married and the expense of this was enough to make me abandon pigs.
>
> 1938 I was Chairman of the Andover Branch of the N.F.U. (National Farmers Union). As I was taking a delayed honeymoon in Ireland I went to my vice-Chairman, John Cherrington and asked him to carry on. I found that he was travelling on the same boat

from Fishguard, the same night. My purpose was fishing, his was buying cattle.

In 1939 I was one of the two Judges of new implements for the Royal Show at Windsor. This involved travelling round and seeing implements at work before the Show. I cannot remember which implements got the medals. I was asked to continue after the war, but matrimonial troubles had me bloody minded.

When I got married in 1937 my wife wanted me to resign from the Reserve of Officers for the T.A. and I did. At the start of the War the authorities wanted me back but with a dud right arm I thought I should be more useful in Food Production. After Dunkirk the Local Defence Volunteers were started and with my wife's permission I joined the night it was formed. This developed into the Home Guard and I became a sergeant in charge of the Tufton Warren and Firgo section. Gen. Grant [Major General Sir Philip Gordon KCB, CMG – a Royal Engineer officer who had served in the Boer War and throughout the Great War and was 71 in the summer of 1940 but who died in 1943] at Hurstbourne was our platoon commander. For the first few months we manned a post each night on the top of the farm to watch for enemy parachutists etc.

Bomford continued:

Afterwards they formed us into a minor army and I became the Platoon Commander. Had there been an invasion I considered we should have been more useful as guerrillas. For a start rifles and ammunition were scarce, but armaments improved afterwards. I remember carrying my shotgun with ball or SSG cartridges. One of our jobs was guarding railway bridges at night. A weary task, I'm glad that we never went into action, but it was good fun…

Before the L.D.V. a peculiar organisation was started based on Fox Hunts in the County [of Hampshire]. This was for sabotage if the Germans landed. I was in demand as an instructor on the use of detonators, fuses etc. Roy Blackadder and I secretly buried a dump of incendiary material in the big pit on top of my farm. It is still there, bushes have grown up and I doubt if I could find it now…

This service added to his medal collection as he was entitled to the Defence Medal (United Kingdom) for his service with the Home Guard.

Was Bomford, a bachelor at forty, late to marriage, more comfortable in the company of men? He appeared to struggle with the apparent constraints of married life or, perhaps, there was marital incompatibility from the outset? He talked and wrote about his war experiences more than most. Perhaps tellingly, he wrote in his *Memoir*: 'While at Epsom [hospital] a doctor tried to persuade me to continue medical studies. Somehow, having unexpectedly survived the war, we didn't worry much about the future'. A view reiterated by Colonel Sir Hugh Boustead at the conclusion of his fascinating autobiography *The Wind of Morning*:

> To those of my generation who fought in the First World War as we were stepping into life at eighteen or nineteen, the experience was indelible. The war stands like a peak on the horizon of one's life; the lengthening perspective of the intervening years never seems to have taken one much further from it. To be alive at the end of it was almost unbelievable, and the fact of survival gave me an even greater zest for life. I have never ceased to be thankful for the gift of life, and in turn life has been good to me. [Boustead ended the War as captain with an MC, and retired in 1965 with post-nominal letters KBE, CMG, DSO, MC* after a life of service in Russia, Sudan, Ethiopia and Arabia – but with two engagements, neither of which led to marriage.]

Lord Portsmouth told of 'a gentle man'. Bomford ploughed his own furrow in his development, both with machinery and with his farming practices. I am inclined to think that the sudden and unexpected death of his father in 1920 with the resultant loss of guidance was a greater influence on his later life than his war experiences – about which he both spoke and wrote, notably in the years after the Second World War. That his two marriages failed cannot be blamed on the War. Bomford was just 22 when the War ended and he had had a most impressive three-year military career. It must be remembered that Bomford went to a Wesleyan school before heading up to Edinburgh University where he was 'billeted with the Reverend Aitken who had been Baptist Minister at Dunnington'. He was there for less than a year before joining the Army. He had little exposure to women beyond his extended family and his *Memoir* included a fascinating observation resulting from this sheltered upbringing. When back in England recovering from being gassed in 1916, he remembered that:

> Sometime when I was back I was billeted in Cheltenham. Brother Douglas was there after shrapnel in his neck. Also Robin [Lt JR] Blake, who wanted to take me to a tea party. I objected saying I couldn't talk to girls. He told me to sit by one, and ask her if she liked kippers for breakfast. Sound advice – this sort of remark breaks the ice. I have tried it again since then.

Capt. J. R. Blake, Bretforton. Wounded & missing.

As the War ended, he still had two years to spend in hospital, so he was well into his twenties before he could begin a normal working and social life. His first wife saw him as a person to admire and as a war-hero, though subsequently she came to realise that she did not really love him. She told their son, Robert, that the only psychological effect of the War was that Leslie suffered occasionally from nightmares and always of the bayonet attack in the enemy trench in Italy.

Bomford was to have a most successful peace and made significant contributions to the service of his country. His son's memories of his father are not until his father was well into his fifties – of his friendship with 'Kinson' [Watkinson] and their fishing trips. A measure of the man is perhaps best summed up by his ongoing friendship with his servant, Pte Sanger MM*. He and his brother set him up in a greengrocer store – sadly, which ultimately failed – and Leslie had him to stay on a number of occasions well into their later lives. Robert remembers Sanger as a small frail man but someone for whom his father had great affection. Robert's other memory is that his father did not hold it against anyone who suffered from shell shock or could not cope at the Front, saying that his father mentioned that one officer was sent back after just a day – obviously 2Lt Lewis back in July 1916. Leslie Bomford was an example of one of life's achievers, and so too were Watkinson, Pawsey, Wedgbury and Wilkes.

Leslie's brother, Douglas, was to have an equally illustrious career, mainly in the field of agricultural engineering. Robert remembered that he had been an important influence in the formation of the Institute of Agricultural Engineering, so much so that he was President from 1955-57 and the Douglas Bomford Trust was formed, initially by a bequest from his widow, Betty, to continue 'his interest and ideals'. A recent report showed that it had investments of over £5m and makes annual awards and prizes of some £150,000.

Watkinson, on being released from the Army in January 1919, returned to the civil service, initially with an appointment as a clerk in the Inland Revenue. He rose subsequently to Board level but in 1931 he transferred to the Board of Trade. It was in this capacity that he rose again to prominence and high office, particularly during the Second World War. From 1940 he worked as Principal Assistant Secretary and was directly involved in a number of vital measures of wartime control, commencing with the limitation of the output of consumer goods industries needed to release labour for war work; continuing with releasing industrial factory space for war purposes; and, as supplies of consumer goods became scarcer, concluding with various measures for rationing – in particular, clothes and furniture. In 1942 he was seconded to the newly established Ministry of Fuel and Power to work on the Beveridge scheme for the 'points' rationing of the various forms of fuel, returning to the Board of Trade at the end of the year. He remained employed as Under-Secretary for the remainder of the war, concentrating on arrangements for post-war reconstruction, in which role he proved inspirational. He was awarded the CB (Companion of the Order of the Bath). Following VE Day, he was concerned with the working parties set up by Sir Stafford Cripps to enquire into some fifteen of the consumer goods industries, ranging from cotton and clothing to carpets and cutlery, and much besides. However, he was transferred as Deputy Secretary in the Ministry of Fuel and Power in the fuel crisis of 1947, in which capacity he had to deal with the problems of the coal-mining industry. He was appointed KBE (Knight Commander of the Most Excellent Order of the British Empire). Watkinson served subsequently as Vice-Chairman of Harris Lebus Ltd (1955-57) and as Chairman (1958-61). He served later as Chairman of the London Electricity Consultative Council and as a Member of the London Electricity Board. He was a Member of the Monopolies Commission (1960-68). He retired to Loughton in Essex where he died in 1974.

The Times published the notice of Watkinson's death on 25th March, including 'Much loved husband of "Chips" and father of "Bill"'. Chips was Doris Pilling from Blackpool. This information comes from Spinks, the auctioneers, who were asked to sell his medals and papers in 2017 by a 'direct descendant'. They sold for just £2,600 and his miniatures appeared on a second auction site and his sword on a third. Enquiries have borne no fruit which means that these treasures, particularly the papers, are in some private collection and unavailable for further research. This seems to indicate that the Watkinsons had one child, 'Bill', who perhaps died shortly before this sale.

A glowing tribute in *The Times* on 28th March 1974 by Sir Francis Meynell included:

> Those who worked with him [at the Board of Trade] felt that he did more than any other man on the home front to contribute to the winning of the war. All the most significant controls over civilian goods other than food were invented and set out by him… Before the war was over his were the plans for winning the peace – such things as the Monopolies Commission and the Development Areas. Short, bright-eyed, confidential voice, utterly un-pompous, with no vestige of the expected Civil Service aura of public school, university and club, Wattie had that essential of a true leader – the capacity to inspire affection in all his staff and to make them all, cleaners and messengers upwards, feel themselves to be essential – and in that sense equal – parts of the job in hand.

Watkinson's service in the First World War did not get a mention but there can be little doubt that his leadership skills were developed and honed with A Company; 1/8th Battalion would have given him both the confidence as well as the ability to talk to those from the 'Other Ranks'. As commander of 2nd Platoon in the autumn of 1917 and in Italy in 1918, he would have learnt what was required to inspire men from all walks of life to trust and follow him. At Beaurevoir, he made the toughest of decisions as other leaders fell. His letter in October 1918 to Leslie Bomford showed a man becoming increasingly confident in his abilities.

Watkinson was not the only one of this bemedalled and gallant group to be knighted, nor to have an obituary in *The Times.* Sir Charles Pawsey MC* died on 21st July 1972, his ashes lying now by the south door of Badingham Church in Suffolk. Upon release from his Prisoner of War camp from the Salzerbad area of Lower Austria, Pawsey immediately displayed his renowned initiative by 'hijacking' a train, as the only other option given was to walk back to the British lines. He was awarded his degree by Oxford University in November 1918 by DDH – 'Declared to Deserve Honours' – and was eventually promoted to captain on 18th November 1919. He was successful in applying to join the Indian civil service, starting on 4th October 1919 – presumably his Oxford degree being a considerable advantage. His first posting was as an Assistant Commissioner in Assam. He was knighted in 1947 for his services to the Indian civil service and to the Naga people. He returned to Liverpool Port on 26th February 1948, his career complete, aged 53. He did not get married until he was 60 – to Rita, widow of Hugh Halliday, who had owned a sawmill in Assam. He lived out his life in Suffolk in the body of the wider Pawsey family. During the Second World War he was District Commissioner for the Naga Hills in Burma as a member of the Indian civil service.

Pawsey was based at Kohima and it was at his bungalow and on his tennis court that the infamous sixteen-day siege took place which was to turn the tide against the Japanese. Pawsey stayed to support the garrison commander, Colonel Richards, throughout the siege. On the memorial to the 2nd British Division at the Kohima Military Cemetery are carved the words of John Maxwell Edmonds:

When You Go Home, Tell Them of Us and Say,
For Your Tomorrow, We Gave Our Today.

Charles Pawsey in Nagaland as District Commissioner

The focus of his obituary was very much on his service in India and the Naga Hills as well as the action at Kohima, although a second appreciation of his life told of his MCs though, perhaps more importantly, that 'he earned a niche in history, and the wholehearted respect and affection of all who knew him, whether in the Naga Hills or, after he retired, in the peace of his Suffolk home, where he and Lady Pawsey were the kindest and most unassuming hosts'. Pawsey was to be awarded the Lawrence of Arabia Medal for 'work of outstanding merit in the fields of exploration, research or literature' in 1947. This is not an annual award but made as and when merited. Amongst other recipients are Lord John Hunt (1953), Sir William Thesiger (1954) and the aforementioned Colonel Sir Hugh Boustead (1965).

In an obituary by Major DE Lloyds-Jones of the Assam Regiment there is lovely story which encapsulates the affection for Pawsey: 'Later when the [Assam] battalion went back into action in Burma … its commanding officer, Lt Col WF Brown DSO, OBE, whose devotion to Pawsey was absolute, would at the least excuse don the old woollen jersey lent to him by Pawsey and which he had worn throughout the siege [of Kohima]. Brown was wearing it when he was killed, leading his battalion out on a night operation on Shwebo, and we buried him in it, as we knew he would have wished'. Brigadier RU Richards CBE, DSO, himself a Worcestershire officer, commanded the British forces at Kohima. He wrote:

> Pawsey had jurisdiction over a proud, brave and intelligent mountain people who, before the coming of the British were engaged in fierce tribal raids in which success was measured by the number of human heads taken. He had a remarkable influence over this primitive people; he and they trusted each other implicitly.
>
> He belonged to that select band of British Administrators who were able to control a district entirely through their personalities, by their selfless devotion which they give, over the years, to the people for whose guidance and welfare they are responsible. Whatever service Pawsey asked of the Nagas in the face of the enemy, was willingly and cheerfully given; from carrying food and ammunition, digging

> trenches, carrying out wounded, to moving through Japanese lines to collect information.
>
> He elected to stay with the Garrison throughout the siege; a decision typical of the man and, by so doing, was able, through his Nagas to provide a flow of accurate information regarding enemy movements when all other sources had been cut off, and this continued until the Garrison was completely surrounded. It was from him I first learned the force moving against Kohima was a division and not a regiment as officially stated. The information which his scouts brought in regarding the movement of the Japanese was invaluable. Wearing civilian clothes and careless of his safety, he would walk round at the height of the battle talking to and encouraging men of the Assam Rifles and the Assam Regiment … British troops were tremendously impressed by his calm and confident bearing and by his relationship with the Naga People.

He was still the soldier so respected by C Company in the Great War. Another Assam officer, Lt Col GA Keene MBE, confirmed this view: 'a more unflappable man, as an unarmed civilian in the midst of all that carnage, you could not imagine'. Every young officer of whatever generation would hope to have such an attribute; there can be no doubt that his demeanour in his Great War actions would have rubbed off on his fellow company commanders and subordinates and helped to set the standard achieved by so many of the gallant officers and men with whom he fought. He was undoubtedly a man of great intellect, courage, and many and varied talents.

My visit to Badingham Church required a call to the Parish Recorder, Victor Warne, for help in finding the small inscribed stones lying in the grass, one for 'Charles Pawsey, Knight' and, to his left, for 'Rita Alejandra Georgina Darrell Pawsey'. When I mentioned Charles Pawsey, Mr Warne's immediate response was: 'Oh, I knew him'. He said that in his retirement, Sir Charles had translated all the Church's records from the twelfth century onwards from the Latin. I mentioned his gallant service in the Great War and his two Military Crosses. Mr Warne said that Sir Charles never once mentioned that War nor his medals. He did talk about Assam and Kohima. Mr Warne visited Cambridge University as part of a World War Two village project as Sir Charles and Lady Pawsey had donated all their papers to the Centre for South East Studies there. Sadly, there is nothing concerning Captain Pawsey's Great War service amongst them, nor his medals; I searched in vain for any indication of a desire to remember these experiences or his comrades. There was, however, a postcard from Midlothian dated 27th November 1964 and signed 'ever yours, Ken Mylne'. It was not long and clearly in response to a letter from Sir Charles, but a sentence in the middle told one all that was necessary about his desire to remember that War:

> Many thanks for delightful reply which I took along to show Gwynne Newman who was undergoing a small operation in the Officers' Association Nursing Home where also I was most of October. I agree fully about not getting too much obsessed with the past. In 1932 I enjoyed visiting Messine Road, Ploegstreet, Bailleul etc, also Hébuterne, Ovillers, Albert & many places with their wonderful memorials esp. in the Beaumont Hamel park, not to mention graves of Hugh Wilson & my two brothers, last repeating this [journey] in 1955…

Gwynne Newman was Captain HG Newman, a fellow company commander of Pawsey in the action at Templeux-le-Guérard. Newman was the man posted to Fettes College OTC back in 1922 when Walford was retired by the Army. He must have stayed in Scotland and continued a friendship with Mylne. It is the words 'not getting too much obsessed with the past' that reveal that Pawsey must have made a comment to the effect that he was one of the many who did not want to discuss the War. Pawsey was a man who threw away none of his paperwork – and almost all his correspondence is now in the Cambridge archive. Beside Mylne's postcard was a typed note below a newspaper cutting advertising the 50th Anniversary of the Regiment's 2nd Battalion at the great Battle of Gheluvelt on 31st October 1914 in front of Ypres, which some historians credit with saving the Allied cause by plugging a gap that would have led the Germans to the Channel ports. Below the notice was typed:

Sir Charles Pawsey CSI, CIE, MC.
Some of the remnants of C. Coy, 1/8th Worc. most respectfully hope that you will be at the reunion on Saturday.

Ellis F.	Slough H.
Hill F.	Faulkner H. [DCM, MM]
Evans F.	Liddell H.
Francis W.	Jelfs W. [DCM, MM]
Williams C.	Walker C.
Malsom R.	Walker S.

There is no indication that Pawsey accepted the invitation, but his correspondence of the following month with Mylne may be an indication that both did indeed attend. He sorted out his affairs in the year before he died, 1972, sending all his Indian papers to Cambridge and an album of photographs to his Regiment with every indication that it was Jack Bate who was the officer with the camera at the Front and from whom Paskin and Burlingham's albums may originate.

After Pawsey died, his wife, Rita, wrote to Watkinson and, via him, to Leslie Bomford asking for stories about his Great War service. She flattered both by addressing them as 'Colonel'. She told Bomford that 'Charles never spoke of the 1914 War and the fact that he had been captured came as a great surprise to me' – Watkinson had mentioned it in his letter. She told Watkinson also that he never mentioned the 1914 War and that 'we can find no citation as to how he got his Military Cross. I should be very grateful if you could give me details as his family also want to know.' Bomford, who was serving when each was earned, filled in the gaps and lent Lady Pawsey his copy of Corbett's book with the caveat that his 'story needs taking with a pinch of salt.'

Remarkable in a different way was Second Lieutenant Edmund (Ted) Wedgbury, who returned to Worcester, married, had three sons and returned to the same company for the remainder of his working life. They were indeed proud of his wartime achievements, as the announcement in the *Journal* of 12th April 1919 showed:

Heenan & Froude pre-war Christmas party with
Wedgbury on the right

A HEENAN AND FROUDE WORTHY

The staff of Heenan and Froude's are very delighted with the latest honour conferred on Lieut. E Wedgbury. He was employed in the general office before war broke out. Though a man of quiet, reserved disposition, he was known to have strength of character, and it demonstrated itself in warfare. Being a native of Tallow Hill, he was a Territorial before the war, and was at Camp when hostilities began in August 1914. He went to France as sergeant with the 1/8th Battalion in March 1915. He received a commission with the 3rd Gloucesters in June 1917, and incidentally came back to England. He went back to France and was attached to the 1/8th Worcesters in August of that year. In December he proceeded to Italy, and returned to France in September 1918 joining the Allies final offensive and continuing in it until he was wounded in the arm on November 4. In the meantime he had been awarded an MM in October 1916, the DCM in January 1917, the MC in October 1918 and now he has received the DSO for his work last October. The staff of the firm entertained him to dinner and presented him with a purse of money on his receiving the DCM but they are more than ever proud of his splendid record, and, as he has returned to business, he is a hero among the staff.

Lieutenant E WEDGBURY DSO MC DCM MM
1/8th Bn The Worcestershire Regiment

If only they knew that he was and remains the only soldier to win each of those medals as well as being Mentioned in Despatches in 1917 and 1919 – imagine their pride. He was to work in the accounts department of Heenan and Froude, an engineering firm best known for building Blackpool Tower, for more than 40 years. He resigned his commission on 23rd September 1921 and was granted his rank of lieutenant – so thoroughly deserved. He anticipated the amalgamation of the two battalions by a week, so went on his own terms. Interestingly, he resigned his commission from the Gloucester Regiment on 14th July 1920 so his final resignation from the Army was from the Worcestershire Regiment, which he had joined some fourteen years before as a private soldier and had served so gallantly and with such distinction.

The writing of this book has much to do with a chance email back in 2015. I was part of a small team organising a Waterloo Dinner at Hatfield House to both celebrate that great victory but, in the main, to raise funds for the Hertfordshire branch of the Army Benevolent Fund. Wine was one of my responsibilities and a diligent ABF Treasurer questioned some of my paperwork. He closed his email with 'Kind regards, Robert Wedgbury'. I answered his questions and closed by asking if he was, by chance, related to an Edmund Wedgbury who 'had a particularly gallant First World War with the Worcestershire Regiment'. Imagine my amazement when he replied that Wedgbury was his father. It did not occur to me that the children of any serving officers of the Great War were still alive. Arthur, his eldest son and Robert, his third son, are still with us. They remember that their father used to go each Friday evening to the British Legion Club in St Nicholas Street to play cards from the early 1920s until the late 1940s. They say that they believe one of Wedgbury's group was Mr Hardy, the Regimental tailor. I have met with Robert on a number of occasions, the first one understandably emotional. He has been kind enough to lend me what family papers he has retained. These eight gallant men had few children and just one daughter but the fact that three of the six sons are alive in 2023 is remarkable.

Wedgbury's medals are displayed at the Worcester City Museum in the case for the Victoria Crosses donated to the Regiment. The honour is deserved but I wonder if they should be displayed beside those of his brother officers and those from the ranks of the Battalion? Presently the Regiment holds those of Wilkes, Bateman, Paskin and Major RHH Creak, the second-in-command when the Battalion crossed to France. The medals of Osborn Walford, Leslie Bomford and Hubert Clarke are still held by their families. Those of Lance Evers MC*, NVH Symons MC and Hugh Davies DSO, MC – all part of this story but who served only with the 2/8th Battalion – are also held by the Regiment. Symons was later to be Private Secretary to the Governor of Bengal in the 1930s and published *The Story of Government House* in 1935, having been promoted to major in the Indian Army on 27th August 1934. He retired to Lymington and to sailing. He was probably the last of these officers to die, living until 24th January 1986, so into his nineties.

As part of my research for this book, I have tried to locate the medals of as many of the central characters as possible. In part, this was with the intention of assembling them all in one place as if reuniting these remarkable men one more time. Having been given the list of those held by the curator of the Regiment, and having established that those of Osborn Walford, Leslie Bomford and Hubert Clarke are still retained by their families, I went in search of the medals of Watkinson, Bate and Pawsey. As I said earlier, I found that those of Watkinson were sold by his family through Spinks in 2017 together with some papers. Enquiries have drawn a blank as to the purchaser.

When asking Pawsey's old school and university college about his years at each, I asked if he had left his medals to either institution. Neither held them nor could help as to their present whereabouts. As a last resort, I put 'Pawsey' and 'Suffolk' into Google and found a 'John Pawsey'. His almost immediate reply linked me to one of Pawsey's nieces, Cilla Steed. To date she has not been able to find out where they are held. This left those of Bate, a fine collection. The *Daily Telegraph* death column showed that his son, Roger, died in a hospice in Harrogate in 2009. The hospice told me that they had no record of other members of the family. Exhaustive Google searches gave me no encouragement. However, and to my amazement, the Regiment's curator, John Paddock, asked me in February 2023 of the name of the officer whose medals I was seeking. When I replied Bate, he said that he felt certain that a month previously a parcel had arrived containing the medals of a 'Bate' as well as some books and papers. I said that they were a notable collection with a DSO and Bar and an MC and Bar. John said that he was certain there was a DSO and Bar. At my next visit to Worcester, John showed me the box. There was a dark blue leather case, another case similar to that in which Walford's MCs were presented as well as the three WW1 medals for service and victory and his Italian gallantry medal. The medals had not been mounted, presumably because Bate had no opportunity to wear them in uniform. The DSO and MC do not appear to have seen daylight very often and are in wonderful condition. Bate's miniatures were not there, if he had ever purchased them – those worn at formal dinners. It seems that they had been given to his old Regiment for safe keeping as well as with the opportunity for display so that his extraordinary service can become more widely known. To me, the timing of their arrival at Worcester was just another of the coincidences which I have encountered throughout my researching of the story of these great men.

Captain S H WILKES MC + 2 Bars, Sidney Herbert Wilkes was born in Dudley and was at Oxford when war broke out in 1914. He joined the 1/8th Battalion The Worcestershire Regiment in France in 1916 and won his first Military Cross on the Somme that winter. The second was awarded in 1917 for leadership and contempt for danger at Ypres, and third for leading a raid on the enemy's lines in Italy in June 1918, for which he was awarded the Italian Commemorative Medal. He returned to Oxford after the war and was later a teacher and a civil servant. He died in 1977, aged 81 years.

Captain Sydney Wilkes MC** returned to St John's College at Oxford University when the War finished. He had interrupted his degree to enlist in 1914. Thereafter he taught at Bembridge School on the Isle of Wight before becoming a civil servant. The school was started by John Howard Whitehouse, a disciple of John Ruskin, a Quaker, a conscientious objector and a leading opponent of the Military Service Bill – the conscription bill – in the House of Commons as a Liberal MP. This would have made an interesting contrast to Wilkes who was Church of England and enlisted to fight for his country at the first opportunity – and did so with great skill and gallantry. In 1925, Wilkes married Helen Latimer who was 24 days his senior. Wilkes described himself as a 'chemist' on his marriage certificate so he must have finished teaching by then. They lived in the same house in Grange Park, North London for over forty years with Wilkes having been HM Engineering Inspector of Factories, the Home Office, dealing with chemical matters in 1939. At the time Helen was a voluntary assistant at the Middlesex branch of the British Red Cross. He died on 2nd June 1977. His widow bequeathed his medals to the Regiment upon her death, aged 100, in 1997. His Victory medal was received from his sister, Alice, upon her death in 1999. It is not believed that the Wilkes had any children.

The last member of the group of eight gallant Worcestershire officers was the commanding officer, Lt Col Hubert Thomas Clarke DSO. His life became increasingly complicated after the War. The announcement in the *Journal* in December 1918 referred to him as having been 'Clerk to the Worcestershire Old-Age Pensions and Insurance Committees'. He was to be cited as a Co-Respondent in the divorce of Harry Ernest Oram and Gertrude Freeman Oram (née Burgess) in 1926 and then as Respondent in 1930 when his wife May Elizabeth Clarke (née Walsey), whom he married in the spring of 1911 at Evesham, sought a divorce. Both files can be read at the National Archives. What is perhaps more surprising is that he appears to have been at a school for Orphans in 1891 at the age of five in Wanstead in Essex. His father, Thomas Richard Clarke, an accountant, died in 1888 but his mother lived until August 1948, having married again, to Frederick Winwood in 1905 in Tufnell Park, Islington. Winwood died only three years later at 46 Britannia Square, Worcester with Hubert Clarke as an executor. Unlike Hubert's father whose assets were some £60, Frederick Winwood left £5,400 (£767,712 in 2023). His first wife had died in 1904 and between them they had six children. This marriage brought Hubert to Worcester, to some money and to the Worcestershire Regiment. His subsequent advancement came entirely through his own skills and ability, as it was when fate took him to War with the Battalion. Clarke did not have the typical background of a county Territorial officer, perhaps why he was not mentioned in the letters and diaries of Bomford or Evers. He remained in command of the 8th Battalion until January 1921, the 2/8th having been disbanded in April 1919 as the Army was rapidly reduced in size. He resigned his commission on 8th February 1921 and was transferred to the Territorial Force Reserve.

Clarke's first marriage to May Walsey produced one child, Eric, who was born in January 1912, shortly after his father's promotion to captain. Sadly, Eric was to be killed serving in the RAF in 1942 having been awarded an Air Force Cross. His second marriage to

Gertrude Oram also produced a son, Richard, born in 1930. Clarke was the clerk to the Worcestershire Health Insurance Committee. He did not hide his war service, indeed he called his house in Malvern after the greatest victory of his command, Landrecies. In 1921, Malvern adopted Landrecies, not at his initiative but rather that of Mrs Tassell (née Manet) who, as part of the Malvern War Memorial Committee, had visited Landrecies and, three years after the War, found that some inhabitants were still living in huts. Clarke would have been aware of the deaths of both Walford and Bate but his family would have been completely unprepared for the tragedy in the summer of 1935.

As with Walford, we need to revert to newspaper reports of an inquest to understand quite what happened but, again, as with Walford, Clarke still possessed his pistol from his military service. The *Daily Herald* of Friday, 12th July 1935 reported under the headline: 'Death of DSO Colonel found shot at desk'. Gallingly, the article starts: 'He was lying by his desk, with two revolver wounds just below the heart, and was rushed to Worcester Royal Infirmary where he died tonight (Thursday)'. *The Citizen* report was more detailed and told of a harrowing 24 hours for all involved. Clarke had shot himself on the Wednesday, presumably in the early evening when all others had left the office:

> George Henry Jones, the caretaker of the offices, said that he went round on Wednesday evening and saw nothing unusual. On Thursday morning he heard a noise of someone hammering and went into the office. Colonel Clarke said, 'Is that you Jones? Fetch Mr Tom Bates. I have had an accident.' He said that he had been lying there all night. Before he was taken away Colonel Clarke said: 'To think that any poor men suffered like this in No Man's Land.'
>
> Tom Bates reported that Clarke said: 'It happened when I was examining the ejector'. As he remained conscious when he reached hospital, he was able to receive and to speak with both his wife and his mother, each of whom visited him before he died. To his wife, Clarke said: 'It was an accident. I have got so many meetings this week. I kept hammering on the floor'. To his mother, Mrs AE Winwood: 'Mother, dear, it was a bad accident'. She continued that

> her son had been worried about financial difficulties for a number of years – though not mentioning the divorces and, perhaps, having to support two households. She said that Clarke had been to talk to her on the Wednesday afternoon, 'and lay down for a time'. Clarke's wife referred to a heart attack some ten days before and, later, some 'awful headaches'. However, there was a note which the Coroner showed to Mrs Clarke and to the jury. Mrs Clarke confirmed it as being in the Colonel's handwriting. The Coroner told the jury: '… that having read the note, they would probably gather Colonel Clarke's intention, and the only verdict they could record was that he took his life, probably in an emotional crisis or brainstorm, though he might have become rational later…' The jury returned a verdict of suicide while temporarily of unsound mind.

Those words were the same as for Walford, excepting that Walford's had been attributed to his war experiences. Like Walford's grandchildren, who did not hear any discussion of the Old Gent from his only child, so Clarke's grandson, Jeremy, wrote to me that: 'my grandfather is a subject never spoken about in my family as I grew up', encouragingly continuing 'so the research that both you and Robert [Jeremy's son-in-law] have done has opened a new world for me and I am most grateful'. We must celebrate the lives and achievements of these men who had to live and fight in such troubled times, not feel any embarrassment at the manner of their going or of those, like Burlingham, who struggled at the Front. As we witnessed with the Company dinner in the 1960s chaired by Burlingham, their men never forgot their contributions and their leadership and neither must we.

There were clearly a number of factors involved in Clarke's death, both poor health and money worries, but to what extent his wartime experiences had been a catalyst to his matrimonial problems will never be known. What is certain is that from the day in October 1917 when he assumed command of the 1/8th Battalion, 11 officers and 97 men lost their lives. He, as with Major Bate, crossed the Channel with their Battalion, arriving in the early hours of Maundy Thursday, 1st April 1915. Excepting for absences for leave and courses, they both served continually with the Battalion until the great success at Landrecies.

During that period, 31 officers – many being friends – and 439 men died. Hubert Clarke and Osborn Walford deserved a less troubled peace. Neither of their names adorn the war memorials of their local town or village but each does have his own grave. As with Bate – and with every man who fell on the battlefields of that war – none of the three shares a grave with his wife. Clarke lies alone at St Thomas Church at Crown East outside Worcester and Jack Bate stands a lonely vigil at the Priory Church of the Annunciation at Woodchester outside Stroud in Gloucestershire. Having organised the renovation of Walford's grave at St Mary's Church at Hanbury, all three graves now tell of their gallantry awards so that the few who visit them will know that they stand at the side of a brave man who gave great service to their country, their King and their fellow soldiers. Such visitors will not know of their later turmoils and endings.

We salute them and all the gallant officers and men who served with the 1/8th Battalion, the Worcestershire Regiment through the Great War and those who were spared and who made such important contributions to their country when world war returned just two decades later.

They all stood FIRM.

The graves of Osborn Walford, Jack Bate, Hubert Clarke

ACKNOWLEDGEMENTS

As I negotiated my way through army, City and family life, it never occurred to me for one moment that 'I had a book in me', let alone that I had the skills to write one. When I took a report which I had drafted to the Senior Partner at Cazenove, John Kemp-Welch, he read it and said that it would be fine. There were two split infinitives, if I could just correct them. I knew from that moment that my O-Level grade 5 English needed much attention.

There have been many kindnesses that have led to the writing of this book, in the main by those who have taken such an interest in Osborn Walford's story. Perhaps I should mention them chronologically as they helped in my search for his grave and his life story. My first thanks go to Judith Berham, churchwarden at St Mary the Virgin's Church, Hanbury – for being at home when I called her number; for having to hand the handwritten ledger of the inscriptions of the older graves; for getting so excited when we found him; and, for her ongoing support over more than a decade. Next, to the team at King Edward's School, Birmingham – firstly to Alison Wheatley for taking an equally keen interest in Walford's sad story and recommending that the City of Birmingham adopt the Old Gent as the focus for the 1914 Centenary Day. To Paul Golightly, the head of History, who suggested and organised the film: *Walford's War*. As my book matured, he allowed me to lean on him in an editorial capacity, particularly to ensure the book had pace from the start and that I attempt to investigate the drivers of the gallantry of these great men. To my aunt, Pam Brooking, for her support in the battlefields during the filming and afterwards, until dementia so cruelly reduced her capacity, as it took my mother, Pam's elder sister, away before this project was even contemplated.

There has been the wonderful support that I have been given by John Paddock at the Worcestershire Regiment archives – correctly, The Mercian Regiment Museum (Worcestershire) – for taking such an interest in my project and being unstinting with his time whenever I visited or telephoned Dannox House. When I got down to the nitty-gritty of wanting to illustrate my text with photographs from various albums in their safe keeping, in stepped Helen Hunter, the archivist. Nothing has been too much trouble as I kept changing my mind or wanting yet more high-resolution copies.

I want to thank two people who gave me the confidence to undertake this project in the first place and then to believe that it had merit. Firstly, Lars Kjear, head of History at the New College of the Humanities. When I wrote to thank him for allowing me on his degree course as a young sixty-year-old, and then making his syllabus so interesting, he wrote back to say that he was looking forward to giving me a reference for a Master's course. It had never occurred to me that I would be accepted onto one, but with his reference even KCL accepted me. Secondly, Sam Carter to whom I sent a very early draft of this book to see if it had any merit and if he would be interested in helping me bring the project to full publication. He has bolstered my confidence throughout our six months working together and even amazed my family by using the word 'awesome' to describe some of my efforts.

Then there have been all the extraordinary coincidences encountered as I sought out Osborn Walford's story. Robert Wedgbury's letter to challenge the price I had paid for the Waterloo Dinner wine and to discover that it was his father who was one of the finest soldiers with whom the Old Gent served. His trust that I should borrow all his father's papers – even those which he wrote after his finest actions – and our lunches together are very special. When I sent him a draft copy of the dust jacket, his immediate reply was: "Wonderful news – the end is in sight. You must let me make a contribution to the publishing cost as my father would have insisted I do." What a lovely son of an extraordinary man. There was Jane Stanley who sought me out after a 2014 story in the *Birmingham Mail* about Walford, just as she was about to publish her great uncle's diaries: *Lance's War*. We had a City lunch and have kept in touch ever since. She showed me all Evers' diaries, papers and photographs. I treasure our recent lunch at Thurlstone. Lastly, I am so grateful to Robert Bomford, Leslie's son, for giving me so much of his time when I have visited his home at Bevington. As with Robert Wedgbury, he has been remarkably generous and trusting in letting me take away whichever papers and photographs I wished from his father's archive. A thank you to John Gilkes who helped me to fulfil a desire to introduce this story on the endpapers with a very smart map of France and Flanders, to allow readers to follow the Battalion's progress and battles, and to Alice and Emily Carter.

Finally, this book would not have been possible without the wonderful support from my wife, Fi. She did not bat an eyelid when I rang from the office one day in March 2017 to say that I had decided to retire from the City and that I had organised a place at university. She has endured my filing all across the kitchen table without too much comment. Also, to our lovely children, Angus, Katie and Rosanna, who have found humour in my fascination for the battlefields and cemeteries of France and Flanders. Daddy is "doing dead people" was the cry! I hope that I have managed to impress them with this telling of the story of their great-great-grandfather, the Old Gent and his extraordinary soldiers and brother officers.

GLOSSARY

Gallantry awards		*can be awarded to*
Victoria Cross	VC	all ranks
Distinguished Service Order	DSO	senior officers
Military Cross	MC	junior officers and WOs
Distinguished Conduct Medal	DCM	all Other Ranks
Military Medal	MM	all Other Ranks
Meritorious Service Medal	MSM	WOs & SNCOs
Mentioned in Despatches	MiD	all ranks

Military Ranks – Field Officers	
Field Marshal	FM
General	Gen
Lieutenant General	Lt Gen
Major General	Maj Gen
Brigadier General	Brig/Brig Gen
Colonel	Col

Army Formations		*commanded by*
British Expeditionary Force (BEF)		Commander-in-Chief (FM/General)
Army	1st, 2nd etc	General/Lt Gen
Corps	I, II, III, IV etc	Lt Gen
Division	Div (1st, 2nd etc)	Maj Gen
Brigade	Bde (1st, 2nd etc)	Brigadier/Brig Gen

Infantry battalion structure

Regiment	Regt		non-field infantry grouping, as with Worcestershire Regt
			commanded by
Battalion	Bn	(as 1/8th, 2/8th)	Lt Col
Company	Coy	(A, B, C, D)	Major/Captain
Platoon	Pl	(1-16)	Lt/2Lt/Sgt
Section	Sect		Sgt/Cpl/LCpl

Infantry Battalion officers

Lieutenant Colonel	Lt Col
Major	Maj
Captain	Capt
Lieutenant	Lt
Second Lieutenant	2Lt

Other Ranks in battalions
Warrant officers (WOs)

Regimental Sergeant Major	RSM
Regt Quartermaster Sergeant	RQMS
Company Sergeant Major	CSM

Senior Non-Commissioned Officers (SNCOs)

Company Quartermaster Sgt	CQMS
Sergeant/Serjeant	Sgt

Non-Commissioned Officers (NCOs)

Corporal	Cpl
Lance Corporal	LCpl

Soldiers

Private	Pte

Battalion Headquarters

Commanding Officer	CO	(Lt Col)
Second-in-Command	2-i-C	(Major)
Adjutant	Adjt	(Capt/Lt)
Quartermaster	QM	(Capt)
Regt Medical Officer	RMO	(Capt)
Padre	Pde	(Capt)

Other arms			*commanded by*
Regiment	Regt	(Cavalry/Tanks/Artillery/Engineers)	Lt Col
Battery	Bty	(Artillery)	Major
Squadron	Sqn	(Cavalry/Engineers)	Major
Troop	Tp	(Cavalry/Engineers)	Lt/2Lt/Sgt

Royal Army Medical Corps (RAMC)		*commanded by*
Field Hospital		Col/Lt Col
Casualty Clearing Station	CCS	Major/Capt
Field Dressing Station	FDS	Capt
Regimental Aid Post	RAP	RMO (Capt)

BIBLIOGRAPHY

Private papers and books

Adams, Herbert Mayow (1922) *1916–1918: A War Diary.* Worcester: Ebenezer Baylis & Son, by kind permission of Trinity College Library, Cambridge.

Bomford Brothers letters – Private collection, kindly loaned by Robert Bomford [son of LR Bomford].

Bomford, Bruce (1983) *The Bomfords of Worcestershire*

Captain Leslie Bomford DSO MC* – Private Memoir and Grasshopper speech – Private Collection, kindly loaned by Robert Bomford (son).

Lance's War. (2015) Diaries of Captain HL Evers MC*, compiled by Jane Stanley (great niece).

Lt Col HT Clarke family papers – Family papers kindly loaned by Robert Whetstone.

Walford, JO (1918) *Letter from Second Battle of Le Cateau* – Private collection.

Wedgbury family papers – Private collection, kindly loaned by Robert Wedgbury [youngest son of E Wedgbury]

Unpublished primary sources

Berrow's Worcester Journal – 1914-1919: weekly editions and fortnightly supplements.

FIRM The Magazine of The Worcestershire Regiment. October 1956 – Wedgbury's obituary.

Imperial War Museum

17711 – Private papers of Captain Richard Henry Burlingham

14176 – Private papers of private AR Read

880 – Private Papers of 2Lt Bertram Warner

6416 – Private papers of Colonel Sir Hugh Chance CBE, DL, MA

10407 – Letters concerning a soldier's [Pte FE Bruton] grave, WWI

16899 – Private papers of Cpl AS Little

13035 – Sound archive of Pte Leonard Lipscombe

LBY 04/1920 – War Office: *Committee of Enquiry into Shell Shock*

National Archives

WO 95/2251/2 – *War Diary* of 1/8th The Worcestershire Regiment (October 1918–February 1919)

The Worcestershire Regiment – Archives

War Diary: 1/8th Battalion, The Worcestershire Regiment: November 1917–September 1918

Centre for South Asian Studies, Cambridge University
Papers donated by Sir Charles Pawsey, Lady Pawsey and Michael Pawsey

Published primary sources – online
Ancestry website – https://www.ancestry.co.uk/search/
Commonwealth War Graves Commission website – https://www.cwgc.org/find-records/
Errington, Lt. Col. F.H.L. (1922) *The Inns of Court Officers Training Corps* – https://archive.org/details/innsofcourtoffic00erri/page/n11/mode/2up
London Gazette website – https://www.thegazette.co.uk/all-notices
Myers, Lt. Col. C.S. (1919) *A Final Contribution: The Study of Shell Shock: Being a consideration of unsettled points needing investigation. The Lancet* – https://www.thelancet.com/journals/lancet/article/PIIS0140-6736(01)25176-9/fulltext
The Progonian Family Memoirs – Sir Hugh Chance CBE – https://1cha.co.uk/sir-hugh-chance/
The Malvernian, Malvern College – https://www.malverniansocietyarchives.co.uk/authenticated/Browse.aspx-?BrowseID=140&tableName=ta_malvernian
The St Edward's School Chronicle, St Edward's School, Oxford – https://archive.stedwardsoxford.org/authenticated/Browse.aspx?BrowseID=1155&tableName=ta_publications
Film: (2018) *Walford's War* – https://kes.org.uk/about-us/history-of-the-school/king-edwards-school-great-war/walfords-war-film/

Published Secondary Sources
Barnett, Lt. Col. H.G. (1923) *With the 48th Division in Italy.* Edinburgh and London: William Blackwood and Sons
Bomford, N.R. (2013) *Brothers in War: Letters from the Western Front 1915–18.* Lulu.com
Carey, G.V. (1921) *The War List of the University of Cambridge.* Cambridge: University Press
Carr, Lt. Col. H.A. (1919) *1/8th Battalion, The Worcestershire Regiment: Notes by Lieut. Col. H.A. Carr, DSO.* Worcester: Journal Co. Ltd
Clarke, Lt. Col. H.T. (1919) *1/8th Battalion, The Worcestershire Regiment 1914–1918.* London: War Narratives Publishing Company
Clayton, D. (2018) *Decisive Victory: The Battle of The Sambre, 4 November 1918.* Warwick: Helion & Co
Corbett, E.C. (1921) *The Worcestershire Regiment: War Story of the 1/8th (Territorial) Battalion.* Worcester: *Worcester Herald*
Craig, E.S. and Gibson, W.M. (1920) *Oxford University Roll of Service.* Oxford: Clarendon Press
Crane, D. (2014) *Empires of The Dead: How one man's vision led to the*

creation of WWI's War Graves. London: William Collins

First World War and Army of Occupation: War Diary: France, Belgium and Germany. *48 DIVISION, 144 Infantry Brigade: Worcestershire Regiment, 1/8th Battalion. (1 April 1915–31) October 1917 (First World War, War Diary, WO92/2759/2).* Uckfield: The Naval & Military Press Ltd

Gale, R. (1970) *The Worcestershire Regiment (The 29th and 36th Regiments of Foot).* London: Leo Cooper Ltd

Hart, P. (2018) *The Last Battle: Endgame on The Western Front, 1918.* London: Profile Books

Holland, J. (2021) *Brothers in Arms.* London: Bantam Press

Keegan, J. (2001) *The First World War: An Illustrated History.* London: Hutchinson

Kenyon, D. (2012) *Horsemen in No Man's Land: British Cavalry & Trench Warfare 1914–1918.* Barnsley: Pen & Sword Military

Kincaid-Smith, Lt. Col. M. (1919) *The 25th Division in France and Flanders.* Uckfield: The Naval & Military Press

Lewis-Stempel, J. (2011) *Six Weeks: The Short and Gallant Life of the British Officer in the First World War.* London: Orion

Lewis-Stempel, J. (2017) *Where Poppies Blow: The British Soldier, Nature, The Great War.* London: Weidenfeld & Nicolson

MacDonald, J. with Compric, Z. (2015) *Caporetto and the Isonzo Campaign: The Italian Front 1915–1918.* Barnsley: Pen & Sword Military.

Mitchinson, K.W. (2017) *The 48th (South Midland) Division 1908–1919.* Solihull: Helion & Company Ltd

Mylne, Captain K.M. (1918) *The History of The Worcestershire Regiment.* Worcester: Littlebury and Company, The Worcester Press

Sassoon, S. (1965) *The Memoirs of an Infantry Officer.* London: Faber and Faber Limited

Snelling, S. (1998) *VCs of The First World War: Passchendaele 1917.* Stroud: Sutton Publishing Ltd

Stacke, Captain H. FiztM. (1929) *The Worcestershire Regiment in The Great War (No. 165).* Kidderminster: G.T. Cheshire & Sons Ltd

Wavell, General Sir Archibald (1940) *Allenby: a study of greatness.* London: George G. Harrap & Co. Ltd

Wearne, S. (2017) *Epitaphs of The Great War: Passchendaele.* London: Uniform Publishing Group

Maps

Stacke, Captain H. FiztM. (1929) *The Worcestershire Regiment in The Great War (No. 165).* Kidderminster: G.T. Cheshire & Sons Ltd

Music & Poetry

Phil Mountford & Kathy Gee (2017) *Suite for the Fallen Soldier.* Feckenham

WW1 Commemoration Committee: http://feckenhamww1.org.uk/suite-for-the-fallen-soldier/

Photographs

Author, pp 16, 17, 71, 85, 98, 116, 147, 160, 176, 192, 195, 220, 221, 237, 336 (both), 339, 341 (both), 342, 361, 363, 369 (both), 373 (both), 396, 407, 413, 419, 439, 463, 488 (all).

Berrow's Worcester Journals (1914–1919), Newsquest Media Group: 41 (both), 50, 52, 54, 69, 71, 95, 128, 136, 138, 163, 183 (both), 190, 191, 196, 197, 208 (both), 234, 244, 249, 293, 380, 406, 446, 471, 480.

The Bomford family papers: pp 111, 441.

Imperial War Museum – HU113678 p242, HU120990 p125

Mercian Regiment Museum (Worcestershire), *WOSWR: Photo Album-93 (Captain CR Pawsey), photograph* no. 1 p64, *12* p74, *15* p62, *17* p167, *39* p332, *50* p82, *63* p140, *68* p149, *80* p139, *84* p125 & 162, *89* p107.

Mercian Regiment Museum (Worcestershire), *WOSWR: Photo Album-95 (Captain RH Burlingham), p12(r)* p98, *17(top)* p73, *22(l)* p125, *25(l)* p435, *30(r)* p86.

Mercian Regiment Museum (Worcestershire), *WOSWR: Photo Album-96, p 1(i)* p45, *3(r)* p52 & 99, *4(l)* p462, *6(l)* p62, *9(r)* p52, *9(l)* p150, *12(l)* p325, *14(r)* p38, *15(l)* p46, *20(l)* p40, *24(l)* p122, *37(l+r)* p173.

Mercian Regiment Museum (Worcestershire), *WOSWR: M1451* p481, *M1972* p484, *2023-4* p464, *2023-6* p43 & 101.

Redditch & Alcester Advertiser, Newsquest Media Group: p 72.

The Royal Scots Dragoon Guards Charity: p 352.

The Walford family papers: p 13, 434.

The Wedgbury family papers: p 277, 450.7

Central plate photographs

Author: Plates 22, 23

Mercian Regiment Museum (Worcestershire), WOSWR:
- Photo Album 93: 72 (Pl 9), 45 (Pl 10), 46 (Pl 11), 81 (Pl 12), 82 (Pl 13), 43 (Pl 14), 44 (Pl 15)
- Photo Album 95: 7 (Pl 17), 29a (Pl 18)
- Photo Album 96: 6a (Pl 6), 6b (Pl 7), 31b (Pl 8)
- M1451: Pl 25
- 2023-4: Pl 24
- 2023-6: Pl 1
- 2023-7: Pl 5
- 2023-8: Pl 2

The Bomford Family Papers: Plates 3, 4, 16

The Walford Family Papers: Plates 19, 21

The Wedgbury Family Papers: Plate 20

INDEX

People

Military Units

Cavalry Regiments

Infantry Regiments

Battles and Places

First published in Great Britain in 2023 by Bertie's Books.

Edited, designed and produced by Tandem Publishing
http://tandempublishing.yolasite.com

ISBN: 978-1-3999-6954-3

10 9 8 7 6 5 4 3 2 1

A CIP catalogue record for this book is available from the British Library.

Printed and bound in Great Britain by CPI Group (UK) Ltd,
Croydon CR0 4YY.

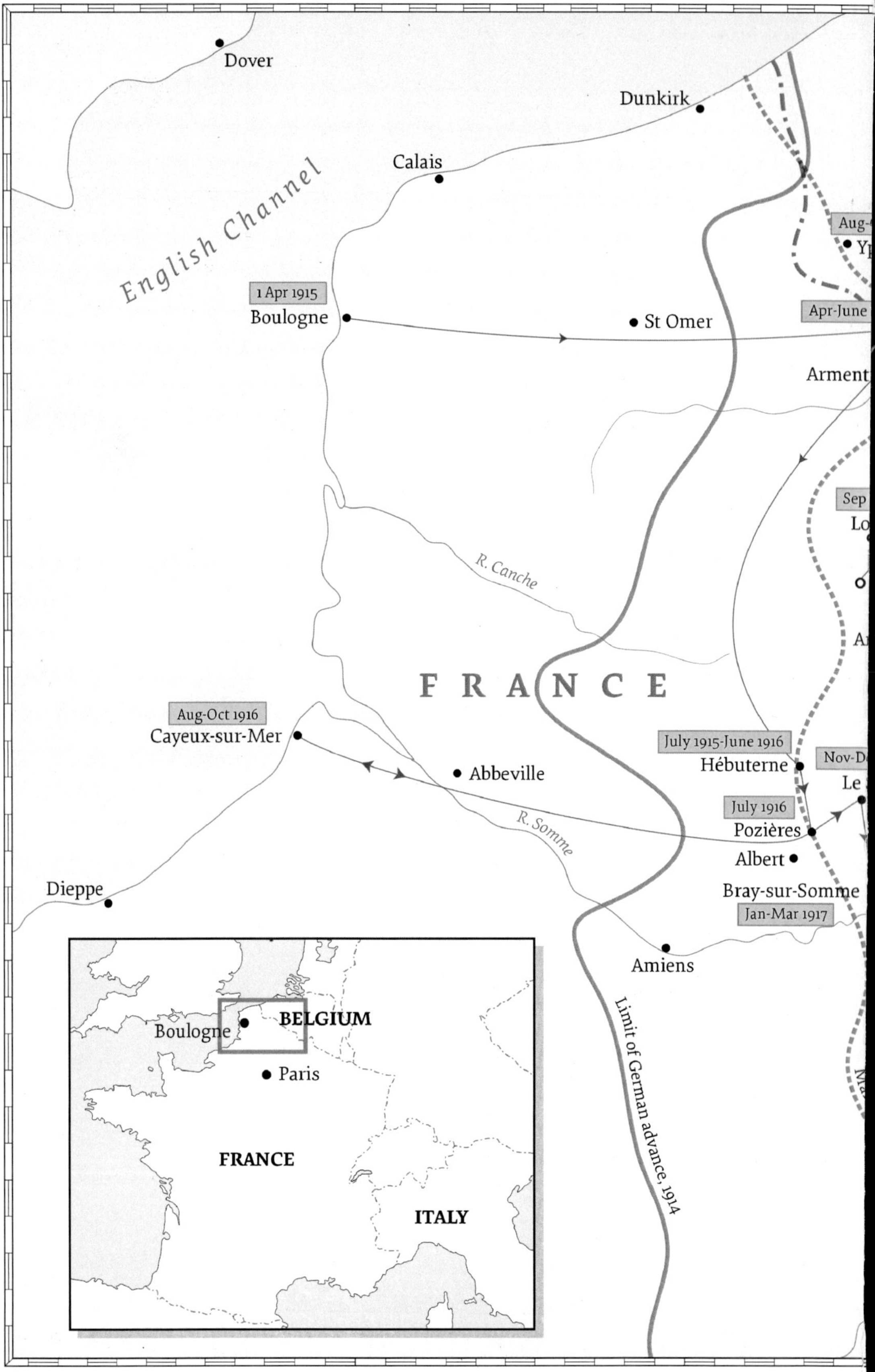

Dover
Dunkirk
Calais
English Channel
1 Apr 1915
Boulogne
St Omer
R. Canche
FRANCE
Aug-Oct 1916
Cayeux-sur-Mer
Abbeville
R. Somme
Dieppe
July 1915-June 1916
Hébuterne
July 1916
Pozières
Albert
Bray-sur-Somme
Jan-Mar 1917
Amiens
Limit of German advance, 1914
Boulogne
BELGIUM
Paris
FRANCE
ITALY